David Livingstone

Livingstone's Travels and Researches in South Africa

David Livingstone

Livingstone's Travels and Researches in South Africa

ISBN/EAN: 9783744758345

Printed in Europe, USA, Canada, Australia, Japan

Cover: Foto ©Andreas Hilbeck / pixelio.de

More available books at **www.hansebooks.com**

The Missionary's Escape from the Lion.

LIVINGSTONE'S
Travels and Researches
IN SOUTH AFRICA;

INCLUDING

A SKETCH OF SIXTEEN YEARS' RESIDENCE IN THE INTERIOR OF AFRICA
AND A JOURNEY FROM THE CAPE OF GOOD HOPE TO LOANDA
ON THE WEST COAST, THENCE ACROSS THE CONTINENT,
DOWN THE RIVER ZAMBESI, TO THE
EASTERN OCEAN.

From the Personal Narrative
OF
DAVID LIVINGSTONE, LL.D., D.C.L.

LLOW OF THE FACULTY OF PHYSICIANS AND SURGEONS, GLASGOW; CORRESPONDING MEM
OF THE GEOGRAPHICAL AND HISTORICAL SOCIETY OF NEW YORK; GOLD MEDALLIST
AND CORRESPONDING MEMBER OF THE ROYAL GEOGRAPHICAL SOCIETIES
OF LONDON AND PARIS, ETC. ETC.

TO WHICH IS ADDED

A HISTORICAL SKETCH OF DISCOVERIES IN AFRICA.

Illustrated with Numerous Engravings.

The Tsetse Fly, magnified.

PHILADELPHIA:
J. W BRADLEY, 48 N. FOURTH STREET.
1861.

Entered according to Act of Congress, in the year 1859, by
J. W. BRADLEY,
in the Clerk's Office of the District Court of the United States in and for the Eastern District of Pennsylvania.

STEREOTYPED BY L. JOHNSON & CO.
PHILADELPHIA.
PRINTED BY KING & BAIRD.

PREFACE

OF THE

AMERICAN PUBLISHER.

Dr. Livingstone is the most remarkable of all the travellers who have visited Africa. His personal narrative is the most important and interesting of all that have yet been published. It will prove the most influential on future discovery. His great journey across the continent was almost entirely over ground hitherto untrodden by the foot of the white man. The information which he gives is therefore fresh, and, in many instances, refutes and explodes the theories of previous travellers. In the matter of personal adventures and hairbreadth escapes it is much richer than the doctor could have desired.

Dr. Livingstone is a very pleasing writer, a man of true Christian benevolence, a man of extensive scientific information, and an indefatigable laborer in the cause of discovery and civilization. His personal narrative contains a vast amount of information on the geology, meteorology, zoology, and history of the countries which he visited, which will be esteemed highly valuable by scientific inquirers. The edition of his book now offered to the public, by omitting a considerable amount of scientific matter and minor details, has been compressed into a compass which will render it perhaps more acceptable to the general reader than if the whole had been given, and at the same time bring it within the reach of those who find it necessary to consult economy in their purchases of books.

The reader will observe that the narrative is all given in the language of Dr. Livingstone, and that it forms a complete account of his various journeys, omitting only incidental details and scientific matter.*

---

* Since the above Preface was written and published, the publisher has issued a work which forms an excellent companion to Dr. Livingstone's Travels and Researches, as the Author has explored thoroughly, and described with wonderfully graphic power, the whole of North Central Africa, while Dr. Livingstone was engaged in his useful labors in South Central Africa. The contrast between the nations and tribes which they respectively visited, in manners, character and civilization, is of the most striking kind. The following is the title of Dr. Barth's work: "Travels and Discoveries in North and Central Africa, from the Journal of an Expedition undertaken under the auspices of H. B. M. Government in the years 1849-1855. By Henry Barth, Ph. D., D. C. L., Fellow of the Royal Geographical and Asiatic Societies, etc.; with notes and extracts from Mr. Richardson's Account of the Expedition, and a Sketch of Denham and Clapperton's Expedition by the American editor."

CONTENTS.

INTRODUCTION.

Personal Sketch—Highland Ancestors—Family Traditions—Grandfather removes to the Lowlands—Parents—Early Labors and Efforts—Evening School—Love of Reading—Religious Impressions—Medical Education—Youthful Travels—Geology—Mental Discipline—Study in Glasgow—London Missionary Society—Native Village—Medical Diploma—Theological Studies—Departure for Africa No Claim to Literary Accomplishments...... Page 9

CHAPTER I.

The Bakwáin Country—Study of the Language—Mabótsa Station—A Lion Encounter—Virus of the Teeth of Lions—Sechéle—Baptism of Seebele—Opposition of the Natives—Purchase Land at Chonuáne—Relations with the People—Their Intelligence—Prolonged Drought—Consequent Trials—The Hunting Hopo.. 18

CHAPTER II.

The Boers—Their Treatment of the Natives—The Tale of the Cannon—The Boers threaten Sechele—In violation of Treaty, they expel Missionaries—They attack the Bakwains—Their Mode of Fighting—The Natives killed and the School-Children carried into Slavery—Destruction of English Property—Continued Hostility of the Boers—The Journey North—Preparations—Fellow-Travellers 28

CHAPTER III.

Departure from Kolobeng, 1st June, 1849—Companions—Our Route—Serotli, a Fountain in the Desert—The Hyena—The Chief Sekomi—Dangers—The Wandering Guide—Cross Purposes—Slow Progress—Want of Water—The Salt-Pan at Nchokotsa—The Mirage—Reach the River Zouga—The Quakers of Africa—Discovery of Lake Ngami, 1st August, 1849—Its Extent—Small Depth of Water—The Bamangwato and their Chief—Desire to visit Sebituane, the Chief of the Makololo—Refusal of Lechulatebe to furnish us with Guides—The Banks of the Zouga... 34

CHAPTER IV.

Leave Kolobeng again for the Country of Sebituane—Reach the Zouga—The Tsétse—A Party of Englishmen—Death of Mr. Ridér—Obtain Guides—Children fall sick with Fever—Relinquish the Attempt to reach Sebituane—Return to Kolobeng—Make a Third Start thence—Reach Nchokotsa—Our

vii

Guide Shobo—The Banajoa—An Ugly Chief—The Tsetse-Bite fatal to Domestic Animals, but harmless to Wild Animals and Man—Operation of the Poison—Losses caused by it—The Makololo—Our Meeting with Sebituane—His Sudden Illness and Death—Succeeded by his Daughter—Her Friendliness to us—Discovery, in June, 1851, of the Zambesi flowing in the Centre of the Continent—Determine to send Family to England—Return to the Cape in April, 1852—Safe Transit through the Caffre Country during Hostilities—Need of a "Special Correspondent"—Kindness of the London Missionary Society—Assistance afforded by the Astronomer-Royal at the Cape .... Page 44

CHAPTER V.

Start, in June, 1852, on the Last and Longest Journey from Cape Town—Companions—Wagon-Travelling—Migration of Springbucks—The Orange River—Territory of the Griquas and Bechuanas—The Griquas—The Chief Waterboer—His Wise and Energetic Government—His Fidelity—Success of the Missionaries among the Griquas and Bechuanas—Manifest Improvement of the Native Character—Dress of the Natives—Articles of Commerce in the Country of the Bechuanas—Their Unwillingness to learn and Readiness to criticize.. 57

CHAPTER VI.

Kuruman—Its fine Fountain—The Bible translated by Mr. Moffat—Capabilities of the Language—Christianity among the Natives—Disgraceful Attack of the Boers on the Bakwains—Letter from Sechele—Details of the Attack—Destruction of House and Property at Kolobeng—The Boers vow Vengeance against me—Consequent Difficulty of getting Servants to accompany me on my Journey—Start in November, 1852—Meet Sechele on his way to England to obtain Redress from the Queen—He is unable to proceed beyond the Cape—Meet Mr. Macabe on his Return from Lake Ngami—Reach Litubaruba—The Cave Lepelole—Superstitions regarding it—Impoverished State of the Bakwains—Retaliation on the Boers—Slavery—Attachment of the Bechuanas to Children. 63

CHAPTER VII.

Departure from the Country of the Bakwains—Large Black Ant—Habits of Old Lions—Cowardice of the Lion—Its Dread of a Snare—Major Vardon's Note—The Roar of the Lion resembles the Cry of the Ostrich—Seldom attacks full-grown Animals—Buffaloes and Lions—Sekomi's Ideas of Honesty—Gordon Cumming's Hunting Adventures—A Word of Advice for Young Sportsmen—Bushwomen drawing Water.. 73

CHAPTER VIII.

Effects of Missionary Efforts—Belief in the Deity—Departure from their Country—Nchokotsa—The Bushmen—Their Superstitions—Elephant-Hunting—The Chief Kaissa—His Fear of Responsibility—Severe Labor in cutting our Way—Party seized with Fever—Discovery of Grape-Bearing Vines—Difficulty of passing through the Forest—Sickness of my Companion—The Bushmen—Their Mode of destroying Lions—Poisons—A Pontooning Expedition—The Chobe—Arrive at the Village of Moremi—Surprise of the Makololo at our Sudden Appearance—Cross the Chobe on our way to Linyanti. 86

CONTENTS.

CHAPTER IX.

Reception at Linyanti—The Court Herald—Sekeletu obtains the Chieftainship from his Sister—Sekeletu's Reason for not learning to read the Bible—Public Religious Services in the Kotla—Unfavorable Associations of the Place—Native Doctors—Proposals to teach the Makololo to read—Sekeletu's Present—Reason for accepting it—Trading in Ivory—Accidental Fire—Presents for Sekeletu.. Page 96

CHAPTER X.

The Fever—Its Symptoms—Remedies of the Native Doctors—Hospitality of Sekeletu and his People—They cultivate largely—The Makalaka or Subject Tribes—Sebituane's Policy respecting them—Their Affection for him—Products of the Soil—Instrument of Culture—The Tribute—Distributed by the Chief—A Warlike Demonstration—Lechulatebe's Provocations—The Makololo determine to punish him... 104

CHAPTER XI.

Departure from Linyanti for Sesheke—Level Country—Ant-Hills—Wild Date-Trees—Appearance of our Attendants on the March—The Chief's Guard—They attempt to ride on Oxback—Reception at the Villages—Presents of Beer and Milk—Eating with the Hand—The Chief provides the Oxen for Slaughter—Social Mode of Eating—Cleanliness of Makololo Huts—Their Construction and Appearance—The Beds—Cross the Leeambye—Aspect of this part of the Country—Hunting—An Eland................................. 109

CHAPTER XII.

Procure Canoes and ascend the Leeambye—Beautiful Islands—Winter Landscape—Industry and Skill of the Banyeti—Rapids—Falls of Gonye—Nalièle, the Capital, built on an Artificial Mound—Santuru, a Great Hunter—The Barotse—More Religious Feeling—Belief in a Future State and in the Existence of Spiritual Beings—Hippopotamus-Hunters—No Healthy Location—Determine to go to Loanda—Buffaloes, Elands, and Lions above Libonta—Two Arabs from Zanzibar—Their Opinion of the Portuguese and the English—Reach the Town of Ma-Sekeletu—Joy of the People at the First Visit of their Chief—Return to Seshoke—Heathenism................ 116

CHAPTER XIII.

Preliminary Arrangements for the Journey—A Picho—Twenty-Seven Men appointed to accompany me to the West—Eagerness of the Makololo for Direct Trade with the Coast—Effects of Fever—A Makololo Question—Reflections—The Outfit for the Journey—11th November, 1853, leave Linyanti and embark on the Chobe—Dangerous Hippopotami—Banks of Chobe—Trees—The Course of the River—The Island Mparia at the Confluence of the Chobe and the Leeambye—Anecdote—Ascend the Leeambye—Public Addresses at Seshoke—Attention of the People—Results—Proceed up the River—The Fruit which yields *Nux vomica*—The Rapids—Hippopotami and their Young... 125

CHAPTER XIV.

Increasing Beauty of the Country—Mode of spending the Day—The People and the Falls of Gonye—A Makololo Foray—A second prevented, and Captives delivered up—Politeness and Liberality of the People—The Rains—Present of Oxen—Death from a Lion's Bite at Libonta—Continued Kindness—Arrangements for spending the Night during the Journey—Cooking and Washing—Abundance of Animal Life—Alligators—Narrow Escape of one of my Men—Superstitious Feelings respecting the Alligator—Large Game—Shoals of Fish—Hippopotami.. Page 138

CHAPTER XV.

Message to Masiko, the Barotse Chief, regarding the Captives—Navigation of the Leeambye—Capabilities of this District—The Leeba—Buffalo-Hunt—Suspicion of the Balonda—Sekelénke's Present—Message from Manénko, a Female Chief—Mambari Traders—A Dream—Sheakóndo and his People—Interview with Nyamoána, another Female Chief—Court Etiquette—Hair versus Wool—Increase of Superstition—Arrival of Manenko: her Appearance and Husband—Mode of Salutation—Anklets—Embassy, with a Present from Masiko—Roast Beef—Manioc—Magic Lantern—Manenko an Accomplished Scold: compels us to wait... 148

CHAPTER XVI.

Nyamoana's Present—Charms—Manenko's Pedestrian Powers—Rain—Hunger—Dense Forests—Artificial Bee-Hives—Villagers lend the Roofs of their Houses—Divination and Idols—Manenko's Whims—Shinte's Messengers and Present—The Proper Way to approach a Village—A Merman—Enter Shinte's Town: its Appearance—Meet two Half-Caste Slave-Traders—The Makololo scorn them—The Balonda Real Negroes—Grand Reception from Shinte—His Kotla—Ceremony of Introduction—The Orators—Women—Musicians and Musical Instruments—A Disagreeable Request—Private Interviews with Shinte—Give him an Ox—Manenko's New Hut—Conversation with Shinte—Kolimbóta's Proposal—Balonda's Punctiliousness—Selling Children—Kidnapping—Shinte's Offer of a Slave—Magic Lantern—Alarm of Women—Delay—Sambánza returns intoxicated—The Last and Greatest Proof of Shinte's Friendship.. 162

CHAPTER XVII.

Leave Shinte—Manioc-Gardens—Presents of Food—Punctiliousness of the Balonda—Cazembe—Inquiries for English Cotton Goods—Intemese's Fiction—Locs of Pontoon—Plains covered with Water—A Night on an Island—Loan of the Roofs of Huts—A Halt—Omnivorous Fish—Natives' Mode of catching them—The Village of a Half-Brother of Katema: his Speech and Present—Our Guide's Perversity—Mozenkwa's Pleasant Home and Family—A Messenger from Katema—Quendende's Village: his Kindness—Crop of Wool—Meet People from the Town of Matiamvo—Fireside Talk—Matiamvo's Character and Conduct—Presentation at Kutema's Court: his Present—Interview on the following Day—Cattle—A Feast and a Makololo Dance—Sagacity of Ants. 186

CHAPTER XVIII.

The Watershed between the Northern and Southern Rivers—A Deep Valley—Rustic Bridge—Fountains on the Slopes of the Valleys—Village of Kabinje—Demand for Gunpowder and English Calico—The Kasai—Vexatious Trick—Want of Food—No Game—Katende's Unreasonable Demand—A Grave Offence—Toll-Bridge Keeper—Greedy Guides—Flooded Valleys—Swim the Suana Loké—Prompt Kindness of my Men—Makololo Remarks on the rich Uncultivated Valleys—Difference in the Color of Africans—Reach a Village of the Chiboque—The Head Man's Impudent Message—Surrounds our Encampment with his Warriors—The Pretence—Their Demand—Prospect of a Fight—Way in which it was averted—Change our Path—The Ox Sinbad—Insubordination suppressed—Beset by Enemies—A Robber Party—More Troubles—Detained by Ionga Panza—His Village—Annoyed by Bangala Traders—My Men discouraged—Their Determination and Precaution Page 199

CHAPTER XIX.

Guides Prepaid—Bark Canoes—Deserted by Guides—Native Traders—Valley of the Quango—The Chief Sansawe—His Hostility—Pass him safely—The River Quango—Chief's Mode of dressing his Hair—Opposition—Opportune Aid by Cypriano—His Generous Hospitality—Arrive at Cassange—A Good Supper—Kindness of Captain Neves—Portuguese Curiosity and Questions—Anniversary of the Resurrection—No Prejudice against Color—Country around Cassange—Sell Sekeletu's Ivory—Makololo's Surprise at the High Price obtained—Proposal to return Home, and Reasons—Soldier-Guide—Tala Mungongo, Village of—Civility of Basongo—Fever—Enter District of Ambaca—Good Fruits of Jesuit Teaching—The Tampan: its Bite—Universal Hospitality of the Portuguese—A Tale of the Mambari—Exhilarating Effects of Highland Scenery—District of Golungo Alto—Fertility—Forests of Gigantic Timber—Native Carpenters—Coffee-Estate—Sterility of Country near the Coast—Fears of the Makololo—Welcome by Mr. Gabriel to Loanda.. 224

CHAPTER XX.

Continued Sickness—Kindness of the Bishop of Angola and her Majesty's Officers—Mr. Gabriel's Unwearied Hospitality—Serious Deportment of the Makololo—They visit Ships of War—Politeness of the Officers and Men—The Makololo attend Mass in the Cathedral—Their Remarks—Find Employment in collecting Firewood and unloading Coal—Their Superior Judgment respecting Goods—Beneficial Influence of the Bishop of Angola—The City of St. Paul de Loanda—The Harbor—Custom-House—No English Merchants—Sincerity of the Portuguese Government in suppressing the Slave-Trade—Convict Soldiers—Presents from Bishop and Merchants for Sekeletu—Outfit—Leave Loanda 20th September, 1854—Accompanied by Mr. Gabriel as far as Icollo i Bengo—Women spinning Cotton—Cazengo: its Coffee-Plantations—South American Trees—Ruins of Iron-Foundry—Native Miners—Coffee-Plantations—Return to Golungo Alto—Self-Complacency of the Makololo—Fever—Jaundice—Insanity.. 251

CHAPTER XXI.

Visit a Deserted Convent—Favorable Report of Jesuits and their Teaching—Marriages and Funerals—Litigation—Mr. Canto's Illness—Bad Behavior of his Slaves—An Entertainment—Ideas on Free Labor—Loss of American

CONTENTS

Cotton-Seed—Abundance of Cotton in the Country—Sickness of Sekeletu's Horse—Eclipse of the Sun—Insects which distill Water—Experiments with them—Proceed to Ambaca—Present from Mr. Schut, of Loanda—Visit Pungo Andongo—Its Good Pasturage, Grain, Fruit, &c.—The Fort and Columnar Rocks—Salubrity of Pungo Andongo—Price of a Slave—A Merchant-Prince —His Hospitality—Hear of the Loss of my Papers in "Forerunner"—Narrow Escape from an Alligator—Ancient Burial-Places—Neglect of Agriculture in Angola—Manioc the Staple Product—Its Cheapness—Sickness—Friendly Visit from a Colored Priest—The Prince of Congo—No Priests in the Interior of Angola.. Page 265

CHAPTER XXII.

Leave Pungo Andongo—Extent of Portuguese Power—Meet Traders and Carriers—Descend the Heights of Tala Mungongo—Cassange Village—Quinine and Cathory—Sickness of Captain Neves's Infant—Loss of Life from the Ordeal—Wide-Spread Superstitions—The Chieftainship—Receive Copies of the "Times"—Trading Pombeiros- Present for Matiamvo—Fever after Westerly Winds—Capabilities of Angola for producing the Raw Materials of English Manufacture—Trading-Parties with Ivory—More Fever—A Hyena's Choice—Makololo Opinion of the Portuguese—Cyprino's Debt—A Funeral—Dread of Disembodied Spirits—Crossing the Quango—Ambakistas called "The Jews of Angola"—Fashions of the Bashinje—Approach the Village of Sansawe—His Idea of Dignity—The Pombeiros' Present—Long Detention—A Blow on the Beard—Attacked in a Forest—Sudden Conversion of a Fighting Chief to Peace-Principles by means of a Revolver—No Blood shed in consequence—Rate of Travelling—Feeders of the Congo or Zaire—Obliged to refuse Presents—Cross the Loajima—Appearance of People: Hair-Fashions... 289

CHAPTER XXIII.

Make a Détour southward—The Chihombo—Cabango—Send a Sketch of the Country to Mr. Gabriel—The Chief Bango—Valley of the Loembwe—Funeral Observances—Agreeable Intercourse with Kawawa—His Impudent Demand 298

CHAPTER XXIV.

Level Plains—Vultures—Twenty-Seventh Attack of Fever—Reach Katema's Town—His Renewed Hospitality—Ford Southern Branch of Lake Dilolo—Hearty Welcome from Shinte—Nyamoana now a Widow—Purchase Canoes and descend the Leeba—Despatch a Message to Manenko—Arrival of her Husband Sambanza—Mambowe Hunters—Charged by a Buffalo—Reception from the People of Libonta—Explain the Causes of our Long Delay—Pitsane's Speech—Thanksgiving Services—Appearance of my "Braves"—Wonderful Kindness of the People... 303

CHAPTER XXV.

Colony of Birds called Linkololo—The Village of Chitlane—Murder of Mpololo's Daughter—Execution of the Murderer and his Wife—My Companions find that their Wives have married other Husbands—Sunday—A Party from Masiko—Freedom of Speech—Canoe struck by a Hippopotamus—Appearance of Trees at the End of Winter—Murky Atmosphere—Surprising Amount of Organic Life—The Packages forwarded by Mr. Moffat—Makololo Suspicions and Reply to the Matebele who brought them—Convey the Goods to an Island and build a Hut over them—Ascertain that Sir R. Murchison had recognised the True Form of African Continent—Arrival at Linyanti—A Grand Picho—Shrewd Inquiry—Sekeletu in his Uniform—A Trading-Party sent to Loanda with Ivory—Mr. Gabriel's Kindness to them—Two Makololo Forays during our Absence—The Makololo desire to be nearer the Market—Opinions upon a Change of Residence—Sekeletu's Hospitality—Sekeletu wishes to purchase a Sugar-Mill, &c.—The Donkeys—Influence among the Natives—"Food fit for a Chief"—Parting Words of Mamire—Motibe's Excuses... Page 311

CHAPTER XXVI.

Departure from Linyanti—A Thunder-Storm—An Act of Genuine Kindness—Fitted out a Second Time by the Makololo—Sail down the Leeambye—Victoria Falls—Native Names—Columns of Vapor—Gigantic Crack—Wear of the Rocks—Second Visit to the Falls—Part with Sekeletu—Night-Travelling—Moyara's Village—Savage Customs of the Batoka—A Chain of Trading-Stations—"The Well of Joy"—First Traces of Trade with Europeans—Knocking out the Front Teeth—Facetious Explanation—Degradation of the Batoka—Description of the Travelling-Party—Cross the Unguesi —Ruins of a Large Town.. 326

CHAPTER XXVII.

Low Hills—A Wounded Buffalo assisted—Buffalo-Bird—Rhinoceros-Bird—The Honey-Guide—The White Mountain—Sebituane's Old Home—Hostile Village—Prophetic Frenzy—Friendly Batoka—Clothing despised—Method of Salutation—The Captive released—The Village of Monze—Aspect of the Country—Visit from the Chief Monze and his Wife—Central Healthy Locations—Friendly Feelings of the People in reference to a White Resident—Kindness and Remarks of Monze's Sister—Generosity of the Inhabitants—Their Anxiety for Medicine—Hooping-Cough............................... 339

CHAPTER XXVIII.

Beautiful Valley—Buffalo—My Young Men kill two Elephants—The Hunt—Semalembue—His Presents—Joy in prospect of living in Peace—Trade—His People's Way of wearing their Hair—Their Mode of Salutation—Old Encampment—Sebituane's former Residence—Ford of Kafue—Prodigious Quantities of Large Game—Their Tameness—Rains—Less Sickness than in the Journey to Loanda—Reason—Charge from an Elephant—Vast Amount of Animal Life on the Zambesi—Water of River discolored—An Island with Buffaloes and Men on it—Native Devices for killing Game—Tsetse now in Country—Agricultural Industry—An Albino murdered by his Mother—"Guilty of Tlolo"—Women who make their Mouths "like those of Ducks" —First Symptom of the Slave-Trade on this Side—Sololê's Hostility—An Armed Party hoaxed—An Italian Marauder slain—Elephant's Tenacity of Life—A Word to Young Sportsmen—Mr. Oswell's Adventure with an Elephant: Narrow Escape—Mburuma's Village—Suspicious Conduct of his People—Guides attempt to detain us—The Village and People of Ma-Mburuma—Character our Guides give of us.................................... 351

CHAPTER XXIX.

Confluence of Loangwa and Zambesi—Hostile Appearances—Ruins of a Church—Turmoil of Spirit—Cross the River—Friendly Parting—The Situation of Zumbo for Commerce—Pleasant Gardens—Dr. Lacerda's Visit to Casembe—Pereira's Statement—Unsuccessful Attempt to establish Trade

CONTENTS.

with the People of Cazembe—One of my Men tossed by a Buffalo—Meet a Man with Jacket and Hat on—Hear of the Portuguese and Native War—Dancing for Corn—Mpende's Hostility—Incantations—A Fight anticipated—Courage and Remarks of my Men—Visit from two old Councillors of Mpende—Their Opinion of the English—Mpende concludes not to fight us—His subsequent Friendship—Aids us to cross the River—Desertion of one of my Men—Meet Native Traders with American Calico—Boroma—Freshets—Leave the River—Loquacious Guide—Nyampungo, the Rain-Charmer—An Old Man—No Silver—Gold-Washing—No Cattle...................... Page 372

CHAPTER XXX.

An Elephant-Hunt—Offering and Prayers to the Barimo for Success—Native Mode of Expression—Working of Game-Laws—A Feast—Laughing Hyenas—Numerous Insects—Curious Notes of Birds of Song—Caterpillars—Butterflies—Silica—The Fruit Makoronga and Elephants—Rhinoceros-Adventure—Honey and Bees'-Wax—Superstitious Reverence for the Lion—Slow Travelling—Grapes—The Ue—Monína's Village—Native Names—Suspected of Falsehood—War-Dance—Insanity and Disappearance of Monahin—Fruitless Search—Monina's Sympathy—The Sand-River Tangwe—The Ordeal Muavi: its Victims—An Unreasonable Man—"Woman's Rights"—Presents—Temperance—A Winding Course to shun Villages—Banyai Complexion and Hair—Mushrooms—The Tubers, Mokuri—The Tree Shekabakadzi—Face of the Country—Pot-Holes—Pursued by a Party of Natives—Unpleasant Threat—Aroused by a Company of Soldiers—A Civilized Breakfast—Arrival at Tete... 387

CHAPTER XXXI.

Kind Reception from the Commandant—His Generosity to my Men—The Village of Tete—The Population—Distilled Spirits—The Fort—Cause of the Decadence of Portuguese Power—Former Trade—Slaves employed in Gold-Washing—Slave-Trade drained the Country of Laborers—The Rebel Nyaude's Stockade—He burns Tete—Extensive Field of Sugarcane—The Commandant's Good Reputation among the Natives—Providential Guidance—Seams of Coal—A Hot Spring—Picturesque Country—Water-Carriage to the Coal-Fields—Workmen's Wages—Exports—Price of Provisions—Visit Gold-Washings—Coal within a Gold-Field—Present from Major Sicard—Natives raise Wheat, &c.—Liberality of the Commandant—Geographical Information from Senhor Candido—Earthquakes—Disinterested Kindness of the Portuguese.. 405

CHAPTER XXXII.

Leave Tete and proceed down the River—Pass the Stockade of Bonga—War-Drum at Shiramba—Reach Senna—Its Ruinous State—Landeens levy Fines upon the Inhabitants—Cowardice of Native Militia—Boat-Building at Senna—Our Departure—Fever: its Effects—Kindly received into the House of Colonel Nunes at Kilimane—Forethought of Captain Nolloth and Dr. Walsh—Joy imbittered—Deep Obligations to the Earl of Clarendon, &c.—Desirableness of Missionary Societies selecting Healthy Stations—Arrangements on leaving my Men—Site of Kilimane—Unhealthiness—Arrival of H.M. Brig "Frolic"—Anxiety of one of my Men to go to England—Rough Passage in the Boats to the Ship—Sekwebu's Alarm—Sail for Mauritius-Sekwebu on board: he becomes insane: drowns himself—Kindness of Major-General C. M. Hay—Escape Shipwreck—Reach Home................... 420

HISTORICAL SKETCH OF DISCOVERY IN AFRICA............................ 434

JOURNEYS AND RESEARCHES

IN

SOUTH AFRICA.

INTRODUCTION

My own inclination would lead me to say as little as possible about myself; but several friends, in whose judgment I have confidence, have suggested that, as the reader likes to know something about the author, a short account of his origin and early life would lend additional interest to this book. Such is my excuse for the following egotism; and, if any apology be necessary for giving a genealogy, I find it in the fact that it is not very long, and contains only one incident of which I have reason to be proud.

Our great-grandfather fell at the battle of Culloden, fighting for the old line of kings; and our grandfather was a small farmer in Ulva, where my father was born. It is one of that cluster of the Hebrides thus alluded to by Walter Scott :—

"And Ulva dark, and Colonsay,
And all the group of islets gay
That guard famed Staffa round."*

Our grandfather was intimately acquainted with all the traditionary legends which that great writer has since made use of in the "Tales of a Grandfather" and other works. As a boy I remember listening to him with de

* Lord of the Isles, canto iv.

light, for his memory was stored with a never-ending stock of stories, many of which were wonderfully like those I have since heard while sitting by the African evening fires. Our grandmother, too, used to sing Gaelic songs, some of which, as she believed, had been composed by captive islanders languishing hopelessly among the Turks.

Grandfather could give particulars of the lives of his ancestors for six generations of the family before him; and the only point of the tradition I feel proud of is this: One of these poor hardy islanders was renowned in the district for great wisdom and prudence; and it is related that, when he was on his death-bed, he called all his children around him and said, "Now, in my lifetime I have searched most carefully through all the traditions I could find of our family, and I never could discover that there was a dishonest man among our forefathers. If, therefore, any of you or any of your children should take to dishonest ways, it will not be because it runs in our blood: it does not belong to you. I leave this precept with you: Be honest." If, therefore, in the following pages I fall into any errors, I hope they will be dealt with as honest mistakes, and not as indicating that I have forgotten our ancient motto. This event took place at a time when the Highlanders, according to Macaulay, were much like the Cape Caffres, and any one, it was said, could escape punishment for cattle-stealing by presenting a share of the plunder to his chieftain. Our ancestors were Roman Catholics: they were made Protestants by the laird coming round with a man having a yellow staff, which would seem to have attracted more attention than his teaching, for the new religion went long afterward, perhaps it does so still, by the name of "the religion of the yellow stick."

Finding his farm in Ulva insufficient to support a numerous family, my grandfather removed to Blantyre Works, a large cotton-manufactory on the beautiful Clyde, above Glasgow; and his sons, having had the best education the

Hebrides afforded, were gladly received as clerks by the proprietors, Monteith and Co. He himself, highly esteemed for his unflinching honesty, was employed in the conveyance of large sums of money from Glasgow to the works, and in old age was, according to the custom of that company, pensioned off, so as to spend his declining years in ease and comfort.

Our uncles all entered his majesty's service during the last French war, either as soldiers or sailors; but my father remained at home, and, though too conscientious ever to become rich as a small tea-dealer, by his kindliness of manner and winning ways he made the heart-strings of his children twine around him as firmly as if he had possessed, and could have bestowed upon them, every worldly advantage. He reared his children in connection with the Kirk of Scotland,—a religious establishment which has been an incalculable blessing to that country; but he afterward left it, and during the last twenty years of his life held the office of deacon of an independent church in Hamilton, and deserved my lasting gratitude and homage for presenting me, from my infancy, with a continuously consistent pious example, such as that the ideal of which is so beautifully and truthfully portrayed in Burns's "Cottar's Saturday Night." He died in February, 1856, in peaceful hope of that mercy which we all expect through the death of our Lord and Saviour. I was at the time on my way below Zumbo, expecting no greater pleasure in this country than sitting by our cottage-fire and telling him my travels. I revere his memory.

The earliest recollection of my mother recalls a picture often seen among the Scottish poor,—that of the anxious housewife striving to make both ends meet. At the age of ten I was put into the factory as a "piecer," to aid by my earnings in lessening her anxiety. With a part of my first week's wages I purchased Ruddiman's "Rudiments of Latin," and pursued the study of that language for many years afterward, with unabated ardor, at an evening school, which met between the hours of eight and ten. The dictionary part of my labors was followed up till twelve o'clock, or later, if my mother did not interfere by jumping up and snatching the books out of my hands. I had to be back in the factory by six in the morning, and continue my work, with intervals for breakfast and dinner, till eight o'clock at night. I read in this way many of the classical authors, and knew Virgil and Horace better at sixteen than I do now. Our schoolmaster—happily still alive—was supported in part by the company; he was attentive and kind, and so moderate in his charges that all who wished for education might have obtained it. Many availed themselves of the privilege; and some of my schoolfellows now rank in positions far above what they appeared ever likely to come to when in the village school. If such a system were established in England, it would prove a never-ending blessing to the poor.

In reading, every thing that I could lay my hands on was devoured except novels. Scientific works and books of travels were my especial delight; though my father, believing, with many of his time who ought to have known better, that the former were inimical to religion, would have preferred to have seen me poring over the "Cloud of Witnesses," or Boston's "Fourfold State." Our difference of opinion reached the point of open rebellion on my part, and his last application of the rod was on my refusal to peruse Wilberforce's "Practical Christianity." This dislike to dry doctrinal reading, and to religious reading of every sort, continued for years afterward; but having lighted on those admirable works of Dr. Thomas Dick, "The Philosophy of Religion" and "The Philosophy of a Future State," it was gratifying to find my own ideas, that religion and science are not hostile, but friendly to each other, fully proved and enforced.

Great pains had been taken by my parents to instil the doctrines of Christianity into my mind, and I had no difficulty in understanding the theory of our free salvation by the atonement of our Saviour; but it was only about this time that I really began to feel the necessity and value of a personal application of the provisions of that atonement to my own case. The change was like what may be supposed would take place were it possible to cure a case of "color-blindness." The perfect freeness with which the pardon of all our guilt is offered in God's book drew forth feelings of affectionate love to Him who bought us with his blood, and a sense of deep obligation to Him for his mercy has influenced, in some small measure, my conduct ever since. But I shall not again refer to the inner spiritual life which I believe then began, nor do I intend to specify with any prominence the evangelistic labors to which the love of Christ has since impelled me. This book will speak, not so much of what has been done, as of what stil remains to be performed before the gospel can be said to be preached to all nations.

In the glow of love which Christianity inspires, I soon resolved to devote my life to the alleviation of human misery. Turning this idea over in my mind, I felt that to be a pioneer of Christianity in China might lead to the material benefit of some portions of that immense empire, and therefore set myself to obtain a medical education, in order to be qualified for that enterprise.

In recognising the plants pointed out in my first medical book, that extraordinary old work on astrological medicine, Culpeper's "Herbal," I had the guidance of a book on the plants of Lanarkshire, by Patrick. Limited as my time was, I found opportunities to scour the whole country-side, "collecting simples." Deep and anxious were my studies on the still deeper and more perplexing profundities of astrology, and I believe I got as far into that abyss of fantasies as my author said he dared to lead me. It seemed perilous ground to tread on farther, for the dark hint seemed to my youthful mind to loom toward "selling soul and body to the devil," as the price of the unfathomable knowledge of the stars These excursions, often in company with brothers, one now in Canada, and the other a clergyman in the United States, gratified my intense love of nature; and though we generally returned so unmercifully hungry and fatigued that the embryo parson shed tears, yet we discovered, to us, so many new and interesting things, that he was always as eager to join us next time as he was the last.

On one of these exploring tours we entered a limestone-quarry,—long before geology was so popular as it is now. It is impossible to describe the delight and wonder with which I began to collect the shells found in the carboniferous limestone which crops out in High Blantyre and Cambuslang. A quarry-man, seeing a little boy so engaged, looked with that pitying eye which the benevolent assume when viewing the insane. Addressing him with, "How ever did these shells come into these rocks?" "When God made the rocks, he made the shells in them," was the damping reply. What a deal of trouble geologists might have saved themselves by adopting the Turk-like philosophy of this Scotchman!

My reading while at work was carried on by placing the book on a portion of the spinning-jenny, so that I could catch sentence after sentence as I passed at my work: I thus kept up a pretty constant study, undisturbed by the roar of the machinery. To this part of my education I owe my present power of completely abstracting the mind from surrounding noises, so as to read and write with perfect comfort amid the play of children or near the dancing and songs of savages. The toil of cotton-spinning, to which I was promoted in my nineteenth year, was excessively severe on a slim, loose-jointed lad, but it was well paid for; and it enabled me to support myself while attending medical and Greek classes in Glasgow in winter, as also the divinity lectures of Dr. Wardlaw by working with my hands in summer. I never received a farthing of aid from any one, and should have accomplished my project of going to China as a medical missionary, in the course of time, by my own efforts, had not some friends advised my joining the London Missionary Society, on account of its perfectly unsectarian character. It "sends neither Episcopacy, nor Presbyterianism, nor Independency, but the gospel of Christ, to the heathen." This exactly agreed with my ideas of what a missionary society ought to do; but it was not without a pang that I offered myself, for 't was not quite agreeable to one accustomed to work his own way to become in a measure dependent on others; and I would not have been much put about though my offer had been rejected.

Looking back now on that life of toil, I cannot but feel thankful that it formed such a material part of my early education; and, were it possible, I should like to begin life over again in the same lowly style, and to pass through the same hardy training.

Time and travel have not effaced the feelings of respect I imbibed for the humble inhabitants of my native village. For morality, honesty, and intelligence, they were, in general, good specimens of the Scottish poor. In a population of more than two thousand souls, we had, of course, a variety of character. In addition to the common run of men, there were some characters of sterling worth and ability, who exerted a most beneficial influence on the children and youth of the place by imparting gratuitous religious instruction.* Much intelligent interest was felt by the villagers in all public questions, and they furnished a proof that the possession of the means of education did not render them an unsafe portion of the population. They felt kindly

---

* The reader will pardon my mentioning the names of two of these most worthy men,—David Hogg, who addressed me on his death-bed with the words, "Now, lad, make religion the every-day business of your life, and not a thing of fits and starts: for if you do not, temptation and other things will get the better of you;" and Thomas Burke, an old Forty-Second Peninsula soldier, who has been incessant and never weary in good works for about forty years. I was delighted to find him still alive: men like these are an honor to their country and profession.

toward each other, and much respected those of the neighboring gentry who, like the late Lord Douglas, placed some confidence in their sense of honor. Through the kindness of that nobleman, the poorest among us could stroll at pleasure over the ancient domains of Bothwell, and other spots hallowed by the venerable associations of which our school-books and local traditions made us well aware; and few of us could view the dear memorials of the past without feeling that these carefully-kept monuments were our own. The masses of the working-people of Scotland have read history, and are no revolutionary levellers. They rejoice in the memories of "Wallace and Bruce and a' the lavè," who are still much revered as the former champions of freedom. And, while foreigners imagine that we want the spirit only to overturn capitalists and aristocracy, we are content to respect our laws till we can change them, and hate those stupid revolutions which might sweep away time-honored institutions, dear alike to rich and poor.

Having finished the medical curriculum and presented a thesis on a subject which required the use of the stethoscope for its diagnosis, I unwittingly procured for myself an examination rather more severe and prolonged than usual among examining bodies. The reason was, that between me and the examiners a slight difference of opinion existed as to whether this instrument could do what was asserted. The wiser plan would have been to have had no opinion of my own. However, I was admitted a Licentiate of Faculty of Physicians and Surgeons. It was with unfeigned delight I became a member of a profession which is pre-eminently devoted to practical benevolence, and which with unwearied energy pursues from age to age its endeavors to lessen human woe.

But, though now qualified for my original plan, the opium war was then raging, and it was deemed inexpedient for me to proceed to China. I had fondly hoped to have gained access to that then closed empire by means of the healing art; but, there being no prospect of an early peace with the Chinese, and as another inviting field was opening out through the labors of Mr. Moffat, I was induced to turn my thoughts to Africa; and, after a more extended course of theological training in England than I had enjoyed in Glasgow, I embarked for Africa in 1840, and, after a voyage of three months, reached Cape Town. Spending but a short time there, I started for the interior by going round to Algoa Bay, and soon proceeded inland, and have spent the following sixteen years of my life, namely, from 1840 to 1856, in medical and missionary labors there without cost to the inhabitants.

As to those literary qualifications which are acquired by habits of writing, and which are so important to an author my African life has not only not been favorable to the growth of such accomplishments, but quite the reverse; it has made composition irksome and laborious. I think I would rather cross the African continent again than undertake to write another book. It is far easier to travel than to write about it. I intended on going to Africa to continue my studies; but as I could not brook the idea of simply entering into other men's labors made ready to my hands, I entailed on myself, in addition to teaching, manual labor in building and other handicraft-work, which made me generally as much exhausted and unfit for study in the evenings as ever I had been when a cotton-spinner. The want of time for self-improvement was the only source of regret that I experienced during my African career. The reader, remembering this, will make allowances for the mere gropings for light of a student who has the vanity to think himself "not yet too old to learn." More precise information on several subjects has necessarily been omitted in a popular work like the present; but I hope to give such details to the scientific reader through some other channel

B

CHAPTER I.

DR. LIVINGSTONE A MISSIONARY IN THE BAKWAIN COUNTRY

THE general instructions I received from the Directors of the London Missionary Society led me, as soon as I reached Kuruman or Lattakoo, then, as it is now, their farthest inland station from the Cape, to turn my attention to the north. Without waiting longer at Kuruman than was necessary to recruit the oxen, which were pretty well tired by the long journey from Algoa Bay, I proceeded, in company with another missionary, to the Bakuéna or Bakwain country, and found Sechele, with his tribe, located at Shokuáne. We shortly after retraced our steps to Kuruman; but as the objects in view were by no means to be attained by a temporary excursion of this sort, I determined to make a fresh start into the interior as soon as possible. Accordingly, after resting three months at Kuruman, which is a kind of head-station in the country, I returned to a spot about fifteen miles south of Shokuáne, called Lepelóle (now Litubarúba.) Here, in order to obtain an accurate knowledge of the language, I cut myself off from all European society for about six months, and gained by this ordeal an insight into the habits, ways of thinking, laws, and language of that section of the Bechuanas called Bakwains, which has proved of incalculable advantage in my intercourse with them ever since.

In this second journey to Lepelóle—so called from a cavern of that name—I began preparations for a settlement, by making a canal to irrigate gardens, from a stream then flowing copiously, but now quite dry. When these preparations were well advanced, I went northward to visit the Bakáa and Bamangwáto, and the Makaláka, living between 22° and 23° south latitude. The Bakáa Mountains had been visited before by a trader, who, with his people, all perished from fever. In going round the northern part of these basaltic hills near Letlóche I was only ten days distant from the lower part of the Souga, which passed by the same name as Lake Ngami; and 1 might then (in 1842) have discovered that lake, had discovery alone been my object. Most part of this journey beyond Shokuane was performed on foot, in consequence of the draught-oxen having become sick. Some of my companions who had recently joined us, and did not know that I understood a little of their speech, were overheard by me discussing my appearance and powers: "He is not strong; he is quite slim, and only appears stout because he puts himself into those bags, (trowsers:) he will soon knock up." This caused my Highland blood to rise, and made me despise the fatigue of keeping them all at the top of their speed for days together, and until I heard them expressing proper opinions of my pedestrian powers.

Returning to Kuruman, in order to bring my luggage to our proposed settlement, I was followed by the news that the tribe of Bakwains, who had shown themselves so friendly toward me, had been driven from Lepelole by the Barolongs, so that my prospects for the time of forming a settlement there were at an end. One of those periodical outbreaks of war, which seem to have occurred from time immemorial, for the possession of cattle, had burst forth in the land, and had so changed the relations of the tribes to each other that I was obliged to set out anew to look for a suitable locality for a mission-station.

As some of the Bamangwato people had accompanied me to Kuruman, I was obliged to restore them and their goods to their chief Sekómi. This made a journey to the residence of that chief again necessary, and, for the first time, I performed a distance of some hundred miles on ox-back.

Returning toward Kuruman, I selected the beautiful valley of Mabotsa (lat. 25° 14' south, long. 26° 30'?) as the site of a missionary station, and thither I removed in 1843. Here an occurrence took place concerning which I have frequently been questioned in England, and which, but for the importunities of friends, I meant to have kept in store to tell my children when in my dotage. The Bakátla of the village Mabotsa were much troubled by lions, which leaped into the cattle-pens by night and destroyed their cows. They even attacked the herds in open day. This was so unusual an occurrence that the people believed that they were bewitched,—"given," as they said, "into the power of the lions by a neighboring tribe." They went once to attack the animals; but, being rather a cowardly people compared to Bechuanas in general on such occasions, they returned without killing any.

It is well known that if one of a troop of lions is killed, the others take the hint and leave that part of the country. So, the next time the herds were attacked, I went with the people, in order to encourage them to rid themselves of the annoyance by destroying one of the marauders. We found the lions on a small hill about a quarter of a mile in length and covered with trees. A circle of men was formed round it, and they gradually closed up, ascending pretty near to each other. Being down below on the plain with a native schoolmaster, named Mebálwe, a most excellent man, I saw one of the lions sitting on a piece of rock within the now closed circle of men. Mebalwe fired at him before I could, and the ball struck the rock on which the animal was sitting. He bit at the spot struck, as a dog does at a stick or stone thrown at him, then, leaping away, broke through the opening circle and escaped unhurt. The men were afraid to attack him, perhaps on account of their belief in witchcraft. When the circle was reformed, we saw two other lions in it; but we were afraid to fire, lest we should strike the men, and they allowed the beasts to burst through also. If the Bakatla had acted according to the custom of the country, they would have speared the lions in their attempt to get out. Seeing we could not get them to kill one of the lions, we bent our footsteps toward the village: in going round the end of the hill, however, I saw one of the beasts sitting on a piece of rock as before, but this time he had a little bush in front. Being about thirty yards off, I took a good aim at his body through the bush, and fired both barrels into it. The men then called out, "He is shot! he is shot!" Others cried, "He has been shot by another man too; let us go to him!" I did not see any one else shoot at him, but I saw the lion's tail erected in anger behind the bush, and, turning to the people, said, "Stop a little, till I load again." When in the act of ramming down the bullets, I heard a shout. Starting, and looking half round, I saw the lion just in the act of springing upon me. I was upon a little height; he caught my shoulder as he sprang, and we both came to the ground below together. Growling horribly close to my ear, he shook me as a terrier dog does a rat. The shock produced a stupor similar to that which seems to be felt by a mouse after the first shake of the cat. It caused a sort of dreaminess, in which there was no sense of pain nor feeling of terror, though quite conscious of all that was happening. It was like what patients partially under the influence of chloroform describe, who see all the operation, but feel not the knife. This singular condition was not the result of any mental process. The shake annihilated fear, and allowed no sense of horror in looking round at the beast. This peculiar state is probably produced in all animals killed by the carnivora, and, if so, is a merciful provision by our benevolent Creator for lessening the pain of death. Turning round to relieve myself of the weight, as he had one paw on the back of my head, I saw his eyes directed to Mebalwe, who was trying to shoot him at a distance of ten or fifteen yards. His gun, a flint one, missed fire in both barrels; the lion immediately left me, and, attacking Mebalwe, bit his thigh. Another man, whose life I had saved before, after he had been tossed by a buffalo, attempted to spear the lion while he was biting Mebalwe. He left Mebalwe and caught this man by the shoulder, but at that moment the bullets he had received took effect, and he fell down dead. The whole was the work of a few moments, and must have been his paroxysms of dying rage In order to take out the charm from him, the Bakatla on the following day made a huge bonfire over the carcass, which was declared to be that of the largest lion they had ever seen. Besides crunching the bone into splinters, he left eleven teeth-wounds on the upper part of my arm.

A wound from this animal's tooth resembles a gun-shot wound; it is generally followed by a great deal of sloughing and discharge, and pains are felt in the part periodically ever afterward. I had on a tartan jacket on the occasion, and I believe that it wiped off all the virus from the teeth that pierced the flesh, for my two companions in this affray have both suffered from the peculiar pains, while I have escaped with only the inconvenience of a false joint in my limb. The man whose shoulder was wounded showed me his wound actually burst forth afresh on the same month of the following year. This curious point deserves the attention of inquirers.

I attached myself to the tribe called Bakuena or Bakwains, the chief of which, named Sechele, was then living with his people at a place called Shokuane. I was from the first struck by his intelligence, and by the marked manner in which we both felt drawn to each other. This remarkable man has not only embraced Christianity, but expounds its doctrines to his people.

Sechele continued to make a consistent profession for about three years; and, perceiving at last some of the difficulties of his case, and also feeling compassion for the poor women, who were by far the best of our scholars, I had no desire that he should be in any hurry to make a full profession by baptism and putting away all his wives but one. His principal wife, too, was about the most unlikely subject in the tribe ever to become any thing else than an out-and-out greasy disciple of the old school. She has since become greatly altered, I hear, for the better; but again and again have I seen Sechele send her out of church to put her gown on, and away she would go with her lips shot out, the very picture of unutterable disgust at his new-fangled notions.

When he at last applied for baptism, I simply asked him how he, having the Bible in his hand, and able to read it, thought he ought to act. He went home, gave each of his superfluous wives new clothing, and all his own goods, which they had been accustomed to keep in their huts for him, and sent them to their parents with an intimation that he had no fault to find with them, but that in parting with them he wished to follow the will of God. On the day on which he and his children were baptized, great numbers came to see the ceremony. Some thought, from a stupid calumny circulated by enemies to Christianity in the south, that the converts would be made to drink an infusion of "dead men's brains," and were astonished to find that water only was used at baptism. Seeing several of the old men actually in tears during the service, I asked them afterward the cause of their weeping; they were crying to see their father, as the Scotch remark over a case of suicide, "*so far left to himself.*" They seemed to think that I had thrown the glamour over him, and that he had become mine. Here commenced an opposition which we had not previously experienced. All the friends of the divorced wives became the opponents of our religion. The attendance at school and church diminished to very few besides the chief's own family. They all treated us still with respectful kindness, but to Sechele himself they said things which, as he often remarked, had they ventured on in former times, would have cost them their lives. It was trying, after all we had done, to see our labors so little appreciated; but we had sown the good seed, and have no doubt but it will yet spring up, though we may not live to see the fruits.

Leaving this sketch of the chief, I proceed to give an equally rapid one of our dealing with his people, the Bakena, or Bakwains. A small piece of land, sufficient for a garden, was purchased when we first went to live with them, though that was scarcely necessary in a country where the idea of buying land was quite new. It was expected that a request for a suitable spot would have been made, and that we should have proceeded to occupy it as any other member of the tribe would. But we explained to them that we wished to avoid any cause of future dispute when land had become more valuable; or when a foolish chief began to reign, and we had erected large or expensive buildings, he might wish to claim the whole. These reasons were considered satisfactory. About £5 worth of goods were given for a piece of land, and an arrangement was come to that a similar piece should be allotted to any other missionary, at any other place to which the tribe might remove. The particulars of the sale sounded strangely in the ears of the tribe, but were nevertheless readily agreed to.

In our relations with this people we were simply strangers, exercising no authority or control whatever. Our influence depended entirely on persuasion; and, having taught them by kind conversation as well as by public instruction, I expected them to do what their own sense of right and wrong dictated. We never wished them to do right merely because it would be pleasing to us, nor thought ourselves to blame when they did wrong, although we were quite aware of the absurd idea to that effect We saw that our teaching did good to the general mind of the people by bringing new and better motives into play. Five instances are positively known to me in which, by our influence on public opinion, war was prevented; and where, in individual cases, we failed, the people did no worse than they did before we came into the country. In general they were slow, like all the African people hereafter to be described, in coming to a decision on religious subjects; but in questions affecting their worldly affairs they were keenly alive to their own interests. They might be called stupid in matters which had not come within the sphere of their observation, but in

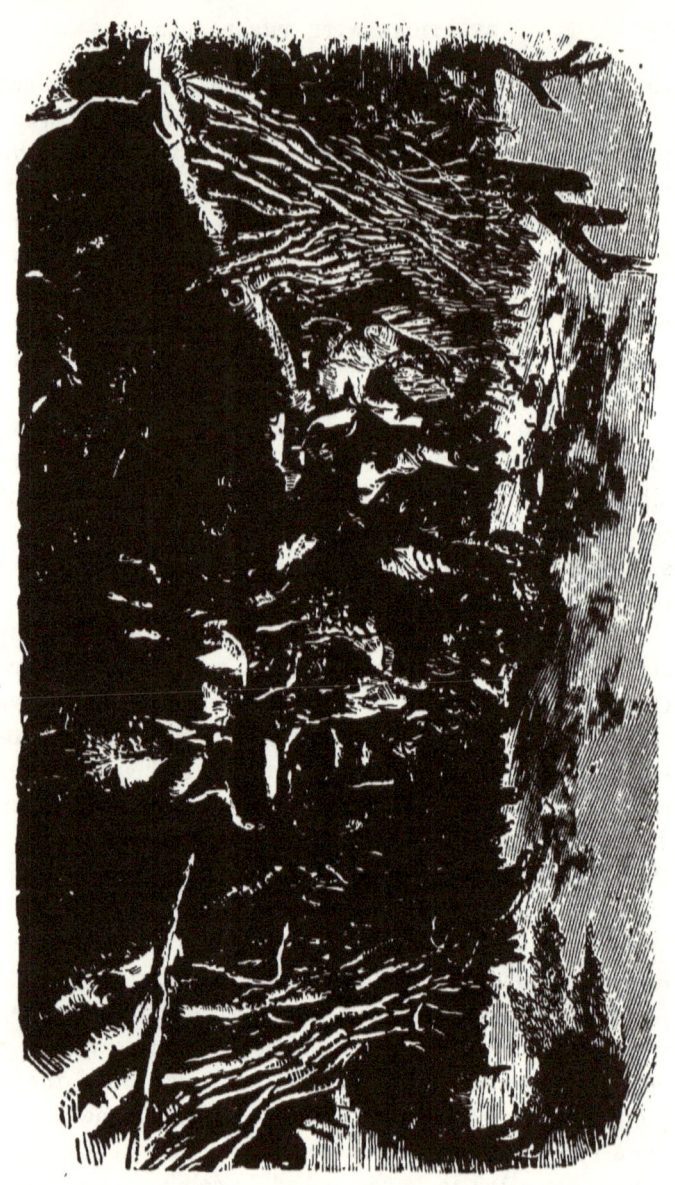

The Pit at the Extremity of the Hope.

other things they showed more intelligence than is to be met with in our own uneducated peasantry. They are remarkably accurate in their knowledge of cattle, sheep, and goats, knowing exactly the kind of pasturage suited to each; and they select with great judgment the varieties of soil best suited to different kinds of grain. They are also familiar with the habits of wild animals, and in general are well up in the maxims which embody their ideas of political wisdom.

The place where we first settled with the Bakwains is called Chonuane, and it happened to be visited, during the first year of our residence there, by one of those droughts which occur from time to time in even the most favored districts of Africa.

The conduct of the people during this long-continued drought was remarkably good. The women parted with most of their ornaments to purchase corn from more fortunate tribes. The children scoured the country in search of the numerous bulbs and roots which can sustain life, and the men engaged in hunting. Very great numbers of the large game, buffaloes, zebras, giraffes, tsessébes, kamas or hartebeests, kokongs or gnus, pallahs, rhinoceroses, &c., congregated at some fountains near Kolobeng, and the trap called "*hopo*" was constructed, in the lands adjacent, for their destruction. The hopo consists of two hedges in the form of the letter V, which are very high and thick near the angle. Instead of the hedges being joined there, they are made to form a lane of about fifty yards in length, at the extremity of which a pit is formed, six or eight feet deep, and about twelve or fifteen in breadth and length. Trunks of trees are laid across the margin of the pit, and more especially over that nearest the lane where the animals are expected to leap in, and over that farthest from the lane where it is supposed they will attempt to escape after they are in. The trees form an overlapping border and render escape almost impossible. The whole is carefully decked with short green rushes, making the pit like a concealed pitfall. As the hedges are frequently about a mile long, and about as much apart at their extremities, a tribe making a circle three or four miles round the country adjacent to the opening, and gradually closing up, are almost sure to enclose a large body of game. Driving it up with shouts to the narrow part of the hopo, men secreted there throw their javelins into the affrighted herds, and on the animals rush to the opening presented at the converging hedges, and into the pit, till that is full of a living mass. Some escape by running over the others, as a Smithfield market-dog does over the sheep's backs. It is a frightful scene. The men, wild with excitement, spear the lovely animals with mad delight; others of the poor creatures, borne down by the weight of their dead and dying companions, every now and then make the whole mass heave in their smothering agonies.

The Bakwains often killed between sixty and seventy head of large game at the different hopos in a single week; and as every one, both rich and poor, partook of the prey, the meat counteracted the bad effects of an exclusively vegetable diet.

CHAPTER II.

DR. LIVINGSTONE PREPARES TO GO TO LAKE NGAMI.

ANOTHER adverse influence with which the mission had to contend was the vicinity of the Boers of the Cashan Mountains, otherwise named "Magaliesberg." These are not to be confounded with the Cape colonists, who sometimes pass by the name. The word Boer simply means "farmer," and is not synonymous with our word boor. Indeed, to the Boers generally the latter term would be quite inappropriate, for they are a sober, industrious, and most hospitable body of peasantry. Those, how-

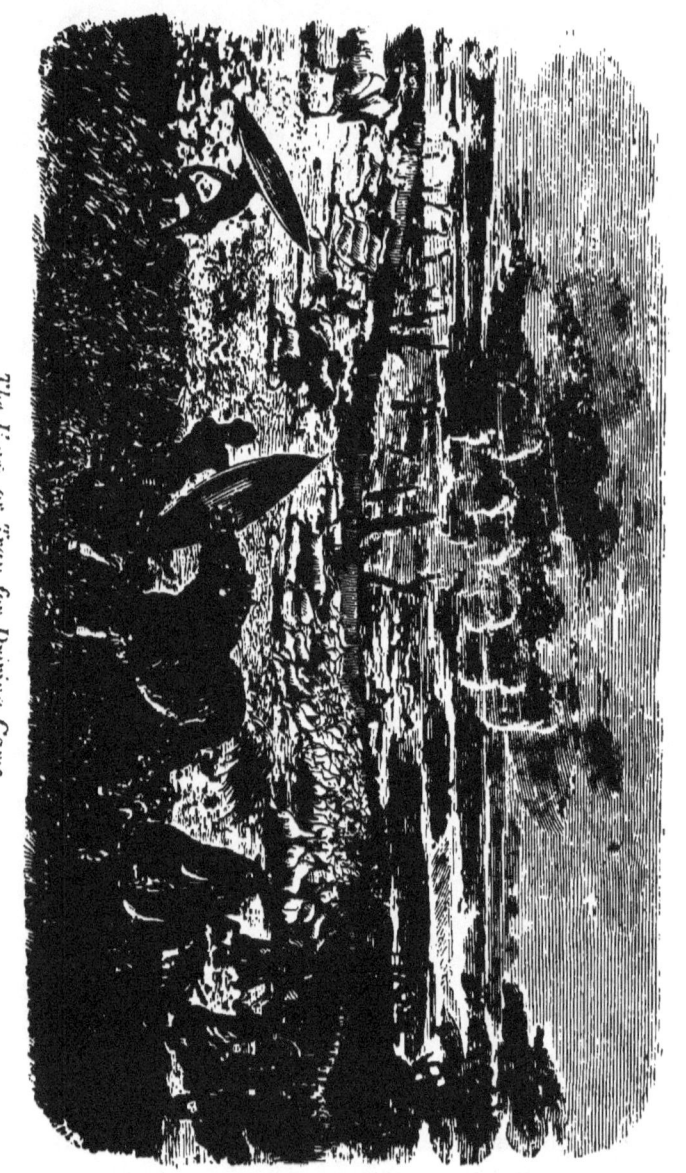

The Hopo, or Trap for Driving Game.

ever who have fled from English law on various pretexts, and have been joined by English deserters and every other variety of bad character in their distant localities, are unfortunately of a very different stamp. The great objection many of the Boers had, and still have, to English law, is that it makes no distinction between black men and white. They felt aggrieved by their supposed losses in the emancipation of their Hottentot slaves, and determined to erect themselves into a republic, in which they might pursue, without molestation, the "proper treatment of the blacks." It is almost needless to add that the "proper treatment" has always contained in it the essential element of slavery, namely, compulsory unpaid labor.

One section of this body, under the late Mr. Hendrick Potgeiter, penetrated the interior as far as the Cashan Mountains, whence a Zulu or Caffre chief, named Mosilikatze, had been expelled by the well-known Caffre Dingaan;* and a glad welcome was given them by the Bechuana tribes, who had just escaped the hard sway of that cruel chieftain. They came with the prestige of white men and deliverers; but the Bechuanas soon found, as they expressed it, "that Mosilikatze was cruel to his enemies, and kind to those he conquered; but that the Boers destroyed their enemies, and made slaves of their friends." The tribes who still retain the semblance of independence are forced to perform all the labor of the fields, such as manuring the land, weeding, reaping, building,

---

* Dingaan was the brother and successor of Chaka, the most cruel and bloodthirsty tyrant that ever disgraced the soil of Africa. He had formed his tribe into a military organization and ravaged all the neighboring tribes; but his horrible cruelties to his own subjects led to a revolt, headed by Dingaan and Umslungani, his two elder brothers, who first attacked him with spears, wounding him in the back. Chaka was enveloped in a blanket, which he cast off and fled. He was overtaken and again wounded. Falling at the feet of his pursuers, he besought them in the most abject terms to let him live, that he might be their slave; but he was instantly speared to death.—*Am. Ed*

making dams and canals, and at the same time to support themselves. I have myself been an eye-witness of Boers coming to a village, and, according to their usual custom, demanding twenty or thirty women to weed their gardens, and have seen these women proceed to the scene of unrequited toil, carrying their own food on their heads, their children on their backs, and instruments of labor on their shoulders. Nor have the Boers any wish to conceal the meanness of thus employing unpaid labor: on the contrary, every one of them, from Mr. Potgeiter and Mr. Gert Krieger, the commandants, downward, lauded his own humanity and justice in making such an equitable regulation. "We make the people work for us, in consideration of allowing them to live in our country."

The Boers determined to put a stop to English traders going past Kolobeng, by dispersing the tribe of Bakwains and expelling all the missionaries. Sir George Cathcart proclaimed the independence of the Boers, the best thing that could have been done had they been between us and the Caffres. A treaty was entered into with these Boers; an article for the free passage of Englishmen to the country beyond, and also another, that no slavery should be allowed in the independent territory, were duly inserted, as expressive of the views of her majesty's government at home. "But what about the missionaries?" inquired the Boers. "*You may do as you please with them,*" is said to have been the answer of the "Commissioner." This remark, if uttered at all, was probably made in joke: designing men, however, circulated it, and caused the general belief in its accuracy which now prevails all over the country, and doubtless led to the destruction of three mission-stations immediately after. The Boers, four hundred in number, were sent by the late Mr. Pretorius to attack the Bakwains in 1852. Boasting that the English had given up all the blacks into their power, and had agreed to aid them in their subjugation by preventing all supplies of ammunition from coming into the Bechuana country, they assaulted the Bakwains, and, besides killing a considerable number of adults, carried off two hundred of our schoolchildren into slavery. The natives under Sechele defended themselves till the approach of night enabled them to flee to the mountains; and, having in that defence killed a number of the enemy, the very first ever slain in this country by Bechuanas, I received the credit of having taught the tribe to kill Boers! My house, which had stood perfectly secure for years under the protection of the natives, was plundered in revenge. English gentlemen, who had come in the footsteps of Mr. Cumming to hunt in the country beyond, and had deposited large quantities of stores in the same keeping, and upward of eighty head of cattle as relays for the return journeys, were robbed of all, and, when they came back to Kolobeng, found the skeletons of the guardians strewed all over the place. The books of a good library—my solace in our solitude—were not, taken away, but handfuls of the leaves were torn out and scattered over the place. My stock of medicines was smashed, and all our furniture and clothing carried off and sold at public auction to pay the expenses of the foray.

In trying to benefit the tribes living under the Boers of the Cashan Mountains, I twice performed a journey of about three hundred miles to the eastward of Kolobeng. Sechele had become so obnoxious to the Boers that, though anxious to accompany me in my journey, he dared not trust himself among them. This did not arise from the crime of cattle-stealing; for that crime, so common among the Caffres, was never charged against his tribe, nor, indeed, against any Bechuana tribe. It is, in fact, unknown in the country, except during actual warfare. His independence and love of the English were his only faults. In my last journey there, of about two hundred miles, on parting at the river Marikwe he gave me two servants, "to be," as he said, "his arms to serve me," and expressed regret that he could not come himself. "Suppose we went north," I said, "would you come?" He then told me the story of

Sebituane having saved his life, and expatiated on the far famed generosity of that really great man. This was the first time I had thought of crossing the Desert to Lake Ngami.

The conduct of the Boers, who had sent a letter designed to procure my removal out of the country, and their well-known settled policy which I have already described, became more fully developed on this than on any former occasion. When I spoke to Mr. Hendrick Potgeiter of the danger of hindering the gospel of Christ among these poor savages, he became greatly excited, and called one of his followers to answer me. He threatened to attack any tribe that might receive a native teacher; yet he promised to use his influence to prevent those under him from throwing obstacles in our way. I could perceive plainly that nothing more could be done in that direction, so I commenced collecting all the information I could about the desert, with the intention of crossing it, if possible. Sekomi, the chief of the Bamangwato, was acquainted with a route which he kept carefully to himself, because the Lake country abounded in ivory, and he drew large quantities thence periodically at but small cost to himself.

Sechele, who valued highly every thing European, and was always fully alive to his own interest, was naturally anxious to get a share of that inviting field. He was most anxious to visit Sebituane too, partly, perhaps, from a wish to show off his new acquirements, but chiefly, I believe, from having very exalted ideas of the benefits he would derive from the liberality of that renowned chieftain.

Sechele, by my advice, sent men to Sekomi, asking leave for me to pass along his path, accompanying the request with the present of an ox. Sekomi's mother, who possesses great influence over him, refused permission, because she had not been propitiated. This produced a fresh message; and the most honorable man in the Bakwain tribe, next to Sechele, was sent with an ox for both Sekomi and his mother. This, too, was met by refusal. It was said,

' The Matebele, the mortal enemies of the Bechuanas, are in the direction of the lake, and, should they kill the white man, we shall incur great blame from all his nation."

The exact position of the Lake Ngami had, for half a century at least, been correctly pointed out by the natives, who had visited it when rains were more copious in the Desert than in more recent times, and many attempts had been made to reach it by passing through the Desert in the direction indicated; but it was found impossible, even for Griquas, who, having some Bushman blood in them, may be supposed more capable of enduring thirst than Europeans. It was clear, then, that our only chance of success was by going round, instead of through, the Desert. The best time for the attempt would have been about the end of the rainy season, in March or April, for then we should have been likely to meet with pools of rain-water, which always dry up during the rainless winter. I communicated my intention to an African traveller, Colonel Steele, then aide-de-camp to the Marquis of Tweedale at Madras, and he made it known to two other gentlemen, whose friendship we had gained during their African travel, namely, Major Vardon and Mr. Oswell. All of these gentlemen were so enamored with African hunting and African discovery that the two former must have envied the latter his good fortune in being able to leave India to undertake afresh the pleasures and pains of desert life. I believe Mr. Oswell came from his high position at a very considerable pecuniary sacrifice, and with no other end in view but to extend the boundaries of geographical knowledge. Before I knew of his coming, I had arranged that the payment of the guides furnished by Sechele should be the loan of my wagon to bring back whatever ivory he might obtain from the chief at the lake. When, at last, Mr. Oswell came, bringing Mr. Murray with him, he undertook to defray the entire expense of the guides, and fully executed his generous intention

Sechele himself would have come with us, but, fearing
C

that the much-talked-of assault of the Boers might take place during our absence, and blame be attached to me for taking him away, I dissuaded him against it by saying that he knew Mr. Oswell "would be as determined as himself to get through the Desert."

CHAPTER III.

DR. LIVINGSTONE DISCOVERS LAKE NGAMI.

Just before the arrival of my companions, a party of the people of the lake came to Kolobeng, stating that they were sent by Lechulatebe, the chief, to ask me to visit that country. They brought such flaming accounts of the quantities of ivory to be found there, (cattle-pens made of elephants' tusks of enormous size, &c.,) that the guides of the Bakwains were quite as eager to succeed in reaching the lake as any one of us could desire. This was fortunate, as we knew the way the strangers had come was impassable for wagons.

Messrs. Oswell and Murray came at the end of May, and we all made a fair start for the unknown region on the 1st of June, 1849. Proceeding northward, and passing through a range of tree-covered hills to Shokuane, formerly the residence of the Bakwains, we soon after entered on the high road to the Bamangwato, which lies generally in the bed of an ancient river or wady that must formerly have flowed N. to S.

Boatlanáma, our next station, is a lovely spot in the otherwise dry region. The wells from which we had to lift out the water for our cattle are deep, but they were well filled. A few villages of Bakahari were found near them, and great numbers of pallahs, springbucks, Guineafowl, and small monkeys.

Lopépe came next. This place afforded **another proof**

Discovery of Lake Ngami by Livingstone, Oswell and Murray.

of the desiccation of the country. The first time I passed it, Lopépo was a large pool with a stream flowing out of it to the south; now it was with difficulty we could get our cattle watered by digging down in the bottom of a well.

At Mashüe—where we found a never-failing supply of pure water in a sandstone rocky hollow—we left the road to the Bamangwato Hills, and struck away to the north into the Desert. Having watered the cattle at a well called Lobotáni, about N. W. of Bamangwato, we next proceeded to a real Kalahari fountain, called Scrotli.

In the evening of our second day at Scrotli, a hyena appearing suddenly among the grass, succeeded in raising a panic among our cattle. This false mode of attack is the plan which this cowardly animal always adopts. His courage resembles closely that of a turkey-cock. He will bite if an animal is running away; but if the animal stand still, so does he. Seventeen of our draught-oxen ran away, and in their flight went right into the hands of Sekomi, whom, from his being unfriendly to our success, we had no particular wish to see. Cattle-stealing, such as in the circumstances might have occurred in Caffraria, is here unknown; so Sekomi sent back our oxen, and a message strongly dissuading us against attempting the Desert. "Where are you going? You will be killed by the sun and thirst, and then all the white men will blame me for not saving you." This was backed by a private message from his mother. "Why do you pass me? I always made the people collect to hear the word that you have got. What guilt have I, that you pass without looking at me?" We replied by assuring the messengers that the white men would attribute our deaths to our own stupidity and "hardheadedness," (tlogo, e thata,) "as we did not intend to allow our companions and guides to return till they had put us into our graves." We sent a handsome present to Sekomi, and a promise that, if he allowed the Bakalahari to keep the wells open for us, we would repeat the gift on our return.

After exhausting all his eloquence in fruitless attempts to persuade us to return, the under-chief, who headed the party of Sekomi's messengers, inquired, "Who is taking them?" Looking round, he exclaimed, with a face expressive of the most unfeigned disgust, "It is Ramotobi!" Our guide belonged to Sekomi's tribe, but had fled to Sechele; as fugitives in this country are always well received, and may even afterward visit the tribe from which they had escaped, Ramotobi was in no danger, though doing that which he knew to be directly opposed to the interests of his own chief and tribe.

For sixty or seventy miles beyond Serotli, one clump of bushes and trees seemed exactly like another; but, as we walked together this morning, Ramotobi remarked, "When we come to that hollow we shall light upon the highway of Sekomi; and beyond that again lies the river Mokóko;" which, though we passed along it, I could not perceive to be a river-bed at all.

After breakfast, some of the men, who had gone forward on a little path with some footprints of water-loving animals upon it, returned with the joyful tidings of "*metse*," water, exhibiting the mud on their knees in confirmation of the news being true. It does one's heart good to see the thirsty oxen rush into a pool of delicious rainwater, as this was. In they dash until the water is deep enough to be nearly level with their throat, and then they stand drawing slowly in the long, refreshing mouthfuls, until their formerly collapsed sides distend as if they would burst. So much do they imbibe, that a sudden jerk, when they come out on the bank, makes some of the water run out again from their mouths; but, as they have been days without food too, they very soon commence to graze, and of grass there is always abundance everywhere. This pool was called Mathuluána; and thankful we were to have obtained so welcome a supply of water.

After giving the cattle a rest at this spot, we proceeded down the dry bed of the river Mokoko.

At Nchokotsa we came upon the first of a great number of salt-pans, covered with an efflorescence of lime, probably the nitrate. A thick belt of mopane-trees (a *Bauhinia*) hides this salt-pan, which is twenty miles in circumference, entirely from the view of a person coming from the southeast; and, at the time the pan burst upon our view, the setting sun was casting a beautiful blue haze over the white incrustations, making the whole look exactly like a lake. Oswell threw his hat up in the air at the sight, and shouted out a huzza which made the poor Bushwoman and the Bakwains think him mad. I was a little behind him, and was as completely deceived by it as he; but, as we had agreed to allow each other to behold the lake at the same instant, I felt a little chagrined that he had, unintentionally, got the first glance. We had no idea that the long-looked-for lake was still more than three hundred miles distant. One reason of our mistake was that the river Zouga was often spoken of by the same name as the lake,—viz.: Noka ea Batletli, ("River of the Batletli.")

On the 4th of July we went forward on horseback toward what we supposed to be the lake, and again and again did we seem to see it; but at last we came to the veritable water of the Zouga, and found it to be a river running to the N.E. A village of Bakurutse lay on the opposite bank: these live among Batletli, a tribe having a click in their language, and who were found by Sebituane to possess large herds of the great horned cattle. They seem allied to the Hottentot family. Mr. Oswell, in trying to cross the river, got his horse bogged in the swampy bank. Two Bakwains and I managed to get over by wading beside a fishing-weir. The people were friendly, and informed us that this water came out of Ngami. This news gladdened all our hearts, for we now felt certain of reaching our goal. We might, they said, be a moon on the way: but we had the river Zouga at our feet, and by following it we should at last reach the broad water.

Next day, when we were quite disposed to be friendly

with every one, two of the Bamangwato, who had been sent on before us by Sekomi to drive away all the Bushmen and Bakalahari from our path, so that they should not assist or guide us, came and sat down by our fire. We had seen their footsteps fresh in the way, and they had watched our slow movements forward, and wondered to see how we, without any Bushmen, found our way to the waters. This was the first time they had seen Ramotobi. "You have reached the river now," said they; and we, quite disposed to laugh at having won the game, felt no ill-will to any one. They seemed to feel no enmity to us, either; but, after an apparently friendly conversation, proceeded to fulfil to the last the instructions of their chief. Ascending the Zouga in our front, they circulated the report that our object was to plunder all the tribes living on the river and lake; but when they had got half-way up the river, the principal man sickened of fever, turned back some distance, and died. His death had a good effect, for the villagers connected it with the injury he was attempting to do us. They all saw through Sekomi's reasons for wishing us to fail in our attempt; and, though they came to us at first armed, kind and fair treatment soon produced perfect confidence.

When we had gone up the bark of this beautiful river about ninety-six miles from the point where we first struck it, and understood that we were still a considerable distance from the Ngami, we left all the oxen and wagons, except Mr. Oswell's, which was the smallest, and one team, at Ngabisáne, in the hope that they would be recruited for the home journey, while we made a push for the lake. The Bechuana chief of the Lake region, who had sent men to Sechele, now sent orders to all the people on the river to assist us, and we were received by the Bakóba, whose language clearly shows that they bear an affinity to the tribes in the north. They call themselves Bayeiye, *i.e.* men; but the Bechuanas call them Bakoba, which contains somewhat of the idea of slaves. They have never been known to fight, and, indeed, have a tradition that their forefathers, in their

Hottentots—Women coming from the water—Men around a dead Hartebeest.

first essays at war, made their bows of the Palma Christi, and, when these broke, they gave up fighting altogether. They have invariably submitted to the rule of every horde which has overrun the countries adjacent to the rivers on which they specially love to dwell. They are thus the Quakers of the body politic in Africa.

Twelve days after our departure from the wagons at Ngabisane we came to the northeast end of Lake Ngami; and on the 1st of August, 1849, we went down together to the broad part, and, for the first time, this fine-looking sheet of water was beheld by Europeans. The direction of the lake seemed to be N.N.E. and S.S.W. by compass. The southern portion is said to bend round to the west, and to receive the Teoughe from the north at its northwest extremity. We could detect no horizon where we stood looking S.S.W., nor could we form any idea of the extent of the lake, except from the reports of the inhabitants of the district; and, as they professed to go round it in three days, allowing twenty-five miles a day would make it seventy-five, or less than seventy geographical miles in circumference. Other guesses have been made since as to its circumference, ranging between seventy and one hundred miles. It is shallow, for I subsequently saw a native punting his canoe over seven or eight miles of the northeast end; it can never, therefore, be of much value as a commercial highway. In fact, during the months preceding the annual supply of water from the north, the lake is so shallow that it is with difficulty cattle can approach the water through the boggy, reedy banks. These are low on all sides, but on the west there is a space devoid of trees, showing that the waters have retired thence at no very ancient date. This is another of the proofs of desiccation met with so abundantly throughout the whole country. A number of dead trees lie on this space, some of them embedded in the mud, right in the water. We were informed by the Bayeiye, who live on the lake, that when the annual inundation begins not only trees of great size, but antelopes, as the springbuck and tsessebe, (*Acronotus lunata*,) **are** swept down by its rushing waters; the trees are gradually driven by the winds to the opposite side, and become embedded in the mud.

The water of the lake is perfectly fresh when full, but brackish when low; and that coming down the Tamunak'le we found to be so clear, cold, and soft, the higher we ascended, that the idea of melting snow was suggested to our minds. We found this region, with regard to that from which we had come, to be clearly a hollow, the lowest point being Lake Kumadau; the point of the ebullition of water, as shown by one of Newman's barometric thermometers, was only between $207\frac{1}{4}°$ and $206°$, giving an elevation of not much more than two thousand feet above the level of the sea. We had descended above two thousand feet in coming to it from Kolobeng. It is the southern and lowest part of the great river-system beyond, in which large tracts of country are inundated annually by tropical rains.

My chief object in coming to the lake was to visit Sebituane, the great chief of the Makololo, who was reported to live some two hundred miles beyond. We had now come to a half-tribe of the Bamangwato, called Batauána. Their chief was a young man named Lechulatébe. Sebituane had conquered his father Morémi, and Lechulatebe received part of his education while a captive among the Bayeiye. His uncle, a sensible man, ransomed him, and, having collected a number of families together, abdicated the chieftainship in favor of his nephew. As Lechulatebe had just come into power, he imagined that the proper way of showing his abilities was to act directly contrary to every thing that his uncle advised. When we came, **the** uncle recommended him to treat us handsomely: therefore the hopeful youth presented us with a goat only. It ought to have been an ox. So I proposed to my companions to loose the animal and let him go, as a hint to his master. They, however, did not wish to insult him. I, being more of a native, and familiar with their customs, knew that this shabby present was an insult to us. We wished to purchase some goats or oxen; Lechulatebe offered us elephants' tusks. "No, we cannot eat these; we want something to fill our stomachs." "Neither can I; but I hear you white men are all very fond of these bones; so I offer them: I want to put the goats into my own stomach." A trader, who accompanied us, was then purchasing ivory at the rate of ten good large tusks for a musket worth thirteen-shillings. They were called "bones;" and I myself saw eight instances in which the tusks had been left to rot with the other bones where the elephant fell. The Batauana never had a chance of a market before; but, in less than two years after our discovery, not a man of them could be found who was not keenly alive to the great value of the article.

On the day after our arrival at the lake, I applied to Lechulatebe for guides to Sebituane. As he was much afraid of that chief, he objected, fearing lest other white men should go thither also, and give Sebituane guns; whereas, if the traders came to him alone, the possession of fire-arms would give him such a superiority that Sebituane would be afraid of him. It was in vain to explain that I would inculcate peace between them,—that Sebituane had been a father to him and Sechele, and was as anxious to see me as he, Lechulatebe, had been. He offered to give me as much ivory as I needed without going to that chief; but, when I refused to take any, he unwillingly consented to give me guides. Next day, however, when Oswell and I were prepared to start, with the horses only, we received a senseless refusal; and like Sekomi, who had thrown obstacles in our way, he sent men to the Bayeiye with orders to refuse us a passage across the river. Trying hard to form a raft at a narrow part, I worked many hours in the water; but the dry wood was so worm-eaten it would not bear the weight of a single person. I was not then aware of the number of alligators which exist in the Zouga, and never think of my labor in the water without feeling thankful that I escaped their jaws. The season was now far advanced; and as Mr. Oswell, with his wonted generous feelings, volunteered, on the spot, to go down to the Cape and bring up a boat, we resolved to make our way south again.

CHAPTER IV.

DR. LIVINGSTONE PERFORMS TWO JOURNEYS IN THE INTERIOR AND DISCOVERS THE RIVER ZAMBESI—HE SENDS HIS FAMILY TO ENGLAND.

HAVING returned to Kolobeng, I remained there till April, 1850, and then left in company with Mrs. Livingstone, our three children, and the chief Sechele,—who had now bought a wagon of his own,—in order to go across the Zouga at its lower end, with the intention of proceeding up the northern bank till we gained the Tamunak'le, and of then ascending that river to visit Sebituane in the north. Sekomi had given orders to fill up the wells which we had dug with much labor at Serotli; so we took the more eastern route through the Bamangwato town and by Letloche. That chief asked why I had avoided him in our former journeys. I replied that my reason was that I knew he did not wish me to go to the lake, and I did not want to quarrel with him. "Well," he said, "you beat me then, and I am content."

Parting with Sechele at the ford, as he was eager to visit Lechulatebe, we went along the northern woody bank of the Zouga with great labor, having to cut down very many trees to allow the wagons to pass. Our losses by oxen falling into pitfalls were very heavy. The Bayeiye kindly opened the pits when they knew of our approach; but, when that was not the case, we could blame no one on finding an established custom of the country inimical to our interests. On approaching the confluence of the Tamunak'le we were informed that the fly called tsétse* abounded on its banks. This was a barrier we never expected to meet; and, as it might have brought our wagons to a complete stand-still in a wilderness, where no supplies for the children could be obtained, we were reluctantly compelled to recross the Zouga.

From the Bayeiye we learned that a party of Englishmen, who had come to the lake in search of ivory, were all laid low by fever; so we travelled hastily down about sixty miles to render what aid was in our power. We were grieved to find, as we came near, that Mr. Alfred Rider, an enterprising young artist who had come to make sketches of this country and of the lake immediately after its discovery, had died of fever before our arrival; but, by the aid of medicines and such comforts as could be made by the only English lady who ever visited the lake, the others happily recovered.

Sechele used all his powers of eloquence with Lechulatebe to induce him to furnish guides, that I might be able to visit Sebituane on ox-back, while Mrs. Livingstone and the children remained at Lake Ngami. He yielded at last. I had a very superior London-made gun, the gift of Lieutenant Arkwright, on which I placed the greatest value, both on account of the donor and the impossibility of my replacing it. Lechulatebe fell violently in love with it, and offered whatever number of elephants' tusks I might ask for it. I too was enamored with Sebituane; and, as he promised in addition that he would furnish Mrs. Livingstone with meat all the time of my absence, his arguments made me part with the gun. Though he had no ivory at the time to pay me, I felt the piece would be well

---

* *Glossina morsitans*, the first specimens of which were brought to England in 1848 by my friend Major Vardon, from the banks of the Limpopo.

spent on those terms, and delivered it to him. All being ready for our departure, I took Mrs. Livingstone about six miles from the town, that she might have a peep at the broad part of the lake. Next morning we had other work to do than part, for our little boy and girl were seized with fever. On the day following, all our servants were down too with the same complaint. As nothing is better in these cases than change of place, I was forced to give up the hope of seeing Sebituane that year; so, leaving my gun as part payment for guides next year, we started for the pure air of the Desert.

Some mistake had happened in the arrangement with Mr. Oswell, for we met him on the Zouga on our return, and he had devoted the rest of this season to elephant-hunting, at which the natives universally declare he is the greatest adept that ever came into the country. He hunted without dogs. It is remarkable that this lordly animal is so completely harassed by the presence of a few yelping curs as to be quite incapable of attending to man. He makes awkward attempts to crush them by falling on his knees, and sometimes places his forehead against a tree ten inches in diameter; glancing on one side of the tree and then on the other, he pushes it down before him, as if he thought thereby to catch his enemies. The only danger the huntsman has to apprehend is the dogs' running toward him, and thereby leading the elephant to their master. Mr. Oswell has been known to kill four large old male elephants a day. The value of the ivory in these cases would be one hundred guineas. We had reason to be proud of his success, for the inhabitants conceived from it a very high idea of English courage, and when they wished to flatter me would say, "If you were not a missionary you would just be like Oswell; you would not hunt with dogs either." When, in 1852, we came to the Cape, my black coat eleven years out of fashion, and without a penny of salary to draw, we found that Mr. Oswell had most generously ordered an outfit for the half-naked children, which cost about £200, and presented it to us, saying he thought Mrs. Livingstone had a right to the game of her own preserves.

Foiled in this second attempt to reach Sebituane, we returned again to Kolobeng, whither we were soon followed by a number of messengers from that chief himself. When he heard of our attempts to visit him, he despatched three detachments of his men with thirteen brown cows to Lechulatebe, thirteen white cows to Sekomi, and thirteen black cows to Sechele, with a request to each to assist the white men to reach him. Their policy, however, was to keep him out of view, and act as his agents in purchasing with his ivory the goods he wanted. This is thoroughly African; and that continent being without friths and arms of the sea, the tribes in the centre have always been debarred from European intercourse by its universal prevalence among all the people around the coasts.

Before setting out on our third journey to Sebituane, it was necessary to visit Kuruman; and Sechele, eager, for the sake of the commission thereon, to get the ivory of that chief into his own hands, allowed all the messengers to leave before our return. Sekomi, however, was more than usually gracious, and even furnished us with a guide, but no one knew the path beyond Nchokotsa which we intended to follow. When we reached that point, we found that the mainspring of the gun of another of his men, who was well acquainted with the Bushmen, through whose country we should pass, had opportunely broken. I never undertook to mend a gun with greater zest than this; for, under promise of his guidance, we went to the north instead of westward. All the other guides were most liberally rewarded by Mr. Oswell.

We passed quickly over a hard country, which is perfectly flat. A little soil lying on calcareous tufa, over a tract of several hundreds of miles, supports a vegetation of fine, sweet short grass, and mopane and baobab trees.

We found a great number of wells in this tufa. A place

called Matlomagan-yána, or the "Links," is quite a chain of these never-failing springs. As they occasionally become full in seasons when no rain falls, and resemble somewhat in this respect the rivers we have already mentioned, it is probable they receive some water by percolation from the river-system in the country beyond. Among these links we found many families of Bushmen; and, unlike those on the plains of the Kalahari, who are generally of short stature and light yellow color, these were tall, strapping fellows, of dark complexion. Heat alone does not produce blackness of skin, but heat with moisture seems to insure the deepest hue.

One of these Bushmen, named Shobo, consented to be our guide over the waste between these springs and the country of Sebituane. Shobo gave us no hope of water in less than a month. Providentially, however, we came sooner than we expected to some supplies of rain-water in a chain of pools. It is impossible to convey an idea of the dreary scene on which we entered after leaving this spot: the only vegetation was a low scrub in deep sand; not a bird or insect enlivened the landscape. It was, without exception, the most uninviting prospect I ever beheld; and, to make matters worse, our guide Shobo wandered on the second day. We coaxed him on at night, but he went to all points of the compass on the trails of elephants which had been here in the rainy season, and then would sit down in the path, and in his broken Sichuána say, "No water, all country only; Shobo sleeps; he breaks down; country only," and then coolly curl himself up and go to sleep. The oxen were terribly fatigued and thirsty; and, on the morning of the fourth day, Shobo, after professing ignorance of every thing, vanished altogether. We went on in the direction in which we last saw him, and about eleven o'clock began to see birds; then the trail of a rhinoceros. At this we unyoked the oxen, and they, apparently knowing the sign, rushed along to find the water in the river Mahábe, which comes from the Tamunak'le, and lay to the west of us. The supply of water in the wagons had been wasted by one of our servants, and by the afternoon only a small portion remained for the children. This was a bitterly anxious night; and next morning the less there was of water the more thirsty the little rogues became. The idea of their perishing before our eyes was terrible. It would almost have been a relief to me to have been reproached with being the entire cause of the catastrophe; but not one syllable of upbraiding was uttered by their mother, though the tearful eye told the agony within. In the afternoon of the fifth day, to our inexpressible relief, some of the men returned with a supply of that fluid of which we had never before felt the true value.

The cattle, in rushing along to the water in the Mahabe, probably crossed a small patch of trees containing tsétse, an insect which was shortly to become a perfect pest to us. Shobo had found his way to the Bayeiye, and appeared, when we came up to the river, at the head of a party; and, as he wished to show his importance before his friends, he walked up boldly and commanded our whole cavalcade to stop, and to bring forth fire and tobacco, while he coolly sat down and smoked his pipe. It was such an inimitably natural way of showing off that we all stopped to admire the acting, and, though he had left us previously in the lurch, we all liked Shobo, a fine specimen of that wonderful people, the Bushmen.

Next day we came to a village of Banajoa, a tribe which extends far to the eastward. They were living on the borders of a marsh in which the Mahabe terminates. They had lost their crop of corn, (*Holcus sorghum*,) and now subsisted almost entirely on the root called "tsitla," a kind of aroidœa, which contains a very large quantity of sweet-tasted starch. When dried, pounded into meal, and allowed to ferment, it forms a not unpleasant article of food. The women shave all the hair off their heads, and seem darker than the Bechuanas. Their huts were built on poles, and a fire is made beneath by night, in order that the smoke may drive away the mosquitos, which abound on the Mababe and Tamunak'le more than in any other part of the country. The head-man of this village, Majáne, seem.ed a little wanting in ability, but had had wit enough to promote a younger member of the family to the office. This person, the most like the ugly negro of the tobacconists' shops I ever saw, was called Moróa Majáne, or son of Majane, and proved an active guide across the river Sonta, and to the banks of the Chobe, in the country of Sebituane. We had come through another tsetse district by night, and at once passed our cattle over to the northern bank to preserve them from its ravages.

A few remarks on the Tsetse, or *Glossina morsitans*, may here be appropriate. It is not much larger than the common house-fly, and is nearly of the same brown color as the common honey-bee; the after-part of the body has three or four yellow bars across it; the wings project beyond this part considerably, and it is remarkably alert, avoiding most dexterously all attempts to catch it with the hand at common temperatures; in the cool of the mornings and evenings it is less agile. Its peculiar buzz when once heard can never be forgotten by the traveller whose means of locomotion are domestic animals; for it is well known that the bite of this poisonous insect is certain death to the ox, horse, and dog. In this journey, though we were not aware of any great number having at any time lighted on our cattle, we lost forty-three fine oxen by its bite. We watched the animals carefully, and believe that not a score of flies were ever upon them.

A most remarkable feature in the bite of the tsetse is its perfect harmlessness in man and wild animals, and even calves so long as they continue to suck the cow. We never experienced the slightest injury from them ourselves, personally, although we lived two months in their *habitat*, which was in this case as sharply defined as in many others, for the south bank of the Chobe was infested by them, and the northern bank, where our cattle were placed, only fifty yards distant, contained not a single specimen. This was the more remarkable as we often saw natives carrying over raw meat to the opposite bank with many tsetse settled upon it.

The poison does not seem to be injected by a sting, or by ova placed beneath the skin; for, when one is allowed to feed freely on the hand, it is seen to insert the middle prong of three portions, into which the proboscis divides, somewhat deeply into the true skin; it then draws it out a little way, and it assumes a crimson color as the mandibles come into brisk operation. The previously-shrunken belly swells out, and, if left undisturbed, the fly quietly departs when it is full. A slight itching irritation follows, but not more than in the bite of a mosquito. In the ox this same bite produces no more immediate effects than in man. It does not startle him as the gad-fly does; but a few days afterward the following symptoms supervene: the eye and nose begin to run, the coat stares as if the animal were cold, a swelling appears under the jaw and sometimes at the navel; and, though the animal continues to graze, emaciation commences, accompanied with a peculiar flaccidity of the muscles, and this proceeds unchecked until, perhaps months afterward, purging comes on, and the animal, no longer able to graze, perishes in a state of extreme exhaustion. Those which are in good condition often perish soon after the bite is inflicted, with staggering and blindness, as if the brain were affected by it. Sudden changes of temperature produced by falls of rain seem to hasten the progress of the complaint; but, in general, the emaciation goes on uninterruptedly for months, and, do what we will, the poor animals perish miserably.

When opened, the cellular tissue on the surface of the body beneath the skin is seen to be injected with air, as if a quantity of soap-bubbles were scattered over it, or a dishonest, awkward butcher had been trying to make it look fat. The fat is of a greenish-yellow color and of an oily consistence. All the muscles are flabby, and the heart often so soft that the fingers may be made to meet through it. The lungs. and liver partake of the disease. The stomach and bowels are pale and empty, and the gall-bladder is distended with bile.

The mule, ass, and goat enjoy the same immunity from the tsetse as man and game. Many large tribes on the Zambesi can keep no domestic animals except the goat, in consequence of the scourge existing in their country. Our children were frequently bitten, yet suffered no harm; and we saw around us numbers of zebras, buffaloes, pigs, pallahs and other antelopes, feeding quietly in the very *habitat* of the tsetse, yet as undisturbed by its bite as oxen are when they first receive the fatal poison.

The Makololo whom we met on the Chobe were delighted to see us; and, as their chief. Sebituane was about twenty miles down the river, Mr. Oswell and I proceeded in canoes to his temporary residence. He had come from the Barótse town of Naliéle down to Sesheke as soon as he heard of white men being in search of him, and now came one hundred miles more to bid us welcome into his country. He was upon an island, with all his principal men around him, and engaged in singing when we arrived. It was more like church-music than the sing-song ō ē ō, œ œ œ, of the Bechuanas of the south, and they continued the tune for some seconds after we approached. We informed him of the difficulties we had encountered, and how glad we were that they were all at an end by at last reaching his presence. He signified his own joy, and added, "Your cattle are ɾ' bitten by the tsetse, and will certainly die; but never min I have oxen, and will give you as many as you need." We, in our ignorance, then thought that as so few tsetse had bitten them no great mischief would follow. He then presented us with an ox and a jar of honey as food, and handed us over to the care of Mahále, who had headed the party to Kolobeng, and would now fain appropriate to himself the whole credit of our coming. Prepared skins of oxen, as soft as cloth, were given to cover us through the night;

and, as nothing could be returned to this chief, Mahalo became the owner of them. Long before it was day, Sebituane came, and sitting down by the fire, which was lighted for our benefit behind the hedge where we lay, he narrated the difficulties he had himself experienced, when a young man, in crossing that same desert which we had mastered long afterward.

He was much pleased with the proof of confidence we had shown in bringing our children, and promised to take us to see his country, so that we might choose a part in which to locate ourselves. Our plan was, that I should remain in the pursuit of my objects as a missionary, while Mr. Oswell explored the Zambesi to the east. Poor Sebituane, however, just after realizing what he had so long ardently desired, fell sick of inflammation of the lungs, which originated in and extended from an old wound got at Melita. I saw his danger, but, being a stranger, I feared to treat him medically, lest, in the event of his death, I should be blamed by his people. I mentioned this to one of his doctors, who said, "Your fear is prudent and wise: this people would blame you." He had been cured of this complaint, during the year before, by the Barotse making a large number of free incisions in the chest. The Makololo doctors, on the other hand, now scarcely cut the skin. On the Sunday afternoon in which he died, when our usual religious service was over, I visited him with my little boy Robert. "Come near," said Sebituane, "and see if I am any longer a man. I am done." He was thus sensible of the dangerous nature of his disease; so I ventured to assent, and added a single sentence regarding hope after death. "Why do you speak of death?" said one of a relay of fresh doctors; "Sebituane will never die." If I had persisted, the impression would have been produced that by speaking about it I wished him to die. After sitting with him some time, and commending him to the mercy of God, I rose to depart, when the dying chieftain, raising himself up a little from his prone position, called a servant, and said, "Take Robert to Maunku, [one of his wives,] and tell her to give him some milk." These were the last words of Sebituane.

We were not informed of his death until the next day. The burial of a Bechuana chief takes place in his cattle-pen, and all the cattle are driven for an hour or two around and over the grave, so that it may be quite obliterated. We went and spoke to the people, advising them to keep together and support the heir. They took this kindly; and in turn told us not to be alarmed, for they would not think of ascribing the death of their chief to us; that Sebituane had just gone the way of his fathers; and, though the father had gone, he had left children, and they hoped that we would be as friendly to his children as we intended to have been to himself.

He was decidedly the best specimen of a native chief I ever met. I never felt so much grieved by the loss of a black man before; and it was impossible not to follow him in thought into the world of which he had just heard before he was called away, and to realize somewhat of the feelings of those who pray for the dead. The deep, dark question of what is to become of such as he must, however, be left where we find it, believing that, assuredly, the "Judge of all the earth will do right."

At Sebituane's death the chieftainship devolved, as her father intended, on a daughter named Ma-mochisane. He had promised to show us his country and to select a suitable locality for our residence. We had now to look to the daughter, who was living twelve days to the north, at Nalicle We were obliged, therefore, to remain until a message came from her; and, when it did, she gave us perfect liberty to visit any part of the country we chose. Mr. Oswell and I then proceeded one hundred and thirty miles to the northeast, to Sesheke; and in the end of June, 1851, we were rewarded by the discovery of the Zambesi, in the centre of the continent. This was a most important point, for that river was not previously known to exist there at all. The Portuguese maps all represent it as rising far to the east of where we now were; and, if ever any thing like a chain of trading-stations had existed across the country between the latitudes 12° and 18° south, this magnificent portion of the river must have been known before. We saw it at the end of the dry season, at the time when the river is about at its lowest; and yet there was a breadth of from three hundred to six hundred yards of deep, flowing water. Mr. Oswell said he had never seen such a fine river even in India. At the period of its annual inundation it rises fully twenty feet in perpendicular height, and floods fifteen or twenty miles of lands adjacent to its banks.

Occasionally the country between the Chobe and Zambesi is flooded, and there are large patches of swamps lying near the Chobe or on its banks. The Makololo were living among these swamps for the sake of the protection the deep reedy rivers afforded them against their enemies.

Now, in reference to a suitable locality for a settlement for myself, I could not conscientiously ask them to abandon their defences for my convenience alone. The healthy districts were defenceless, and the safe localities were so deleterious to human life that the original Basutos had nearly all been cut off by the fever: I therefore feared to subject my family to the scourge.

As there was no hope of the Boers allowing the peaceable instruction of the natives at Kolobeng, I at once resolved to save my family from exposure to this unhealthy region by sending them to England, and to return alone, with a view to exploring the country in search of a healthy district that might prove a centre of civilization and open up the interior by a path to either the east or west coast. This resolution led me down to the Cape in April, 1852, being the first time during eleven years that I had visited the scenes of civilization. Our route to Cape Town led us to pass through the centre of the colony during the twentieth month of a Caffre war; and if those who periodically pay enormous sums for these inglorious affairs wish to know how our little unprotected party could quietly travel through the heart of the colony to the capital with as little sense or sign of danger as if we had been in England, they must engage a "*Times* Special Correspondent" for the next outbreak to explain where the money goes, and who have been benefited by the blood and treasure expended.

Having placed my family on board a homeward-bound ship, and promised to rejoin them in two years, we parted, for, as it subsequently proved, nearly five years. The Directors of the London Missionary Society signified their cordial approval of my project, by leaving the matter entirely to my own discretion; and I have much pleasure in acknowledging my obligations to the gentlemen composing that body for always acting in an enlightened spirit and with as much liberality as their constitution would allow.

I have the like pleasure in confessing my thankfulness to the Astronomer Royal at the Cape, Thomas Maclear, Esq., for enabling me to recall the little astronomical knowledge which constant manual labor and the engrossing nature of missionary duties had effaced from my memory, and in adding much that I did not know before. The promise he made on parting, that he would examine and correct all my observations, had more effect in making me persevere in overcoming the difficulties of an unassisted solitary observer than any thing else; so, whatever credit may be attached to the geographical positions laid down in my route must be attributed to the voluntary aid of the excellent and laborious astronomer of the Cape Observatory.

Having given the reader as rapid a sketch as possible events which attracted notice between 1840 and 1852, I ,w proceed to narrate the incidents of the last and ngest journey of all, performed in 1852-56

CHAPTER V.

DR. LIVINGSTONE STARTS IN JUNE, 1852, ON THE LAST AND LONGEST JOURNEY FROM CAPE TOWN.

.HAVING sent my family home to England, I started in the beginning of June, 1852, on my last journey from Cape Town. This journey extended from the southern extremity of the continent to St. Paul de Loando, the capital of Angola, on the west coast, and thence across South Central Africa in an oblique direction to Kilimane (Quilimane) in Eastern Africa. I proceeded in the usual conveyance of the country, the heavy lumbering Cape wagon drawn by ten oxen, and was accompanied by two Christian Bechuanas from Kuruman,—than whom I never saw better servants anywhere,—by two Bakwain men, and two young girls, who, having come as nurses with our children to the Cape, were returning to their home at Kolobeng. Wagon-travelling in Africa has been so often described that I need say no more than that it is a prolonged system of picnicking, excellent for the health, and agreeable to those who are not over-fastidious about trifles, and who delight in being in the open air.

Our route to the north lay near the centre of the cone-shaped mass of land which constitutes the promontory of the Cape.

The slow pace at which we wound our way through the colony made almost any subject interesting. The attention is attracted to the names of different places, because they indicate the former existence of buffaloes, elands, and elephants, which are now to be found only hundreds of miles beyond. A few blesbucks, (*Antilope pygarga*,) gnus, bluebucks, (*A. cerulea*,) steinbucks, and the ostrich, (*Struthio camelus*,) continue, like the Bushmen, to maintain a precarious existence when all the rest are gone. The ciephant, the most sagacious, flees the sound of fire-arms first; the gnu and ostrich, the most wary and the most stupid, last. The first emigrants found the Hottentots in possession of prodigious herds of fine cattle, but no horses, asses, or camels. The original cattle, which may still be seen in some parts of the frontier, must have been brought south from the north-northeast, for from this point the natives universally ascribe their original migration. They brought cattle, sheep, goats, and dogs : why not the horse, the delight of savage hordes ? Horses thrive well in the Cape Colony when imported. Naturalists point out certain mountain-ranges as limiting the habitat of certain classes of animals; but there is no Cordillera in Africa to answer that purpose, there being no visible barrier between the northeastern Arabs and the Hottentot tribes to prevent the different hordes, as they felt their way southward, from indulging their taste for the possession of this noble animal.

I am here led to notice an invisible barrier, more insurmountable than mountain-ranges, but which is not opposed to the southern progress of cattle, goats, and sheep. The tsetse would prove a barrier only until its well-defined habitat was known; but the disease passing under the term of horse-sickness (*peripneumonia*) exists in such virulence over nearly seven degrees of latitude that no precaution would be sufficient to save these animals. The horse is so liable to this disease, that only by great care in stabling can he be kept anywhere between 20° and 27° S. during the time between December and April. The winter, beginning in the latter month, is the only period in which Englishmen can hunt on horseback, and they are in danger of losing all their studs some months before December. To this disease the horse is especially exposed, and it is almost always fatal. One attack, however, seems to secure immunity from a second. Cattle, too, are subject to it, but only at intervals of a few, sometimes many, years; but it never makes a clean sweep of the whole cattle of a village, as it would do of a troop of fifty horses. This barrier, then, seems to explain the absence of the horse among the Hottentots, though it is not opposed to the southern migration of cattle, sheep, and goats.

When the flesh of animals that have died of this disease is eaten, it causes a malignant carbuncle, which, when it appears over any important organ, proves rapidly fatal. It is more especially dangerous over the pit of the stomach. The effects of the poison have been experienced by missionaries who had eaten properly-cooked food,—the flesh of sheep really but not visibly affected by the disease. The virus in the flesh of the animal is destroyed neither by boiling nor roasting. This fact, of which we have had innumerable examples, shows the superiority of experiments on a large scale to those of acute and able physiologists and chemists in the laboratory; for a well-known physician of Paris, after careful investigation, considered that the virus in such cases was completely neutralized by boiling.

This disease attacks wild animals too. During our residence at Chonuan, great numbers of tolos, or koodoos, were attracted to the gardens of the Bakwains, abandoned at the usual period of harvest because there was no prospect of the corn (*Holcus sorghum*) bearing that year. The koodoo is remarkably fond of the green stalks of this kind of millet. Free feeding produced that state of fatness favorable for the development of this disease, and no fewer than twenty-five died on the hill opposite our house. Great numbers of gnus and zebras perished from the same cause; but the mortality produced no sensible diminution in the numbers of the game, any more than the deaths of many of the Bakwains who persisted, in spite of every remonstrance, in eating the dead meat, caused any sensible decrease in the strength of the tribe.

Before we came to the Orange River, we saw the last portion of a migration of springbucks, (*Gazella euchore*, or tsépe.) They came from the great Kalahari Desert, and, when first seen after crossing the colonial boundary, are said often to exceed forty thousand in number. I cannot give an estimate of their numbers, for they appear spread over a vast expanse of country, and make a quivering motion as they feed, and move, and toss their graceful horns. They feed chiefly on grass; and, as they come from the north about the time when the grass most abounds, it cannot be want of food that prompts the movement. Nor is it want of water; for this antelope is one of the most abstemious in that respect. Their nature prompts them to seek as their favorite haunts level plains with short grass, where they may be able to watch the approach of an enemy. The Bakalahari take advantage of this feeling, and burn off large patches of grass, not only to attract the game by the new crop when it comes up, but also to form bare spots for the springbuck to range over.

On crossing the Orange River we come into independent territory inhabited by Griquas and Bechuanas. By Griquas is meant any mixed race sprung from natives and Europeans. Those in question were of Dutch extraction through association with Hottentot and Bush women. Half-castes of the first generation consider themselves superior to those of the second, and all possess in some degree the characteristics of both parents. They were governed for many years by an elected chief, named Waterboer, who, by treaty, received a small sum per annum from the colonial government for the support of schools in his country, and proved a most efficient guard of our northwest boundary.

Many hundreds of both Griquas and Bechuanas have become Christians and partially civilized through the teaching of English missionaries. My first impressions of the progress made were that the accounts of the effects of the gospel among them had been too highly colored. I expected a higher degree of Christian simplicity and purity than exists either among them or among ourselves. I was not anxious for a deeper insight in detecting shams than others; but I expected character, such as we imagine the primitive disciples had,—and was disappointed. When, however, I passed on to the true heathen in the countries beyond the sphere of missionary influence, and could compare the people there with the Christian natives, I came to the conclusion that, if the question were examined in the most rigidly severe or scientific way, the change effected by the missionary movement would be considered unquestionably great.

We cannot fairly compare these poor people with ourselves, who have an atmosphere of Christianity and enlightened public opinion, the growth of centuries, around us, to influence our deportment; but let any one from the natural and proper point of view behold the public morality of Griqua Town, Kuruman, Likatlong, and other villages, and remember what even London was a century ago, and he must confess that the Christian mode of treating aborigines is incomparably the best.

The Griquas and Bechuanas were in former times clad much like the Caffres, if such a word may be used where there is scarcely any clothing at all. A bunch of leather strings about eighteen inches long hung from the lady's waist in front, and a prepared skin of a sheep or antelope covered the shoulders, leaving the breast and abdomen bare: the men wore a patch of skin, about the size of the crown of one's hat, which barely served for the purposes of decency, and a mantle exactly like that of the women. To assist in protecting the pores of the skin from the influence of the sun by day and of the cold by night, all smeared themselves with a mixture of fat and ochre; the head is anointed with pounded blue mica schist mixed with fat; and the fine particles of shining mica, falling on the body and on strings of beads and brass rings, were considered as highly ornamental, and fit for the most fastidious dandy. Now these same people come to church in decent though poor clothing, and behave with a decorum certainly superior to what seems to have been the case in the time of Mr. Samuel Pepys in London Sunday is well observed, and, even in localities where no missionary lives, religious meetings are regularly held, and children and adults taught to read by the more advanced of their own fellow-countrymen; and no one is allowed to make a profession of faith by baptism unless he knows how to read and understands the nature of the Christian religion.

The Bechuana Mission has been so far successful that, when coming from the interior, we always felt, on reaching Kuruman, that we had returned to civilized life. But I would not give any one to understand by this that they are model Christians,—we cannot claim to be model Christians ourselves,—or even in any degree superior to the members of our country churches. They are more stingy and greedy than the poor at home; but in many respects the two are exactly alike. On asking an intelligent chief what he thought of them, he replied, "You white men have no idea of how wicked we are; we know each other better than you: some feign belief to ingratiate themselves with the missionaries; some profess Christianity because they like the new system, which gives so much more importance to the poor, and desire that the old system may pass away; and the rest—a pretty large number—profess because they are really true believers." This testimony may be considered as very nearly correct.

There is not much prospect of this country ever producing much of the materials of commerce except wool At present the chief articles of trade are karosses or mantles,—the skins of which they are composed come from the Desert; next to them, ivory, the quantity of which cannot now be great, inasmuch as the means of shooting elephants is sedulously debarred entrance into the country. A few skins and horns, and some cattle, make up the remainder of the exports. English goods, sugar, tea, and coffee are the articles received in exchange. All the natives of these parts soon become remarkably fond of coffee. The acme of respectability among the Bechuanas is the possession of cattle and a wagon. It is remarkable that, though these latter require frequent repairs, none of the Bechuanas have ever learned to mend them. Forges and tools have been at their service, and teachers willing to aid them, but, beyond putting together a camp-stool, no effort has ever been made to acquire a knowledge of the trades. They observe most carefully a missionary at work until they understand whether a tire is well welded or not, and then pronounce upon its merits with great emphasis; but there their ambition rests satisfied. It is the same peculiarity among ourselves which leads us in other matters, such as book-making, to attain the excellence of fault-finding without the wit to indite a page. It was in vain I tried to indoctrinate the Bechuanas with the idea that criticism did not imply any superiority over the workman, or even equality with him.

CHAPTER VI.

DR. LIVINGSTONE VISITS HIS FATHER-IN-LAW, MR. MOFFAT, AT KURUMAN.

The permanence of the station called Kuruman depends entirely on the fine ever-flowing fountain of that name. It comes from beneath the trap-rock, and, as it usually issues at a temperature of 72° Fahr., it probably comes from the old silurian schists which formed the bottom of the great primeval valley of the continent. I could not detect any diminution in the flow of this gushing fountain during my residence in the country; but when Mr. Moffat first attempted a settlement here, thirty-five years ago, he made a dam six or seven miles below the present one, and led out the stream for irrigation, where not a drop of the fountain-water ever now flows. Other parts, fourteen miles below the Kuruman gardens, are pointed out as having contained, within the memory of people now living, hippopotami, and pools sufficient to drown both men and cattle. This failure of water must be chiefly ascribed to the general desiccation of the country, but partly also to the amount of irrigation carried on along both banks of the stream at the mission-station. This latter circumstance would have more weight were it not coincident with the failure of fountains over a wide extent of country

Without at present entering minutely into this feature of the climate, it may be remarked that the Kuruman district presents evidence of this dry southern region having at no very distant date, been as well watered as the country north of Lake Ngami is now. Ancient river-beds and water-courses abound, and the very eyes of fountains long since dried up may be seen, in which the flow of centuries has worn these orifices from a slit to an oval form, having on their sides the tufa so abundantly deposited from these primitive waters; and just where the splashings, made when the stream fell on the rock below, may be supposed to have reached and evaporated, the same phenomenon appears. Many of these failing fountains no longer flow, because the brink over which they ran is now too high, or because the elevation of the western side of the country lifts the land away from the water-supply below; but let a cutting be made from a lower level than the brink, and through it to a part below the surface of the water, and water flows perennially. Several of these ancient fountains have been resuscitated by the Bechuanas near Kuruman, who occasionally show their feelings of self-esteem by laboring for months at deep cuttings, which, having once begun, they feel bound in honor to persevere in, though told by a missionary that they can never force water to run up hill.

During the period of my visit at Kuruman, Mr. Moffat, who has been a missionary in Africa during upward of forty years, and is well known by his interesting work, "Scenes and Labors in South Africa," was busily engaged in carrying through the press, with which his station is furnished, the Bible in the language of the Bechuanas, which is called Sichuana. This has been a work of immense labor; and as he was the first to reduce their speech to a written form, and has had his attention directed to the study for at least thirty years, he may be supposed to be better adapted for the task than any man living. Some idea of the copiousness of the language may be formed from the fact that even he never spends a week at his work without discovering new words; the phenomenon, therefore, of any man who, after a few months' or years' study of a native tongue, cackles forth a torrent of vocables, may well be wondered at, if it is meant to convey instruction. In my own case, though I have had as much intercourse with the purest idiom as most Englishmen, and have studied the language carefully, yet I can never utter an important statement without doing so very slowly, and repeating it too, lest the foreign accent, which is distinctly perceptible in all Europeans, should render the sense unintelligible. In this I follow the example of the Bechuana orators, who, on important matters, always speak slowly, deliberately, and with reiteration. The capabilities of this language may be inferred from the fact that the Pentateuch is fully expressed in Mr. Moffat's translation in fewer words than in the Greek Septuagint, and in a very considerably smaller number than in our own English version. The language is, however, so simple in its construction, that its copiousness by no means requires the explanation that the people have fallen from a former state of civilization and culture.

The fact of the complete translation of the Bible at a station seven hundred miles inland from the Cape naturally suggests the question whether it is likely to be permanently useful, and whether Christianity, as planted by modern missions, is likely to retain its vitality without constant supplies of foreign teaching. It would certainly be no cause for congratulation if the Bechuana Bible seemed at all likely to meet the fate of Elliot's Choctaw version, a specimen of which may be seen in the library of one of the American colleges,—as God's word in a language which no living tongue can articulate, nor living mortal understand; but a better destiny seems in store for this, for the Sichuana language has been introduced into the new country beyond Lake Ngami. There it is the court language, and will take a stranger anywhere through a district larger than France. The Bechuanas, moreover, in all probability possess that imperishability which forms so remarkable a feature in the entire African race.

Protestant missionaries of every denomination in South Africa all agree in one point, that no mere profession of Christianity is sufficient to entitle the converts to the Christian name. They are all anxious to place the Bible in the hands of the natives, and, with ability to read that, there can be little doubt as to the future. We believe Christianity to be divine, and equal to all it has to perform; then let the good seed be widely sown, and, no matter to what sect the converts may belong, the harvest will be glorious. Let nothing that I have said be interpreted as indicative of feelings inimical to any body of Christians, for I never, as a missionary, felt myself to be either Presbyterian, Episcopalian, or Independent, or called upon in any way to love one denomination less than another. My earnest desire is, that those who really have the best interests of the heathen at heart should go to them; and assuredly, in Africa at least, self-denying labors among real heathen will not fail to be appreciated. Christians have never yet dealt fairly by the heathen and been disappointed.

When Sechele understood that we could no longer remain with him at Kolobeng, he sent his children to Mr. Moffat, at Kuruman, for instruction in all the knowledge of the white men. Mr Moffat very liberally received at once an accession of five to his family, with their attendants.

Having been detained at Kuruman about a fortnight by the breaking of a wagon-wheel, I was thus providentially prevented from being present at the attack of the Boers on the Bakwains, news of which was brought, about the end of that time, by Masebele, the wife of Sechele. She had herself been hidden in a cleft of a rock, over which a number of Boers were firing. Her infant began to cry, and, terrified lest this should attract the attention of the men, the muzzles of whose guns appeared at every discharge over her head, she took off her armlets as playthings to quiet the child. She brought Mr. Moffat a letter, which tells its own tale. Nearly literally translated it was as follows:—

"Friend of my heart's love, and of all the confidence of my heart, I am Sechele. I am undone by the Boers, who attacked me, though I had no guilt with them. They demanded that I should be in their kingdom, and I refused. They demanded that I should prevent the English and Griquas from passing (northward). I replied, These are my friends, and I can prevent no one (of them). They came on Saturday, and I besought them not to fight on Sunday, and they assented. They began on Monday morning at twilight, and fired with all their might, and burned the town with fire, and scattered us. They killed sixty of my people, and captured women, and children, and men. And the mother of Baleriling (a former wife of Sechele) they also took prisoner. They took all the cattle and all the goods of the Bakwains; and the house of Livingstone they plundered, taking away all his goods. The number of wagons they had was eighty-five, and a cannon; and after they had stolen my own wagon and that of Macabe, then the number of their wagons (counting the cannon as one) was eighty-eight. All the goods of the hunters (certain English gentlemen hunting and exploring in the north) were burned in the town; and of the Boers were killed twenty-eight. Yes, my beloved friend, now my wife goes to see the children, and Kobus Hae will convey her to you.   "I am SECHELE,

"The son of Mochoasele."

This statement is in exact accordance with the account given by the native teacher Mebalwe, and also that sent by some of the Boers themselves to the public colonial papers. The crime of cattle-stealing, of which we hear so much near Caffreland, was never alleged against these people; and, if a single case had occurred when I was in the country, I must have heard of it, and would at once say so. But the only crime imputed in the papers was that "Sechele was getting too saucy." The demand made for his subjection and service in preventing the English traders passing to the north was kept out of view.

Very soon after Pretorius had sent the marauding-party against Kolobeng, he was called away to the tribunal of infinite justice. His policy is justified by the Boers generally from the instructions given to the Jewish warriors in Deuteronomy xx. 10-14. Hence, when he died, the obituary notice ended with "Blessed are the dead who die in the Lord." I wish he had not "forbidden us to preach unto the Gentiles that they may be saved."

The report of this outrage on the Bakwains, coupled with denunciations against myself for having, as it was alleged, taught them to kill Boers, produced such a panic in the country that I could not engage a single servant to accompany me to the north. I have already alluded to their mode of warfare, and in all previous Boerish forays the killing had all been on one side; now, however, that a tribe where an Englishman had lived had begun to shed *their* blood as well, it was considered the strongest presumptive evidence against me. Loud vows of vengeance were uttered against my head, and threats of instant pursuit by a large party on horseback, should I dare to go into or beyond their country; and as these were coupled with the declaration that the English Government had given over the whole of the native tribes to their rule, and would assist in their entire subjection by preventing fire-arms and ammunition from entering the country except for the use of the Boers, it was not to be wondered at that I was detained for months at Kuruman from sheer inability to get wagon-drivers. The English name, from being honored and respected all over the country, had become somewhat more than suspected; and as the policy of depriving those friendly tribes of the means of defence was represented by the Boers as proof positive of the wish of the English that they should be subjugated, the conduct of a government which these tribes always thought the paragon of justice and friendship was rendered totally incomprehensible to them; they could neither defend themselves against their enemies, nor shoot the animals in the produce of which we wished them to trade.

At last I found three servants willing to risk a journey to the north; and a man of color named George Fleming, who had generously been assisted by Mr. H. E. Rutherford, a mercantile gentleman of Cape Town, to endeavor to establish a trade with the Makololo, had also managed to get a similar number; we accordingly left Kuruman on the 20th of November, and proceeded on our journey. Our servants were the worst possible specimens of those who imbibe the vices without the virtues of Europeans; but we had no choice, and were glad to get away on any terms.

When we reached Motito, forty miles off, we met Sechele on his way, as he said, "to the Queen of England." Two of his own children, and their mother, a former wife, were among the captives seized by the Boers; and, being strongly imbued with the then very prevalent notion of England's justice and generosity, he thought that in consequence of the violated treaty he had a fair case to lay before her majesty. He employed all his eloquence and powers of persuasion to induce me to accompany him, but I excused myself on the ground that my arrangements were already made for exploring the north. On explaining the difficulties of the way, and endeavoring to dissuade him from the attempt, on account of the knowledge I possessed of the governor's policy, he put the pointed question, "Will the queen not listen to me, supposing I should reach her?"

I replied, "I believe she would listen, but the difficulty is to get to her." "Well, I shall reach her," expressed his final determination. Others explained the difficulties more fully, but nothing could shake his resolution. When he reached Bloemfontein he found the English army just returning from a battle with the Basutos, in which both parties claimed the victory, and both were glad that a second engagement was not tried. Our officers invited Sechele to dine with them, heard his story, and collected a handsome sum of money to enable him to pursue his journey to England.* The commander refrained from noticing him, as a single word in favor of the restoration of the children of Sechele would have been a virtual confession of the failure of his own policy at the very outset. Sechele proceeded as far as the Cape; but, his resources being there expended, he was obliged to return to his own country, one thousand miles distant, without accomplishing the object of his journey.

On his return he adopted a mode of punishment which he had seen in the colony, namely, making criminals work on the public roads. And he has since, I am informed, made himself the missionary to his own people. He is tall, rather corpulent, and has more of the negro feature than common, but has large eyes. He is very dark, and his people swear by "Black Sechele." He has great intelligence, reads well, and is a fluent speaker. Great numbers of the tribes formerly living under the Boers have taken refuge under his sway, and he is now greater in power than he was before the attack on Kolobeng.

Having parted with Sechele, we skirted along the Kalahari Desert, and sometimes within its borders, giving the Boers a wide berth. A larger fall of rain than usual had occurred in 1852, and that was the completion of a cycle of eleven or twelve years, at which the same phenomenon is reported to have happened on three occasions. An unusually large crop of melons had appeared in consequence We had the pleasure of meeting with Mr. J. Macabe returning from Lake Ngami, which he had succeeded in reaching by going right across the Desert from a point a little to the south of Kolobeng. The accounts of the abundance of water-melons were amply confirmed by this energetic traveller; for, having these in vast quantities, his cattle subsisted on the fluid contained in them for a period of no less than twenty-one days; and when at last they reached a supply of water they did not seem to care much about it. Coming to the lake from the southeast, he crossed the Teoughe, and went round the northern part of it, and is the only European traveller who had actually seen it all. His estimate of the extent of the lake is higher than that given by Mr. Oswell and myself, or from about ninety to one hundred miles in circumference.

On the 31st of December, 1852, we reached the town of Sechele, called, from the part of the range on which it is situated, Litubaruba. Near the village there exists a cave named Lepelole; it is an interesting evidence of the former existence of a gushing fountain. No one dared to enter the Lohaheng, or cave, for it was the common belief that it was the habitation of the Deity. As we never had a holiday from January to December, and our Sundays were the periods of our greatest exertions in teaching, I projected an excursion into the cave on a weekday to see the god of the Bakwains. The old men said that every one who went in remained there forever, adding, "If the teacher is so mad as to kill himself, let him do so alone: we shall not be to blame." The declaration of Sechele, that he would follow where I led, produced the greatest consternation. It is curious that in all their pretended dreams or visions of their god he has always a crooked leg, like the Egyptian Thau. Supposing that those who were reported to have perished in this cave had fallen over some precipice, we went well provided with lights, ladder, lines, &c.; but it turned out to be only an open cave, with an entrance about ten feet square, which contracts into two water-worn branches, ending in round orifices through which the water once flowed. The only inhabitants it seems ever to have had were baboons. I left at the end of the upper branch one of Father Mathew's leaden teetotal tickets.

I never saw the Bakwains looking so haggard and lean as at this time. Most of their cattle had been swept away by the Boers, together with about eighty fine draught-oxen; and much provision left with them by two officers, Captains Codrington and Webb, to serve for their return journey south, had been carried off also. On their return these officers found the skeletons of the Bakwains where they expected to find their own goods. All the corn, clothing, and furniture of the people, too, had been consumed in the flames which the Boers had forced the subject tribes to apply to the town during the fight, so that its inhabitants were now literally starving.

Sechele had given orders to his people not to commit any act of revenge pending his visit to the Queen of England; but some of the young men ventured to go to meet a party of Boers returning from hunting, and, as the Boers became terrified and ran off, they brought their wagons to Litubaruba. This seems to have given the main body of Boers an idea that the Bakwains meant to begin a guerrilla war upon them. This "Caffre war" was, however, only in embryo, and not near that stage of development in which the natives have found out that the hide-and-seek system is the most successful.

The Boers, in alarm, sent four of their number to ask for peace! I, being present, heard the condition:—"Sechele's children must be restored to him." I never saw men so completely and unconsciously in a trap as these four Boers were. Strong parties of armed Bakwains occupied every pass in the hills and gorges around; and had they not promised much more than they intended, or did perform, that day would have been their last. The commandant Schols had appropriated the children of Sechele to be his own domestic slaves. I was present when one little boy, Khari, son of Sechele, was returned to his mother; the child had been allowed to roll into the fire, and there were three large unbound open sores upon different parts of his body. His mother and the women received him with a flood of silent tears.

Slavery is said to be mild and tender-hearted in some places. The Boers assert that they are the best of masters, and that, if the English had possessed the Hottentot slaves, they would have received much worse treatment than they did: what that would have been it is difficult to imagine. I took down the names of some scores of boys and girls, many of whom I knew as our scholars; but I could not comfort the weeping mothers by any hope of their ever returning from slavery.

The Bechuanas are universally much attached to children. A little child toddling near a party of men while they are eating is sure to get a handful of the food. This love of children may arise in a great measure from the patriarchal system under which they dwell. Every little stranger forms an increase of property to the whole community, and is duly reported to the chief,—boys being more welcome than girls. The parents take the name of the child, and often address their children as Ma, (mother,) or Ra, (father.) Our oldest boy being named Robert, Mrs. Livingstone was, after his birth, always addressed as Ma-Robert instead of Mary, her Christian name.

CHAPTER VII.

LIVINGSTONE LEAVES THE COUNTRY OF THE BAKWAINS.

HAVING remained five days with the wretched Bakwains seeing the effects of war, of which only a very inadequate idea can ever be formed by those who have not been eyewitnesses of its miseries, we prepared to depart on the 15th of January, 1853. Several dogs, in better condition by far than any of the people, had taken up their residence at the water. No one would own them; there they had remained, and, coming on the trail of the people, long after their departure from the scene of conflict, it was plain they had

"Held o'er the dead their carnival."

Hence the disgust with which they were viewed.

On our way from Khopong, along the ancient river-bed which forms the pathway to Boatlanama, I found a species of cactus, being the third I had seen in the country, namely, one in the colony with a bright red flower, one at Lake Ngami, the flower of which was liver-colored, and the present one, flower unknown. That the plant is uncommon may be inferred from the fact that the Bakwains find so much difficulty in recognising the plant again after having once seen it, that they believe it has the power of changing its locality.

On the 21st of January we reached the wells of Boatlanama, and found them for the first time empty. Lopepe, which I had formerly seen a stream running from a large reedy pool, was also dry. The hot salt spring of Serináne, east of Lopepe, being undrinkable, we pushed on to Mashüe for its delicious waters. In travelling through this country, the olfactory nerves are frequently excited by a strong disagreeable odor. This is caused by a large jet-bla ant named "Leshónya." It is nearly an inch in length, and emits a pungent smell when alarmed, in the same manner as the skunk. The scent must be as volatile as ether, for, on irritating the insect with a stick six feet long, the odor is instantly perceptible.

That the fear of man often remains excessively strong in the carnivora is proved from well-authenticated cases in which the lioness, in the vicinity of towns where the large game had been unexpectedly driven away by fire-arms, has been known to assuage the paroxysms of hunger by devouring her own young. It must be added that, though the effluvium which is left by the footsteps of man is in general sufficient to induce lions to avoid a village, there are exceptions: so many came about our half-deserted houses at Chonuane while we were in the act of removing to Kolobeng, that the natives who remained with Mrs. Livingstone were terrified to stir out of doors in the evening. Bitches, also, have been known to be guilty of the horridly unnatural act of eating their own young, probably from the great desire for animal food, which is experienced by the inhabitants as well.

When a lion is met in the daytime, a circumstance by no means unfrequent to travellers in these parts, if preconceived notions do not lead them to expect something very "noble" or "majestic," they will see merely an animal somewhat larger than the biggest dog they ever saw, and partaking very strongly of the canine features: the face is not much like the usual drawings of a lion, the nose being prolonged like a dog's; not exactly such as our painters make it,—though they might learn better at the Zoological Gardens,—their ideas of majesty being usually shown by making their lions' faces like old women in nightcaps. When encountered in the daytime, the lion stands a second or two, gazing, then turns slowly round, and walks as slowly away for a dozen paces, looking over his shoulder, then begins to trot, and, when he thinks himself out of sight, bounds off like a greyhound. By day there is not, as a rule, the smallest danger of lions which are not molested attacking man, nor even on a clear moonlight night, except when they possess the breeding $\sigma\tau o\rho\gamma\bar{\eta}$, (natural affection :) this makes them brave almost any danger; and if a man happens to cross to the windward of them, both lion and lioness will rush at him, in the manner of a bitch with whelps. This does not often happen, as I only became aware of two or three instances of it. In one case a man, passing where the wind blew from him to the animals, was bitten before he could climb a tree; and occasionally a man on horseback has been caught by the leg under the same circumstances. So general, however, is the sense of security on moonlight nights, that we seldom tied up our oxen, but let them lie loose by the wagons; while on a dark, rainy night, if a lion is in the neighborhood, he is almost sure to venture to kill an ox. His approach is always stealthy, except when wounded; and any appearance of a trap is enough to cause him to refrain from making the last spring. This seems characteristic of the feline species: when a goat is picketed in India for the purpose of enabling the huntsmen to shoot a tiger by night, if on a plain, he would whip off the animal so quickly by a stroke of the paw that no one could take aim; to obviate this, a small pit is dug, and the goat is picketed to a stake in the bottom; a small stone is tied in the ear of the goat, which makes him cry the whole night. When the tiger sees the appearance of a trap, he walks round and round the pit, and allows the hunter, who is lying in wait, to have a fair shot.

When a lion is very hungry, and lying in wait, the sight of an animal may make him commence stalking it. In one case a man, while stealthily crawling toward a rhinoceros, happened to glance behind him, and found to his horror a lion *stalking him;* he only escaped by springing up a tree like a cat. At Lopepe a lioness sprang on the after-quarter of Mr. Oswell's horse, and when we came up to him we found the marks of the claws on the horse, and a scratch on Mr. O.'s hand. The horse, on feeling the lion on him, sprang away, and the rider, caught by a wait-a-bit thorn, was brought to the ground and rendered insensible. His dogs saved him. Another English gentleman (Captain Codrington) was surprised in the same way, though not hunting the lion at the time, but turning round he shot him dead in the neck. By accident a horse belonging to Codrington ran away, but was stopped by the bridle catching a stump; there he remained a prisoner two days, and when found the whole space around was marked by the footprints of lions. They had evidently been afraid to attack the haltered horse, from fear that it was a trap. Two lions came up by night to within three yards of oxen tied to a wagon, and a sheep tied to a tree, and stood roaring, but afraid to make a spring. On another occasion, one of our party was lying sound asleep and unconscious of danger between two natives behind a bush at Mashüe; the fire was nearly out at their feet in consequence of all being completely tired out by the fatigues of the previous day: a lion came up to within three yards of the fire, and there commenced roaring instead of making a spring: the fact of their riding-ox being tied to the bush was the only reason the lion had for not following his instinct and making a meal of flesh. He then stood on a knoll three hundred yards distant, and roared all night, and continued his growling as the party moved off by daylight next morning.

Nothing that I ever learned of the lion would lead me to attribute to it either the ferocious or noble character ascribed to it elsewhere. It possesses none of the nobility of the Newfoundland or St. Bernard dogs. With respect to its great strength there can be no doubt. The immense masses of muscle around its jaws, shoulders, and forearms proclaim tremendous force. They would seem, however, to be inferior in power to those of the Indian tiger. Most of those feats of strength that I have seen performed by lions, such as the taking away of an ox, were not carrying, but dragging or trailing the carcass along the ground: they have sprung on some occasions on to the hind-quarters of a horse, but no one has ever seen them on the withers of a giraffe. They do not mount on the hind-quarters of an eland even, but try to tear him down with their claws. Messrs. Oswell and Vardon once saw three lions endeavoring to drag down a buffalo, and they were unable to do so for a time, though he was then mortally wounded by a two-ounce ball.*

---

* This singular encounter, in the words of an eye-witness, happened as follows:—

"My South African Journal is now before me, and I have got hold of the account of the lion and buffalo affair; here it is:—'15th September, 1846. Oswell and I were riding this afternoon along the banks of the

In general the lion seizes the animal he is attacking by the flank near the hind-leg, or by the throat below the jaw. It is questionable whether he ever attempts to seize an animal by the withers. The flank is the most common point of attack, and that is the part he begins to feast on first. The natives and lions are very similar in their tastes in the selection of titbits: an eland may be seen disembowelled by a lion so completely that he scarcely seems cut up at all. The bowels and fatty parts form a full meal for even the largest lion. The jackal comes sniffing about, and sometimes suffers for his temerity by a stroke from the lion's paw

---

Limpopo, when a waterbuck started in front of us. I dismounted, and was following it through the jungle, when three buffaloes got up, and after going a little distance, stood still, and the nearest bull turned round and looked at me. A ball from the two-ouncer crashed into his shoulder, and they all three made off. Oswell and I followed as soon as I had reloaded, and when we were in sight of the buffalo, and gaining on him at every stride, three lions leaped on the unfortunate brute; he bellowed most lustily as he kept up a kind of running fight, but he was, of course, soon overpowered and pulled down. We had a fine view of the struggle, and saw the lions on their hind-legs tearing away with teeth and claws in most ferocious style. We crept up within thirty yards, and, kneeling down, blazed away at the lions. My rifle was a single barrel, and I had no spare gun. One lion fell dead almost *on* the buffalo; he had merely time to turn toward us, seize a bush with his teeth, and drop dead with the stick in his jaws. The second made off immediately; and the third raised his head, coolly looked round for a moment, then went on tearing and biting at the carcass as hard as ever. We retired a short distance to load, then again advanced and fired. The lion made off, but a ball that he received *ought* to have stopped him, as it went clean through his shoulder-blade. He was followed up and killed, after having charged several times. Both lions were males. It is not often that one *bags* a **brace** of lions and a bull-buffalo in about ten minutes. It was an exciting adventure, and I shall never forget it.'

"Such, my dear Livingstone, is the plain unvarnished account. The buffalo had, of course, gone close to where the lions were lying down for the day; and they, seeing him lame and bleeding, thought the opportunity too good a one to be lost. Ever yours,

"FRANK VARDON.

Three Lions Attempting to Drag Down a Buffalo.

laying him dead. When gorged, the lion falls fast asleep, and is then easily despatched. Hunting a lion with dogs involves very little danger compared with hunting the Indian tiger, because the dogs bring him out of cover and make him stand at bay, giving the hunter plenty of time for a good deliberate shot.

Where game is abundant, there you may expect lions in proportionately large numbers. They are never seen in herds, but six or eight, probably one family, occasionally hunt together. One is in much more danger of being run over when walking in the streets of London than he is of being devoured by lions in Africa, unless engaged in hunting the animal. Indeed, nothing that I have seen or heard about lions would constitute a barrier in the way of men of ordinary courage and enterprise.

The same feeling which has induced the modern painter to caricature the lion has led the sentimentalist to consider the lion's roar the most terrific of all earthly sounds. We hear of the "majestic roar of the king of beasts." It is, indeed, well calculated to inspire fear if you hear it in combination with the tremendously loud thunder of that country, on a night so pitchy dark that every flash of the intensely vivid lightning leaves you with the impression of stone-blindness, while the rain pours down so fast that your fire goes out, leaving you without the protection of even a tree, or the chance of your gun going off. But when you are in a comfortable house or wagon, the case is very different, and you hear the roar of the lion without any awe or alarm. The silly ostrich makes a noise as loud; yet he never was feared by man. To talk of the majestic roar of the lion is mere majestic twaddle. On my mentioning this fact some years ago, the assertion was doubted, so I have been careful ever since to inquire the opinions of Europeans, who have heard both, if they could detect any difference between the roar of a lion and that of an ostrich; the invariable answer was, that they could not when the animal was at any distance. The natives assert that they can detect a variation between the commencement of the noise of each. There is, it must be admitted, considerable difference between the singing noise of a lion when full, and his deep, gruff growl when hungry. In general the lion's voice seems to come deeper from the chest than that of the ostrich; but to this day I can distinguish between them with certainty only by knowing that the ostrich roars by day and the lion by night.

The African lion is of a tawny color, like that of some mastiffs. The mane in the male is large, and gives the idea of great power. In some lions the ends of the hair of the mane are black; these go by the name of blackmaned lions, though as a whole all look of the yellow tawny color. At the time of the discovery of the lake, Messrs. Oswell and Wilson shot two specimens of another variety. One was an old lion, whose teeth were mere stumps, and his claws worn quite blunt; the other was full grown, in the prime of life, with white, perfect teeth: both were entirely destitute of mane. The lions in the country near the lake give tongue less than those farther south. We scarcely ever heard them roar at all.

The lion has other checks on inordinate increase besides man. He seldom attacks full-grown animals; but frequently, when a buffalo-calf is caught by him, the cow rushes to the rescue, and a toss from her often kills him. One we found was killed thus; and on the Leeambye another, which died near Sesheke, had all the appearance of having received his death-blow from a buffalo. It is questionable if a single lion ever attacks a full-grown buffalo. The amount of roaring heard at night, on occasions when a buffalo is killed, seems to indicate there are always more than one lion engaged in the onslaught.

On the plain, south of Sebituane's ford, a herd of buffaloes kept a number of lions from their young by the males turning their heads to the enemy. The young and the cows were in the rear. One toss from a bull would kill the strongest lion that ever breathed I have been in-

Female Buffalo Defending her Young.

formed that in one part of India even the tame buffaloes feel their superiority to some wild animals, for they have been seen to chase a tiger up the hills, bellowing as if they enjoyed the sport. Lions never go near any elephants except the calves, which, when young, are sometimes torn by them; every living thing retires before the lordly elephant, yet a full-grown one would be an easier prey than the rhinoceros; the lion rushes off at the mere sight of this latter beast.

When we reached the Bamangwato, the chief, Sekomi, was particularly friendly, collected all his people to the religious services we held, and explained his reasons for compelling some Englishmen to pay him a horse. "They would not sell him any powder, though they had plenty; so he compelled them to give it and the horse for nothing. He would not deny the extortion to me; that would be 'boherehere,' (swindling.)" He thus thought extortion better than swindling. I could not detect any difference in the morality of the two transactions; but Sekomi's ideas of honesty are the lowest I have met with in any Bechuana chief, and this instance is mentioned as the only approach to demanding payment for leave to pass that I have met with in the south. In all other cases the difficulty has been to get a chief to give us men to show the way, and the payment has only been for guides. Englishmen have always very properly avoided giving that idea to the native mind which we shall hereafter find prove troublesome, that payment ought to be made for passage through a country

January 28.—Passing on to Letloche, about twenty miles beyond the Bamangwato, we found a fine supply of water. This is a point of so much interest in that country that the first question we ask of passers-by is, "Have you had water?" the first inquiry a native puts to a fellow-countryman is, "Where is the rain?" and, though they are by no means an untruthful nation, the answer generally is, "I don't know: there is none: we are killed with hunger and by the sun." If news is asked for, they commence with, "There is no news; I heard some lies only," and then tell all they know.

This spot was Mr. Gordon Cumming's farthest station north. Our house at Kolobeng having been quite in the hunting-country, rhinoceros and buffaloes several times rushed past, and I was able to shoot the latter twice from our own door. We were favored by visits from this famous hunter during each of the five years of his warfare with wild animals. Many English gentlemen following the same pursuits paid their guides and assistants so punctually that in making arrangements for them we had to be careful that four did not go where two only were wanted: they knew so well that an Englishman would pay that they depended implicitly on his word of honor, and not only would they go and hunt for five or six months in the north, enduring all the hardships of that trying mode of life, with little else but meat of game to subsist on, but they willingly went seven hundred or eight hundred miles to Graham's Town, receiving for wages only a musket worth fifteen shillings.

No one ever deceived them, except one man; and, as I believed that he was afflicted with a slight degree of the insanity of greediness, I upheld the honor of the English name by paying his debts. As the guides of Mr. Cumming were furnished through my influence, and usually got some strict charges as to their behavior before parting, looking upon me in the light of a father, they always came to give me an account of their service, and told most of those hunting-adventures which have since been given to the world, before we had the pleasure of hearing our friend relate them himself by our own fireside. I had thus a tolerably good opportunity of testing their accuracy, and I have no hesitation in saying that, for those who love that sort of thing, Mr. Cumming's book conveys a truthful idea of South African hunting. Some things in it require explanation, but the numbers of animals said to have been met with and killed are by no means improbable, considering the amount of large game then in the country. Two other gentlemen hunting in the same region destroyed in one season no fewer than seventy-eight rhinoceroses alone. Sportsmen, however, would not now find an equal number; for, as guns are introduced among the tribes, all these fine animals melt away like snow in spring. In the more remote districts, where fire-arms have not yet been introduced, with the single exception of the rhinoceros, the game is to be found in numbers much greater than Mr. Cumming ever saw. The tsetse is, however, an insuperable barrier to hunting with horses there, and Europeans can do nothing on foot. The step of the elephant when charging the hunter, though apparently not quick, is so long that the pace equals the speed of a good horse at a canter. A young sportsman, no matter how great among pheasants, foxes, and hounds, would do well to pause before resolving to brave fever for the excitement of risking such a terrific charge; the scream or trumpeting of this enormous brute when infuriated is more like what the shriek of a French steam-whistle would be to a man standing on the dangerous part of a railroad than any other earthly sound: a horse unused to it will sometimes stand shivering instead of taking his rider out of danger. It has happened often that the poor animal's legs do their duty so badly that he falls and causes his rider to be trodden into a mummy; or, losing his presence of mind, the rider may allow the horse to dash under a tree and crack his cranium against a branch. As one charge from an elephant has made embryo Nimrods bid a final adieu to the chase, incipient Gordon Cummings might try their nerves by standing on railways till the engines were within a few yards of them. Hunting elephants on foot would be not less dangerous,* unless the Ceylon mode of killing them by

---

* Since writing the above statement, it has received confirmation in the reported death of Mr. Wahlberg while hunting elephants on foot at Lake Ngami.

one shot could be followed: it has never been tried in Africa.

Advancing to some wells beyond Letloche, at a spot named Kanne, we found them carefully hedged round by the people of a Bakalahari village situated near the spot. We had then sixty miles of country in front without water, and very distressing for the oxen, as it is generally deep soft sand. There is one sucking-place, around which were congregated great numbers of Bushwomen with their eggshells and reeds. Mathuluane now contained no water, and Motlatsa only a small supply; so we sent the oxen across the country to the deep well Nkauane, and half were lost on the way. When found at last, they had been five whole days without water. Very large numbers of elands were met with, as usual, though they seldom can get a sip of drink. Many of the plains here have large expanses of grass without trees; but you seldom see a treeless horizon.

CHAPTER VIII.

DR. LIVINGSTONE REACHES THE COUNTRY OF THE MAKOLOLO.

The Bakalahari, who live at Motlatsa Wells, have always been very friendly to us, and listen attentively to instruction conveyed to them in their own tongue. It is, however, difficult to give an idea to a European of the little effect teaching produces; because no one can realize the degradation to which their minds have been sunk by centuries of barbarism and hard struggling for the necessaries of life: like most others, they listen with respect and attention; but, when we kneel down and address an unseen Being, the position and the act often appear to them so ridiculous that they cannot refrain from bursting into uncontrollable laughter. After a few services they get over this tendency. I was once present when a missionary attempted to sing among a wild heathen tribe of Bechuanas, who had no music in their composition: the effect on the risible faculties of the audience was such that the tears actually ran down their cheeks. Nearly all their thoughts are directed to the supply of their bodily wants; and this has been the case with the race for ages. If asked, then, what effect the preaching of the gospel has at the commencement on such individuals, I am unable to tell, except that some have confessed long afterward that they then first began to pray in secret. Of the effects of a long-continued course of instruction there can be no reasonable doubt, as mere nominal belief has never been considered sufficient proof of conversion by any body of missionaries; and, after the change which has been brought about by this agency, we have good reason to hope well for the future: those I have myself witnessed behaving in the manner described, when kindly treated in sickness, often utter imploring words to Jesus, and, I believe, sometimes really do pray to him in their afflictions. As that great Redeemer of the guilty seeks to save all he can, we may hope that they find mercy through his blood, though little able to appreciate the sacrifice he made.

Leaving Motlatsa on the 8th of February, 1853, we passed down the Mokoko, which, in the memory of persons now living, was a flowing stream.

At Nchokotsa, the rainy season having this year been delayed beyond the usual time, we found during the day the thermometer stand at 96° in the coolest possible shade.

We dug out several wells; and, as we had on each occasion to wait till the water flowed in again, and then allow our cattle to feed a day or two and slake their thirst thoroughly, as far as that could be done, before starting, our progress was but slow. At Koobe there was such a mass of mud in the pond, worked up by the wallowing rhinoceros to the consistency of mortar, that only by great labor could we get a space cleared at one side for the water to ooze through and collect in for the oxen.

At Rapesh we came among our old friends the Bushmen, under Horoye. This man, Horoye, a good specimen of that tribe, and his son Mokantsa, and others, were at least six feet high, and of a darker color than the Bushmen of the south. They have always plenty of food and water; and, as they frequent the Zouga as often as the game in company with which they live, their life is very different from that of the inhabitants of the thirsty plains of the Kalahari.

Those among whom we now were kill many elephants, and, when the moon is full, choose that time for the chase, on account of its coolness. Hunting this animal is the best test of courage this country affords. The Bushmen choose the moment succeeding a charge, when the elephant is out of breath, to run in and give him a stab with their long-bladed spears. In this case the uncivilized have the advantage over us; but I believe that, with half their training, Englishmen would beat the Bushmen.

At Maila we spent a Sunday with Kaisa, the head-man of a village of Mashona, who had fled from the iron sway of Mosilikatse, whose country lies east of this. I wished him to take charge of a packet of letters for England, to be forwarded when, as is the custom of the Bamangwato, the Bechuanas come hither in search of skins and food among the Bushmen; but he could not be made to comprehend that there was no danger in the consignment. He feared the responsibility and guilt if any thing should happen to them; so I had to bid adieu to all hope of letting my family hear of my welfare till I should reach the west coast.

At Unku we came into a tract of country which had been visited by refreshing showers long before, and every spot was covered with grass run up to seed, and the flowers of the forest were in full bloom. Instead of the dreary prospect around Koobe and Nchokotsa, we had here a delightful scene,—all the ponds full of water, and the birds twittering joyfully As the game can now obtain water everywhere, they become very shy, and cannot be found in their accustomed haunts.

1st March.—The thermometer in the shade generally stood at 98° from 1 to 3 P.M.; but it sank as low as 65° by night; so that the heat was by no means exhausting. At the surface of the ground, in the sun, the thermometer marked 125°, and, three inches below it, 138°. The hand cannot be held on the ground, and even the horny soles of the feet of the natives must be protected by sandals of hide; yet the ants were busy working on it. The water in the ponds was as high as 100°; but, as water does not conduct heat readily downward, deliciously-cool water may be obtained by any one walking into the middle and lifting up the water from the bottom to the surface with his hands.

Proceeding to the north, from Kama-kama, we entered into dense Mohonono bush, which required the constant application of the axe by three of our party for two days. This bush has fine silvery leaves, and the bark has a sweet taste. The elephant, with his usual delicacy of taste, feeds much on it. On emerging into the plains beyond, we found a number of Bushmen, who afterward proved very serviceable. The rains had been copious; but now great numbers of pools were drying up. Lotus-plants abounded in them, and a low, sweet-scented plant covered their banks. Breezes came occasionally to us from these drying-up pools; but the pleasant odor they carried caused sneezing in both myself and people; and on the 10th of March (when in lat. 19° 16′ 11″ S., long. 24° 24′ E.) we were brought to a stand by four of the party being seized with fever. I had seen this disease before; but did not at once recognise it as the African fever: I imagined it was only a bilious attack arising from full feeding on flesh; for, the large game having been very abundant, we always had a good supply. But, instead of the first sufferers recovering soon, every man of our party was in a few days laid low, except a Bakwain and myself. He managed the oxen, while I attended to the wants of the patients and went out occasionally with the Bushmen to get a zebra or buffalo, so as to induce them to remain with us.

Here for the first time I had leisure to follow the instructions of my kind teacher, Mr. Maclear, and calculated several longitudes from lunar distances. The hearty manner in which that eminent astronomer and frank, friendly man had promised to aid me in calculating and verifying my work conduced more than any thing else to inspire me with perseverance in making astronomical observations throughout the journey.

We wished to avoid the tsetse of our former path, so kept a course on the magnetic meridan from Lurilopepe. The necessity of making a new path much increased our toil. We were, however, rewarded in lat. 18° with a sight we had not enjoyed the year before, namely, large patches of grape-bearing vines. There they stood before my eyes; but the sight was so entirely unexpected that I stood some time gazing at the clusters of grapes with which they were loaded, with no more thought of plucking than if I had been beholding them in a dream. The Bushmen know and eat them; but they are not well flavored, on account of the great astringency of the seeds, which are in shape and size like split peas. The elephants are fond of the fruit, plant, and root alike.

The forest, through which we were slowly toiling, daily became more dense, and we were kept almost constantly at work with the axe; there was much more leafiness in the trees here than farther south. The leaves are chiefly of the pinnate and bi-pinnate forms, and are exceedingly beautiful when seen against the sky : a great variety of the papilionaceous family grow in this part of the country.

Fleming had until this time always assisted to drive his own wagon, but about the end of March he knocked up, as well as his people As I could not drive two wagons, I shared with him the remaining water, half a caskful, and went on, with the intention of coming back for him as soon as we should reach the next pool. Heavy rain now commenced; I was employed the whole day in cutting down trees, and every stroke of the axe brought down a thick shower on my back, which in the hard work was very refreshing, as the water found its way down into my shoes In the evening we met some Bushmen, who volunteered to show us a pool; and, having unyoked, I walked some miles in search of it. As it became dark they showed their politeness—a quality which is by no means confined entirely to the civilized—by walking in front, breaking the branches which hung across the path, and pointing out the fallen trees. On returning to the wagon, we found that being left alone had brought out some of Fleming's energy, for he had managed to come up.

As the water in this pond dried up, we were soon obliged to move again. One of the Bushmen took out his dice, and, after throwing them, said that God told him to go home. He threw again, in order to show me the command, but the opposite result followed; so he remained and was useful, for we lost the oxen again by a lion driving them off to a very great distance. The lions here are not often heard. They seem to have a wholesome dread of the Bushmen, who, when they observe evidence of a lion's having made a full meal, follow up his spoor so quietly that his slumbers are not disturbed. One discharges a poisoned arrow from a distance of only a few feet, while his companion simultaneously throws his skin cloak on the beast's head. The sudden surprise makes the lion lose his presence of mind, and he bounds away in the greatest confusion and terror. Our friends here showed me the poison which they use on these occasions. It is the entrails of a caterpillar called N'gwa, half an inch long. They squeeze out these, and place them all around the bottom of the barb, and allow the poison to dry in the sun. They are very careful in cleaning their nails after working with it, as a small portion introduced into a scratch acts like morbid matter in dissection-wounds.' The agony is so great that the person cuts himself, calls for his mother's breast as if he were returned in idea to his childhood again, or flies from human habitations a raging maniac. The effects on the lion are equally terrible. He is heard moaning in distress, and becomes furious, biting the trees and ground in rage.

As the Bushmen have the reputation of curing the wounds of this poison, I asked how this was effected. They said that they administer the caterpillar itself in combination with fat; they also rub fat into the wound, saying that "the N'gwa wants fat, and, when it does not find it in the body, kills the man: we give it what it wants, and it is content:" a reason which will commend itself to the enlightened among ourselves.

None of the men of our party had died, but two seemed unlikely to recover; and Kibopechoe, my willing Mokwain, at last became troubled with boils, and then got all the symptoms of fever. As he lay down, the others began to move about, and complained of weakness only. Believing that frequent change of place was conducive to their recovery, we moved along as much as we could, and came to the hill N'gwa, (lat. 18° 27' 20" S., long. 24° 13' 36" E.) This being the only hill we had seen since leaving Bamangwato, we felt inclined to take off our hats to it. It is three or four hundred feet high, and covered with trees.

Our Bushmen wished to leave us, and, as there was no use in trying to thwart these independent gentlemen, I paid them, and allowed them to go. The payment, however, acted as a charm on some strangers who happened to be present, and induced them to volunteer their aid.

We at last came to the Sanshureh, which presented an impassable barrier; so we drew up under a magnificent baobab-tree, (lat. 18° 4' 27" S., long. 24° 6' 20" E.,) and resolved to explore the river for a ford. The great quantity of water we had passed through was part of the annual inundation of the Chobe; and this, which appeared a large, deep river, filled in many parts with reeds, and having hippopotami in it, is only one of the branches by which it sends its superabundant water to the southeast.

We made so many attempts to get over the Sanshureh, both to the west and east of the wagon, in the hope of reaching some of the Makololo on the Chobe, that my Bushmen friends became quite tired of the work. By means of presents I got them to remain some days; but at last they slipped away by night, and I was fain to take one of the strongest of my still weak companions and cross the river in a pontoon, the gift of Captains Codrington and Webb. We each carried some provisions and a blanket, and penetrated about twenty miles to the westward, in the hope of striking the Chobe. It was much nearer to us in a northerly direction, but this we did not then know. The plain, over which we splashed the whole of the first day, was covered with water ankle deep, and thick grass which reached above the knees. In the evening we came to an immense wall of reeds, six or eight feet high, without any opening admitting of a passage. When we tried to enter, the water always became so deep that we were fain to desist. We concluded that we had come to the banks of the river we were in search of; so we directed our course to some trees which appeared in the south, in order to get a bed and a view of the adjacent locality. Having shot a leche, and made a glorious fire, we got a good cup of tea and had a comfortable night.

Next morning, by climbing the highest trees, we could see a fine large sheet of water, but surrounded on all sides by the same impenetrable belt of reeds. This is the broad part of the river Chobe, and is called Zabesa. Two tree-covered islands seemed to be much nearer to the water than the snore on which we were; so we made an attempt to get to them first. It was not the reeds alone we had to pass through; a peculiar serrated grass, which at certain angles cut the hands like a razor, was mingled with the reed, and the climbing convolvulus, with stalks which felt as strong as whipcord, bound the mass together. We felt like pygmies in it, and often the only way we could get on was by both of us leaning against a part and bending it down till we could stand upon it. The perspiration streamed off our bodies, and as the sun rose high, there being no ventilation among the reeds, the heat was stifling, and the water, which was up to the knees, felt agreeably refreshing. After some hours' toil we reached one of the islands. Here we met an old friend, the bramble-bush. My strong moleskins were quite worn through at the knees, and the leather trousers of my companion were torn and his legs bleeding. Tearing my handkerchief in two, I tied the pieces round my knees, and then encountered another difficulty. We were still forty or fifty yards from the clear water, but now we were opposed by great masses of papyrus, which are like palms in miniature, eight or ten feet high, and an inch and a half in diameter. These were laced together by twining convolvulus so strongly that the weight of both of us could not make way into the clear water. At last we fortunately found a passage prepared by a hippopotamus. Eager as soon as we reached the island to look along the vista to clear water, I stepped in and found it took me at once up to the neck.

Returning nearly worn out, we proceeded up the bank of the Chobe till we came to the point of departure of the branch Sanshureh; we then went in the opposite direction, or down the Chobe, though from the highest trees we could see nothing but one vast expanse of reed, with here and there a tree on the islands. This was a hard day's work; and, when we came to a deserted Bayeiye hut on an ant-hill, not a bit of wood or any thing else could be got for a fire except the grass and sticks of the dwelling itself. I dreaded the "*Tampans,*" so common in all old huts; but outside of it we had thousands of mosquitos, and cold dew began to be deposited, so we were fain to crawl beneath its shelter.

We were close to the reeds, and could listen to the strange sounds which are often heard there. By day I had seen water-snakes putting up their heads and swimming about There were great numbers of otters, (*Lutra inunguis*, F. Cuvier,) which have made little spoors all over the plains in search of the fishes, among the tall grass of these flooded prairies; curious birds, too, jerked and wriggled among these reedy masses, and we heard human-like voices and unearthly sounds, with splash, guggle, jupp, as if rare fun were going on in their uncouth haunts. After a damp, cold night, we set to, early in the morning, at our work of exploring again, but left the pontoon in order to lighten our labor. The ant-hills are here very high, some thirty feet, and of a base so broad that trees grow on them; while the lands, annually flooded, bear nothing but grass. From one of these ant-hills we discovered an inlet to the Chobe; and, having gone back for the pontoon, we launched ourselves on a deep river, here from eighty to one hundred yards wide. I gave my companion strict injunctions to stick by the pontoon in case a hippopotamus should look at us; nor was this caution unnecessary, for one came up at our side and made a desperate plunge off. We had passed over him. The wave he made caused the pontoon to glide quickly away from him.

We paddled on from mid-day till sunset. There was nothing but a wall of reed on each bank, and we saw every prospect of spending a supperless night in our float; but, just as the short twilight of these parts was commencing, we perceived on the north bank the village of Moremi, one of the Makololo, whose acquaintance I had made on our former visit, and who was now located on the island Mahonta, (lat. 17° 58' S., long. 24° 6' E.) The villagers looked as we may suppose people do who see a ghost, and in their figurative way of speaking said, "He has dropped among us from the clouds, yet came riding on the back of a hippopotamus! We Makololo thought no one could cross the

Chobe without our knowledge, but here he drops among us like a bird."

Next day we returned in canoes across the flooded lands, and found that, in our absence, the men had allowed the cattle to wander into a very small patch of wood to the west containing the tsetse; this carelessness cost me ten fine large oxen. After remaining a few days, some of the head-men of the Makololo came down from Linyanti, with a large party of Barotse, to take us across the river. This they did in fine style, swimming and diving among the oxen more like alligators than men, and taking the wagons to pieces and carrying them across on a number of canoes lashed together. We were now among friends; so, going about thirty miles to the north, in order to avoid the still flooded lands on the north of the Chobe, we turned westward toward Linyanti, (lat. 18° 17' 20" S., long. 23° 50' 9" E.,) where we arrived on the 23d of May, 1853. This is the capital town of the Makololo, and only a short distance from our wagon-stand of 1851, (lat. 18° 20' S., long. 23° 50' E.)

CHAPTER IX.

DR. LIVINGSTONE LABORS AS A MISSIONARY AMONG THE MAKOLOLO.

The whole population of Linyanti, numbering between six and seven thousand souls, turned out *en masse* to see the wagons in motion. They had never witnessed the phenomenon before, we having on the former occasion departed by night. Sekeletu, now in power, received us in what is considered royal style, setting before us a great number of pots of boyaloa, the beer of the country. These were brought by women, and each bearer takes a good draught of the beer when she sets it down, by way of "tasting," to show that there is no poison

The court herald, an old man who occupied the post also in Sebituane's time, stood up, and after some antics, such as leaping, and shouting at the top of his voice, roared out some adulatory sentences, as, "Don't I see the white man? Don't I see the comrade of Sebituane? Don't I see the father of Sekeletu?"—"We want sleep."—"Give your son sleep, my lord," &c. &c. The perquisites of this man are the heads of all the cattle slaughtered by the chief, and he even takes a share of the tribute before it is distributed and taken out of the kotla. He is expected to utter all the proclamations, call assemblies, keep the kotla clean, and the fire burning every evening, and when a person is executed in public he drags away the body.

I found Sekeletu a young man of eighteen years of age, of that dark yellow or coffee-and-milk color of which the Makololo are so proud, because it distinguishes them considerably from the black tribes on the rivers. He is about five feet seven in height, and neither so good-looking nor of so much ability as his father was, but is equally friendly to the English. Sebituane installed his daughter Mamochisáne into the chieftainship long before his death, but, with all his acuteness, the idea of her having a husband who should not be her lord did not seem to enter his mind. He wished to make her his successor, probably in imitation of some of the negro tribes with whom he had come into contact; but, being of the Bechuana race, he could not look upon the husband except as the woman's lord; so he told her all the men were hers,—she might take any one, but ought to keep none. In fact, he thought she might do with the men what he could do with the women; but these men had other wives; and, according to a saying in the country, "the tongues of women cannot be governed," they made her miserable by their remarks. One man whom she chose was even called her wife, and her son the child of Mamochisane's wife; but the arrangement was so distasteful to Mamochisane herself that, as soon as Sebituane died, she said she never would consent to govern the Makololo so long as she had a brother living Sekeletu, being afraid of another member of the family, Mpépe, who had pretensions to the chieftainship, urged his sister strongly to remain as she had always been, and allow him to support her authority by leading the Makololo when they went forth to war. Three days were spent in public discussion on the point. Mpepe insinuated that Sekeletu was not the lawful son of Sebituane, on account of his mother having been the wife of another chief before her marriage with Sebituane; Mamochisane, however, upheld Sekeletu's claims, and at last stood up in the assembly and addressed him with a womanly gush of tears: —"I have been a chief only because my father wished it. I always would have preferred to be married and have a family like other women. You, Sekeletu, must be chief, and build up your father's house." This was a death-blow to the hopes of Mpepe, who was soon after speared for an attempt to assassinate Sekeletu.

Soon after our arrival at Linyanti, Sekeletu took me aside, and pressed me to mention those things I liked best and hoped to get from him. Any thing, either in or out of his town, should be freely given if I would only mention it. I explained to him that my object was to elevate him and his people to be Christians; but he replied he did not wish to learn to read the Book, for he was afraid " it might change his heart, and make him content with only one wife, like Sechele." It was of little use to urge that the change of heart implied a contentment with one wife equal to his present complacency in polygamy. Such a preference after the change of mind could not now be understood by him any more than the real, unmistakable pleasure of religious services can by those who have not experienced what is known by the term the "new heart." I assured him that nothing was expected but by his own voluntary decision. "No, no; he wanted always to have five wives at least." I liked the frankness of Sekeletu, for nothing is so wearying to the spirit as talking to those who agree with every thing advanced.

At our public religious services in the kotla, the Makololo women always behaved with decorum from the first, except at the conclusion of the prayer. When all knelt down, many of those who had children, in following the example of the rest, bent over their little ones: the children, in terror of being crushed to death, set up a simultaneous yell, which so tickled the whole assembly there was often a subdued titter, to be turned into a hearty laugh as soon as they heard Amen.

The numbers who attended at the summons of the herald, who acted as beadle, were often from five to seven hundred. The service consisted of reading a small portion of the Bible and giving an explanatory address, usually short enough to prevent weariness or want of attention. So long as we continue to hold services in the kotla, the associations of the place are unfavorable to solemnity; hence it is always desirable to have a place of worship as soon as possible; and it is of importance, too, to treat such place with reverence, as an aid to secure that serious attention which religious subjects demand. This will appear more evident when it is recollected that, in the very spot where we had been engaged in acts of devotion, half an hour after a dance would be got up; and these habits cannot be at first opposed without the appearance of assuming too much authority over them. It is always unwise to hurt their feelings of independence.

To give an idea of the routine followed for months together, on other days as well as on Sundays, I may advert to my habit of treating the sick for complaints which seemed to surmount the skill of their own doctors. I refrained from going to any one unless his own doctor wished it or had given up the case. This led to my having a selection of the severer cases only, and prevented the doctors' being offended at my taking their practice out of their hands. When attacked by fever myself, and wish ing to ascertain what their practices were, I could safely intrust myself in their hands, on account of their wellknown friendly feelings.

I proposed to teach the Makololo to read; but, for the reasons mentioned, Sekeletu at first declined: after some weeks, however, Motibe, his father-in-law, and some others, determined to brave the mysterious book. To all who have not acquired it, the knowledge of letters is quite unfathomable; there is naught like it within the compass of their observation; and we have no comparison with any thing except pictures, to aid them in comprehending the idea of signs of words. It seems to them supernatural that we see in a book things taking place or having occurred at a distance. No amount of explanation conveys the idea unless they learn to read. Machinery is equally inexplicable, and money nearly as much so until they see it in actual use. They are familiar with barter alone; and in the centre of the country, where gold is totally unknown, if a button and sovereign were left to their choice, they would prefer the former on account of its having an eye.

In beginning to learn, Motibe seemed to himself in the position of the doctor, who was obliged to drink his potion before the patient, to show that it contained nothing detrimental; after he had mastered the alphabet, and reported the thing so far safe, Sekeletu and his young companions came forward to try for themselves. He must have resolved to watch the effects of the book against his views on polygamy, and abstain whenever he perceived any tendency, in reading it, toward enforcing him to put his wives away A number of men learned the alphabet in a short time, and were set to teach others, but before much progress could be made I was on my way to Loanda.

As I had declined to name any thing as a present from Sekeletu, except a canoe to take me up the river, he brought ten fine elephants' tusks and laid them down beside my wagon. He would take no denial, though I told him I should prefer to see him trading with Fleming, a man of color from the West Indies, who had come for the purpose I had, during the eleven years of my previous course, invariably abstained from taking presents of ivory, from an idea that a religious instructor degraded himself by accepting gifts from those whose spiritual welfare he professed to seek. My precedence of all traders in the line of discovery put me often in the way of very handsome offers; but I always advised the donors to sell their ivory to traders, who would be sure to follow, and when at some future time they had become rich by barter they might remember me or my children. When Lake Ngami was discovered, I might have refused permission to a trader who accompanied us; but when he applied for leave to form part of our company, knowing that Mr. Oswell would no more trade than myself, and that the people of the lake would be disappointed if they could not dispose of their ivory, I willingly granted a sanction, without which his people would not at that time have ventured so far. This was surely preferring the interest of another to my own. The return I got for this was a notice in one of the Cape papers that this "man was the true discoverer of the lake!"

The conclusion I had come to was that it is quite lawful, though perhaps not expedient, for missionaries to trade; but barter is the only means by which a missionary in the interior can pay his way, as money has no value. In all the journeys I had previously undertaken for wider diffusion of the gospel, the extra expenses were defrayed from my salary of £100 per annum. This sum is sufficient to enable a missionary to live in the interior of South Africa, supposing he has a garden capable of yielding corn and vegetables; but should he not, and still consider that six or eight months cannot lawfully be spent simply in getting goods at a lower price than they can be had from itinerant traders, the sum mentioned is barely sufficient for the poorest fare and plainest apparel. As we never felt ourselves justified in making journeys to the colony for the sake of securing bargains, the most frugal living was necessary to enable us to be a little charitable to others; but when to this were added extra travelling-expenses, the wants of an increasing family, and liberal gifts to chiefs, it was difficult to make both ends meet. The pleasure of missionary labor would be enhanced if one could devote his life to the heathen without drawing a salary from a society at all. The luxury of doing good from one's own private resources, without appearing to either natives or Europeans to be making a gain of it, is far preferable, and an object worthy the ambition of the rich. But few men of fortune, however, now devote themselves to Christian missions, as of old. Presents were always given to the chiefs whom we visited, and nothing accepted in return; but when Sebituane (in 1851) offered some ivory, I took it, and was able by its sale to present his son with a number of really useful articles of a higher value than I had ever been able to give before to any chief. In doing this, of course, I appeared to trade, but, feeling I had a right to do so, I felt perfectly easy in my mind; and, as I still held the view of the inexpediency of combining the two professions, I was glad of the proposal of one of the most honorable merchants of Cape Town, Mr. H. E. Rutherford, that he should risk a sum of money in Fleming's hands for the purpose of attempting to develop a trade with the Makololo. It was to this man I suggested Sekeletu should sell the tusks which he had presented for my acceptance; but the chief refused to take them back from me. The goods which Fleming had brought were ill adapted for the use of the natives, but he got a pretty good load of ivory in exchange; and though it was his first attempt at trading, and the distance travelled over made the expenses enormous, he was not a loser by the trip. Other traders followed, who demanded 90 lbs. of ivory for a musket. The Makololo, knowing nothing of steelyards, but supposing that they were meant to cheat them, declined to trade except by exchanging one bull and one cow elephant's tusk for each gun. This would average 70 lbs. of ivory, which sells at the Cape for 5s. per pound, for a secondhand musket worth 10s. I, being sixty miles distant, did not witness this attempt at barter, but, anxious to enable my countrymen to drive a brisk trade, told the Makololo to sell my ten tusks on their own account for whatever they would bring. Seventy tusks were for sale, but, the parties not understanding each other's talk, no trade was established; and when I passed the spot some time afterward I found that the whole of that ivory had been destroyed by an accidental fire, which broke out in the village when all the people were absent. Success in trade is as much dependent on knowledge of the language as success in travelling.

I had brought with me as presents an improved breed of goats, fowls, and a pair of cats. A superior bull was bought, also as a gift to Sekeletu; but I was compelled to leave it on account of its having become foot-sore. As the Makololo are very fond of improving the breed of their domestic animals, they were much pleased with my selection. I endeavored to bring the bull, in performance of a promise made to Sebituane before he died. Admiring a calf which we had with us, he proposed to give me a cow for it, which in the native estimation was offering three times its value. I presented it to him at once, and promised to bring him another and a better one. Sekeletu was much gratified by my attempt to keep my word given to his father

CHAPTER X

SICKNESS OF DR. LIVINGSTONE.—ACCOUNT OF SEKELETU AND HIS SUBJECTS.

On the 30th of May I was seized with fever, for the first time. We reached the town of Linyanti on the 23d; and, as my habits were suddenly changed from great exertion to comparative inactivity, at the commencement of the cold season I suffered from a severe attack of stoppage of the secretions, closely resembling a common cold. Warm baths and drinks relieved me, and I had no idea but that I was now recovering from the effects of a chill got by leaving the warm wagon in the evening in order to conduct family worship at my people's fire. But on the 2d of June a relapse showed to the Makololo, who knew the complaint, that my indisposition was no other than the fever, with which I have since made a more intimate acquaintance. Cold east winds prevail at this time; and as they come over the extensive flats inundated by the Chobe, as well as many other districts where pools of rain-water are now drying up, they may be supposed to be loaded with malaria and watery vapor, and many cases of fever follow. The usual symptoms of stopped secretion are manifested,—shivering and a feeling of coldness, though the skin is quite hot to the touch of another. The heat in the axillæ, over the heart and region of the stomach, was in my case 100°, but along the spine and at the nape of the neck 103° The internal processes were all, with the exception of the kidneys and liver, stopped; the latter, in its efforts to free the blood of noxious particles, often secretes enormous quantities of bile. There were pains along the spine, and frontal headache. Anxious to ascertain whether the natives possessed the knowledge of any remedy of which we were ignorant, I requested the assistance of one of Sekeletu's doctors He put some roots into a pot with water, and,

NATIVE REMEDIES.

when it was boiling, placed it on a spot beneath a blanket thrown around both me and it. This produced no immediate effect: he then got a small bundle of different kinds of medicinal woods, and, burning them in a potsherd nearly to ashes, used the smoke and hot vapor arising from them as an auxiliary to the other in causing diaphoresis. I fondly hoped that they had a more potent remedy than our own medicines afford; but after being stewed in their vapor-baths, smoked like a red herring over green twigs, and charmed *secundum artem*, I concluded that I could cure the fever more quickly than they can. If we employ a wet sheet and a mild aperient in combination with quinine, in addition to the native remedies, they are an important aid in curing the fever, as they seem to have the same stimulating effects on the alimentary canal as these means have on the external surface. Purgatives, general bleeding, or indeed any violent remedies, are injurious; and the appearance of a herpetic eruption near the mouth is regarded as an evidence that no internal organ is in danger. There is a good deal in not "giving in" to this disease. He who is low-spirited, and apt to despond at every attack, will die sooner than the man who is not of such a melancholic nature.

The Makololo had made a garden and planted maize for me, that, as they remarked when I was parting with them to proceed to the Cape, I might have food to eat when I returned, as well as other people. The maize was now pounded by the women into fine meal. This they do in large wooden mortars, the counterpart of which may be seen depicted on the Egyptian monuments. Sekeletu added to this good supply of meal ten or twelve jars of honey, each of which contained about two gallons. Liberal supplies of groundnuts were also furnished every time the tributary tribes brought their dues to Linyanti, and an ox was given for slaughter every week or two. Sekeletu also appropriated two cows to be milked for us every morning and evening. This was in accordance with the acknowledged rule throughout the country, that the chief should feed all the strangers who come on any special business to him and take up their abode in his kotla.

The Makololo cultivate a large extent of land around their villages. Those of them who are real Basutos still retain the habits of that tribe, and may be seen going out with their wives with their hoes in hand,—a state of things never witnessed at Kolobeng, or among any other Bechuana or Caffre tribe. The great chief Moshesh affords an example to his people annually, by not only taking the hoe in hand, but working hard with it on certain public occasions. His Basutos are of the same family with the Makololo to whom I refer. The younger Makololo, who have been accustomed from their infancy to lord it over the conquered Makalaka, have unfortunately no desire to imitate the agricultural tastes of their fathers, and expect their subjects to perform all the manual labor. They are the aristocracy of the country, and once possessed almost unlimited power over their vassals. Their privileges were, however, much abridged by Sebituane himself.

The tribes which Sebituane subjected in this great country pass by the general name of Makalaka. The Makololo were composed of a great number of other tribes, as well as these central negroes. The nucleus of the whole were Basuto, who came with Sebituane from a comparatively cold and hilly region in the south. When he conquered various tribes of the Bechuanas, as Bakwains, Bangwaketze, Bamangwato, Batauana, &c., he incorporated the young of these tribes into his own. Great mortality by fever having taken place in the original stock, he wisely adopted the same plan of absorption on a large scale with the Makalaka. So we found him with even the sons of the chiefs of the Barotse closely attached to his person; and they say to this day, if any thing else but natural death had assailed their father, every one of them would have laid down his life in his defence. One reason for their strong affection was their emancipation by the decree of Sebituane, "all are children of the chief."

Sekeletu receives tribute from a great number of tribes in corn or dura, groundnuts, hoes, spears, honey, canoes, paddles, wooden vessels, tobacco, mutokuane, (*Cannabis sativa*,) various wild fruits, (dried,) prepared skins, and ivory. When these articles are brought into the kotla, Sekeletu has the honor of dividing them among the loungers who usually congregate there. A small portion only is reserved for himself. The ivory belongs nominally to him too, but this is simply a way of making a fair distribution of the profits. The chief sells it only with the approbation of his counsellors, and the proceeds are distributed in open day among the people as before. He has the choice of every thing; but, if he is not more liberal to others than to himself, he loses in popularity. I have known instances in this and other tribes in which individuals aggrieved, because they had been overlooked, fled to other chiefs. One discontented person, having fled to Lechulatebe, was encouraged to go to a village of the Bapálleng, on the river Chō or Tsō, and abstracted the tribute of ivory thence which ought to have come to Sekeletu. This theft enraged the whole of the Makololo, because they all felt it to be a personal loss. Some of Lechulatebe's people having come on a visit to Linyanti, a demonstration was made, in which about five hundred Makololo, armed, went through a mimic fight; the principal warriors pointed their spears toward the lake where Lechulatebe lives, and every thrust in that direction was answered by all with the shout, "Hōō!" while every stab on the ground drew out a simultaneous "Huzz!" On these occasions all capable of bearing arms, even the old, must turn out at the call. In the time of Sebituane, any one remaining in his house was searched for and killed without mercy.

This offence of Lechulatebe was aggravated by repetition, and by a song sung in his town accompanying the dances, which manifested joy at the death of Sebituane. He had enjoined his people to live in peace with those at the lake, and Sekeletu felt disposed to follow his advice;

but Lechulatebe had now got possession of fire-arms, and considered himself more than a match for the Makololo. His father had been dispossessed of many cattle by Sebituane; and, as forgiveness is not considered among the virtues by the heathen, Lechulatebe thought he had a right to recover what he could. As I had a good deal of influence with the Makololo, I persuaded them that, before they could have peace, they must resolve to give the same blessing to others, and they never could do that without forgiving and forgetting ancient feuds. It is hard to make them feel that shedding of human blood is a great crime; they must be conscious that it is wrong, but, having been accustomed to bloodshed from infancy, they are remarkably callous to the enormity of the crime of destroying human life.

I sent a message at the same time to Lechulatebe, advising him to give up the course he had adopted, and especially the song; because, though Sebituane was dead, the arms with which he had fought were still alive and strong.

Sekeletu, in order to follow up his father's instructions and promote peace, sent ten cows to Lechulatebe to be exchanged for sheep; these animals thrive well in a bushy country like that around the lake, but will scarcely live in the flat prairies between the network of waters north of the Chobe. The men who took the cows carried a number of hoes to purchase goats besides. Lechulatebe took the cows and sent back an equal number of sheep. Now, according to the relative value of sheep and cows in these parts, he ought to have sent sixty or seventy.

One of the men who had hoes was trying to purchase in a village without formal leave from Lechulatebe; this chief punished him by making him sit some hours on the broiling hot sand, (at least 130°.) This further offence put a stop to amicable relations between the two tribes altogether. It was a case in which a very small tribe, commanded by a weak and foolish chief, had got possession of fire-arms, and felt conscious of ability to cope with a numerous and warlike race. Such cases are the only ones in which the possession of fire-arms does evil. The universal effect of the diffusion of the more potent instruments of warfare in Africa is the same as among ourselves. Fire-arms render wars less frequent and less bloody. It is indeed exceedingly rare to hear of two tribes having guns going to war with each other; and, as nearly all the feuds, in the south at least, have been about cattle, the risk which must be incurred from long shots generally proves a preventive to the foray.

The Makololo were prevailed upon to keep the peace during my residence with them, but it was easy to perceive that public opinion was against sparing a tribe of Bechuanas for whom the Makololo entertained the most sovereign contempt. The young men would remark, "Lechulatebe is herding our cows for us; let us only go, we shall 'lift' the price of them in sheep," &c.

CHAPTER XI.

DR. LIVINGSTONE LEAVES LINYANTI.

HAVING waited a month at Linyanti, (lat. 18° 17' 20" S., long. 23° 50' 9" E.,) we again departed, for the purpose of ascending the river from Seshcke, (lat. 17° 31' 38" S., long 25° 13' E.) To the Barotse country, the capital of which is Nariéle or Naliéle, (lat. 15° 24' 17" S., long. 23° 5' 54" E.,) I went in company with Se'keletu and about one hundred and sixty attendants. We had most of the young men with us, and many of the under-chiefs besides. The country between Linyanti and Seshcke is perfectly flat, except patches elevated only a few feet above the surrounding level. There are also many mounds where the gigantic ant-hills of the country have been situated or still appear: these mounds are evidently the work of the termites. No one who has not seen their gigantic structures can fancy the industry of these little laborers; they seem to impart fertility to the soil which has once passed through their mouths, for the Makololo find the sides of ant-hills the choice spots for rearing early maize, tobacco, or any thing on which they wish to bestow especial care. We had the Chobe on our right, with its scores of miles of reed occupying the horizon there. It was pleasant to look back on the long extended line of our attendants, as it twisted and bent according to the curves of the footpath, or in and out behind the mounds, the ostrich-feathers of the men waving in the wind. Some had the white ends of ox-tails on their heads, hussar fashion, and others great bunches of black ostrich-feathers, or caps made of lions' manes. Some wore red tunics, or various-colored prints which the chief had bought from Fleming; the common men carried burdens; the gentlemen walked with a small club of rhinoceros-horn in their hands, and had servants to carry their shields; while the "Machaka," battle-axe men, carried their own, and were liable at any time to be sent off a hundred miles on an errand, and expected to run all the way.

Sekeletu is always accompanied by his own Mopato, a number of young men of his own age. When he sits down they crowd around him; those who are nearest eat out of the same dish, for the Makololo chiefs pride themselves on eating with their people. He eats a little, then beckons his neighbors to partake. When they have done so, he perhaps beckons to some one at a distance to take a share; that person starts forward, seizes the pot, and removes it to his own companions. The comrades of Sekeletu, wishing to imitate him in riding on my old horse, leaped on the backs of a number of half-broken Batoka oxen as they ran; but, having neither saddle nor bridle, the number of tumbles they met with was a source of much amusement to the rest.

When we arrived at any village, the women all turned out to lulliloo their chief. Their shrill voices, to which they give a tremulous sound by a quick motion of the tongue, pour forth, "Great lion!" "Great chief!" "Sleep, my lord!" &c. The men utter similar salutations; and Sekeletu receives all with becoming indifference. After a few minutes' conversation and telling the news, the head man of the village, who is almost always a Makololo, rises and brings forth a number of large pots of beer. Calabashes, being used as drinking-cups, are handed round, and as many as can partake of the beverage do so, grasping the vessels so eagerly that they are in danger of being broken.

They bring forth also large pots and bowls of thick milk; some contain six or eight gallons; and each of these, as well as of the beer, is given to a particular person, who has the power to divide it with whom he pleases. The headman of any section of the tribe is generally selected for this office. Spoons not being generally in fashion, the milk is conveyed to the mouth with the hand. I often presented my friends with iron spoons, and it was curious to observe how the habit of hand-eating prevailed, though they were delighted with the spoons. They lifted out a little with the utensil, then put it on the left hand, and ate it out of that.

As the Makololo have great abundance of cattle, and the chief is expected to feed all who accompany him, he either selects an ox or two of his own from the numerous cattle-stations that he possesses at different spots all over the country, or is presented by the head-men of the villages he visits with as many as he needs, by way of tribute. The animals are killed by a thrust from a small javelin in the region of the heart, the wound being purposely small in order to avoid any loss of blood, which, with the internal parts, are the perquisites of the men who perform the work of the butcher; hence all are eager to render service in that line. Each tribe has its own way of cutting up and distributing an animal. Among the Makololo the hump and ribs belong to the chief; among the Bakwains the breast is his perquisite. After the oxen are cut up, the different joints are placed before Sekeletu, and he apportions them among the gentlemen of the party. The whole is rapidly divided by their attendants, cut into long strips, and so many of these are thrown into the fires at once that they are nearly put out. Half broiled and burning hot, the meat is quickly handed round; every one gets a mouthful, but no one except the chief has time to masticate. It is not the enjoyment of eating they aim at, but to get as much of the food into the stomach as possible during the short time the others are cramming as well as themselves, for no one can eat more than a mouthful after the others have finished. They are eminently gregarious in their eating; and, as they despise any one who eats alone, I always poured out two cups of coffee at my own meals, so that the chief, or some one of the principal men, might partake along with me. They all soon become very fond of coffee; and, indeed, some of the tribes attribute greater fecundity to the daily use of this beverage. They were all well acquainted with the sugarcane, as they cultivate it in the Barotse country, but knew nothing of the method of extracting the sugar from it. They use the cane only for chewing. Sekeletu, relishing the sweet coffee and biscuits, of which I then had a store, said "he knew my heart loved him by finding his own heart warming to my food." He had been visited during my absence at the Cape by some traders and Griquas, and "their coffee did not taste half so nice as mine, because they loved his ivory and not himself." This was certainly an original mode of discerning character.

Sekeletu and I had each a little gipsy-tent in which to sleep. The Makololo huts are generally clean, while those of the Makalaka are infested with vermin. The cleanliness of the former is owing to the habit of frequently smearing the floors with a plaster composed of cow-dung and earth. If we slept in the tent in some villages, the mice ran over our faces and disturbed our sleep, or hungry prowling dogs would eat our shoes and leave only the soles. When they were guilty of this and other misdemeanors, we got the loan of a hut. The best sort of Makololo huts consist of three circular walls, with small holes as doors, each similar to that in a dog-house; and it is necessary to bend down the body to get in, even when on all-fours. The roof is formed of reeds or straight sticks, in shape like a Chinaman's-hat, bound firmly together with circular bands, which are lashed with the strong inner bark of the mimosa-tree. When all prepared except the thatch, it is lifted on to the circular wall, the rim resting on a circle of poles, between each of which the third wall is built. The roof is thatched with fine grass, and sewed with the same material as the lashings; and, as it projects far beyond the walls, and reaches within four feet of the ground, the shade is the best to be found in the country. These huts are very cool in the hottest day, but are close and deficient in ventilation by night.

The bed is a mat made of rushes sewn together with twine; the hip-bone soon becomes sore on the hard flat surface, as we are not allowed to make a hole in the floor to receive the prominent part called trochanter by anatomists, as we do when sleeping on grass or sand.

Our course at this time led us to a part above Seshekc, called Katonga, where there is a village belonging to a Bashubia man named Sekhosi,—latitude 17° 29' 13", longitude 24° 33'. The river here is somewhat broader than at Seshcke, and certainly not less than six hundred yards. It flows somewhat slowly in the first part of its eastern course. When the canoes came from Sekhosi to take us over, one of the comrades of Sebituane rose, and, looking to Sekeletu, called out, "The elders of a host always take the lead in an attack." This was understood at once; and Sekeletu, with all the young men, were obliged to give the elders the precedence, and remain on the southern bank and see that all went orderly into the canoes. It took a considerable time to ferry over the whole of our large party, as, even with quick paddling, from six to eight minutes were spent in the mere passage from bank to bank.

Several days were spent in collecting canoes from different villages on the river, which we now learned is called by the whole of the Barotse the Liambai or Leeambye. This we could not ascertain on our first visit, and, consequently, called the river after the town "Sesheke." This term Sesheke means "white sand-banks," many of which exist at this part. There is another village in the valley of the Barotse likewise called Sesheke, and for the same reason; but the term Leeambye means "the large river," or the river *par excellence*. Luambéji, Luambési, Ambézi, Ojimbési, and Zambési, &c., are names applied to it at different parts of its course, according to the dialect spoken, and all possess a similar signification, and express the native idea of this magnificent stream being the main drain of the country.

In order to assist in the support of our large party, and at the same time to see the adjacent country, I went several times, during our stay, to the north of the village for game. The country is covered with clumps of beautiful trees, among which fine open glades stretch away in every direction; when the river is in flood these are inundated, but the tree-covered elevated spots are much more numerous here than in the country between the Chobe and the Leeambye. The soil is dark loam, as it is everywhere on spots reached by the inundation, while among the trees it is sandy, and not covered so densely with grass as elsewhere. A sandy ridge covered with trees, running parallel to and about eight miles from the river, is the limit of the inundation on the north; there are large tracts of this sandy forest in that direction, till you come to other districts of alluvial soil and fewer trees. The latter soil 'e always found in the vicinity of rivers which either now overflow their banks annually or formerly did so. The people enjoy rain in sufficient quantity to raise very large supplies of grain and groundnuts.

Great numbers of buffaloes, zebras, tsessebes, tahaetsi, and eland, or pohu, grazed undisturbed on these plains, so that very little exertion was required to secure a fair supply of meat for the party during the necessary delay. Hunting on foot, as all those who have engaged in it in this country will at once admit, is very hard work indeed. The heat of the sun by day is so great, even in winter, as it now was, that, had there been any one on whom I could have thrown the task, he would have been most welcome to all the sport the toil is supposed to impart. But the Makololo shot so badly, that, in order to save my powder, I was obliged to go myself.

We shot a beautiful cow-eland, standing in the shade of a fine tree. It was evident that she had lately had her calf killed by a lion, for there were five long deep scratches on both sides of her hind-quarters, as if she had run to the rescue of her calf, and the lion, leaving it, had attacked herself, but was unable to pull her down. When lying on the ground, the milk flowing from the large udder showed that she must have been seeking the shade, from the distress its non-removal in the natural manner caused. She was a beautiful creature, and Lebeóle, a Makololo gentleman who accompanied me, speaking in reference to its size and beauty, said, "Jesus ought to have given us these instead of cattle." It was a new, undescribed variety of this splendid antelope. It was marked with narrow white bands across the body, exactly like those of the koodoo, and had a black patch of more than a hand-breadth on the outer side of the forearm.

CHAPTER XII.

DR. LIVINGSTONE ASCENDS THE LEEAMBYE, AND DETERMINES TO OPEN A COMMUNICATION WITH THE WEST COAST OF AFRICA.

HAVING at last procured a sufficient number of canoes, we began to ascend the river. I had the choice of the whole fleet, and selected the best, though not the largest; it was thirty-four feet long by twenty inches wide. I had six paddlers, and the larger canoe of Sekeletu had ten They stand upright, and keep the stroke with great precision, though they change from side to side as the course demands. The men at the head and stern are selected from the strongest and most expert of the whole. The canoes, being flat-bottomed, can go into very shallow water; and whenever the men can feel the bottom they use the paddles, which are about eight feet long, as poles to punt with. Our fleet consisted of thirty-three canoes, and about one hundred and sixty men. It was beautiful to see then skimming along so quickly and keeping the time so well On land the Makalala fear the Makololo; on water the Makololo fear them, and cannot prevent them from racing with each other, dashing along at the top of their speed, and placing their masters' lives in danger. In the event of a capsize, many of the Makololo would sink like stones. A case of this kind happened on the first day of our voyage up. The wind, blowing generally from the east, raises very large waves on the Leeambye. An old doctor of the Makololo had his canoe filled by one of these waves, and, being unable to swim, was lost. The Barotse who were in the canoe with him saved themselves by swimming, and were afraid of being punished with death in the evening for not saving the doctor as well. Had he been a man of more influence, they certainly would have suffered death.

We proceeded rapidly up the river, and I felt the pleasure of looking on lands which had never been seen by a European before. The river is, indeed, a magnificent one, often more than a mile broad, and adorned with many islands of from three to five miles in length. Both islands and banks are covered with forests, and most of the trees on the brink of the water send down roots from their branches like the banian, or *Ficus Indica*. The islands at a little distance seem great rounded masses of sylvan vegetation reclining on the bosom of the glorious stream. The beauty of the scenery of some of the islands is greatly increased by the date-palm, with its gracefully-curved fronds and refreshing light-green color, near the bottom of the picture, and the lofty palmyra towering far above, and casting its feathery foliage against a cloudless sky. It being winter, we had the strange coloring on the banks which many parts of African landscape assume. The country adjacent to the river is rocky and undulating, abounding in elephants and all other large game, except leches and nakongs, which seem generally to avoid stony ground. The soil is of a reddish color, and very fertile, as is attested by the great quantity of grain raised annually by the Banyeti. A great many villages of this poor and very industrious people are situated on both banks of the river: they are expert hunters of the hippopotami and other animals, and very proficient in the manufacture of articles of wood and iron. The whole of this part of the country being infested with the tsetse, they are unable to rear domestic animals. This may have led to their skill in handicraft works. Some make large wooden vessels with very neat lids, and wooden bowls of all sizes; and, since the idea of sitting on stools has entered the Makololo mind, they have shewn great taste in the different forms given to the legs of these pieces of furniture.

Other Banyeti, or Manyeti, as they are called, make neat and strong baskets of the split roots of a certain tree, while others excel in pottery and iron. I cannot find that they have ever been warlike. Indeed, the wars in the centre of the country, where no slave-trade existed, have seldom been about any thing else but cattle. So well known is this, that several tribes refuse to keep cattle, because they tempt their enemies to come and steal. Nevertheless, they have no objection to eat them when offered, and their country admits of being well stocked. I have heard of but one war having occurred from another cause. Three brothers, Barolongs, fought for the possession of a woman who was considered worth a battle, and the tribe has remained permanently divided ever since.

From the bend up to the north, called Katima-molelo, (I quenched fire,) the bed of the river is rocky, and the stream runs fast, forming a succession of rapids and cataracts, which prevent continuous navigation when the water is low. The rapids are not visible when the river is full, but the cataracts of Nambwe, Bombwe, and Kale must always be dangerous. The fall at each of these is between four and six feet. But the falls of Gonye present a much more serious obstacle. There we were obliged to take the canoes out of the water, and carry them more than a mile by land. The fall is about thirty feet. The main body of water, which comes over the ledge of rock when the river is low, is collected into a space seventy or eighty yards wide before it takes the leap, and, a mass of rock being thrust forward against the roaring torrent, a loud sound is produced.

As we passed up the river, the different villages of Banyeti turned out to present Sekeletu with food and skins, as their tribute. One large village is placed at Gonye, the inhabitants of which are required to assist the Makololo to carry their canoes past the falls. The tsetse here lighted on us even in the middle of the stream. This we crossed repeatedly, in order to make short cuts at bends of the river. The course is, however, remarkably straight among the rocks; and here the river is shallow, on account of the great breadth of surface which it covers.

When we came to about 16° 16' S. latitude, the high wooded banks seemed to leave the river, and no more tsetse appeared.

This visit was the first Sekeletu had made to these parts since he attained the chieftainship. Those who had taken part with Mpepe were consequently in great terror. When we came to the town of Mpepe's father, as he and another man had counselled Mamochisane to put Sekeletu to death and marry Mpepe, the two were led forth and tossed into the river. Nokuane was again one of the executioners. When I remonstrated against human blood being shed in the off-hand way in which they were proceeding, the counsellors justified their acts by the evidence given by Mamochisane, and calmly added, "You see we are still Boers: we are not yet taught."

Naliele, the capital of the Barotse, is built on a mound which was constructed artificially by Santuru, and was his storehouse for grain. His own capital stood about five hundred yards to the south of that, in what is now the bed of the river. All that remains of the largest mound in the valley are a few cubic yards of earth, to erect which cost the whole of the people of Santuru the labor of many years. The same thing has happened to another ancient site of a town, Linangelo, also on the left bank. It would seem, therefore, that the river in this part of the valley must be wearing eastward.

Santuru, at whose ancient granary we are staying, was a great hunter, and very fond of taming wild animals. His people, aware of his taste, brought to him every young antelope they could catch, and, among other things, two young hippopotami. These animals gambolled in the river by day, but never failed to remember to come up to Naliele for their suppers of milk and meal. They were the wonder of the country, till a stranger, happening to come to visit Santuru, saw them reclining in the sun, and speared one of them, on the supposition that it was wild. The same unlucky accident happened to one of the cats I had brought to Sekeletu. A stranger, seeing an animal he had never viewed before, killed it, and brought the trophy to the chief, thinking that he had made a very remarkable discovery: we thereby lost the breed of cats, of which, from the swarms of mice, we stood in great need.

On making inquiries to ascertain whether Santuru, the Molōiana, had ever been visited by white men, I could find no vestige of any such visit; there is no evidence of any of Santuru's people having ever seen a white man before the arrival of Mr. Oswell and myself in 1851. The people have, it is true, no written records; but any remarkable event here is commemorated in names, as was observed by Park to be the case in the countries he traversed. The year of our arrival is dignified by the name of the year when the white men came, or of Sebituane's death; but they prefer the former, as they avoid, if possible, any direct reference to the departed. After my wife's first visit, great numbers of children were named Ma-Robert, or mother of Robert, her eldest child; others were named Gun, Horse, Wagon, Monare, Jesus, &c.; but though our names, and those of the native Portuguese who came in 1853, were adopted, there is not a trace of any thing of the sort having happened previously among the Barotse: the visit of a white man is such a remarkable event, that, had any taken place during the last three hundred years, there must have remained some tradition of it.

The town or mound of Santuru's mother was shown to me: this was the first symptom of an altered state of feeling with regard to the female sex that I had observed. There are few or no cases of women being elevated to the headships of towns farther south. The Barotse also showed some relics of their chief, which evinced a greater amount of the religious feeling than I had ever known displayed among Bechuanas. His more recent capital, Lilonda, built, too, on an artificial mound, is covered with different kinds of trees, transplanted when young by himself. They form a grove on the end of the mound, in which are to be seen various instruments of iron just in the state he left them. One looks like the guard of a basket-hilted sword; another has an upright stem of the metal, on which are placed branches worked at the ends into miniature axes, hoes, and spears; on these he was accustomed to present offerings, according as he desired favors to be conferred in undertaking hewing, agriculture, or fighting. The people still living there, in charge of these articles, were supported by presents from the chief; and the Makololo sometimes follow the example. This was the nearest approach to a priesthood I met. When I asked them to part with one of these relics, they replied, "Oh, no: he refuses." "Who refuses?" "Santuru," was their reply, showing their belief in a future state of existence. After explaining to them, as I always did when opportunity offered, the nature of true worship, and praying with them in the simple form which needs no offering from the worshipper except that of the heart, and planting some fruit-tree seeds in the grove, we departed.

Another incident, which occurred at the confluence of the Leeba and Leeambye, may be mentioned here, as showing a more vivid perception of the existence of spiritual beings, and greater proneness to worship, than among the Bechuanas. Having taken lunar observations in the morning, I was waiting for a meridian altitude of the sun for the latitude; my chief boatman was sitting by, in order to pack up the instruments as soon as I had finished; there was a large halo, about 20° in diameter, round the sun; thinking that the humidity of the atmosphere, which this indicated, might betoken rain, I asked him if his experience did not lead him to the same view. "Oh, no," replied he; "it is the Barimo, [gods or departed spirits,] who have called a picho; don't you see they have the Lord [sun] in the centre?"

While still at Naliele, I walked out to Katongo, (lat. 15° 16' 33",) on the ridge which bounds the valley of the Barotse in that direction, and found it covered with trees. It is only the commencement of the lands which are never inundated; their gentle rise from the dead level of the valley much resembles the edge of the Desert in the valley of the Nile.

I imagined the slight elevation (Katongo) might be healthy, but was informed that no part of this region is exempt from fever. When the waters begin to retire from this valley, such masses of decayed vegetation and mud are exposed to the torrid sun that even the natives suffer severely from attacks of fever. The grass is so rank in its growth that one cannot see the black alluvial soil of the bottom of this periodical lake. Even when the grass falls down in winter, or is "laid" by its own weight, one is obliged to lift the feet so high, to avoid being tripped up by it, as to make walking excessively fatiguing. Young leches are hidden beneath it by their dams; and the Makololo youth complain of being unable to run in the Barotse land on this account. There was evidently no healthy spot in this quarter; and, the current of the river being about four and a half miles per hour, (one hundred yards in sixty seconds,) I imagined we might find what we needed in the higher lands, from which the river seemed to come. I resolved, therefore, to go to the utmost limits of the Barotse country before coming to a final conclusion. Katongo was the best place we had seen; but, in order to accomplish a complete examination, I left Sekeletu at Naliele, and ascended the river. He furnished me with men, besides my rowers, and among the rest a herald, that I might enter his villages in what is considered a dignified manner. This, it was supposed, would be effected by the herald shouting out, at the top of his voice, "Here comes the lord, the great lion;" the latter phrase being "tau e tŏna," which, in his imperfect way of pronunciation, became "sau e tŏna," and so like "the great sow" that I could not receive the honor with becoming gravity, and had to entreat him, much to the annoyance of my party, to be silent.

In our ascent we visited a number of Makololo villages,

and were always received with a hearty welcome, as messengers to them of peace, which they term "sleep." They behave well in public meetings, even on the first occasion of attendance, probably from the habit of commanding the Makalaka, crowds of whom swarm in every village, and whom the Makololo women seem to consider as especially under their charge.

The river presents the same appearance of low banks without trees as we have remarked it had after we came to 16° 16', until we arrive at Libonta, (14° 59' S. lat.) Twenty miles beyond that, we find forests down to the water's edge, and tsetse. Here I might have turned back, as no locality can be inhabited by Europeans where that scourge exists; but, hearing that we were not far from the confluence of the river of Londa or Lunda, named Leeba or Loiba, and the chiefs of that country being reported to be friendly to strangers, and therefore likely to be of use to me on my return from the west coast, I still pushed on to latitude 14° 11' 2" S. There the Leeambye assumes the name Kabompo, and seems to be coming from the east. It is a fine large river, about three hundred yards wide, and the Leeba two hundred and fifty. The Loeti, a branch of which is called Langebongo, comes from W.N.W., through a level grassy plain named Mango; it is about one hundred yards wide, and enters the Leeambye from the west; the waters of the Loeti are of a light color, and those of the Leeba of a dark mossy hue. After the Loeti joins the Leeambye, the different-colored waters flow side by side for some distance unmixed.

Before reaching the Loeti, we came to a number of people from the Lobale region, hunting hippopotami. They fled precipitately as soon as they saw the Makololo, leaving their canoes and all their utensils and clothing. My own Makalaka, who were accustomed to plunder wherever they went, rushed after them like furies, totally regardless of my shouting. As this proceeding would have destroyed my character entirely at Lobale, I took my stand on a commanding position as they returned, and forced them to lay down all the plunder on a sand-bank, and leave it there for its lawful owners.

It was now quite evident that no healthy location could be obtained in which the Makololo would be allowed to live in peace. I had thus a fair excuse, if I had chosen to avail myself of it, of coming home and saying that the "door was shut," because the Lord's time had not yet come. But believing that it was my duty to devote some portion of my life to these (to me at least) very confiding and affectionate Makololo, I resolved to follow out the second part of my plan, though I had failed in accomplishing the first. The Leeba seemed to come from the N. and by W.; or N.N.W.; so, having an old Portuguese map, which pointed out the Coanza as rising from the middle of the continent in 9° S. lat., I thought it probable that, when we had ascended the Leeba (from 14° 11') two or three degrees, we should then be within one hundred and twenty miles of the Coanza, and find no difficulty in following it down to the coast near Loanda. This was the logical deduction; but, as is the case with many a plausible theory, one of the premises was decidedly defective. The Coanza, as we afterward found, does not come from anywhere near the centre of the country.

The numbers of large game above Libonta are prodigious, and they proved remarkably tame. Eighty-one buffaloes defiled in slow procession before our fire one evening, within gunshot; and herds of splendid elands stood by day, without fear, at two hundred yards' distance. They were all of the striped variety, and, with their forearm markings, large dewlaps, and sleek skins, were a beautiful sight to see. The lions here roar much more than in the country near the lake, Zouga, and Chobe. One evening we had a good opportunity of hearing the utmost exertions the animal can make in that line. We had made our beds on a large sand-bank, and could be easily seen from all sides. A lion on the opposite shore amused himself for hours by roaring as loudly as he could, putting, as is usual in such cases, his mouth near the ground, to make the sound reverberate. The river was too broad for a ball to reach him, so we let him enjoy himself, certain that he durst not have been guilty of the impertinence in the Bushman country. Wherever the game abounds, these animals exist in proportionate numbers. Here they were very frequently seen, and two of the largest I ever saw seemed about as tall as common donkeys; but the mane made their bodies appear rather larger.

A party of Arabs from Zanzibar were in the country at this time. Sekeletu had gone from Naliele to the town of his mother before we arrived from the north, but left an ox for our use, and instructions for us to follow him thither. We came down a branch of the Leeambye called Marile, which departs from the main river in latitude 15° 15′ 43″ S., and is a fine deep stream about sixty yards wide. It makes the whole of the country around Naliele an island. When sleeping at a village in the same latitude as Naliele town, two of the Arabs mentioned made their appearance. They were quite as dark as the Makololo, but, having their heads shaved, I could not compare their hair with that of the inhabitants of the country. When we were about to leave, they came to bid adieu; but I asked them to stay and help us to eat our ox. As they had scruples about eating an animal not blooded in their own way, I gained their good-will by saying I was quite of their opinion as to getting quit of the blood, and gave them two legs of an animal slaughtered by themselves. They professed the greatest detestation of the Portuguese, "because they eat pigs;" and disliked the English, "because they thrash them for selling slaves." I was silent about pork; though, had they seen me at a hippopotamus two days afterward, they would have set me down as being as much a heretic as any of that nation; but I ventured to tell them that I agreed with the English, that it was better to let the children grow up and comfort their mothers when they became old, than to carry them away and sell them across the sea. This they never attempt to justify; "they want them only to cultivate the land, and take care of them as their children." It is the same old story, justifying a monstrous wrong on pretence of taking care of those degraded portions of humanity which cannot take care of themselves; doing evil that good may come.

These Arabs, or Moors, could read and write their own language readily; and, when speaking about our Savior, I admired the boldness with which they informed me "that Christ was a very good prophet, but Mohammed was far greater." And with respect to their loathing of pork, it may have some foundation in their nature; for I have known Bechuanas who had no prejudice against the wild animal, and ate the tame without scruple, yet, unconscious of any cause of disgust, vomit it again. The Bechuanas south of the lake have a prejudice against eating fish, and allege a disgust to eating any thing like a serpent. This may arise from the remnants of serpent-worship floating in their minds, as, in addition to this horror of eating such animals, they sometimes render a sort of obeisance to living serpents by clapping their hands to them, and refuisng to destroy the reptiles; but in the case of the hog they are conscious of no superstitious feeling.

Having parted with our Arab friends, we proceeded down the Marile till we re-entered the Leeambye, and went to the town of Ma-Sekeletu (mother of Sekeletu,) opposite the island of Loyela. Sekeletu had always supplied me most liberally with food, and, as soon as I arrived, presented me with a pot of boiled meat, while his mother handed me a large jar of butter, of which they make great quantities for the purpose of anointing their bodies. He had himself sometimes felt the benefit of my way of putting aside a quantity of the meat after a meal, and had now followed my example by ordering some to be kept for me. According to their habits, every particle of an ox is devoured at one meal; and as the chief cannot, without a deviation from their customs, eat alone, he is often compelled to suffer severely from hunger before another meal is ready. We henceforth always worked into each other's hands by saving a little for each other; and when some of the sticklers for use and custom grumbled, I advised them to eat like men, and not like vultures.

As this was the first visit which Sekeletu had paid to this part of his dominions, it was to many a season of great joy. The head-men of each village presented oxen, milk, and beer, more than the horde which accompanied him could devour, though their abilities in that line are something wonderful. The people usually show their joy and work off their excitement in dances and songs.

As Sekeletu had been waiting for me at his mother's, we left the town as soon as I arrived, and proceeded down the river. Our speed with the stream was very great, for in one day we went from Litofe to Gonye, a distance of forty-four miles of latitude; and if we add to this the windings of the river, in longitude the distance will not be much less than sixty geographical miles. At this rate we soon reached Seshcke, and then the town of Linyanti.

I had been, during a nine weeks' tour, in closer contact with heathenism than I had ever been before; and though all, including the chief, were as kind and attentive to me as possible, and there was no want of food, (oxen being slaughtered daily, sometimes ten at a time, more than sufficient for the wants of all,) yet to endure the dancing, roaring, and singing, the jesting, anecdotes, grumbling, quarrelling, and murdering of these children of nature, seemed more like a severe penance than any thing I had before met with in the course of my missionary duties. I took thence a more intense disgust at heathenism than I had before, and formed a greatly-elevated opinion of the latent effects of missions in the south, among tribes which are reported to have been as savage as the Makololo. The indirect benefits which, to a casual observer, lie beneath the surface and are inappreciable, in reference to the probable wide diffusion of Christianity at some future time, are worth all the money and labor that have been expended to produce them.

CHAPTER XIII.

DR. LIVINGSTONE SETS OUT ON THE EXPEDITION TO THE WEST COAST.

LINYANTI, *September*, 1853.—The object proposed to the Makololo seemed so desirable that it was resolved to proceed with it as soon as the cooling influence of the rains should be felt in November. The longitude and latitude of Linyanti (lat. 18° 17′ 20″ S., long. 23° 50′ 9″ E.) showed that St. Philip de Benguela was much nearer to us than Loanda; and I might have easily made arrangements with the Mambari to allow me to accompany them as far as Bihe, which is on the road to that port; but it is so undesirable to travel in a path once trodden by slave-traders that I preferred to find out another line of march.

Accordingly, men were sent at my suggestion to examine all the country to the west, to see if any belt of country free from tsetse could be found to afford us an outlet. The search was fruitless. The town and district of Linyanti are surrounded by forests infested by this poisonous insect, except at a few points, as that by which we entered at Sanshureh and another at Sesheke. But the lands both east and west of the Barotse valley are free from this insect-plague. There, however, the slave-trade had defiled the path, and no one ought to follow in its wake unless well armed. The Mambari had informed me that many English lived at Loanda; so I prepared to go thither. The prospect of meeting with countrymen seemed to overbalance the toils of the longer march.

A "picho" was called to deliberate on the steps proposed
In these assemblies great freedom of speech is allowed;
and on this occasion one of the old diviners said, "Where
s he taking you to? This white man is throwing you
away. Your garments already smell of blood." It is
curious to observe how much identity of character appears
all over the world. This man was a noted croaker. He
always dreamed something dreadful in every expedition,
and was certain that an eclipse or comet betokened the
propriety of flight. But Sebituane formerly set his visions
down to cowardice, and Sekeletu only laughed at him now.
The general voice was in my favor; so a band of twenty
seven were appointed to accompany me to the west
These men were not hired, but sent to enable me to
accomplish an object as much desired by the chief and
most of his people as by me. They were eager to obtain
free and profitable trade with white men. The prices
which the Cape merchants could give, after defraying the
great expenses of a long journey hither, being very small,
made it scarce worth while for the natives to collect produce for that market; and the Mambari, giving only a few
bits of print and baize for elephants' tusks worth more
pounds than they gave yards of cloth, had produced the
belief that trade with them was throwing ivory away.
The desire of the Makololo for direct trade with the sea-
coast coincided exactly with my own conviction that no
permanent elevation of a people can be effected without
commerce. Neither could there be a permanent mission
here, unless the missionaries should descend to the level of
the Makololo, for even at Kolobeng we found that traders
demanded three or four times the price of the articles we
needed, and expected us to be grateful to them besides for
letting us have them at all.

The three men whom I had brought from Kuruman had
frequent relapses of the fever; so, finding that instead of
serving me I had to wait on them, I decided that they
should return to the south with Fleming as soon as he had

finished his trading. I was then entirely dependent on my twenty-seven men, whom I might name Zambesians, for there were two Makololo only, while the rest consisted of Barotse, Batoka, Bashubia, and two of the Ambonda.

The fever had caused considerable weakness in my own frame, and a strange giddiness when I looked up suddenly to any celestial object, for every thing seemed to rush to the left, and if I did not catch hold of some object I fell heavily on the ground: something resembling a gush of bile along the duct from the liver caused the same fit to occur at night, whenever I turned suddenly round.

The Makololo now put the question, "In the event of your death, will not the white people blame us for having allowed you to go away into an unhealthy, unknown country of enemies?" I replied that none of my friends would blame them, because I would leave a book with Sekeletu, to be sent to Mr. Moffat in case I did not return, which would explain to him all that had happened until the time of my departure. The book was a volume of my Journal; and, as I was detained longer than I expected at Loanda, this book, with a letter, was delivered by Sekeletu to a trader, and I have been unable to trace it. I regret this now, as it contained valuable notes on the habits of wild animals, and the request was made in the letter to convey the volume to my family. The prospect of passing away from this fair and beautiful world thus came before me in a pretty plain, matter-of-fact form, and it did seem a serious thing to leave wife and children,—to break up all connection with earth and enter on an untried state of existence; and I find myself in my journal pondering over that fearful migration which lands us in eternity, wondering whether an angel will soothe the fluttering soul, sadly flurried as it must be on entering the spirit-world, and hoping that Jesus might speak but one word of peace, for that would establish in the bosom an everlasting calm.

But, as I had always believed that, if we serve God at all, it ought to be done in a manly way, I wrote to my brother, commending our little girl to his care, as I was determined to "succeed or perish" in the attempt to open up this part of Africa. The Boers, by taking possession of all my goods, had saved me the trouble of making a will; and, considering the light heart now left in my bosom, and some faint efforts to perform the duty of Christian forgiveness, I felt that it was better to be the plundered party than one of the plunderers.

When I committed the wagon and remaining goods to the care of the Makololo, they took all the articles except one box into their huts; and two warriors—Ponuane and Mahale—brought forward each a fine heifer-calf. After performing a number of warlike evolutions, they asked the chief to witness the agreement made between them, that whoever of the two should kill a Matebele warrior first, in defence of the wagon, should possess both the calves.

I had three muskets for my people, a rifle and a double-barrelled smooth-bore for myself; and, having seen such great abundance of game in my visit to the Leeba, I imagined that I could easily supply the wants of my party. Wishing also to avoid the discouragement which would naturally be felt on meeting any obstacles if my companions were obliged to carry heavy loads, I took only a few biscuits, a few pounds of tea and sugar, and about twenty of coffee, which, as the Arabs find, though used without either milk or sugar, is a most refreshing beverage after fatigue or exposure to the sun. We carried one small tin canister, about fifteen inches square, filled with spare shirting, trousers, and shoes, to be used when we reached civilized life, and others in a bag, which were expected to wear out on the way; another of the same size for medicines; and a third for books, my stock being a Nautical Almanac, Thomson's Logarithm Tables, and a Bible; . fourth box contained a magic lantern, which we found of much use. The sextant and artificial horizon, thermometer, and compasses were carried apart. My ammunition was distributed in portions through the whole luggage; so that, if an accident should befall one part, we could still have others to fall back upon. Our chief hopes for food were upon that; but, in case of failure, I took about twenty pounds of beads, worth forty shillings, which still remained in the stock I brought from Cape Town, a small gypsy tent, just sufficient to sleep in, a sheep-skin mantle as a blanket, and a horse-rug as a bed. As I had always found that the art of successful travel consisted in taking as few "impediments" as possible, and not forgetting to carry my wits about me, the outfit was rather spare, and intended to be still more so when we should come to leave the canoes. Some would consider it injudicious to adopt this plan; but I had a secret conviction that, if I did not succeed, it would not be for want of the "knick-knacks" advertised as indispensable for travellers, but from want of "pluck," or because a large array of baggage excited the cupidity of the tribes through whose country we wished to pass.

The instruments I carried, though few, were the best of their kind. A sextant, by the famed makers Troughton and Sims, of Fleet Street; a chronometer watch, with a stop to the seconds-hand,—an admirable contrivance for enabling a person to take the exact time of observations. It was constructed by Dent, of the Strand, (61,) for the Royal Geographical Society, and selected for the service by the President, Admiral Smythe, to whose judgment and kindness I am in this and other matters deeply indebted. It was pronounced by Mr. Maclear to equal most chronometers in performance. For these excellent instruments I have much pleasure in recording my obligations to my good friend Colonel Steel, and at the same time to Mr. Maclear for much of my ability to use them. Besides these, I had a thermometer by Dollond; a compass from the Cape Observatory, and a small pocket one in addition;

a good small telescope with a stand capable of being screwed into a tree.

11th of November, 1853.—Left the town of Linyanti, accompanied by Sekeletu and his principal men, to embark on the Chobe. The chief came to the river in order to see that all was right at parting. We crossed five branches of the Chobe before reaching the main stream: this ramification must be the reason why it appeared so small to Mr. Oswell and myself in 1851. When all the departing branches re-enter, it is a large, deep river. The spot of embarkation was the identical island where we met Sebituane, first known as the island of Mannku, one of his wives. The chief lent me his own canoe; and, as it was broader than usual, I could turn about in it with ease.

The Chobe is much infested by hippopotami, and, as certain elderly males are expelled the herd, they become soured in their temper, and so misanthropic as to attack every canoe that passes near them.

The course of the river we found to be extremely tortuous; so much so, indeed, as to carry us to all points of the compass every dozen miles. Some of us walked from a bend at the village of Moremi to another nearly due east of that point in six hours, while the canoes, going at more than double our speed, took twelve to accomplish the voyage between the same two places. And though the river is from thirteen to fifteen feet in depth at its lowest ebb, and broad enough to allow a steamer to ply upon it, the suddenness of the bendings would prevent navigation; but, should the country ever become civilized, the Chobe would be a convenient natural canal. We spent forty-two and a half hours, paddling at the rate of five miles an hour, in coming from Linyanti to the confluence; there we found a dike of amygdaloid lying across the Leeambye.

The actual point of confluence of the Chobe and the Leeambye is ill defined, on account of each dividing into several branches as they inosculate; but when the whole body of water collects into one bed it is a goodly sight for one who has spent many years in the thirsty south Standing on one bank, even the keen eye of the natives cannot detect whether two large islands, a few miles east of the junction, are mainland or not.

After spending one night at the Makololo village on Mparia, we left the Chobe, and, turning round, began to ascend the Leeambye; on the 19th of November we again reached the town of Sesheke. It stands on the north bank of the river, and contains a large population of Makalaka, under Moriantsane, brother-in-law of Sebituane. There are parties of various tribes here, assembled under their respective head-men, but a few Makololo rule over all. Their sway, though essentially despotic, is considerably modified by certain customs and laws.

The following circumstance, which happened here when I was present with Sekeletu, shows that the simple mode of punishment by forcing a criminal to work out a fine did not strike the Makololo mind until now.

A stranger, having visited Sesheke for the purpose of barter, was robbed by one of the Makalaka of most of his goods. The thief, when caught, confessed the theft, and that he had given the articles to a person who had removed to a distance. The Makololo were much enraged at the idea of their good name being compromised by this treatment of a stranger. Their customary mode of punishing a crime which causes much indignation is to throw the criminal into the river; but, as this would not restore the lost property, they were sorely puzzled how to act. The case was referred to me, and I solved the difficulty by paying for the loss myself and sentencing the thief to work out an equivalent with his hoe in a garden. This system was immediately introduced, and thieves are now sentenced to raise an amount of corn proportioned to their offences. Among the Bakwains, a woman who had stolen from the garden of another was obliged to part with her own entirely: it became the property of her whose field was injured by the crime.

There is no stated day of rest in any part of this country, except the day after the appearance of the new moon; and the people then refrain only from going to their gardens. A curious custom, not to be found among the Bechuanas, prevails among the black tribes beyond them. They watch most eagerly for the first glimpse of the new moon, and, when they perceive the faint outline after the sun has set deep in the west, they utter a loud shout of "Kuā!" and vociferate prayers to it. My men, for instance, called out, "Let our journey with the white man be prosperous! Let our enemies perish, and the children of Nake become rich! May he have plenty of meat on this journey!" &c. &c.

I gave many public addresses to the people of Seshcko under the outspreading camel-thorn-tree, which serves as a shade to the kotla on the high bank of the river. It was pleasant to see the long lines of men, women, and children winding along from different quarters of the town, each party following behind their respective head-men. They often amounted to between five and six hundred souls, and required an exertion of voice which brought back the complaint for which I had got the uvula excised at the Cape. They were always very attentive; and Moriantsane, in order, as he thought, to please me, on one occasion rose up in the middle of the discourse, and hurled his staff at the heads of some young fellows whom he saw working with a skin instead of listening. My hearers sometimes put very sensible questions on the subjects brought before them; at other times they introduced the most frivolous nonsense immediately after hearing the most solemn truths. Some begin to pray to Jesus in secret as soon as they hear of the white man's God, with but little idea of what they are about, and no doubt are heard by Him who, like a father, pitieth his children. Others, waking by night, recollect what has been said about the future world so clearly that, they tell next day what a fright they got by it, and resolve not to listen to the teaching again; and not a few keep to the determination not to believe, as certain villagers in the south, who put all their cocks to death because they crowed the words, "Tlang lo rapelong,"—"Come along to prayers."

On recovering partially from a severe attack of fever which remained upon me ever since our passing the village of Moremi on the Chobe, we made ready for our departure up the river by sending messages before us to the villages to prepare food. We took four elephants' tusks, belonging to Sekeletu, with us, as a means of testing the difference of prices between the Portuguese, whom we expected to reach, and the white traders from the south. Moriantsane supplied us well with honey, milk, and meal. The rains were just commencing in this district; but, though showers sufficient to lay the dust had fallen, they had no influence whatever on the amount of water in the river, yet never was there less in any part than three hundred yards of a deep flowing stream.

Our progress up the river was rather slow: this was caused by waiting opposite different villages for supplies of food. We might have done with much less than we got; but my Makololo man, Pitsane, knew of the generous orders of Sekeletu, and was not at all disposed to allow them to remain a dead letter. The villages of the Banyeti contributed large quantities of mosibe, a bright-red bean yielded by a large tree. The pulp enclosing the seed is not much thicker than a red wafer, and is the portion used. It requires the addition of honey to render it at all palatable.

To these were added great numbers of the fruit which yields a variety of the nux vomica, from which we derive that virulent poison strychnia. The pulp between the nuts is the part eaten, and it is of a pleasant juicy nature, having a sweet acidulous taste. The fruit itself resembles a large yellow orange, but the rind is hard, and, with the pips and bark, contains much of the deadly poison. They evince their noxious qualities by an intensely bitter taste. The nuts, swallowed inadvertently, cause considerable pain, but not death; and, to avoid this inconvenience, the people dry the pulp before the fire, in order to be able the more easily to get rid of the noxious seed.

The rapids in the part of the river between Katimamolelo and Naméta are relieved by several reaches of still, deep water, fifteen or twenty miles long. In these very large herds of hippopotami are seen; and the deep furrows they make, in ascending the banks to graze during the nights, are everywhere apparent. They are guided back to the water by the scent; but a long-continued pouring rain makes it impossible to perceive by that means in which direction the river lies, and they are found bewildered on the land. The hunters take advantage of their helplessness on these occasions to kill them.

It is impossible to judge of the numbers in a herd, for they are almost always hidden beneath the waters; but, as they require to come up every few minutes to breathe, when there is a constant succession of heads thrown up, then the herd is supposed to be large. They love a still reach of the stream, as in the more rapid parts of the channel they are floated down so quickly that much exertion is necessary to regain the distance lost, by frequently swimming up again: such constant exertion disturbs them in their nap. They prefer to remain by day in a drowsy, yawning state, and, though their eyes are open, they take little notice of things at a distance. The males utter a loud succession of snorting grunts, which may be heard a mile off. The canoe in which I was, in passing over a wounded one, elicited a distinct grunting, though the animal lay entirely under the water.

The young, when very little, take their stand on the neck of the dam, and the small head, rising above the large, comes soonest to the surface. The dam, knowing the more urgent need of her calf, comes more frequently to the surface when it is in her care. But in the rivers of Londa, where they are much in danger of being shot, even the hippopotamus gains wit by experience; for, while those in the Zambesi put up their heads openly to blow, those referred to keep their noses among water-plants, and breathe so quietly that one would not dream of their existence in the river except by footprints on the banks.

CHAPTER XIV.

VOYAGE ON THE LEEAMBYE, CONTINUED.

30th of November, 1853.—At Gonye Falls. No rain has fallen here; so it is excessively hot. The trees have put on their gayest dress, and many flowers adorn the landscape yet the heat makes all the leaves droop at mid-day and look languid for want of rain. If the country increases as much in beauty in front as it has done within the last four degrees of latitude, it will be indeed a lovely land.

We all felt great lassitude in travelling. The atmosphere is oppressive both in cloud and sunshine. The evaporation from the river must be excessively great; and I feel as if the fluids of the system joined in the general motion of watery vapor upward, as enormous quantities of water must be drunk to supply its place.

When under way our usual procedure is this :—We get up a little before five in the morning; it is then beginning to dawn. While I am dressing, coffee is made; and, having filled my pannikin, the remainder is handed to my companions, who eagerly partake of the refreshing beverage The servants are busy loading the canoes, while the principal men are sipping the coffee, and, that being soon over we embark. The next two hours are the most pleasant part of the day's sail. The men paddle away most vigorously: the Barotse, being a tribe of boatmen, have large deeply-developed chests and shoulders, with indifferent lower extremities. They often engage in loud scolding of each other, in order to relieve the tedium of their work. About eleven we land, and eat any meat which may have remained from the previous evening meal, or a biscuit with honey, and drink water.

After an hour's rest, we again embark and cower under an umbrella. The heat is oppressive, and, being weak from the last attack of fever, I cannot land and keep the camp supplied with flesh. The men, being quite uncovered in the sun, perspire profusely, and in the afternoon begin to stop, as if waiting for the canoes which have been left behind. Sometimes we reach a sleeping-place two hours before sunset, and, all being troubled with languor, we gladly remain for the night. Coffee again, and a biscuit, or a piece of coarse bread made of maize-meal, or that of the native corn, make up the bill of fare for the evening, unless we have been fortunate enough to kill something,—when we boil a potful of flesh. This is done by cutting it up into long strips and pouring in water till it is covered. When that is boiled dry, the meat is considered ready.

The people at Gonye carry the canoes over the space requisite to avoid the falls by slinging them on poles tied on diagonally. They place these on their shoulders, and, setting about the work with good humor, soon accomplish the task. They are a merry set of mortals; a feeble joke sets them off in a fit of laughter. Here, as elsewhere, all petitioned for the magic lantern; and, as it is a good means of conveying instruction, I willingly complied.

The falls of Gonye have not been made by wearing back like those of Niagara, but are of a fissure form. For many miles below, the river is confined in a narrow space of not more than one hundred yards wide. The water goes boiling along, and gives the idea of great masses of it rolling over and over, so that even the most expert swimmer would find it difficult to keep on the surface. Here it is that the river, when in flood, rises fifty or sixty feet in perpendicular height. The islands above the falls are covered with foliage as beautiful as can be seen anywhere. Viewed from the mass of rock which overhangs the fall, the scenery was the loveliest I had seen.

Nothing worthy of note occurred on our way to Name

There we heard that a party of the Makololo, headed by Lerimo, had made a foray to the north and up the Leeba, in the very direction in which we were about to proceed. Mpololo, the uncle of Sekeletu, is considered the head-man of the Barotse valley; and the perpetrators had his full sanction, because Masiko, a son of Santuru, the former chief of the Barotse, had fled high up the Leeambye, and, establishing himself there, had sent men down to the vicinity of Naliele to draw away the remaining Barotse from their allegiance. Lerimo's party had taken some of this Mesiko's subjects prisoners, and destroyed several villages of the Balonda, to whom we were going. This was in direct opposition to the policy of Sekeletu, who wished to be at peace with these northern tribes; and Pitsáne, my head-man, was the bearer of orders to Mpololo to furnish us with presents to the very chiefs they had attacked. Thus, we were to get large pots of clarified butter and bunches of beads, in confirmation of the message of peace we were to deliver.

When we reached Litofe, we heard that a fresh foray was in contemplation; but I sent forward orders to disband the party immediately. At Ma-Sekeletu's town we found the head-offender, Mpololo himself, and I gave him a bit of my mind, to the effect that, as I was going with the full sanction of Sekeletu, if any harm happened to me in consequence of his ill-advised expedition the guilt would rest with him. Ma-Sekeletu, who was present, heartily approved all I said, and suggested that all the captives taken by Lerimo should be returned by my hand, to show Masiko that the guilt of the foray lay not with the superior persons of the Makololo, but with a mere servant. Her good sense appeared in other respects besides; and, as this was exactly what my own party had previously resolved to suggest, we were pleased to hear Mpololo agree to do what he was advised. He asked me to lay the matter before the under-chiefs of Naliele, and when we reached that place, on the 9th of December, I did so in a picho, called expressly for the purpose. Lerimo was present, and felt rather crestfallen when his exploit was described by Moharisi, one of my companions, as one of extreme cowardice, he having made an attack upon the defenceless villagers of Londa, while, as we had found on our former visit, a lion had actually killed eight people of Naliele without his daring to encounter it. The Makololo are cowardly in respect to animals, but brave against men. Mpololo took all the guilt upon himself before the people, and delivered up a captive child whom his wife had in her possession; others followed his example, till we procured the release of five of the prisoners. Some thought, as Masiko had tried to take their children by stratagem, they ought to take his by force, as the two modes suited the genius of each people: the Makalaka delight in cunning, and the Makololo in fighting; and others thought, if Sekeletu meant them to be at peace with Masiko, he ought to have told them so.

It is rather dangerous to tread in the footsteps of a marauding-party with men of the same tribe as the aggressors, but my people were in good spirits, and several volunteers even offered to join our ranks. We, however, adhered strictly to the orders of Sekeletu as to our companions, and refused all others.

The people of every village treated us most liberally, presenting, besides oxen, butter, milk, and meal, more than we could stow away in our canoes. The cows in this valley are now yielding, as they frequently do, more milk than the people can use, and both men and women present butter in such quantity that I shall be able to refresh my men as we move along. Anointing the skin prevents the excessive evaporation of the fluids of the body, and acts as clothing in both sun and shade. They always made their presents gracefully. When an ox was given, the owner would say, "Here is a little bit of bread for you." This was pleasing, for I had been accustomed to the Bechuanas presenting a miserable goat, with the pompous exclamation, "Behold an ox!" The women persisted in giving me copious supplies of shrill praises, or "lullilooing;" but, though I frequently told them to modify their "great lords" and "great lions" to more humble expressions, they so evidently intended to do me honor that I could not help being pleased with the poor creatures' wishes for our success.

The rains began while we were at Naliele; this is much later than usual; but, though the Barotse valley has been in need of rain, the people never lack abundance of food The showers are refreshing, but the air feels hot and close; the thermometer, however, in a cool hut, stands only at $84\frac{1}{2}°$. The access of the external air to any spot at once raises its temperature above $90°$. A new attack of fever here caused excessive languor; but, as I am already getting tired of quoting my fevers, and never liked to read travels myself where much was said about the illnesses of the traveller, I shall henceforth endeavor to say little about them.

We here sent back the canoe of Sekeletu, and got the loan of others from Mpololo. Eight riding-oxen, and seven for slaughter, were, according to the orders of that chief, also furnished; some were intended for our own use, and others as presents to the chiefs of the Balonda. Mpololo was particularly liberal in giving all that Sekeletu ordered, though, as he feeds on the cattle he has in charge, he might have felt it so much abstracted from his own perquisites.

Leaving Naliele, amid abundance of good wishes for the success of our expedition, and hopes that we might return accompanied with white traders, we began again our ascent of the river. It was now beginning to rise, though the rains had but just commenced in the valley. The banks are low, but cleanly cut, and seldom sloping. At low-water they are from four to eight feet high, and make the river always assume very much the aspect of a canal.

These perpendicular banks afford building-places to a pretty bee-eater,* which loves to breed in society. The

---

* *Merops apiaster* and *M. bullockoides*, (Smith.)

face of the sand-bank is perforated with hundreds of holes leading to their nests, each of which is about a foot apart from the other; and as we pass they pour out of their hiding-places and float overhead.

17th December.—At Libonta. We were detained for days together collecting contributions of fat and butter, according to the orders of Sekeletu, as presents to the Balonda chiefs. Much fever prevailed, and ophthalmia was rife, as is generally the case before the rains begin. Some of my own men required my assistance, as well as the people of Libonta. A lion had done a good deal of mischief here, and when the people went to attack it two men were badly wounded; one of them had his thigh-bone quite broken, showing the prodigious power of this animal's jaws. The inflammation produced by the teeth-wounds proved fatal to one of them.

Here we demanded the remainder of the captives, and got our number increased to nineteen. They consisted of women and children, and one young man of twenty. One of the boys was smuggled away in the crowd as we embarked. The Makololo under-chiefs often act in direct opposition to the will of the head-chief, trusting to circumstances and brazen-facedness to screen themselves from his open displeasure; and, as he does not always find it convenient to notice faults, they often go to considerable lengths in wrong-doing.

Libonta is the last town of the Makololo; so, when we parted from it, we had only a few cattle-stations and outlying hamlets in front, and then an uninhabited border-country till we came to Londa or Lunda. Libonta is situated on a mound, like the rest of the villages in the Barotse valley, but here the tree-covered sides of the valley begin to approach nearer the river. The village itself belongs to two of the chief wives of Sebituane, who furnished us with an ox and abundance of other food. The same kindness was manifested by all who could afford to give any thing; and, as I glance over their deeds of generosity recorded in my journal, my heart glows with gratitude to them, and I hope and pray that God may spare me to make them some return

Before leaving the villages entirely, we may glance at our way of spending the nights. As soon as we land, some of the men cut a little grass for my bed, while Mashauána plants the poles of the little tent. These are used by day for carrying burdens, for the Barotse fashion is exactly like that of the natives of India, only the burden is fastened near the ends of the pole, and not suspended by long cords. The bed is made, and boxes ranged on each side of it, and then the tent pitched over all. Four or five feet in front of my tent is placed the principal or kotla fire, the wood for which must be collected by the man who occupies the post of herald and takes as his perquisite the heads of all the oxen slaughtered and of all the game too. Each person knows the station he is to occupy in reference to the post of honor at the fire in front of the door of the tent. The two Makololo occupy my right and left, both in eating and sleeping, as long as the journey lasts. But Mashauana, my head-boatman, makes his bed at the door of the tent as soon as I retire. The rest, divided into small companies according to their tribes, make sheds all round the fire, leaving a horseshoe-shaped space in front sufficient for the cattle to stand in. The fire gives confidence to the oxen; so the men are always careful to keep them in sight of it. The sheds are formed by planting two stout forked poles in an inclined direction, and placing another over these in a horizontal position. A number of branches are then stuck in the ground in the direction to which the poles are inclined, the twigs drawn down to the horizontal pole and tied with strips of bark. Long grass is then laid over the branches in sufficient quantity to draw off the rain, and we have sheds open to the fire in front but secure from beasts behind. In less than an hour we were usually all under cover. We never lacked abundance of grass during the whole journey. It is a picturesque sight at night, when the clear bright moon of these climates glances on the sleeping forms around, to look out upon the attitudes of profound repose both men and beasts assume. There being no danger from wild animals on such a night, the fires are allowed almost to go out; and, as there is no fear of hungry dogs coming over sleepers and devouring the food, or quietly eating up the poor fellows' blankets, which at best were but greasy skins, which sometimes happened in the villages, the picture was one of perfect peace.

The cooking is usually done in the natives' own style; and, as they carefully wash the dishes, pots, and the hands before handling food, it is by no means despicable. Sometimes alterations are made at my suggestion, and then they believe that they can cook in thorough white man's fashion. The cook always comes in for something left in the pot; so all are eager to obtain the office.

I taught several of them to wash my shirts, and they did it well, though their teacher had never been taught that work himself. Frequent changes of linen and sunning of my blanket kept me more comfortable than might have been anticipated, and I feel certain that the lessons of cleanliness rigidly instilled by my mother in childhood helped to maintain that respect which these people entertain for European ways. It is questionable if a descent to barbarous ways ever elevates a man in the eyes of savages.

Part of our company marched along the banks with the oxen, and part went in the canoes, but our pace was regulated by the speed of the men on shore. Their course was rather difficult, on account of the numbers of departing and re-entering branches of the Leeambye, which they had to avoid or wait at till we ferried them over. The number of alligators is prodigious, and in this river they are more savage than in some others. Many children are carried off annually at Seshoke and other towns; for, notwithstanding the danger, when they go down for water they almost always must play a while. This reptile is said by the natives to strike the victim with his tail, then drag him in and drown him. When lying in the water watching for prey, the body never appears. Many calves are lost also, and it is seldom that a number of cows can swim over at Seshcke without some loss. I never could avoid shuddering on seeing my men swimming across these branches, after one of them had been caught by the thigh and taken below. He, however, retained, as nearly all of them in the most trying circumstances do, his full presence of mind, and, having a small, square, ragged-edged javelin with him, when dragged to the bottom gave the alligator a stab behind the shoulder. The alligator, writhing in pain, left him, and he came out with the deep marks of the reptile's teeth on his thigh. Here the people have no antipathy to persons who have met with such an adventure; but in the Bamangwato and Bakwain tribes, if a man is either bitten or even has had water splashed over him by the reptile's tail, he is expelled his tribe.

When we had gone thirty or forty miles above Libonta, we sent eleven of our captives to the west, to the chief called Makoma, with an explanatory message. This caused some delay; but as we were loaded with presents of food from the Makololo, and the wild animals were in enormous herds, we fared sumptuously. It was grievous, however, to shoot the lovely creatures, they were so tame. With but little skill in stalking, one could easily get within fifty or sixty yards of them. There I lay, looking at the graceful forms and motions of beautiful pokus, leches, and other antelopes, often till my men, wondering what was the matter, came up to see, and frightened them away If we had been starving, I could have slaughtered them with as little hesitation as I should cut off a patient's leg; but I felt a doubt, and the antelopes got the benefit of it.

My men, having never had fire-arms in their hands before, found it so difficult to hold the musket steady at the flash of fire in the pan, that they naturally expected me to furnish them with "gun-medicine," without which, it is almost universally believed, no one can shoot straight.

Great expectations had been formed when I arrived among the Makololo on this subject; but, having invariably declined to deceive them, as some for their own profit have done, my men now supposed that I would at last consent, and thereby relieve myself from the hard work of hunting by employing them after due medication. This I was most willing to do, if I could have done it honestly; for, having but little of the hunting-*furore* in my composition, I always preferred eating the game to killing it. Sulphur is the remedy most admired, and I remember Sechele giving a large price for a very small bit. He also gave some elephants' tusks, worth £30, for another medicine which was to make him invulnerable to musket-balls. As I uniformly recommended that these things should be tested by experiment, a calf was anointed with the charm and tied to a tree. It proved decisive, and Sechele remarked it was "pleasanter to be deceived than undeceived." I offered sulphur for the same purpose, but that was declined, even though a person came to the town afterward and rubbed his hands with a little before a successful trial of shooting at a mark.

I explained to my men the nature of a gun, and tried to teach them, but they would soon have expended all the ammunition in my possession. I was thus obliged to do all the shooting myself ever afterward. Their inability was rather a misfortune; for, in consequence of working too soon after having been bitten by the lion, the bone of my left arm had not united well. Continual hard manual labor, and some falls from ox-back, lengthened the ligament by which the ends of the bones were united, and a false joint was the consequence. The limb has never been painful, as those of my companions on the day of the rencounter with the lion have been; but, there being a joint too many, I could not steady the rifle, and was always obliged to shoot with the piece resting on the left shoulder. I wanted steadiness of aim, and it generally happened that the more hungry the party became, the more frequently I missed the animals.

Before we came to the junction of the Leeba and Leeambye we found the banks twenty feet high, and composed of marly sandstone. They are covered with trees, and the left bank has the tsetse and elephants. I suspect the fly has some connection with this animal, and the Portuguese in the district of Tete must think so too, for they call it the *Musca da elephant*, (the elephant-fly.)

We passed great numbers of hippopotami. They are very numerous in the parts of the river where they are never hunted. The males appear of a dark color, the females of yellowish brown. There is not such a complete separation of the sexes among them as among elephants. They spend most of their time in the water, lolling about in a listless, dreamy manner. When they come out of the river by night, they crop off the soft succulent grasses very neatly. When they blow, they puff up the water about three feet high.

CHAPTER XV.

DR. LIVINGSTONE VISITS THE FEMALE CHIEFS MANENKO AND NYAMOANA.

On the 27th of December we were at the confluence of the Leeba and Leeambye, (lat. 14° 10′ 52″ S., long. 23° 35′ 4J″ E) Masiko, the Barotse chief, for whom we had some captives, lived nearly due east of this point. They were two little boys, a little girl, a young man, and two middle-aged women. One of these as a member of a Babimpe tribe, who knock out both upp r and lower front teeth as a distinction. As we had been informed by the captives on the previous Sunday that Masiko was in the habit of seizing all orphans, and those wh have no powerful friend in the tribe whose protection they can claim, and selling them for clothing to the Mambari, we thought the objection of the women to go first to his town before seeing their friends quite reasonable, and resolved to send a party of our own people to see them safely among their relatives I told the captive young man to inform Masiko that he was very unlike his father Santuru, who had refused to sell his people to Mambari. He will probably be afraid to deliver such a message himself, but it is meant for his people, and they will circulate it pretty widely, and Masiko may yet feel a little pressure from without. We sent Mosántu, a Batoka man, and his companions, with the captives. The Barotse whom we had were unwilling to go to Masiko, since they owe him allegiance as the son of Santuru, and while they continue with Makololo are considered rebels. The message by Mosantu was that " I was sorry to find that Santuru had not borne a wiser son. Santuru loved to govern men, but Masiko wanted to govern wild beasts only, as he sold his people to the Mambari;" adding an explanation of the return of the captives, and an injunction to him to live in peace, and prevent his people kidnapping the children and canoes of the Makololo, as a continuance in these deeds would lead to war, which I wished to prevent. He was also instructed to say, if Masiko wanted fuller explanation of my views, he must send a sensible man to talk with me at the first town of the Balonda, to which I was about to proceed.

We ferried Mosantu over to the left bank of the Leeba. The journey required five days, but it could not have been at a quicker rate than ten or twelve miles per day; the children were between seven and eight years of age, and unable to walk fast in a hot sun.

Leaving Mosantu to pursue his course, we shall take but one glance down the river, which we are now about to leave, for it comes at this point from the eastward, and our course is to be directed to the northwest, as we mean to go to Loanda in Angola. From the confluence, where we now are, down to Mosioatúnya, there are many long reaches, where a vessel equal to the Thames steamers plying between the bridges could run as freely as they do on the Thames. It is often, even here, as broad as that river at London Bridge; but, without accurate measurement of the depth, one could not say which contained most water. There are, however, many and serious obstacles to a continued navigation for hundreds of miles at a stretch. About ten miles below the confluence of the Locti, for instance, there are many large sand-banks in the stream; then you have a hundred miles to the river Simáh, where a Thames steamer could ply at all times of the year; but, again, the space between Simah and Katima-molelo has five or six rapids with cataracts, one of which—Gonye—could not be passed at any time without portage. Between these rapids there are reaches of still, deep water, of several miles in length. Beyond Katima-molelo to the confluence of the Chobe you have nearly a hundred miles, again, of a river capable of being navigated in the same way as in the Barotse valley.

Now, I do not say that this part of the river presents a very inviting prospect for extemporaneous European enterprise; but when we have a pathway which requires only the formation of portages to make it equal to our canals for hundreds of miles, where the philosophers supposed there was naught but an extensive sandy desert, we must confess that the future partakes at least of the elements of hope. My deliberate conviction was and is that the part of the country indicated is as capable of supporting millions of inhabitants as it is of its thousands. The grass of the Barotse valley, for instance, is such a densely-matted mass, that, when "laid," the stalks bear each other up, so that one feels as if walking on the sheaves of a haystack, and the leches nestle under it to bring forth their young The soil which produces this, if placed under the plough, instead of being mere pasturage, would yield grain sufficient to feed vast multitudes.

We now began to ascend the Leeba. The water is black in color as compared with the main stream, which here assumes the name of Kabompo. The Leeba flows placidly, and, unlike the parent river, receives numbers of little rivulets from both sides. It winds slowly through the most charming meadows, each of which has either a soft, sedgy centre, large pond, or trickling rill down the middle.

A large buffalo was wounded, and ran into the thickest part of the forest, bleeding profusely. The young men went on his trail; and, though the vegetation was so dense that no one could have run more than a few yards, most of them went along quite carelessly, picking and eating a fruit of the melon-family called mponko. When the animal heard them approach, he always fled, shifting his stand and doubling on his course in the most cunning manner. In other cases I have known them to turn back to a point a few yards from their own trail, and then lie down in a hollow waiting for the hunter to come up. Though a heavy, lumbering-looking animal, his charge is then rapid and terrific. More accidents happen by the buffalo and the black rhinoceros than by the lion. Though all are aware of the mischievous nature of the buffalo when wounded, our young men went after him quite carelessly. They never lose their presence of mind, but, as a buffalo charges back in a forest, dart dexterously out of his way behind a tree, and, wheeling round, stab him as he passes.

On the 28th we slept at a spot on the right bank from which had just emerged two broods of alligators. We had seen many young ones as we came up; so this seems to be their time of coming forth from the nests, for we saw them sunning themselves on sand-banks in company with the old ones. We made our fire in one of the deserted nests, which were strewed all over with the broken shells. At the Zouga we saw sixty eggs taken out of one such nest alone. They are about the size of those of a goose, only the eggs of the alligator are of the same diameter at both ends, and the white shell is partially elastic, from having a strong internal membrane and but little lime in its composition. The distance from the water was about ten feet and there were evidences of the same place having been used for a similar purpose in former years. A broad path led up from the water to the nest, and the dam, it was said by my companions, after depositing the eggs, covers them up, and returns afterward to assist the young out of the place of confinement and out of the egg. She leads them to the edge of the water, and then leaves them to catch small fish for themselves.

When we reached the part of the river opposite to the village of Manenko, the first female chief whom we encountered, two of the people called Balunda, or Balŏnda, came to us in their little canoe. From them we learned that Kolimbóta, one of our party, who had been in the habit of visiting these parts, was believed by the Balonda to have acted as a guide to the marauders under Lerimo, whose captives we were now returning. They very naturally suspected this, from the facility with which their villages had been found; and, as they had since removed them to some distance from the river, they were unwilling to lead us to their places of concealment. We were in bad repute; but, having a captive boy and girl to show in evidence of, Sekeletu and ourselves not being partakers in the guilt of inferior men, I could fully express my desire that all should live in peace. They evidently felt that I ought to have taught the Makololo first, before coming to them; for they remarked that what I advanced was very good, but guilt lay at the door of the Makololo for disturbing the previously-existing peace. They then went away to report us to Manenko.

When the strangers visited us again in the evening, they were accompanied by a number of the people of an Ambŏnda chief named Sekelenke. The Ambonda live far to the N.W.; their language (the Bŏnda) is the common dialect in Angola. Sekelenke had fled, and was now living with his village as a vassal of Masiko. Sekelenke had gone with his villagers to hunt elephants on the right bank of the Leeba, and was now on his way back to Masiko. He sent me a dish of boiled zebra's flesh, and a request that I should lend him a canoe to ferry his wives and family across the river to the bank on which we were encamped. Many of Sekelenke's people came to salute the first white man they ever had an opportunity of seeing; but Sekelenke himself did not come near. We heard he was offended with some of his people for letting me know he was among the company. He said that I should be displeased with him for not coming and making some present. This was the only instance in which I was shunned in this quarter.

Sekelenke and his people, twenty-four in number, defiled past our camp, carrying large bundles of dried elephants' meat. Most of them came to say good-bye, and Sekelenke himself sent to say that he had gone to visit a wife living in the village of Manenko. It was a mere African manœuvre to gain information, and not to commit himself to either one line of action or another with respect to our visit. As he was probably in the party before us, I replied that it was all right, and when my people came up from Masiko I would go to my wife too.

To our first message offering a visit of explanation to Manenko, we got an answer, with a basket of manioc-roots, that we must remain where we were till she should visit us. Having waited two days already for her, other messengers arrived with orders for me to come to her. After four days of rains and negotiation, I declined going at all, and proceeded up the river to the small stream Makondo, (lat. 13° 23′ 12″ S.,) which enters the Leeba from the east, and is between twenty and thirty yards broad.

January 1, 1854.—We had heavy rains almost every day: indeed, the rainy season had fairly set in. Baskets of the purple fruit called mawa were frequently brought to us by the villagers; not for sale, but from a belief that their chiefs would be pleased to hear that they had treated us well: we gave them pieces of meat in return.

When crossing at the confluence of the Leeba and Makondo, one of my men picked up a bit of a steel watch chain of English manufacture, and we were informed that this was the spot where the Mambari cross in coming to Masiko. Their visits explain why Sekelenke kept his tusks so carefully. These Mambari are very enterprising merchants: when they mean to trade with a town, they deliberately begin the affair by building huts, as if they knew that little business could be transacted without a liberal allowance of time for palaver. They bring Manchester goods into the heart of Africa; these cotton prints look so wonderful that the Makololo could not believe them to be the work of mortal hands. On questioning the Mambari, they were answered that English manufactures came out of the sea, and beads were gathered on its shore. To Africans our cotton-mills are fairy dreams. "How can the irons spin, weave, and print so beautifully?" Our country is like what Taprobane was to our ancestors,—a strange realm of light, whence came the diamond, muslin, and peacocks; an attempt at explanation of our manufactures usually elicits the expression, "Truly ye are gods!"

When about to leave the Makondo, one of my men had dreamed that Mosántu was shut up a prisoner in a stockade: this dream depressed the spirits of the whole party, and when I came out of my little tent in the morning, they were sitting the pictures of abject sorrow. I asked if we were to be guided by dreams, or by the authority I derived from Sekeletu, and ordered them to load the boats at once; they seemed ashamed to confess their fears; the Makololo picked up courage and upbraided the others for having such superstitious views, and said this was always their way: if even a certain bird called to them, they would turn back from an enterprise, saying it was unlucky. They entered the canoes at last, and were the better of a little scolding for being inclined to put dreams before authority.

It rained all the morning, but about eleven we reached the village of Sheakóndo, on a small stream named Lonkónyo. We sent a message to the head-man, who soon appeared with two wives, bearing handsome presents of manioc: Sheakondo could speak the language of the Barotse well, and seemed awe-struck when told some of the "words of God." He manifested no fear, always spoke frankly, and, when he made an asseveration, did so by simply pointing up to the sky above him.

Sheakondo's old wife presented some manioc-roots, and then politely requested to be anointed with butter: as I had been bountifully supplied by the Makololo, I gave her as much as would suffice, and, as they have little clothing, I can readily believe that she felt her comfort greatly enhanced thereby.

The favorite wife, who was also present, was equally anxious for butter. She had a profusion of iron rings on her ankles, to which were attached little pieces of sheet-iron, to enable her to make a tinkling as she walked in her mincing African style; the same thing is thought pretty by our own dragoons in walking jauntingly.

On the 6th of January we reached the village of another female chief, named Nyamoána, who is said to be the mother of Manenko, and sister of Shinté or Kabómpo, the greatest Balonda chief in this part of the country. Her people had but recently come to the present locality, and had erected only twenty huts. Her husband, Samoána, was clothed in a kilt of green and red baize, and was armed with a spear and a broadsword of antique form, about eighteen inches long and three broad. The chief and her husband were sitting on skins placed in the middle of a circle thirty paces in diameter, a little raised above the ordinary level of the ground, and having a trench round it. Outside the trench sat about a hundred persons of all ages and both sexes. The men were well armed with bows, arrows, spears, and broadswords. Beside the husband sat a rather aged woman having a bad outward squint in the left eye. We put down our arms about forty yards off, and I walked up to the centre of the circular bench, and saluted him in the usual way by clapping the hands together in their fashion. He pointed to his wife, as much as to say, The honor belongs to her. I saluted her in the same way, and, a mat having been brought, I squatted down in front of them.

The talker was then called, and I was asked who was my spokesman. Having pointed to Kolimbota, who knew their dialect best, the palaver began in due form. I explained the real objects I had in view, without any attempt to mystify or appear in any other character than my own, for I have always been satisfied that, even though there were no other considerations, the truthful way of dealing with the uncivilized is unquestionably the best. Kolimbota repeated to Nyamoana's talker what I had said to him He delivered it all verbatim to her husband, who repeated it again to her. It was thus all rehearsed four times over, in a tone loud enough to be heard by the whole party of auditors. The response came back by the same round-about route, beginning at the lady to her husband, &c.

After explanations and re-explanations, I perceived that our new friends were mixing up my message of peace and friendship with Makololo affairs, and stated that it was not delivered on the authority of any one less than that of their Creator, and that if the Makololo did again break his laws and attack the Balonda, the guilt would rest with the Makololo and not with me. The palaver then came to a close.

By way of gaining their confidence, I showed them my hair, which is considered a curiosity in all this region. They said, "Is that hair? It is the mane of a lion, and not hair at all." Some thought that I had made a wig of lion's mane, as they sometimes do with fibres of the "ife," and dye it black and 'twist it so as to resemble a mass of their own wool. I could not return the joke by telling them that theirs was not hair, but the wool of sheep, for they have none of these in the country; and even though they had, as Herodotus remarked, "the African sheep are clothed with hair, and men's heads with wool." So I had to be content with asserting that mine was the real original hair, such as theirs would have been had it not been scorched and frizzled by the sun. In proof of what the sun could do, I compared my own bronzed face and hands, then about the same in complexion as the lighter-colored Makololo, with the white skin of my chest. They readily believed that, as they go nearly naked and fully exposed to that influence, we might be of common origin after all. Here, as everywhere when heat and moisture are combined, the people are very dark, but not quite black. There is always a shade of brown in the most deeply colored. I showed my watch and pocket-compass, which are considered great curiosities; but, though the lady was called on by her husband to look, she would not be persuaded to approach near enough.

These people are more superstitious than any we had yet encountered: though still only building their village, they had found time to erect two little sheds at the chief dwelling in it, in which were placed two pots having charms in them. When asked what medicine they contained, they replied, "Medicine for the Barimo;" but when I rose and looked into them they said they were medicine for the game. Here we saw the first evidence of the existence of idolatry, in the remains of an old idol at a deserted village. It was simply a human head carved on a block of wood. Certain charms mixed with red ochre and white pipe-clay are dotted over them when they are in use; and a crooked stick is used in the same way for an idol when they have no professional carver.

As the Leeba seemed still to come from the direction in which we wished to go, I was desirous of proceeding farther up with the canoes; but Nyamoana was anxious that we should allow her people to conduct us to her brother Shinte; and, when I explained to her the advantage of water-carriage, she represented that her brother did not live near the river, and, moreover, there was a cataract in front, over which it would be difficult to convey the canoes. She was afraid, too, that the Balobále, whose country lies to the west of the river, not knowing the objects for which we had come, would kill us. To my reply that I had been so often threatened with death if I visited a new tribe that I was now more afraid of killing any one than of being killed, she rejoined that the Balobale would not kill me, but the Makololo would all be sacrificed as their enemies. This produced considerable effect on my companions, and inclined them to the plan of Nyamoana, of going to the town of her brother rather than ascending the Leeba. The arrival of Manenko herself on the scene threw so much weight into the scale on their side that I was forced to yield the point.

Manenko was a tall, strapping woman about twenty, distinguished by a profusion of ornaments and medicines hung round her person; the latter are supposed to act as charms. Her body was smeared all over with a mixture of fat and red ochre, as a protection against the weather; a necessary precaution, for, like most of the Balonda ladies, she was otherwise in a state of frightful nudity. This was not from want of clothing; for, being a chief, she might have been as well clad as any of her subjects, but from her peculiar ideas of elegance in dress. When she arrived with her husband, Sambánza, they listened for some time to the statements I was making to the people of Nyamoana, after which the husband, acting as spokesman, commenced an oration, stating the reasons for their coming; and, during every two or three seconds of the delivery, he picked up a little sand and rubbed it on the upper part of his arms and chest. This is a common mode of salutation in Londa; and when they wish to be excessively polite they bring a quantity of ashes or pipe-clay in a piece of skin, and, taking up handfuls, rub it on the chest and upper front part of each arm; others, in saluting, drum their ribs with their elbows; while others still touch the ground with one cheek after the other, and clap their hands. The chiefs go through the manœuvre of rubbing the sand on the arms, but only make a feint of picking up some. When Sambanza had finished his oration, he rose up and showed his ankles ornamented with a bundle of copper rings: had they been very heavy they would have made him adopt a straggling walk. Some chiefs have really so many as to be forced, by the weight and size, to keep one foot apart from the other, the weight being a serious inconvenience in walking. The gentlemen like Sambanza, who wish to imitate their betters, do so in their walk; so you see men with only a few ounces of ornament on their legs strutting along as if they had double the number of pounds. When I smiled at Sambanza's walk, the people remarked, " That is the way in which they show off their lordship in these parts."

Manenko was quite decided in the adoption of the policy of friendship with the Makololo which we recommended; and, by way of cementing the bond, she and her counsellors proposed that Kolimbota should take a wife among them. Kolimbota, I found, thought favorably of the proposition, and it afterward led to his desertion from us.

On the evening of the day in which Manenko arrived, we were delighted by the appearance of Mosántu and an imposing embassy from Masiko. It consisted of all his under-chiefs; and they brought a fine elephant's tusk, two calabashes of honey, and a large piece of blue baize, as a present. The last was intended perhaps to show me that he was a truly great chief, who had such stores of white men's goods at hand that he could afford to give presents of them; it might also be intended for Mosantu, for chiefs usually remember the servants: I gave it to him. Masiko expressed delight, by his principal men, at the return of the captives, and at the proposal of peace and alliance with the Makololo. He stated that he never sold any of his own people to the Mambari, but only captives whom his people kidnapped from small neighboring tribes. When the question was put whether his people had been in the habit of molesting the Makololo by kidnapping their servants and stealing canoes, it was admitted that two of his men, when hunting, had gone to the Makololo gardens, to see if any of their relatives were there. As the great object in all native disputes is to get both parties to turn over a new leaf, I explained the desirableness of forgetting past feuds, accepting the present Makololo professions as genuine, and avoiding in future to give them any cause for marauding. I presented Masiko with an ox furnished by Sekeletu as provision for ourselves.

We were now without any provisions, except a small dole of manioc-roots each evening from Nyamoana, which, when eaten raw, produce poisonous effects. A small loaf, made from nearly the last morsel of maize-meal from Libonta, was my stock, and our friends from Masiko were still more destitute; yet we all rejoiced so much at their arrival that we resolved to spend a day with them. The Barotse of our party, meeting with relatives and friends among the Barotse of Masiko, had many old tales to tell; and, after pleasant hungry converse by day, we regaled our friends with the magic lantern by night; and, in order to make the thing of use to all, we removed our camp up to the village of Nyamoana. This is a good means of arresting the attention and conveying important facts to the minds of these people.

When erecting our sheds at the village, Manenko fell upon our friends from Masiko in a way that left no doubt on our minds but that she is a most accomplished scold. Masiko had, on a former occasion, sent to Samoána for a cloth,—a common way of keeping up intercourse,—and, after receiving it, sent it back, because it had the appearance of having had "witchcraft-medicine" on it: this was a grave offence, and now Manenko had a good excuse for venting her spleen, the ambassadors having called at her village and slept in one of the huts without leave. If her family was to be suspected of dealing in evil charms, why were Masiko's people not to be thought guilty of leaving the same in her hut? She advanced and receded in true oratorical style, belaboring her own servants as well for allowing the offence, and, as usual in more civilized feminine lectures, she leaned over the objects of her ire, and screamed forth all their faults and failings ever since they were born, and her despair of ever seeing them become better until they were all "killed by alligators." Masiko's people followed the plan of receiving this torrent of abuse in silence, and, as neither we nor they had any thing to eat, we parted next morning. In reference to Masiko selling slaves to the Mambari, they promised to explain the relationship which exists between even the most abject of his people and our common Father; and that no more kidnapping ought to be allowed, as he ought to give that peace and security to the smaller tribes on his eastern borders which he so much desired to obtain himself from the Makololo. We promised to return through his town when we came back from the sea-coast.

Manenko gave us some manioc-roots in the morning, and had determined to carry our baggage to her uncle's, Kabompo or Shinte. We had heard a sample of what she could do with her tongue; and, as neither my men nor myself had much inclination to encounter a scolding from this black Mrs. Caudle, we made ready the packages; but she came and said the men whom she had ordered for the service had not yet come: they would arrive to-morrow. Being on low and disagreeable diet, I felt annoyed at this further delay, and ordered the packages to be put into the canoes to proceed up the river without her servants. But Manenko was not to be circumvented in this way: she came forward with her people, and said her uncle would be angry if she did not carry forward the tusks and goods of Sekeletu, seized the luggage, and declared that she would carry it in spite of me. My men succumbed sooner to this petticoat-government than I felt inclined to do, and left me no power; and, being unwilling to encounter her tongue, I was moving off to the canoes, when she gave me a kind explanation, and, with her hand on my shoulder, put on a motherly look, saying, "Now, my little man, just do as the rest have done." My feelings of annoyance of course vanished.

CHAPTER XVI.

DR. LIVINGSTONE VISITS SHINTE, CHIEF OF THE BALONDA.

11th of January, 1854.—On starting this morning, Samoana (or rather Nyamoana, for the ladies are the chiefs here) presented a string of beads, and a shell highly valued among them, as an atonement for having assisted Manenko, as they thought, to vex me the day before. They seemed anxious to avert any evil which might arise from my displeasure; but, having replied that I never kept my anger up all night, they were much pleased to see me satisfied. We had to cross, in a canoe, a stream which flows past the village of Nyamoana. Manenko's doctor waved some charms over her, and she took some in her hand and on her body before she ventured upon the water. One of my men spoke rather loudly when near the doctor's basket of medicines. The doctor reproved him, and always spoke in a whisper himself, glancing back to the basket as if afraid of being heard by something therein. So much superstition is quite unknown in the south, and is mentioned here to show the difference in the feelings of this new people, and the comparative want of reverence on these points among Caffres and Bechuanas.

Manenko was accompanied by her husband and her drummer, the latter continued to thump most vigorously until a heavy, drizzling mist set in and compelled him to desist. Her husband used various incantations and vociferations to drive away the rain, but down it poured incessantly, and on our Amazon went, in the very lightest marching-order, and at a pace that few of the men could keep up with. Being on ox-back, I kept pretty close to our leader, and asked her why she did not clothe herself during the rain, and learned that it is not considered proper for a chief to appear effeminate. He or she must always wear the appearance of robust youth and bear vicissitudes without wincing. My men, in admiration of her pedestrian powers, every now and then remarked, "Manenko is a soldier;" and, thoroughly wet and cold, we were all glad when she proposed a halt to prepare our night's lodging on the banks of a stream.

Next day we passed through a piece of forest so dense that no one could have penetrated it without an axe. It was flooded, not by the river, but by the heavy rains which poured down every day and kept those who had clothing constantly wet. I observed in this piece of forest a very strong smell of sulphuretted hydrogen. This I had observed repeatedly in other parts before. I had attacks of fever of the intermittent type again and again, in consequence of repeated drenchings in these unhealthy spots.

On the 11th and 12th we were detained by incessant rains, and so heavy I never saw the like in the south. I had a little tapioca and a small quantity of Libonta meal, which I still reserved for worse times. The patience of my men under hunger was admirable; the actual want of the present is never so painful as the thought of getting nothing in the future. We thought the people of some large hamlets very niggardly and very independent of their chiefs, for they gave us and Manenko nothing, though they had large fields of maize in an eatable state around them. When she went and kindly begged some for me, they gave her five ears only. They were subjects of her uncle, and, had they been Makololo, would have been lavish in their gifts to the niece of their chief. I suspected that they were dependents of some of Shinte's principal men, and had no power to part with the maize of their masters.

The forests became more dense as we went north. We travelled much more in the deep gloom of the forest than in open sunlight. No passage existed on either side of the narrow path made by the axe. Large climbing plants entwined themselves around the trunks and branches of gigantic trees like boa-constrictors, and they often do constrict the trees by which they rise, and, killing them, stand erect themselves. The bark of a fine tree found in abundance here, and called "motuia," is used by the Barotse for making fish-lines and nets, and the "molompi," so well adapted for paddles by its lightness and flexibility, was abundant. There were other trees quite new to my companions: many of them ran up to a height of fifty feet of one thickness, and without branches.

In these forests we first encountered the artificial beehives so commonly met with all the way from this to Angola. They consist of about five feet of the bark of a tree fifteen or eighteen inches in diameter. Two incisions are made right·round the tree at points five feet apart, then one longitudinal slit from one of these to the other; the workman next lifts up the bark on each side of this slit, and detaches it from the trunk, taking care not to break it, until the whole comes from the tree. The elasticity of the bark makes it assume the form it had before; the slit is sewed or pegged up with wooden pins, and ends made of coiled grass rope are inserted, one of which has a hole for the ingress of the bees in the centre, and the hive is complete. These hives are placed in a horizontal position on high trees in different parts of the forest, and in this way all the wax exported from Benguela and Loanda is collected. It is all the produce of free labor. A "piece of medicine" is tied round the trunk of the tree, and proves sufficient protection against thieves. The natives seldom rob each other, for all believe that certain medicines can inflict disease and death· and, though they consider that these are only known to a few, they act on the principle that it is best to let them all alone. The gloom of these forests strengthens the superstitious feelings of the people. In other quarters, where they are not subjected to this influence, I have heard the chiefs issue proclamations to the effect that real witchcraft-medicines had been placed at certain gardens from which produce had been stolen, the thieves having risked the power of the ordinary charms previously placed there.

There was considerable pleasure, in spite of rain and fever, in this new scenery. The deep gloom contrasted strongly with the shadeless glare of the Kalahari, which had left an indelible impression on my memory. Though drenched day by day at this time, and for months afterward, it was long before I could believe that we were getting too much of a good thing. Nor could I look at water being thrown away without a slight, quick impression flitting across the mind that we were guilty of wasting it. Every now and then we emerged from the deep gloom into a pretty little valley, having a damp portion in the middle; which, though now filled with water, at other times contains moisture enough for wells only. These wells have shades put over them in the form of little huts.

We crossed, in canoes, a little never-failing stream, which passes by the name of Lefuje, or "the rapid." It comes from a goodly high mountain, called Monakadzi, (the woman,) which gladdened our eyes as it rose to our sight about twenty or thirty miles to the east of our course. It is of an oblong shape, and seemed at least eight hundred feet above the plains. The Lefuje probably derives its name from the rapid descent of the short course it has to flow from Monakadzi to the Leeba.

The number of little villages seemed about equal to the number of valleys. At some we stopped and rested, the people becoming more liberal as we advanced. Others we found deserted, a sudden panic having seized the inhabitants, though the drum of Nanenko was kept beaten pretty constantly, in order to give notice of the approach of great people. When we had decided to remain for the night at any village, the inhabitants lent us the roofs of their huts, which in form resemble those of the Makololo, or a Chinaman's hat, and can be taken off the walls at pleasure. They lifted them off, and brought them to the spot we had selected as our lodging, and, when my men had propped them up with stakes, they were then safely housed for the night. Every one who comes to salute either Manenko or ourselves rubs the upper parts of the arms and chest with ashes; those who wish to show profounder reverence put some also on the face.

We found that every village had its idols near it. This is the case all through the country of the Balonda, so that, when we came to an idol in the woods, we always knew that we were within a quarter of an hour of human habitations. One very ugly idol we passed rested on a horizontal beam placed on two upright posts. This beam was furnished with two loops of cord, as of a chain, to suspend offerings before it On remarking to my companions that these idols had ears, but that they heard not, &c., I learned that the Balonda, and even the Barotse, believe that divination may be performed by means of these blocks of wood and clay; and, though the wood itself could not hear, the owners had medicines by which it could be made to hear and give responses, so that if an enemy were approaching they would have full information. Manenko having brought us to a stand on account of slight indisposition and a desire to send forward notice of our approach to her uncle, I asked why it was necessary to send forward information of our movements if Shinte had idols who could tell him every thing. "She did it only,"* was the reply. It is seldom of much use to show one who worships idols the folly of idolatry without giving something else as an object

---

* This is a curious African idiom, by which a person implies he had no particular reason for his act.

of adoration instead. They do not love them. They fear them, and betake themselves to their idols only when in perplexity and danger.

While delayed, by Manenko's management, among the Balonda villages, a little to the south of the town of Shinte, we were well supplied by the villagers with sweet potatoes and green maize: Sambanza went to his mother's village for supplies of other food. I was laboring under fever, and did not find it very difficult to exercise patience with her whims; but, it being Saturday, I thought we might as well go to the town for Sunday, (15th.) "No: her messenger must return from her uncle first." Being sure that the answer of the uncle would be favorable, I thought we might go on at once, and not lose two days in the same spot. "No: it is our custom;" and every thing else I could urge was answered in the genuine pertinacious lady style. She ground some meal for me with her own hands, and when she brought it told me she had actually gone to a village and begged corn for the purpose. She said this with an air as if the inference must be drawn by even a stupid white man, "I know how to manage, don' I?" It was refreshing to get food which could be eaten without producing the unpleasantness described by the Rev. John Newton, of St. Mary's, Woolnoth, London, when obliged to eat the same roots while a slave in the West Indies. The day, (January 14th,) for a wonder, was fair, and the sun shone, so as to allow us to dry our clothing and other goods, many of which were mouldy and rotten from the long-continued damp. The guns rusted, in spite of being oiled every evening.

On Sunday afternoon, messengers arrived from Shinte, expressing his approbation of the objects we had in view in our journey through the country, and that he was glad of the prospect of a way being opened by which white men might visit and allow him to purchase ornaments at pleasure. Manenko now threatened in sport to go on, and I soon afterward perceived that what now seemed to me the dilly-dallying way of this lady was the proper mode of making acquaintance with the Balonda; and much of the favor with which I was received in different places was owing to my sending forward messengers to state the object of our coming before entering each town and village. When we came in sight of a village, we sat down under the shade of a tree and sent forward a man to give notice who we were and what were our objects. The headman of the village then sent out his principal men, as Shinte now did, to bid us welcome and show us a tree under which we might sleep. Before I had profited by the rather tedious teaching of Manenko, I sometimes entered a village and created unintentional alarm. The villagers would continue to look upon us with suspicion as long as we remained. Shinte sent us two large baskets of manioc and six dried fishes. His men had the skin of a monkey, called in their tongue "poluma," (*Colobus guereza*,) of a jet-black color, except the long mane, which is pure white: it is said to be found in the north, in the country of Matiámvo, the paramount chief of all the Balonda. We learned from them that they are in the habit of praying to their idols when unsuccessful in killing game or in any other enterprise. They behaved with reverence at our religious services. This will appear important if the reader remembers the almost total want of prayer and reverence we encountered in the south.

Our friends informed us that Shinte would be highly honored by the presence of three white men in his town at once. Two others had sent forward notice of their approach from another quarter, (the west;) could it be Barth or Krapf? How pleasant to meet with Europeans in such an out-of-the-way region! The rush of thoughts made me almost forget my fever. Are they of the same color as I am? "Yes; exactly so." And have the same hair? "Is that hair? we thought it was a wig; we never saw the like before: this white man must be of the sort that lives in the sea." Henceforth my men took the hint, and always sounded my praises as a true specimen of the variety of white men who live in the sea. "Only look at his hair; it is made quite straight by the sea-water!"

I explained to them again and again that, when it was said we came out of the sea, it did not mean that we came from beneath the water; but the fiction has been widely spread in the interior by the Mambari that the real white men live in the sea, and the myth was too good not to be taken advantage of by my companions: so, notwithstanding my injunctions, I believe that, when I was out of hearing, my men always represented themselves as led by a genuine merman: "Just see his hair!" If I returned from walking to a little distance, they would remark of some to whom they had been holding forth, "These people want to see your hair."

As the strangers had woolly hair like themselves, I had to give up the idea of meeting any thing more European than two half-caste Portuguese engaged in trading for slaves, ivory, and bees'-wax.

16th.—After a short march we came to a most lovely valley about a mile and a half wide, and stretching away eastward up to a low prolongation of Monakádzi. A small stream meanders down the centre of this pleasant green glen; and on a little rill, which flows into it from the western side, stands the town of Kabompo, or, as he likes best to be called, Shinte. (Lat. 12° 37' 35" S., long. 22° 47' E.) When Manenko thought the sun was high enough for us to make a lucky entrance, we found the town embowered in banana and other tropical trees having great expansion of leaf; the streets are straight, and present a complete contrast to those of the Bechuanas, which are all very tortuous. Here, too, we first saw native huts with square walls and round roofs. Goats were browsing about, and, when we made our appearance, a crowd of negroes, all fully armed, ran toward us as if they would eat us up: some had guns, but the manner in which they were held showed that the owners were more accustomed to bows and arrows than to white men's weapons. After surrounding and staring at us for an hour, they began to disperse.

The two native Portuguese traders of whom we had heard had erected a little encampment opposite the place where ours was about to be made. One of them, whose spine had been injured in youth,—a rare sight in this country,—came and visited us. I returned the visit next morning. His tall companion had that sickly yellow hue which made him look fairer than myself, but his head was covered with a crop of unmistakable wool. They had a gang of young female slaves in a chain, hoeing the ground in front of their encampment to clear it of weeds and grass; these were purchased recently in Lobale, whence the traders had now come. There were many Mambari with them, and the establishment was conducted with that military order which pervades all the arrangements of the Portuguese colonists. A drum was beaten and trumpet sounded at certain hours, quite in military fashion. It was the first time most of my men had seen slaves in chains. "They are not men," they exclaimed, (meaning, they are beasts,) "who treat their children so."

The Balonda are real negroes, having much more wool on their heads and bodies than any of the Bechuana or Caffre tribes. They are generally very dark in color, but several are to be seen of a lighter hue; many of the slaves who have been exported to Brazil have gone from this region; but, while they have a general similarity to the typical negro, I never could, from my own observation, think that our ideal negro, as seen in tobacconists' shops, is the true type. A large proportion of the Balonda, indeed, have heads somewhat elongated backward and upward, thick lips, flat noses, elongated *ossa calces*, &c. &c.; but there are also many good-looking, well-shaped heads and persons among them.

17th, Tuesday.—We were honored with a grand reception by Shinte about eleven o'clock. Sambanza claimed the honor of presenting us, Manenko being slightly indisposed The native Portuguese and Mambari went fully armed with guns, in order to give Shinte a salute, their drummer and trumpeter making all the noise that very old instruments would produce. The kotla, or place of audience, was about a hundred yards square, and two graceful specimens of a species of banian stood near one end; under one of these sat Shinte, on a sort of throne covered with a leopard's skin. He had on a checked jacket and a kilt of scarlet baize edged with green; many strings of large beads hung from his neck, and his limbs were covered with iron and copper armlets and bracelets, on his head he wore a helmet made of beads woven neatly together and crowned with a great bunch of goose-feathers. Close to him sat three lads with large sheaves of arrows over their shoulders.

When we entered the kotla, the whole of Manenko's party saluted Shinte by clapping their hands, and Sambanza did obeisance by rubbing his chest and arms with ashes. One of the trees being unoccupied, I retreated to it for the sake of the shade, and my whole party did the same. We were now about forty yards from the chief, and could see the whole ceremony. The different sections of the tribe came forward in the same way that we did, the head-man of each making obeisance with ashes which he carried with him for the purpose; then came the soldiers, all armed to the teeth, running and shouting toward us, with their swords drawn and their faces screwed up so as to appear as savage as possible, for the purpose, I thought, of trying whether they could not make us take to our heels. As we did not, they turned round toward Shinte and saluted him, then retired. When all had come and were seated, then began the curious capering usually seen in pichos. A man starts up, and imitates the most approved attitudes observed in actual fight, as throwing one javelin, receiving another on the shield, springing to one side to avoid a third, running backward or forward, leaping, &c. This over, Sambanza and the spokesman of

Nyamoana stalked backward and forward in front of Shinte, and gave forth, in a loud voice, all they had been able to learn, either from myself or people, of my past history and connection with the Makololo; the return of th captives; the wish to open the country to trade; the Bible as a word from heaven; the white man's desire for the tribes to live in peace: he ought to have taught the Makololo that first, for the Balonda never attacked them, yet they had assailed the Balonda: perhaps he is fibbing, perhaps not: they rather thought he was; but as the Balonda had good hearts, and Shinte had never done harm to any one, he had better receive the white man well, and send him on his way. Sambanza was gayly attired, and, besides a profusion of beads, had a cloth so long that a boy carried it after him as a train.

Behind Shinte sat about a hundred women, clothed in their best, which happened to be a profusion of red baize The chief wife of Shinte, one of the Matebele or Zulus, sat in front with a curious red cap on her head. During the intervals between the speeches, these ladies burst forth into a sort of plaintive ditty; but it was impossible for any of us to catch whether it was in praise of the speaker, of Shinte, or of themselves. This was the first time I had ever seen females present in a public assembly. In the south the women are not permitted to enter the kotla, and, even when invited to come to a religious service there, would not enter until ordered to do so by the chief; but here they expressed their approbation by clapping their hands and laughing to different speakers; and Shinte frequently turned round and spoke to them.

A party of musicians, consisting of three drummers and four performers on the piano, went round the kotla several times, regaling us with their music. Their drums are neatly carved from the trunk of a tree, and have a small hole in the side covered with a bit of spider's web: the ends are covered with the skin of an antelope pegged on; and, when they wish to tighten it, they hold it to the fire to make it contract: the instruments are beaten with the hands.

The piano, named "marimba," consists of two bars of wood placed side by side, here quite straight, but, farther north, bent round so as to resemble half the tire of a carriage-wheel; across these are placed about fifteen wooden keys, each of which is two or three inches broad and fifteen or eighteen inches long; their thickness is regulated according to the deepness of the note required: each of the keys has a calabash beneath it; from the upper part of each a portion is cut off to enable them to embrace the bars, and form hollow sounding-boards to the keys, which also are of different sizes, according to the note required; and little drumsticks elicit the music. Rapidity of execution seems much admired among them, and the music is pleasant to the ear. In Angola the Portuguese use the marimba in their dances.

When nine speakers had concluded their orations, Shinte stood up, and so did all the people. He had maintained true African dignity of manner all the while, but my people remarked that he scarcely ever took his eyes off me for a moment. About a thousand people were present, according to my calculation, and three hundred soldiers. The sun had now become hot; and the scene ended by the Mambari discharging their guns.

18*th*.—We were awakened during the night by a message from Shinte, requesting a visit at a very unseasonable hour. As I was just in the sweating-stage of an intermittent, and the path to the town lay through a wet valley, I declined going. Kolimbota, who knows their customs best, urged me to go; but, independent of sickness, I hated words of the night and deeds of darkness. "I was neither a hyena nor a witch." Kolimbota thought that we ought to conform to their wishes in every thing: I thought we ought to have some choice in the matter as well, which put him into high dudgeon. However, at ten next morning we went, and were led into the courts of Shinte, the walls of which were woven rods, all very neat and high. Many trees stood within the enclosure and afforded a grateful shade. These had been planted, for we saw some recently put in, with grass wound round the trunk to protect them from the sun. The otherwise waste corners of the streets were planted with sugarcane and bananas, which spread their large light leaves over the walls.

The Ficus Indica tree, under which we now sat, had very large leaves, but showed its relationship to the Indian banian by sending down shoots toward the ground. Shinte soon came, and appeared a man of upward of fifty-five years of age, of frank and open countenance, and about the middle height. He seemed in good humor, and said he had expected yesterday "that a man who came from the gods would have approached and talked to him." That had been my own intention in going to the reception; but when we came and saw the formidable preparations, and all his own men keeping at least forty yards off from him, I yielded to the solicitations of my men, and remained by the tree opposite to that under which he sat. His remark confirmed my previous belief that a frank, open, fearless manner is the most winning with all these Africans. I stated the object of my journey and mission, and to all I advanced the old gentleman clapped his hands in approbation. He replied through a spokesman; then all the company joined in the response by clapping of hands too.

After the more serious business was over, I asked if he had ever seen a white man before. He replied, "Never: you are the very first I have seen with a white skin and straight hair: your clothing, too, is different from any we have ever seen." They had been visited by native Portuguese and Mambari only.

On learning from some of the people that "Shinte's mouth was bitter for want of tasting ox-flesh," I presented him with an ox, to his great delight; and, as his country is so well adapted for cattle, I advised him to begin a trade in cows with the Makololo. He was pleased with the idea, and when we returned from Loanda we found that he had profited by the hint, for he had got three, and one of them justified my opinion of the country, for it was more like a prize-heifer for fatness than any we had seen in Africa. He soon afterward sent us a basket of green maize boiled, another of manioc-meal, and a small fowl.

During this time Manenko had been extremely busy with all her people in getting up a very pretty hut and court-yard, to be, as she said, her residence always when white men were brought by her along the same path. When she heard that we had given an ox to her uncle, she came forward to us with the air of one wronged, and explained that "this white man belonged to her; she had brought him here, and therefore the ox was hers, not Shinte's." She ordered her men to bring it, got it slaughtered by them, and presented her uncle with a leg only. Shinte did not seem at all annoyed at the occurrence.

19th.—I was awakened at an early hour by a messenger from Shinte; but, the thirst of a raging fever being just assuaged by the bursting forth of a copious perspiration, I declined going for a few hours. Violent action of the heart all the way to the town did not predispose me to be patient with the delay which then occurred, probably on account of the divination being unfavorable:—"They could not find Shinte." When I returned to bed, another message was received:—"Shinte wished to say all he had to tell me at once." This was too tempting an offer; so we went, and he had a fowl ready in his hand to present, also a basket of manioc-meal, and a calabash of mead. Referring to the constantly-recurring attacks of fever, he remarked that it was the only thing which would prevent a successful issue to my journey, for he had men to guide me who knew all the paths which led to the white men. He had himself travelled far when a young man. On asking what he would recommend for the fever, "Drink plenty of the mead, and as it gets in it will drive the fever out." It was, rather strong, and I suspect he liked the remedy pretty well, even though he had no fever. He had always been a friend to Sebituane; and, now that his son Sekeletu was in his place, Shinte was not merely a friend, but a father to him; and if a son asks a favor the father must give it. He was highly pleased with the large calabashes of clarified butter and fat which Sekeletu had sent him, and wished to detain Kolimbota, that he might send a present back to Sekeletu by his hands. This proposition we afterward discovered was Kolimbota's own, as he had heard so much about the ferocity of the tribes through which we were to pass that he wished to save his skin. It will be seen farther on that he was the only one of our party who returned with a wound.

An incident which occurred while we were here may be mentioned, as of a character totally unknown in the south. Two children, of seven and eight years old, went out to collect firewood a short distance from their parents' home, which was a quarter of a mile from the village, and were kidnapped; the distracted parents could not find a trace of them. This happened so close to the town, where there are no beasts of prey, that we suspect some of the high men of Shinte's court were the guilty parties: they can sell them by night. The Mambari erect large huts of a square shape to stow these stolen ones in; they are well fed, but aired by night only. The frequent kidnapping from outlying hamlets explains the stockades we saw around them: the parents have no redress, for even Shinte himself seems fond of working in the dark. One night he sent for me, though I always stated I liked all my dealings to be aboveboard. When I came, he presented me with a slave-girl about ten years old: he said he had always been in the habit of presenting his visitors with a child. On my thanking him, and saying that I thought it wrong to take away children from their parents, that I wished him to give up this system altogether and trade in cattle, ivory, and bees'-wax, he urged that she was "to be a child" to bring me water, and that a great man ought to have a child for the purpose, yet I had none. As I replied that I had four children, and should be very sorry if my chief were to take my little girl and give her away, and that I would prefer this child to remain and carry water for her own mother, he thought I was dissatisfied with her size, and sent for one a head taller. After many explanations of our abhorrence of slavery, and how displeasing it must be to God to see his children selling one another and giving each other so much grief as this child's mother must feel, I declined her also. If I could have taken her into my family for the purpose of instruction, and then returned her as a free woman, according to a promise I should have made to the parents, I might have done so; but to take her away, and probably never be able to secure her return, would have produced no good effect on the minds of the Balonda; they would not then have seen evidence of our hatred to slavery, and the kind attentions of my friends would, as it almost always does in similar cases, have turned the poor thing's head.

Shinte was most anxious to see the pictures of the magic lantern; but fever had so weakening an effect, and I had such violent action of the heart, with buzzing in the ears, that I could not go for several days; when I did go for the purpose he had his principal men and the same crowd of court beauties near him as at the reception. The first picture exhibited was Abraham about to slaughter his son Isaac: it was shown as large as life, and the uplifted knife was in the act of striking the lad; the Balonda men remarked that the picture was much more like a god than the things of wood and clay they worshipped. I explained that this man was the first of a race to whom God had given the Bible we now held, and that among his children our Savior appeared. The ladies listened with silent awe; but, when I moved the slide, the uplifted dagger moving toward them, they thought it was to be sheathed in their bodies instead of Isaac's. "Mother! mother!" all shouted at once, and off they rushed, helter-skelter, tumbling pell-

M

mell over each other, and over the little idol-huts and tobacco-bushes; we could not get one of them back again. Shinte, however, sat bravely through the whole, and afterward examined the instrument with interest. An explanation was always added after each time of showing its powers, so that no one should imagine there was aught supernatural in it; and had Mr. Murray, who kindly brought it from England, seen its popularity among both Makololo and Balonda, he would have been gratified with the direction his generosity then took. It was the only mode of instruction I was ever pressed to repeat. The people came long distances for the express purpose of seeing the objects and hearing the explanations.

One cannot get away quickly from these chiefs; they like to have the honor of strangers residing in their villages. Here we had an additional cause of delay in frequent rains: twenty-four hours never elapsed without heavy showers; every thing is affected by the dampness; surgical instruments become all rusty, clothing mildewed, and shoes mouldy; my little tent was now so rotten and so full of small holes that every smart shower caused a fine mist to descend on my blanket, and made me fain to cover the head with it. Heavy dews lay on every thing in the morning, even inside the tent; there is only a short time of sunshine in the afternoon, and even that is so interrupted by thunder-showers that we cannot dry our bedding.

The winds coming from the north always bring heavy clouds and rain; in the south, the only heavy rains noticed are those which come from the northeast or east. The thermometer falls as low as 72° when there is no sunshine, though, when the weather is fair, the protected thermometer generally rises as high as 82° even in the mornings and evenings.

24th.—We expected to have started to-day; but Sambanza, who had been sent off early in the morning for guides, returned at mid-day without them, and drunk. As far as we could collect from his incoherent sentences, Shinte had said the rain was too heavy for our departure, and the guides still required time for preparation. Shinte himself was busy getting some meal ready for my use in the journey. As it rained nearly all day, it was no sacrifice to submit to his advice and remain. Sambanza staggered to Manenko's hut: she, however, who had never promised "to love, honor, and obey him," had not been "nursing her wrath to keep it warm;" so she coolly bundled him into the hut, and put him to bed.

As the last proof of friendship, Shinte came into my tent, though it could scarcely contain more than one person, looked at all the curiosities, the quicksilver, the looking-glass, books, hair-brushes, comb, watch, &c. &c., with the greatest interest; then, closing the tent, so that none of his own people might see the extravagance of which he was about to be guilty, he drew out from his clothing a string of beads and the end of a conical shell, which is considered, in regions far from the sea, of as great value as the Lord Mayor's badge is in London. He hung it round my neck, and said, "There, now you *have* a proof of my friendship."

My men informed me that these shells are so highly valued in this quarter, as evidences of distinction, that for two of them a slave might be bought, and five would be considered a handsome price for an elephant's tusk worth ten pounds. At our last interview old Shinte pointed out our principal guide, Intemése, a man about fifty, who was, he said, ordered to remain by us till we should reach the sea; that I had now left Sekeletu far behind, and must henceforth look to Shinte alone for aid, and that it would always be most cheerfully rendered. This was only a polite way of expressing his wishes for my success. It was the good words only of the guides which were to aid me from the next chief, Katema, on to the sea; they were to turn back on reaching him; but he gave a good supply of food for the journey before us, and, after mentioning as a reason for letting us go even now that no one could say that we had been driven away from the town, since we had been several days with him, he gave a most hearty salutation, and we parted with the wish that God might bless him.

CHAPTER XVII.

DR. LIVINGSTONE PASSES THROUGH LONDA AND VISITS KATEMA.

26th.—LEAVING Shinte, with eight of his men to aid in carrying our luggage, we passed, in a northerly direction, down the lovely valley on which the town stands, then went a little to the west through pretty open forest, and slept at a village of Balonda. In the morning we had a fine range of green hills, called Saloisho, on our right, and were informed that they were rather thickly inhabited by the people of Shinte, who worked in iron, the ore of which abounds in these hills.

The country through which we passed possessed the same general character of flatness and forest that we noticed before The soil is dark with a tinge of red—in some places it might be called red—and appeared very fertile Every valley contained villages of twenty or thirty huts. with gardens of manioc, which here is looked upon as the staff of life. Very little labor is required for its cultivation The earth is drawn up into oblong beds, about three feet broad and one in height, and in these are planted pieces of the manioc-stalk, at four feet apart A crop of beans or groundnuts is sown between them, and when these are reaped the land around the manioc is cleared of weeds In from ten to eighteen months after planting, according to the quality of the soil, the roots are fit for food. There is no necessity for reaping soon, as the roots do not become bitter and dry until after three years. When a woman takes up the roots, she thrusts a piece or two of the upper stalks into the hole she has made, draws back the soil, and a new crop is thereby begun. The plant grows to a height of six feet, and every part of it is useful; the leaves may be cooked as a vegetable. The roots are from three to four inches in diameter, and from twelve to eighteen inches long.

There are two varieties of the manioc or cassava,—one sweet and wholesome, the other bitter and containing poison, but much more speedy in its growth than the former This last property causes its perpetuation.

Our chief guide, Intemese, sent orders to all the villages around our route that Shinte's friends must have abundance of provisions. Our progress was impeded by the time requisite for communicating the chief's desire and consequent preparation of meal. We received far more food from Shinte's people than from himself. Kapende, for instance, presented two large baskets of meal, three of manioc-roots steeped and dried in the sun and ready to be converted into flour, three fowls, and seven eggs, with three smoke-dried fishes; and others gave with similar liberality. I gave to the head-men small bunches of my stock of beads, with an apology that we were now on our way to the market for these goods. The present was always politely received.

After crossing the Lonaje, we came to some pretty villages. embowered, as the negro villages usually are, in bananas, shrubs, and manioc, and near the banks of the Leeb* we formed our encampment in a nest of serpents, one of which bit one of our men; but the wound was harmless. The people of the surrounding villages presented us with large quantities of food, in obedience to the mandate of Shinte, without expecting any equivalent One village had lately been transferred hither from the country of Matiamvo. They, of course, continue to acknowledge him as paramount chief; but the frequent instances which occur of people changing from one part of the country to another show that the great chiefs possess only a limited power. The only peculiarity we observed in these people is the habit of plaiting the beard into a threefold cord.

The town of the Balonda chief Cazembe was pointed out to us as lying to the N.E. and by E. from the town of Shinte, and great numbers of people in this quarter have gone thither for the purpose of purchasing copper anklets, made at Cazembe's, and report the distance to be about five days' journey.

It took us about four hours to cross the Leeba, which is considerably smaller here than where we left it,—indeed, only about a hundred yards wide. It has the same dark mossy hue. The villagers lent us canoes to effect our passage; and, having gone to a village about two miles beyond the river, I had the satisfaction of getting observations for both longitude and latitude,—for the former, the distance between Saturn and the moon, and for the latter, a meridian altitude of Canopus. Long. 22° 57' E., lat. 12° 6' 6" S.

Here we were surprised to hear English cotton cloth much more eagerly inquired after than beads and ornaments. They are more in need of clothing than the Bechuana tribes living adjacent to the Kalahari Desert, who have plenty of skins for the purpose. Animals of all kinds are rare here, and a very small piece of calico is of great value.

As the people on the banks of the Leeba were the last of Shinte's tribe over which Intemese had power, he was naturally anxious to remain as long as possible. He was not idle, but made a large wooden mortar and pestle for his wife during our journey. He also carved many wooden spoons and a bowl; then commenced a basket; but, as what he considered good living was any thing but agreeable to us, who had been accustomed to milk and maize, we went forward on the 2d without him. He soon followed, but left our pontoon, saying it would be brought by the head-man of the village. This was a great loss, as we afterward found: it remained at this village more than a year, and, when we returned, a mouse had eaten a hole in it.

We entered on an extensive plain beyond the Leeba, at least twenty miles broad, and covered with water ankle deep in the shallowest parts. We deviated somewhat from our N.W. course, by the direction of Intemese, and kept the hills Piri nearly on our right during a great part of the first day, in order to avoid the still more deeply-flooded plains of Lobale (Luval?) on the west. These, according to Intemese, are at present impassable on account of being thigh deep. The plains are so perfectly level that rain-water, which this was, stands upon them for months together They were not flooded by the Leeba, for that was still far within its banks. Here and there, dotted over the surface, are little islands, on which grow stunted date-bushes and scraggy trees.

We made our beds on one of the islands, and were wretchedly supplied with firewood. The booths constructed by the men were but sorry shelter, for the rain poured down without intermission till mid-day. There is no drainage for the prodigious masses of water on these plains, except slow percolation into the different feeders of the Leeba and into that river itself. The quantity of vegetation has prevented the country from becoming furrowed by many rivulets or "nullahs." Were it not so remarkably flat, the drainage must have been effected by torrents, even in spite of the matted vegetation.

When released from our island by the rain ceasing, we marched on till we came to a ridge of dry inhabited land in the N.W. The inhabitants, according to custom, lent us the roofs of some huts to save the men the trouble of booth-making. I suspect that the story in Park's "Travels," of the men lifting up the hut to place it on the lion, referred to the roof only. We leave them for the villagers to replace at their leisure. No payment is expected for the use of them. By night it rained so copiously that all our beds were flooded from below; and from this time forth we always made a furrow round each booth, and used the earth to raise our sleeping-places. My men turned out to work in the wet most willingly: indeed, they always did. I could not but contrast their conduct with that of Intemese. He was thoroughly imbued with the slave-spirit, and lied on all occasions without compunction. Untruthfulness is a sort of refuge for the weak and oppressed. We expected to move on the 4th, but he declared that we were so near Katema's, if we did not send forward to apprize that chief of our approach, he would certainly impose a fine. It rained the whole day, so we were reconciled to the delay; but on Sunday, the 5th, he let us know that we were still two days distant from Katema. We unfortunately could not manage without him, for the country was so deluged we should have been brought to a halt, before we went many miles, by some deep valley, every one of which was full of water. Intemese continued to plait his basket with all his might, and would not come to our religious service. He seemed to be afraid of our incantations, but was always merry and jocular.

6th.—Soon after starting, we crossed a branch of the Lokalueje by means of a canoe, and in the afternoon passed over the main stream by a like conveyance. The former, as is the case with all branches of rivers in this country, is called ñuana Kalueje, (child of the Kalueje.) Hippopotami exist in the Lokalueje, so it may be inferred to be perennial, as the inhabitants asserted. We cannot judge of the size of the stream from what we now saw. It had about forty yards of deep, fast-flowing water, but probably not more than half that amount in the dry season. Besides these, we crossed numerous feeders in our N.N.W. course, and, there being no canoes, got frequently wet in the course of the day. The oxen in some places had their heads only above water, and the stream, flowing over their backs, wetted our blankets, which we used as saddles. The armpit was the only safe spot for carrying the watch, for there it was preserved from rains above and waters below T men on foot crossed these gullies holding up their burdens at arms' length.

Great numbers of the omnivorous-feeding fish *Glanis siluris*, or mosala, spread themselves over the flooded plains, and, as the waters retire, try to find their way back again to the rivers. The Balonda make earthen dikes and hedges across the outlets of the retreating waters, leaving only small spaces through which the chief part of the water flows. In these open spaces they plant creels, similar in shape to our own, into which the fish can enter but cannot return. They secure large quantities of fish in this way, which, when smoke-dried, make a good relish for their otherwise-insipid food. They use also a weir of mats made of reeds sewed together, with but half an inch between each. Open spaces are left for the insertion of the creels as before.

In still water, a fish-trap is employed of the same shape and plan as the common round wire mouse-trap, which has an opening surrounded with wires pointing inward. This is made of reeds and supple wands, and food is placed inside to attract the fish.

Besides these means of catching fish, they use a hook of iron without a barb; the point is bent inward instead, so as not to allow the fish to escape. Nets are not so common as in the Zouga and Leeambye; but they kill large quantities of fishes by means of the bruised leaves of a shrub which may be seen planted beside every village in the country.

On the 7th we came to the village of Soána Molópo, a half-brother of Katema, a few miles beyond the Lokalueje. When we went to visit him, we found him sitting with about one hundred men. He called on Intemese to give some account of us, though no doubt it had been done in private before. He then pronounced the following sentences:—"The journey of the white man is very proper; but Shinte has disturbed us by showing the path to the Makololo who accompany him. He ought to have taken them through the country without showing them the towns. We are afraid of the Makololo." He then gave us a handsome present of food, and seemed perplexed by my sitting down familiarly and giving him a few of our ideas When we left, Intemese continued busily imparting an account of all we had given to Shinte and Masiko, and instilling the hope that Soana Molopo might obtain as much as they had received. Accordingly, when we expected to move on the morning of the 8th, we got some hints about the ox which Soana Molopo expected to eat; but we recommended him to get the breed of cattle for himself, seeing his country was so well adapted for rearing stock. Intemese also refused to move: he, moreover, tried to frighten us into parting with an ox by saying that Soana Molopo would send forward a message that we were a marauding-party; but we packed up and went on without him. We did not absolutely need him; but he was useful in preventing the inhabitants of secluded villages from betaking themselves to flight. We wished to be on good terms with all, and therefore put up with our guide's peccadilloes. His good word respecting us had considerable influence; and he was always asked if we had behaved ourselves like men on the way. The Makololo are viewed as great savages; but Intemese could not justly look with scorn on them, for he has the mark of a large gash on his arm, got in fighting; and he would never tell the cause of battle, but boasted of his powers, as the Makololo do, till asked about a scar on his back, betokening any thing but bravery.

Intemese was useful in cases like that of Monday, when we came upon a whole village in a forest enjoying their noonday nap. Our sudden appearance in their midst so terrified them that one woman nearly went into convulsions from fear. When they saw and heard Intemese, their terror subsided.

As usual, we were caught by rains after leaving Soana Molopo's, and made our booths at the house of Mozinkwa, a most intelligent and friendly man belonging to Katema. He had a fine large garden in cultivation, and well hedged round. He had made the walls of his compound, or court-yard, of branches of the banian, which, taking root, had grown to be a live hedge of that tree. Mozinkwa's wife had cotton growing all round her premises, and several plants used as relishes to the insipid porridge of the country. She cultivated also the common castor-oil plant, and a larger shrub (*Jatropha curcas*) which also yields a purgative oil. Here, however, the oil is used for anointing the heads and bodies alone. We saw in her garden likewise the Indian bringalls, yams, and sweet potatoes. Several trees were planted in the middle of the yard, and in the deep shade they gave stood the huts of his fine family. His children, all by one mother, very black, but comely to view, were the finest negro family I ever saw. We were much pleased with the frank friendship and liberality of this man and his wife. She asked me to bring her a cloth from the white man's country; but, when we returned, poor Mozinkwa's wife was in her grave, and he, as is the custom, had abandoned trees, garden, and huts to ruin. They cannot live on a spot where a favorite wife has died, probably because unable to bear the remembrance of the happy times they have spent there, or afraid to remain in a spot where death has once visited the establishment. If ever the place is revisited, it is to pray to her or make some offering. This feeling renders any permanent village in the country impossible.

We learned from Mozinkwa that Soana Molopo was the elder brother of Katema, but that he was wanting in wisdom; and Katema, by purchasing cattle and receiving in a kind manner all the fugitives who came to him, had secured the birthright to himself, so far as influence in the country is concerned. Soana's first address to us did not savor much of African wisdom.

Friday, 10th.—On leaving Mozinkwa's hospitable mansion, we crossed another stream, about forty yards wide, in canoes. While this tedious process was going on, I was informed that it is called the Mona-Kaluejo, or brother of Kaluoje, as it flows into that river; that both the Kaluoje and Livóa flow into the Leebe; and that the Chifumádze, swollen by the Lotembwa, is a feeder of that river also, below the point where we lately crossed it.

As we were crossing the river, we were joined by a messenger from Katema, called Shakatwála. This person was a sort of steward or factotum to his chief. Every chief has one attached to his person, and, though generally poor, they are invariably men of great shrewdness and ability. They act the part of messengers on all important occasions, and possess considerable authority in the chief's household. Shakatwala informed us that Katema had not received precise information about us, but if we were peaceably disposed, as he loved strangers, we were to come to his town. We proceeded forthwith, but were turned aside, by the strategy of our friend Intemese, to the village of Quendénde, the father-in-law of Katema. This fine old man was so very polite that we did not regret being obliged to spend Sunday at his village. He expressed his pleasure at having a share in the honor of a visit as well as Katema, though it seemed to me that the conferring that pleasure required something like a pretty good stock of impudence, in leading twenty-seven men through the country without the means of purchasing food. My men did a little business for themselves in the begging line: they generally commenced every interview with new villagers by saying, "1 have come from afar; give me something to eat." I forbade this at first, believing that, as the Makololo had a bad name, the villagers gave food from fear. But, after some time, it was evident that in many cases maize and manioc were given from pure generosity. The first time I came to this conclusion was at the house of Mozinkwa: scarcely any one of my men returned from it without something in his hand; and as they protested they had not begged, I asked himself, and found that it was the case, and that he had given spontaneously.

Quendende's head was a good specimen of the greater crop of wool with which the negroes of Londa are furnished. The front was parted in the middle, and plaited into two thick rolls, which, falling down behind the ears, reached the shoulders: the rest was collected into a large knot, which lay on the nape of the neck. As he was an intelligent man, we had much conversation together: he had just come from attending the funeral of one of his people, and I found that the great amount of drum-beating which takes place on these occasions was with the idea that the Barimo, or spirits, could be drummed to sleep. There is a drum in every village, and we often hear it going from sunset to sunrise. They seem to look upon the departed as vindictive beings, and, I suspect, are more influenced by fear than by love. In beginning to speak on religious subjects with those who have never heard of Christianity, the great fact of the Son of God having come down from heaven to die for us is the prominent theme. No fact more striking can be mentioned. "He actually came to men. He himself told us about his Father and the dwelling-place whither he has gone. We have his words in this book, and he really endured punishment in our stead from pure love," &c. If this fails to interest them, nothing else will succeed.

We here met with some people just arrived from the town of Matiamvo, (Muata yánvo,) who had been sent to announce the death of the late chieftain of that name. Matiamvo is the hereditary title, muáta meaning lord or chief. The late Matiamvo seems, from the report of these men, to have become insane, for he is said to have sometimes indulged the whim of running a muck in the town and beheading whomsoever he met, until he had quite a heap of human heads. Matiamvo explained this conduct by saying that his people were too many, and he wanted to diminish them. He had absolute power of life and death.

On inquiring whether human sacrifices were still made, as in the time of Pereira, at Cazembe's, we were informed that these had never been so common as was represented to Pereira, but that it occasionally happened, when certain charms were needed by the chief, that a man was slaughtered for the sake of some part of his body. He added that he hoped the present chief would not act like his (mad) predecessor, but kill only those who were guilty of witchcraft or theft. These men were very much astonished at the liberty enjoyed by the Makololo; and, when they found that all my people had cattle, we were told that Matiamvo alone had a herd. One very intelligent man among them asked, "If he should make a canoe, and take it down the river to the Makololo, would he get a cow for it?" This question, which my men answered in the affirmative, was important, as showing the knowledge of water-communication from the country of Matiamvo to the Makololo; and the river runs through a fertile country abounding in large timber. If the tribes have intercourse with each other, it exerts a good influence on their chiefs to hear what other tribes think of their deeds. The Makololo have such a bad name, on account of their perpetual forays, that they have not been known in Londa except as ruthless destroyers. The people in Matiamvo's country submit to much wrong from their chiefs, and no voice can be raised against cruelty, because they are afraid to flee elsewhere.

We left Quendende's village in company with Quendende himself, and the principal man of the ambassadors of Matiamvo, and, after two or three miles' march to the N.W., came to the ford of the Lotembwa, which flows southward. A canoe was waiting to ferry us over, but it was very tedious work; for, though the river itself was only eighty yards wide, the whole valley was flooded, and we were obliged to paddle more than half a mile to get free of the water. A fire was lit to warm old Quendende and enable him to dry his tobacco-leaves. The leaves are taken from the plant and spread close to the fire until they are quite dry and crisp; they are then put into a snuff-box, which, with a little pestle, serves the purpose of a mill to grind them into powder: it is then used as snuff. As we sat by the fire, the ambassadors communicated their thoughts freely respecting the customs of their race. When a chief dies, a number of servants are slaughtered with him to form his company in the other world. The Barotse followed the same custom; and this and other usages show them to be genuine negroes, though neither they nor the Balonda resemble closely the typical form of that people. Quendende said if he were present on these occasions he would aide his people, so that they might not be slaughtered. As we go north, the people become more bloodily superstitious.

We were assured that if the late Matiamvo took a fancy to any thing,—such, for instance, as my watch-chain, which was of silver wire, and was a great curiosity, as they had never seen metal plaited before,—he would order a whole village to be brought up to buy it from a stranger. When a slave-trader visited him, he took possession of all his goods; then, after ten days or a fortnight, he would send out a party of men to pounce upon some considerable village, and, having killed the head-men, would pay for all the goods by selling the inhabitants. This has frequently been the case, and nearly all the visitants he ever had were men of color. On asking if Matiamvo did not know he was a man, and would be judged, in company with those he destroyed, by a Lord who is no respecter of persons, the ambassador replied, "We do not go up to God, as you do: we are put into the ground." I could not ascertain that even those who have such a distinct perception of the continued existence of departed spirits had any notion of heaven: they appear to imagine the souls to be always near the place of sepulture.

After crossing the river Lotembwa, we travelled about eight miles, and came to Katema's straggling town, (lat

11° 35′ 49″ S., long. 22° 27′ E.) It is more a collection of villages than a town. We were led out about half a mile from the houses, that we might make for ourselves the best lodging we could of the trees and grass, while Intemese was taken to Katema to undergo the usual process of pumping as to our past conduct and professions. Katema soon afterward sent a handsome present of food.

Next morning we had a formal presentation, and found Katema seated on a sort of throne, with about three hundred men on the ground around, and thirty women, who were said to be his wives, close behind him. The main body of the people were seated in a semicircle, at a distance of fifty yards. Each party had its own head-man stationed at a little distance in front, and, when beckoned by the chief, came near him as councillors. Intemese gave our history, and Katema placed sixteen large baskets of meal before us, half a dozen fowls, and a dozen eggs, and expressed regret that we had slept hungry: he did not like any stranger to suffer want in his town; and added, "Go home and cook and eat, and you will then be in a fit state to speak to me at an audience I will give you to-morrow." He was busily engaged in hearing the statements of a large body of fine young men who had fled from Kangénke, chief of Lobale, on account of his selling their relatives to the native Portuguese who frequent his country. Katema is a tall man, about forty years of age, and his head was ornamented with a helmet of beads and feathers. He had on a snuff-brown coat, with a broad band of tinsel down the arms, and carried in his hand a large tail made of the caudal extremities of a number of gnus. This has charms attached to it, and he continued waving it in front of himself all the time we were there. He seemed in good spirits, laughing heartily several times. This is a good sign, for a man who shakes his sides with mirth is seldom difficult to deal with. When we rose to take leave, all rose with us, as at Shinte's.

Returning next morning, Katema addressed me thus:—

"I am the great Moene (lord) Katema, the fellow of Matiamvo. There is no one in the country equal to Matiamvo and me I have always lived here, and my forefathers too. There is the house in which my father lived. You found no human skulls near the place where you are encamped I never killed any of the traders: they all come to me. I am the great Moene Katema, of whom you have heard." He looked as if he had fallen asleep tipsy and dreamed of his greatness. On explaining my objects to him, he promptly pointed out three men who would be our guides, and explained that the northwest path was the most direct, and that by which all traders came, but that the water at present standing on the plains would reach up to the loins: he would therefore send us by a more northerly route, which no trader had yet traversed. This was more suited to our wishes, for we never found a path safe that had been trodden by slave-traders.

We presented a few articles which pleased him highly,— a small shawl, a razor, three bunches of beads, some buttons, and a powder-horn. Apologizing for the insignificance of the gift, I wished to know what I could bring him from Loanda, saying, not a large thing, but something small. He laughed heartily at the limitation, and replied, "Every thing of the white people would be acceptable, and he would receive any thing thankfully; but the coat he then had on was old, and he would like another." I introduced the subject of the Bible; but one of the old councillors broke in, told all he had picked up from the Mambari, and glided off into several other subjects. It is a misery to speak through an interpreter, as I was now forced to do. With a body of men like mine, composed as they were of six different tribes, and all speaking the language of the Bechuanas, there was no difficulty in communicating on common subjects with any tribe we came to; but doling out a story in which they felt no interest, and which I understood only sufficiently well to perceive that a mere abridgment was given, was uncommonly slow work. Neither could Katema's attention be arrested, except by compliments, of which they have always plenty to bestow as well as receive. We were strangers, and knew that, as Makololo, we had not the best of characters; yet his treatment of us was wonderfully good and liberal.

I complimented him on the possession of cattle, and pleased him by telling him how he might milk the cows. He has a herd of about thirty, really splendid animals, all reared from two which he brought from the Balobale when he was young. They are generally of a white color, and are quite wild, running off with graceful ease like a herd of elands on the approach of a stranger. They excited the unbounded admiration of the Makololo, and clearly proved that the country was well adapted for them. When Katema wishes to slaughter one, he is obliged to shoot it as if it were a buffalo. Matiamvo is said to possess a herd of cattle in a similar state. I never could feel certain as to the reason why they do not all possess cattle in a country containing such splendid pasturage.

As Katema did not offer an ox, as would have been done by a Makololo or Caffre chief, we slaughtered one of our own, and all of us were delighted to get a meal of meat, after subsisting so long on the light porridge and green maize of Londa. On occasions of slaughtering an animal, some pieces of it are in the fire before the skin is all removed from the body. A frying-pan full of these pieces having been got quickly ready, my men crowded about their father, and I handed some all round. It was a strange sight to the Balonda, who were looking on wondering. I offered portions to them too, but these were declined, though they are excessively fond of a little animal food to eat with their vegetable diet. They would not eat with us, but they would take the meat and cook it in their own way, and then use it. I thought at one time that they had imported something from the Mohammedans, and the more especially as an exclamation of surprise, "Allah!" sounds like the Illah of the Arabs; but we found, a little farther

Bechuana Reed-Dance by Moonlight.

on, another form of salutation, of Christian (?) origin, "Ave-rie," (Ave Marie.) The salutations probably travel farther than the faith. My people, when satisfied with a meal like that which they enjoy so often at home, amused themselves by an uproarious dance. Katema sent to ask what I had given them to produce so much excitement. Intemese replied it was their custom, and they meant no harm. The companion of the ox we slaughtered refused food for two days, and went lowing about for him continually. He seemed inconsolable for his loss, and tried again and again to escape back to the Makololo country. My men remarked, "He thinks, They will kill me as well as my friend." Katema thought it the result of art, and had fears of my skill in medicine, and, of course, witchcraft. He refused to see the magic lantern.

On Sunday, the 19th, both I and several of our party were seized with fever, and I could do nothing but toss about in my little tent, with the thermometer about 90°,—though this was the beginning of winter, and my men made as much shade as possible by planting branches of trees all round and over it. We have, for the first time in my experience in Africa, had a cold wind from the north. All the winds from that quarter are hot, and those from the south are cold; but they seldom blow from either direction.

20th.—We were glad to get away, though not on account of any scarcity of food; for my men, by giving small presents of meat as an earnest of their sincerity, formed many friendships with the people of Katema. We went about four or five miles in a N.N.W. direction, then two in a westerly one, and came round the small end of Lake Dilolo. It seemed, as far as we could at this time discern, to be like a river a quarter of a mile wide.

Immediately beyond Dilolo there is a large flat about twenty miles in breadth. Here Shakatwala insisted on our remaining to get supplies of food from Katema's subjects before entering the uninhabited watery plains.

Heavy rains prevented us from crossing the plain in ; ont (N.N.W.) in one day, and the constant wading among the grass hurt the feet of the men. There is a footpath all the way across, but, as this is worn down beneath the level of the rest of the plain, it is necessarily the deepest portion, and the men, avoiding it, make a new walk by its side. A path, however narrow, is a great convenience, as any one who has travelled on foot in Africa will admit. The virtual want of it here caused us to make slow and painful progress.

Ants surely are wiser than some men, for they learn by experience. They have established themselves even on these plains, where water stands so long annually as to allow the lotus, and other aqueous plants, to come to maturity. When all the ant-horizon is submerged a foot deep, they manage to exist by ascending to little houses built of black tenacious loam on stalks of grass and placed higher than the line of inundation. This must have been the result of experience; for, if they had waited till the water actually invaded their terrestrial habitations, they would not have been able to procure materials for their aerial quarters unless they dived down to the bottom for every mouthful of clay. Some of these upper chambers are about the size of a bean, and others as large as a man's thumb. They must have built in anticipation; and, if so, let us humbly hope that the sufferers by the late inundations in France may be possessed of as much common sense as the little black ants of the Dilolo plains.

CHAPTER XVIII.

DR. LIVINGSTONE ADVANCES TO THE NORTHWEST—VISITS KATENDE AND IONGA PANZA.

24th of February.—On reaching unflooded lands beyond the plain, we found the villages there acknowledged the authority of the chief named Katénde, and we discovered, also, to our surprise, that the almost level plain we had passed forms the watershed between the southern and northern rivers, for we had now entered a district in which the rivers flowed in a northerly direction into the Kasai or Loké, near to which we now were, while the rivers we had hitherto crossed were all running southward. Having met with kind treatment and aid at the first village, Katema's guides returned, and we were led to the N.N.W. by the inhabitants, and descended into the very first really-deep valley we had seen since leaving. Kolobeng. A stream ran along the bottom of a slope of three or four hundred yards from the plains above.

We crossed this by a rustic bridge at present submerged thigh deep by the rains. The trees growing along the stream of this lovely valley were thickly planted and very high. Many had sixty or eighty feet of clean straight trunk, and beautiful flowers adorned the ground beneath them. Ascending the opposite side, we came, in two hours' time, to another valley, equally beautiful, and with a stream also in its centre.

Reaching the village of Kabinje, in the evening he sent us a present of tobacco, Mutokuane or "bang," (*Cannabis sativa,*) and maize, by the man who went forward to announce our arrival, and a message expressing satisfaction at the prospect of having trade with the coast. The westing we were making brought us among people who are frequently visited by the Mambari as slave-dealers.

This trade causes bloodshed; for when a poor family is selected as the victims it is necessary to get rid of the older members of it, because they are supposed to be able to give annoyance to the chief afterward by means of enchantments. The belief in the power of charms for good or evil produces not only honesty, but a great amount of gentle dealing. The powerful are often restrained in their despotism from a fear that the weak and helpless may injure them by their medical knowledge.

When we wished to move on, Kabinje refused a guide to the next village, because he was at war with it; but, after much persuasion, he consented, provided that the guide should be allowed to return as soon as he came in sight of the enemy's village. This we felt to be a misfortune, as the people all suspect a man who comes telling his own tale; but, there being no help for it, we went on, and found the head-man of a village on the rivulet Kalómba, called Kangénke, a very different man from what his enemy represented. We found, too, that the idea of buying and selling took the place of giving for friendship. As I had nothing with which to purchase food except a parcel of beads, which were preserved for worse times, I began to fear that we should soon be compelled to suffer more from hunger than we had done. The people demanded gunpowder for every thing. If we had possessed any quantity of that article, we should have got on well, for here it is of great value. On our return, near this spot we found a good-sized fowl was sold for a single charge of gunpowder. Next to that, English calico was in great demand, and so were beads; but money was of no value whatever. Gold is quite unknown; it is thought to be brass: trade is carried on by barter alone. The people know nothing of money. A purse-proud person would here feel the ground move from beneath his feet. Occasionally a large piece of copper, in the shape of a St. Andrew's cross, is offered for sale.

February 27.—Kangenke promptly furnished guides

River Scenery on the West Coast.

this morning, so we went briskly on a short distance, and came to a part of the Kasye, Kasai, or Loke, where he had appointed two canoes to convey us across. This is a most beautiful river, and very much like the Clyde in Scotland. The slope of the valley down to the stream is about five hundred yards, and finely wooded. It is perhaps one hundred yards broad, and was winding slowly from side to side in the beautiful green glen, in a course to the north and northeast. In both the directions from which it came and to which it went it seemed to be alternately embowered in sylvan vegetation or rich meadows covered with tall grass. The men pointed out its course, and said " Though you sail along it for months, you will turn without seeing the end of it."

While at the ford of the Kasai we were subjected to a trick, of which we had been forewarned by the people of Shinte. A knife had been dropped by one of Kangenka's people, in order to entrap my men; it was put down near our encampment, as if lost, the owner in the mean time watching till one of my men picked it up. Nothing was said until our party was divided, one half on this and the other on that bank of the river. Then the charge was made to me that one of my men had stolen a knife. Certain of my people's honesty, I desired the man, who was making a great noise, to search the luggage for it; the unlucky lad who had taken the bait then came forward and confessed that he had the knife in a basket which was already taken over the river. When it was returned, the owner would not receive it back unless accompanied with a fine. The lad offered beads, but these were refused with scorn. A shell hanging round his neck, similar to that which Shinte had given me, was the object demanded, and the victim of the trick, as we all knew it to be, was obliged to part with his costly ornament. I could not save him from the loss, as all had been forewarned; and it is the universal custom among the Makololo and many other tribes to show whatever they may find to the chief person of their company, and make a sort of offer of it to him. This lad ought to have done so to me: the rest of the party always observed this custom. I felt annoyed at the imposition, but the order we invariably followed in crossing a river forced me to submit. The head of the party remained to be ferried over last; so, if I had not come to terms, I would have been, as I always was in crossing rivers which we could not swim, completely in the power of the enemy. It was but rarely we could get a head-man so witless as to cross a river with us and remain on the opposite bank in a convenient position to be seized as a hostage in case of my being caught.

This trick is but one of a number equally dishonorable which are practised by tribes that lie adjacent to the more civilized settlements. The Balonda farther east told us, by way of warning, that many parties of the more central tribes had at various periods set out, in order to trade with the white men themselves, instead of through the Mambari, but had always been obliged to return without reaching their destination, in consequence of so many pretexts being invented by the tribes encountered in the way for fining them of their ivory.

This ford was in 11° 15′ 47″ S. latitude, but the weather was so excessively cloudy we got no observation for longitude.

We were now in want of food; for, to the great surprise of my companions, the people of Kangenke gave nothing except by way of sale, and charged the most exorbitant prices for the little meal and manioc they brought. The only article of barter my men had was a little fat saved from the ox we slaughtered at Katema's; so I was obliged to give them a portion of the stock of beads. One day (29th) of westing brought us from the Kasai to near the village of Katende, and we saw that we were in a land where no hope could be entertained of getting supplies of animal food, for one of our guides caught a light-blue-colored mole and two mice for his supper. The care with which he wrapped them up in a leaf and slung them on his spear told that we could not hope to enjoy any larger game. We saw no evidence of any animals besides; and, on coming to the villages beyond this, we often saw boys and girls engaged in digging up these tiny quadrupeds.

Katende sent for me on the day following our arrival, and, being quite willing to visit him, I walked, for this purpose, about three miles from our encampment. When we approached the village we were desired to enter a hut, and, as it was raining at the time, we did so. After a long time spent in giving and receiving messages from the great man, we were told that he wanted either a man, a tusk, beads, copper rings, or a shell, as payment for leave to pass through his country. No one, we were assured, was allowed that liberty, or even to behold him, without something of the sort being presented. Having humbly explained our circumstances, and that he could not expect to "catch an humble cow by the horns,"—a proverb similar to ours that "you can't draw milk out of a stone,"—we were told to go home, and he would speak again to us next day. I could not avoid a hearty laugh at the cool impudence of the savage, and made the best of my way home in the still pouring rain. My men were rather nettled at this want of hospitality; but, after talking over the matter with one of Katende's servants, he proposed that some small article should be given, and an attempt made to please Katende. I turned out my shirts, and selected the worst one as a sop for him, and invited Katende to come and choose any thing else I had, but added that, when I should reach my own chief naked, and was asked what I had done with my clothes, I should be obliged to confess that I had left them with Katende. The shirt was despatched to him, and some of my people went along with the servant: they soon returned, saying that the shirt had been accepted, and guides and food too would be sent to us next day. The chief had, moreover, expressed a hope to see me on my return. He is reported to be very corpulent. The traders who have come here seem to have been very timid, yielding to every demand made on the most frivolous pretences. One of my men, seeing another much like an acquaintance at home, addressed him by the name of the latter in sport, telling him, at the same time, why he did so; this was pronounced to be a grave offence, and a large fine demanded: when the case came before me I could see no harm in what had been done, and told my people not to answer the young fellow. The latter felt himself disarmed, for it is chiefly in a brawl they have power; then words are spoken in anger which rouse the passions of the complainant's friends. In this case, after vociferating some time, the would-be offended party came and said to my man that, if they exchanged some small gift, all would be right, but, my man taking no notice of him, he went off rather crest-fallen.

My men were as much astonished as myself at the demand for payment for leave to pass, and the almost entire neglect of the rules of hospitality. Katende gave us only a little meal and manioc, and a fowl. Being detained two days by heavy rains, we felt that a good stock of patience was necessary in travelling through this country in the rainy season.

Passing onward without seeing Katende, we crossed a small rivulet, the Sengko, by which we had encamped, and after two hours came to another, the Totélo, which was somewhat larger and had a bridge over it. At the farther end of this structure stood a negro, who demanded fees. He said the bridge was his, the path his; the guides were his children; and if we did not pay him he would prevent farther progress. This piece of civilization I was not prepared to meet, and stood a few seconds looking at our bold toll-keeper, when one of my men took off three copper bracelets, which paid for the whole party. The negro was a better man than he at first seemed, for he immediately went to his garden and brought us some leaves of tobacco as a present.

When we got fairly away from the villages, the guides from Kangenke sat down and told us that there were we paths in front, and if we did not at once present them with a cloth they would leave us to take whichever we might like best. As I had pointed out the direction in which Loanda lay, and had only employed them for the sake of knowing the paths between villages which lay along our route, and always objected when they led us in any other than the Loanda direction, I wished my men now to go on without the guides, trusting to ourselves to choose the path which would seem to lead us in the direction we had always followed. But Mashauana, fearing lest we might wander, asked leave to give his own cloth, and when the guides saw that they came forward, shouting, "Averié! Averié!"

In the afternoon of this day we came to a valley about a mile wide, filled with clear, fast-flowing water. The men on foot were chin deep in crossing, and we three on ox-back got wet to the middle, the weight of the animals preventing them from swimming. A thunder-shower descending completed the partial drenching of the plain, and gave a cold, uncomfortable "packing in a wet blanket" that night. Next day we found another flooded valley about half a mile wide, with a small and now deep rivulet in its middle, flowing rapidly to the S.S.E., or toward the Kasai. The middle part of this flood, being the bed of what at other times is the rivulet, was so rapid that we crossed by holding on to the oxen, and the current soon dashed them to the opposite bank: we then jumped off, and, the oxen being relieved of their burdens, we could pull them on to the shallower part. The rest of the valley was thigh deep and boggy, but, holding on by the belt which fastened the blanket to the ox, we each floundered through the nasty slough as well as we could.

In the afternoon we came to another stream, ñuana Loke, (or child of Loke,) with a bridge over it. The men had to swim off to each end of the bridge, and when on it were breast deep: some preferred holding on by the tails of the oxen the whole way across. I intended to do this too;

but, riding to the deep part, before I could dismount and seize the helm the ox dashed off with his companions, and his body sank so deep that I failed in my attempt even to catch the blanket-belt, and if I pulled the bridle the ox seemed as if he would come backward upon me; so I struck out for the opposite bank alone. My poor fellows were dreadfully alarmed when they saw me parted from the cattle, and about twenty of them made a simultaneous rush into the water for my rescue, and just as I reached the opposite bank one seized my arm, and another threw his around my body. When I stood up it was most gratifying to see them all struggling toward me. Some had leaped off the bridge and allowed their cloaks to float down the stream. Part of my goods, abandoned in the hurry, were brought up from the bottom after I was safe. Great was the pleasure expressed when they found that I could swim like themselves, without the aid of a tail, and I did and do feel grateful to these poor heathens for the promptitude with which they dashed in to save, as they thought, my life. I found my clothes cumbersome in the water: they could swim quicker from being naked. They swim like dogs, not frog-fashion as we do.

In the evening we crossed the small rivulet Lozéze, and came to some villages of the Kasábi, from whom we got some manioc in exchange for beads. They tried to frighten us by telling of the deep rivers we should have to cross in our way. I was drying my clothes by turning myself round and round before the fire. My men laughed at the idea of being frightened by rivers. "We can all swim: who carried the white man across the river but himself?" I felt proud of their praise.

Saturday, 4th March.—Came to the outskirts of the territory of the Chiboque. We crossed the Kondo and Kalúze rivulets. The former is a deep, small stream with a bridge, the latter insignificant; the valleys in which these rivulets run are beautifully fertile. My companions are continually lamenting over the uncultivated vales in such words as these:—"What a fine country for cattle! My heart is sore to see such fruitful valleys for corn lying waste."

While at the villages of the Kasabi we saw no evidences of want of food among the people. Our beads were very valuable, but cotton cloth would have been still more so; as we travelled along, men, women, and children came running after us, with meal and fowls for sale, which we would gladly have purchased had we possessed any English manufactures. When they heard that we had no cloth, they turned back much disappointed.

The amount of population in the central parts of the country may be called large only as compared with the Cape Colony or the Bechuana country. The cultivated land is as nothing compared with what might be brought under the plough. There are flowing streams in abundance, which, were it necessary, could be turned to the purpose of irrigation with but little labor. Miles of fruitful country are now lying absolutely waste, for there is not even game to eat off the fine pasturage, and to recline under the evergreen, shady groves which we are ever passing in our progress. The people who inhabit the central region are not all quite black in color. Many incline to that of bronze, and others are as light in hue as the Bushmen, who, it may be remembered, afford a proof that heat alone does not cause blackness, but that heat and moisture combined do very materially deepen the color.

Having, on the aforementioned date, reached the village of Njambi, one of the chiefs of the Chiboque, we intended to pass a quiet Sunday; and, our provisions being quite spent, I ordered a tired riding-ox to be slaughtered. As we wished to be on good terms with all, we sent the hump and ribs to Njambi, with the explanation that this was the customary tribute to chiefs in the part from which we had come, and that we always honored men in his position. He returned thanks, and promised to send food. Next morning he sent an impudent message, with a very small present of meal; scorning the meat he had accepted, he demanded either a man, an ox, a gun, powder, cloth, or a shell; and, in the event of refusal to comply with his demand, he intimated his intention to prevent our farther progress. We replied, we should have thought ourselves fools if we had scorned his small present and demanded other food instead; and, even supposing we had possessed the articles named, no black man ought to impose a tribute on a party that did not trade in slaves. The servants who brought the message said that, when sent to the Mambari, they had always got a quantity of cloth from them for their master, and now expected the same, or something else as an equivalent, from me.

We heard some of the Chiboque remark, "They have only five guns;" and about mid-day Njambi collected all his people and surrounded our encampment. Their object was evidently to plunder us of every thing. My men seized their javelins, and stood on the defensive, while the young Chiboque had drawn their swords and brandished them with great fury. Some even pointed their guns at me, and nodded to each other, as much as to say, "This is the way we shall do with him." I sat on my camp-stool, with my double-barrelled gun across my knees, and invited the chief to be seated also. When he and his counsellors had sat down on the ground in front of me, I asked what crime we had committed that he had come armed in that way. He replied that one of my men, Pitsane, while sitting at the fire that morning, had, in spitting, allowed a small quantity of the saliva to fall on the leg of one of his men, and this "guilt" he wanted to be settled by the fine of a man, ox, or gun. Pitsane admitted the fact of a little saliva having fallen on the Chiboque, and, in proof of its being a pure accident, mentioned that he had given the man a piece of meat, by way of making friends, just before it happened, and wiped it off with his hand as soon as it fell. In reference to a man being given, I declared that we were all ready to die rather than give up one of our num-

but to be a slave; that my men might as well give me as I give one of them, for we were all free men. "Then you can give the gun with which the ox was shot." As we heard some of his people remarking even now that we had only "five guns," we declined, on the ground that, as they were intent on plundering us, giving a gun would be helping them to do so.

This they denied, saying they wanted the customary tribute only. I asked what right they had to demand payment for leave to tread on the ground of God, our common Father. If we trod on their gardens, we would pay, but not for marching on land which was still God's, and not theirs. They did not attempt to controvert this, because it is in accordance with their own ideas, but reverted again to the pretended crime of the saliva.

My men now entreated me to give something; and, after asking the chief if he really thought the affair of the spitting a matter of guilt, and receiving an answer in the affirmative, I gave him one of my shirts. The young Chiboque were dissatisfied, and began shouting and brandishing their swords for a greater fine.

As Pitsane felt that he had been the cause of this disagreeable affair, he asked me to add something else. I gave a bunch of beads, but the counsellors objected this time; so I added a large handkerchief. The more I yielded, the more unreasonable their demands became, and at every fresh demand a shout was raised by the armed party, and a rush made around us with brandishing of arms. One young man made a charge at my head from behind; but I quickly brought round the muzzle of my gun to his mouth, and he retreated. I pointed him out to the chief, and he ordered him to retire a little. I felt anxious to avoid the effusion of blood; and though sure of being able, with my Makololo, who had been drilled by Sebituane, to drive off twice the number of our assailants, though now a large body and well armed with spears, swords, arrows, and guns, I strove to avoid actual collision. My men were quite unprepared for this exhibition, but behaved with admirable coolness. The chief and counsellors, by accepting my invitation to be seated, had placed themselves in a trap, for my men very quietly surrounded them, and made them feel that there was no chance of escaping their spears. I then said that, as one thing after another had failed to satisfy them, it was evident that *they* wanted to fight, while *we* only wanted to, pass peaceably through the country; that they must begin first, and bear the guilt before God: we would not fight till they had struck the first blow. I then sat silent for some time. It was rather trying for me, because I knew that the Chiboque would aim at the white man first; but I was careful not to appear flurried, and, having four barrels ready for instant action, looked quietly at the savage scene around. The Chiboque countenance, by no means handsome, is not improved by the practice which they have adopted of filing the teeth to a point. The chief and counsellors, seeing that they were in more danger than I, did not choose to follow our decision that they should begin by striking the first blow and then see what we could do, and were perhaps influenced by seeing the air of cool preparation which some of my men displayed at the prospect of a work of blood.

The Chiboque at last put the matter before us in this way:—" You come among us in a new way, and say you are quite friendly: how can we know it unless you give us some of your food, and you take some of ours? If you give us an ox, we will give you whatever you may wish, and then we shall be friends." In accordance with the entreaties of my men, I gave an ox, and, when asked what I should like in return, mentioned food as the thing which we most needed. In the evening, Njambi sent us a very small basket of meal, and two or three pounds of the flesh of our own ox! with the apology that he had no fowls, and very little of any other food. It was impossible to avoid a laugh at the coolness of the generous creatures. I was truly thankful, nevertheless, that, though resolved to lie rather than deliver up one of our number to be a slave, we had so far gained our point as to be allowed to pass on without having shed human blood.

In the midst of the commotion, several Chiboque stole pieces of meat out of the sheds of my people, and Mohorisi, one of the Makololo, went boldly into the crowd and took back a marrow-bone from one of them. A few of my Batoka seemed afraid, and would perhaps have fled had the affray actually begun, but, upon the whole, I thought my men behaved admirably. They lamented having left their shields at home by command of Sekeletu, who feared that, if they carried these, they might be more disposed to be overbearing in their demeanor to the tribes we should meet. We had proceeded on the principles of peace and conciliation, and the foregoing treatment shows in what light our conduct was viewed: in fact, we were taken for interlopers trying to cheat the revenue of the tribe. They had been accustomed to get a slave or two from every slave-trader who passed them, and, now that we disputed the right, they viewed the infringement on what they considered lawfully due with most virtuous indignation.

March 6.—We were informed that the people on the west of the Chiboque of Njambi were familiar with the visits of slave-traders; and it was the opinion of our guides from Kangenke that so many of my companions would be demanded from me, in the same manner as the people of Njambi had done, that I should reach the coast without a single attendant. I therefore resolved to alter our course and strike away to the N.N.E., in the hope that at some point farther north I might find an exit to the Portuguese settlement of Cassange. We proceeded at first due north, with the Kasabi villages on our right and the Kasau on our left. During the first twenty miles we crossed many small, but now swollen, streams, having the usual boggy banks; and wherever the water had stood for any length of time it was discolored with rust of iron.

On the 8th, one of the men had left an ounce or two of

powder at our sleeping-place, and went back several miles for it. My clothing being wet from crossing a stream, I was compelled to wait for him: had I been moving in the sun I should have felt no harm; but the inaction led to a violent fit of fever. The continuance of this attack was a source of much regret; for we went on next day to a small rivulet called Chihuné, in a lovely valley, and had, for a wonder, a clear sky and a clear moon; but such was the confusion produced in my mind by the state of my body, that I could scarcely manage, after some hours' trial, to get a lunar observation in which I could repose confidence. The Chihune flows into the Longe, and that into the Chihómbo, a feeder of the Kasai. Those who know the difficulties of taking altitudes, times, and distances, and committing all of them to paper, will sympathize with me in this and many similar instances While at Chihune, the men of a village brought wax for sale, and, on finding that we wished honey, went off and soon brought a hive. All the bees in the country are in possession of the natives; for they place hives sufficient for them all. After having ascertained this, we never attended the call of the honey-guide, for we were sure it would only lead us to a hive which we had no right to touch. The bird continues its habit of inviting attention to the honey, though its services in this district are never actually needed. My Makololo lamented that they never knew before that wax could be sold for any thing of value.

In passing through these narrow paths I had an opportunity of observing the peculiarities of my ox "Sinbad." He had a softer back than the others, but a much more intractable temper. His horns were bent downward and hung loosely, so he could do no harm with them; but, as we wended our way slowly along the narrow path, he would suddenly dart aside. A string tied to a stick put through the cartilage of the nose serves instead of a bridle: if you jerk this back, it makes him run faster on; if you pull it to one side, he allows the nose and head to go, but keeps the opposite eye directed to the forbidden spot and goes in spite of you. The only way he can be brought to a stand is by a stroke with a wand across the nose. When Sinbad ran in below a climber stretched over the path so low that I could not stoop under it, I was dragged off and came down on the crown of my head; and he never allowed an opportunity of the kind to pass without trying to inflict a kick, as if I neither had nor deserved his love.

On leaving the Chihune, we crossed the Longe, and, as the day was cloudy, our guides wandered in a forest away to the west till we came to the river Chihombo, flowing to the E.N.E. My men depended so much on the sun for guidance, that, having seen nothing of the luminary all day, they thought we had wandered back to the Chiboque; and, as often happens when bewildered, they disputed as to the point where the sun should r ͵e next morning. As soon as the rains would allow next day, we went off to the N.E. It would have been better to have travelled by compass alone; for the guides took advantage of any fears expressed by my people, and threatened to return if presents were not made at once. But my men had never left their own country before except for rapine and murder. When they formerly came to a village, they were in the habit of killing numbers of the inhabitants and then taking a few young men to serve as guides to the next place. As this was their first attempt at an opposite line of conduct, and as they were without their shields, they felt defenceless among the greedy Chiboque, and some allowance must be made for them on that account.

Saturday, 11*th.*—Reached a small village on the banks of a narrow stream. I was too ill to go out of my little covering except to quell a mutiny which began to show itself among some of the Batoka and Ambonda of our party. They grumbled, as they often do against their chiefs when they think them partial in their gifts, because they supposed that I had shown a preference in the distribution of the beads; but the beads I had given to my principal, men were only sufficient to purchase a scanty meal, and I had hastened on to this village in order to slaughter a tired ox and give them all a feast as well as a rest on Sunday, as preparation for the journey before us. I explained this to them, and thought their grumbling was allayed. I soon sank into a state of stupor, which the fever sometimes produced, and was oblivious to all their noise in slaughtering. On Sunday the mutineers were making a terrible din in preparing a skin they had procured. I requested them twice, by the man who attended me, to be more quiet, as the noise pained me; but, as they paid no attention to this civil request, I put out my head, and, repeating it myself, was answered by an impudent laugh. Knowing that discipline would be at an end if this mutiny were not quelled, and that our lives depended on vigorously upholding authority, I seized a double-barrelled pistol and darted forth from the domicile, looking, I suppose, so savage as to put them to a precipitate flight. As some remained within hearing, I told them that I must maintain discipline, though at the expense of some of their limbs; so long as we travelled together they must remember that I was master, and not they. There being but little room to doubt my determination, they immediately became very obedient, and never afterward gave me any trouble or imagined that they had any right to my property.

13th.—We went forward some miles, but were brought to a stand by the severity of my fever on the banks of a branch of the Loajima, another tributary of the Kasai. I was in a state of partial coma until late at night, when it became necessary for me to go out; and I was surprised to find that my men had built a little stockade, and some of them took their spears and acted as a guard. I found that we were surrounded by enemies, and a party of Chiboquo lay near the gateway, after having preferred the demand of "a man, an ox, a gun, or a tusk." My men had prepared for defence in case of a night-attack, and, when the Chiboque wished to be shown where I lay sick, the very properly refused to point me out. In the morning went out to the Chiboque, and found that they answered me civilly regarding my intentions in opening the country, teaching them, &c. &c. They admitted that their chief would be pleased with the prospect of friendship, and not only wished to exchange tokens of good-will with me, and offered three pigs, which they hoped I would accept. The people here are in the habit of making a present and then demanding whatever they choose in return. We had been forewarned of this by our guides; so I tried to decline, by asking if they would eat one of the pigs in company with us. To this proposition they said that they durst not accede. I then accepted the present, in hope that the blame of deficient friendly feeling might not rest with me, and presented a razor, two bunches of beads, and twelve copper rings, contributed by my men from their arms. They went off to report to their chief; and, as I was quite unable to move from excessive giddiness, we continued in the same spot on Tuesday evening, when they returned with a message couched in very plain terms, that a man, tusk, gun, or even an ox, alone would be acceptable; that he had every thing else in his possession but oxen, and that, whatever I should please to demand from him, he would gladly give it. As this was all said civilly, and there was no help for it if we refused but bloodshed, I gave a tired riding-ox. My late chief mutineer, an Ambonda man, was now overloyal, for he armed himself and stood at the gateway. He would rather die than see his father imposed on; but I ordered Mosantu to take him out of the way, which he did promptly, and allowed the Chiboque to march off well pleased with their booty. I told my men that I esteemed one of their lives of more value than all the oxen we had, and that the only cause which could induce me to fight would be to save the lives and liberties of the majority. In the propriety of this they all agreed, and said that, if the Chiboque molested us who behaved so peaceably, the guilt would be on their heads This is a favourite mode of expression throughout the whole country. All are anxious to give explanation of any acts they have performed, and conclude the narration with, "I have no guilt or blame," ("molatu.") "They have the guilt." I never could be positive whether the idea in their minds is guilt in the sight of the Deity, or of mankind only.

Next morning the robber-party came with about thirty yards of strong striped English calico, an axe, and two hoes for our acceptance, and returned the copper rings, as the chief was a great man and did not need the ornaments of my men, but we noticed that they were taken back again. I divided the cloth among my men, and pleased them a little by thus compensating for the loss of the ox. I advised the chief, whose name we did not learn, as he did not deign to appear except under the *alias* Matiamvo, to get cattle for his own use, and expressed sorrow that I had none wherewith to enable him to make a commencement. Rains prevented our proceeding till Thursday morning, and then messengers appeared to tell us that their chief had learned that all the cloth sent by him had not been presented; that the copper rings had been secreted by the persons ordered to restore them to us, and that he had stripped the thievish emissaries of their property as a punishment. Our guides thought these were only spies of a larger party concealed in the forest through which we were now about to pass. We prepared for defence by marching in a compact body and allowing no one to straggle far behind the others. We marched through many miles of gloomy forest in gloomier silence, but nothing disturbed us. We came to a village, and found all the men absent,—the guides thought, in the forest, with their countrymen. I was too ill to care much whether we were attacked or not. Though a pouring rain came on, as we were all anxious to get away out of a bad neighborhood, we proceeded. The thick atmosphere prevented my seeing the creeping plants in time to avoid them; so

Pitsane, Mohorisi, and I, who alone were mounted, were often caught; and, as there is no stopping the oxen when they have the prospect of giving the rider a tumble, we came frequently to the ground. In addition to these mishaps, Sinbad went off at a plunging gallop, the bridle broke, and I came down backward on the crown of my head. He gave me a kick on the thigh at the same time. I felt none the worse for this rough treatment, but would not recommend it to others as a palliative in cases of fever. This last attack of fever was so obstinate that it reduced me almost to a skeleton. The blanket which I used as a saddle on the back of the ox, being frequently wet, remained so beneath me even in the hot sun, and, aided by the heat of the ox, caused extensive abrasion of the skin, which was continually healing and getting sore again. To this inconvenience was now added the chafing of my projecting bones on the hard bed.

On Friday we came to a village of civil people on the banks of the Loajima itself, and we were wet all day in consequence of crossing it. The bridges over it, and another stream which we crossed at mid-day, were submerged, as we have hitherto invariably found, by a flood of perfectly-clear water. At the second ford we were met by a hostile party, who refused us farther passage. I ordered my men to proceed in the same direction we had been pursuing, but our enemies spread themselves out in front of us with loud cries. Our numbers were about equal to theirs this time, so I moved on at the head of my men. Some ran off to other villages, or back to their own village, on pretence of getting ammunition; others called out that all traders came to them, and that we must do the same. As these people had plenty of iron-headed arrows and some guns, when we came to the edge of the forest I ordered my men to put the luggage in our centre, and, if our enemies did not fire, to cut down some young trees and make a screen as quickly as possible, but do nothing to them except in case of actual attack. I then dismounted, and, advancing a little toward our principal opponent, showed him how easily I could kill him, but pointed upward, saying, "I fear God." He did the same, placing his hand on his heart, pointing upward, and saying, "I fear to kill; but come to our village; come: do come." At this juncture, the old head-man, Ionga Panza, a venerable negro, came up, and I invited him and all to be seated, that we might talk the matter over. Ionga Panza soon let us know that he thought himself very ill treated in being passed by. As most skirmishes arise from misunderstanding, this might have been a serious one; for, like all the tribes near the Portuguese settlements, people here imagine that they have a right to demand payment from every one who passes through the country; and now, though Ionga Panza was certainly no match for my men, yet they were determined not to forego their right without a struggle. I removed with my men to the vicinity of the village, thankful that no accident had as yet brought us into actual collision.

The reason why the people have imbibed the idea so strongly that they have a right to demand payment for leave to pass through the country is probably this. They have seen no traders except those either engaged in purchasing slaves or who have slaves in their employment. These slave-traders have always been very much at the mercy of the chiefs through whose country they have passed; for, if they afforded a ready asylum for runaway slaves, the traders might be deserted at any moment, and stripped of their property altogether. They are thus obliged to curry favor with the chiefs, so as to get a safe-conduct from them. The same system is adopted to induce the chiefs to part with their people, whom all feel to be the real source of their importance in the country. On the return of the traders from the interior with chains of slaves, it is so easy for a chief who may be so disposed to take away a chain of eight or ten unresisting slaves, that the merchant is fain to give any amount of presents in order to secure the good-will of the rulers. The independent chiefs, not knowing why their favor is so eagerly sought, become excessively proud and supercilious in their demands, and look upon white men with the greatest contempt. To such lengths did the Bangála, a tribe near to which we had now approached, proceed a few years ago, that they compelled the Portuguese traders to pay for water, wood, and even grass, and every possible pretext was invented for levying fines; and these were patiently submitted to so long as the slave-trade continued to flourish. We had unconsciously come in contact with a system which was quite unknown in the country from which my men had set out. An English trader may there hear a demand for payment of guides, but never, so far as I am aware, is he asked to pay for leave to traverse a country. The idea does not seem to have entered the native mind, except through slave-traders; for the aborigines all acknowledge that the untilled land, not needed for pasturage, belongs to God alone, and that no harm is done by people passing through it. I rather believe that, wherever the slave-trade has not penetrated, the visits of strangers are esteemed a real privilege

The village of old Ionga Panza (lat. 10° 25′ S., long. 20° 15′ E.) is small, and embowered in lofty evergreen trees, which were hung around with fine festoons of creepers. He sent us food immediately, and soon afterward a goat, which was considered a handsome gift, there being but few domestic animals, though the country is well adapted for them. I suspect this, like the country of Shinte and Katema, must have been a tsetse district, and only recently rendered capable of supporting other domestic animals besides the goat by the destruction of the game through the extensive introduction of fire-arms. We might all have been as ignorant of the existence of this insect-plague as the Portuguese, had it not been for the numerous migrations of pastoral tribes which took place in the south in consequence of Zulu irruptions.

During these exciting scenes I always forgot my fever;

but a terrible sense of sinking came back with the feeling of safety. The same demand of payment for leave to pass was made on the 20th by old Ionga Panza as by the other Chiboque. I offered the shell presented by Shinte, but Ionga Panza said he was too old for ornaments. We might have succeeded very well with him, for he was by no means unreasonable, and had but a very small village of supporters; but our two guides from Kangenke complicated our difficulties by sending for a body of Bangala traders, with a view to force us to sell the tusks of Sekeletu and pay them with the price. We offered to pay them handsomely if they would perform their promise of guiding us to Cassange, but they knew no more of the paths than we did; and my men had paid them repeatedly and tried to get rid of them, but could not. They now joined with our enemies, and so did the traders. Two guns and some beads belonging to the latter were standing in our encampment, and the guides seized them and ran off. As my men knew that we should be called upon to replace them, they gave chase, and when the guides saw that they would be caught they threw down the guns, directed their flight to the village, and rushed into a hut. The doorway is not much higher than that of a dog's kennel. One of the guides was reached by one of my men as he was in the act of stooping to get in, and a cut was inflicted on a projecting part of the body which would have made any one in that posture wince. The guns were restored, but the beads were lost in the flight. All I had remaining of my stock of beads could not replace those lost; and, though we explained that we had no part in the guilt of the act, the traders replied that we had brought the thieves into the country; these were of the Bangala, who had been accustomed to plague the Portuguese in the most vexatious way. We were striving to get a passage through the country, and, feeling anxious that no crime whatever should be laid to our charge, tried the concilia tory plan here, though we were not, as in the other instances, likely to be overpowered by numbers.

My men offered all their ornaments, and I offered all my beads and shirts; but, though we had come to the village against our will, and the guides had also followed us contrary to our desire, and had even sent for the Bangala traders without our knowledge or consent, yet matters could not be arranged without our giving an ox and one of the tusks. We were all becoming disheartened, and could not wonder that native expeditions from the interior to the coast had generally failed to reach their destinations. My people were now so much discouraged that some proposed to return home: the prospect of being obliged to return when just on the threshold of the Portuguese settlements distressed me exceedingly. After using all my powers of persuasion, I declared to them that if they returned I would go on alone, and went into my little tent with the mind directed to Him who hears the sighing of the soul, and was soon followed by the head of Mohorisi, saying, "We will never leave you. Do not be disheartened. Wherever you lead we will follow. Our remarks were made only on account of the injustice of these people." Others followed, and with the most artless simplicity of manner told me to be comforted: "they were all my children; they knew no one but Sekeletu and me, and they would die for me; they had not fought, because I did not wish it; they had just spoken in the bitterness of their spirit, and when feeling that they could do nothing; but if these enemies begin you will see what we can do." One of the oxen we offered to the Chiboque had been rejected because he had lost part of his tail, as they thought that it had been cut off and witchcraft-medicine inserted; and some mirth was excited by my proposing to raise a similar objection to all the oxen we still had in our possession. The remaining four soon presented a singular shortness of their caudal extremities, and, though no one ever asked whether they had medicine in the stumps or no, we were no more troubled by the demand for an ox! We now slaughtered another ox, that the spectacle might not be seen of the owners of the cattle fasting while the Chiboque were feasting.

CHAPTER XIX.

DR. LIVINGSTONE REACHES THE WEST COAST OF AFRICA.

24th.—IONGA PANZA's sons agreed to act as guides into the territory of the Portuguese if I would give them the shell given by Shinte. I was strongly averse to this, and especially to give it beforehand, but yielded to the entreaty of my people to appear as if showing confidence in these hopeful youths. They urged that they wished to leave the shell with their wives as a sort of payment to them for enduring their husbands' absence so long. Having delivered the precious shell, we went west-by-north to the river Chikápa, which here (lat. 10° 22′ S.) is forty or fifty yards wide, and at present was deep; it was seen flowing over a rocky, broken cataract with great noise about half a mile above our ford. We were ferried over in a canoe made out of a single piece of bark sewed together at the ends, and having sticks placed in it at different parts to act as ribs.

Next morning our guides went only about a mile, and then told us they would return home. I expected this when paying them beforehand, in accordance with the entreaties of the Makololo, who are rather ignorant of the world. Very energetic remonstrances were addressed to the guides, but they slipped off one by one in the thick forest through which we were passing, and I was glad to hear my companions coming to the conclusion that, as we were now in parts visited by traders, we did not require the guides, whose chief use had been to prevent misapprehension of our objects in the minds of the villagers.

26th.—We spent Sunday on the banks of the Quilo or Kweelo, here a stream of about ten yards wide. It runs in a deep glen, the sides of which are almost five hundred yards of slope, and rocky, the rocks being hardened calcareous tufa lying on clay shale and sandstone below, with a capping of ferruginous conglomerate The scenery would have been very pleasing, but fever took away much of the joy of life, and severe daily intermittents rendered me very weak and always glad to recline.

In continuing our W.N.W. course, we met many parties of native traders, each carrying some pieces of cloth and salt, with a few beads to barter for bees'-wax. They are all armed with Portuguese guns, and have cartridges with iron balls. When we meet, we usually stand a few minutes They present a little salt, and we give a bit of ox-hide, or some other trifle, and then part with mutual good wishes. The hide of the oxen we slaughtered had been a valuable addition to our resources, for we found it in so great repute for girdles all through Loanda that we cut up every skin into strips about two inches broad, and sold them for meal and manioc as we went along. As we came nearer Angola we found them of less value, as the people there possess cattle themselves.

The village on the Kweelo, at which we spent Sunday, was that of a civil, lively old man, called Sakandála, who offered no objections to our progress. We found we should soon enter on the territory of the Bashinjé, (Chinge of the Portuguese,) who are mixed with another tribe, named Bangala, which have been at war with the Babindéle or Portuguese. Rains and fever, as usual, helped to impede our progress until we were put on the path which leads from Cassange and Bihe to Matiamvo by a head-man named Kamboóla. This was a well-beaten footpath, and soon after entering upon it we met a party of half-caste traders from Bihe, who confirmed the information we had already got of this path leading straight to Cassange, through which they had come on their way from Bihe to

Cabángo   They kindly presented my men with some tobacco, and marvelled greatly when they found that I had never been able to teach myself to smoke.

As we were now alone, and sure of being on the way to the abodes of civilization, we went on briskly.

On the 30th we came to a sudden descent from the high land, indented by deep, narrow valleys, over which we had lately been travelling. It is generally so steep that it can only be descended at particular points, and even there I was obliged to dismount, though so weak that I had to be led by my companions to prevent my toppling over in walking down. It was annoying to feel myself so helpless, for I never liked to see a man, either sick or well, give in effeminately. Below us lay the valley of the Quango. If you sit on the spot where Mary Queen of Scots viewed the battle of Langside, and look down on the vale of Clyde, you may see in miniature the glorious sight which a much greater and richer valley presented to our view. It is about a hundred miles broad, clothed with dark forest, except where the light-green grass covers meadow-lands on the Quango, which here and there glances out in the sun as it wends its way to the north. The opposite side of this great valley appears like a range of lofty mountains, and the descent into it about a mile, which, measured perpendicularly, may be from a thousand to twelve hundred feet. Emerging from the gloomy forests of Londa, this magnificent prospect made us all feel as if a weight had been lifted off our eyelids. A cloud was passing across the middle of the valley, from which rolling thunder pealed, while above all was glorious sunlight; and when we went down to the part where we saw it passing we found that a very heavy thunder-shower had fallen under the path of the cloud, and the bottom of the valley, which from above seemed quite smooth, we discovered to be intersected by great numbers of deep-cut streams. Looking back from below, the descent appears as the edge of a table-land, with numerous indented dells and spurs jutting out all along.

giving it a serrated appearance. Both the top and sides of the sierra are covered with trees; but large patches of the more perpendicular parts are bare, and exhibit the red soil which is general over the region we have now entered.

The hollow affords a section of this part of the country; and we find that the uppermost stratum is the ferruginous conglomerate already mentioned. The matrix is rust of iron, (or hydrous peroxide of iron and hematite,) and in it are embedded water-worn pebbles of sandstone and quartz. As this is the rock underlying the soil of a large part of Londa, its formation must have preceded the work of denudation by an arm of the sea which washed away the enormous mass of matter required before the valley of Cassange could assume its present form. The strata under the conglomerate are all of red clay shale of different degrees of hardness, the most indurated being at the bottom. This red clay shale is named "keele" in Scotland, and has always been considered as an indication of gold; but the only thing we discovered was that it had given rise to a very slippery clay soil, so different from that which we had just left that Mashauana, who always prided himself on being an adept at balancing himself in the canoe on water, and so sure of foot on land that he could afford to express contempt for any one less gifted, came down in a very sudden and undignified manner, to the delight of all whom he had previously scolded for falling.

Sunday, April 2.—We rested beside a small stream, and our hunger being now very severe, from having lived on manioc alone since leaving Ionga Panza's, we slaughtered one of our four remaining oxen. We could get neither meal nor manioc, but should have been comfortable had not the Bashinje chief Sansáwé pestered us for the customary present. The native traders informed us that a display of force was often necessary before they could pass this man.

Sansawe, the chief of a portion of the Bashinje, having sent the usual formal demand for a man, an ox, or a tusk, spoke very contemptuously of the poor things we offered him instead. We told his messengers that the tusks were Sekeletu's: every thing was gone except my instruments, which could be of no use to them whatever. One of them begged some meat, and, when it was refused, said to my men, "You may as well give it, for we shall take all after we have killed you to-morrow." The more humbly we spoke, the more insolent the Bashinje became, till at last we were all feeling savage and sulky, but continued to speak as civilly as we could. They are fond of argument, and, when I denied their right to demand tribute from a white man who did not trade in slaves, an old white-headed negro put rather a posing question:—"You know that God has placed chiefs among us whom we ought to support. How is it that you, who have a book that tells you about him, do not come forward at once to pay this chief tribute like every one else?" I replied by asking, "How could I know that this was a chief, who had allowed me to remain a day and a half near him without giving me any thing to eat?" This, which to the uninitiated may seem sophistry, was to the Central Africans quite a rational question; for he at once admitted that food ought to have been sent, and added that probably his chief was only making it ready for me, and that it would come soon.

After being wearied by talking all day to different parties sent by Sansawe, we were honored by a visit from himself: he is quite a young man, and of rather a pleasing countenance. There cannot have been much intercourse between real Portuguese and these people even here, so close to the Quango, for Sansawe asked me to show him my hair, on the ground that, though he had heard of it, and some white men had even passed through his country, he had never seen straight hair before. This is quite possible, as most of the slave-traders are not Portuguese, but half-castes. The difference between their wool and our hair caused him to burst into a laugh, and the contrast between the exposed and unexposed parts of my skin, when exhibited in evidence of our all being made of one stock originally, and the children of one Maker, seemed to strike him with wonder. I then showed him my watch, and wished to win my way into his confidence by conversation; but, when about to exhibit my pocket-compass, he desired me to desist, as he was afraid of my wonderful things. I told him, if he knew my aims as the tribes in the interior did, and as I hoped he would yet know them and me, he would be glad to stay, and see also the pictures of the magic lantern; but, as it was now getting dark, he had evidently got enough of my witchery, and began to use some charms to dispel any kindly feelings he might have found stealing round his heart. He asked leave to go, and when his party moved off a little way he sent for my spokesman, and told him that, "if we did not add a red jacket and a man to our gift of a few copper rings and a few pounds of meat, we must return by the way we had come." I said, in reply, "that we should certainly go forward next day, and if he commenced hostilities the blame before God would be that of Sansawe;" and my man added, of his own accord, "How many white men have you killed in this path?" which might be interpreted into, "You have never killed any white man; and you will find ours more difficult to manage than you imagine." It expressed a determination, which we had often repeated to each other, to die rather than yield one of our party to be a slave.

Hunger has a powerful effect on the temper. When we had got a good meal of meat, we could all bear the petty annoyances of these borderers on the more civilized region in front with equanimity; but, having suffered considerably of late, we were all rather soured in our feelings, and not unfrequently I overheard my companions remark in their own tongue, in answer to threats of attack, "That's what we want: only begin, then;" or with clenched teeth they would exclaim to each other, "These things have never travelled, and do not know what men are." The worrying, of which I give only a slight sketch, had considerable influence on my mind, and more especially as it was impossible to make any allowance for the Bashinje such as I was willing to award to the Chiboque. They saw that we had nothing to give, nor would they be benefited in the least by enforcing the impudent order to return whence we had come. They were adding insult to injury, and this put us all into a fighting spirit, and, as nearly as we could judge, we expected to be obliged to cut our way through the Bashinje next morning.

3d April.—As soon as day dawned we were astir, and, setting off in a drizzling rain, passed close to the village. This rain probably damped the ardor of the robbers. We, however, expected to be fired upon from every clump of trees, or from some of the rocky hillocks among which we were passing; and it was only after two hours' march that we began to breathe freely, and my men remarked, in thankfulness, "We are children of Jesus." We continued our course, notwithstanding the rain, across the bottom of the Quango valley, which we found broken by clay shale rocks jutting out, though lying nearly horizontally. We passed many villages during this drenching, one of which possessed a flock of sheep; and after six hours we came to a stand near the river Quango, (lat. 9° 53' S., long. 18° 37' E.,) which may be called the boundary of the Portuguese claims to territory on the west. As I had now no change of clothing, I was glad to cower under the shelter of my blanket, thankful to God for his goodness in bringing us so far without losing one of the party.

4th April.—We were now on the banks of the Quango, a river one hundred and fifty yards wide, and very deep. The water was discolored,—a circumstance which we had observed in no other river in Londa or in the Makololo country. This fine river flows among extensive meadows clothed with gigantic grass and reeds, and in a direction nearly north.

We were advised not to sleep near it; but, **as we were**

anxious to cross to the western side, we tried to induce some of the Bashinje to lend us canoes for the purpose. This brought out the chief of these parts, who informed us that all the canoe-men were his children, and nothing could be done without his authority. He then made the usual demand for a man, an ox, or a gun, adding that otherwise we must return to the country from which we had come. As I did not believe that this man had any power over the canoes of the other side, and suspected that

BASHINJE CHIEF'S MODE OF WEARING THE HAIR.

if I gave him my blanket—the only thing I now had in reserve—he might leave us in the lurch after all, I tried to persuade my men to go at once to the bank, about two miles off, and obtain possession of the canoes before we gave up the blanket; but they thought that this chief might attack us in the act of crossing, should we do so. The chief came himself to our encampment and made his demand again. My men stripped off the last of their copper rings and gave them; but he was still intent on a man.

He thought, as others did, that my men were slaves. He was a young man, with woolly hair elaborately dressed: that behind was made up into a cone, about eight inches in diameter at the base, carefully swathed round with red and black thread. As I resisted the proposal to deliver up my blanket until they had placed us on the western bank, this chief continued to worry us with his demands till I was tired. My little tent was now in tatters, and, having a wider hole behind than the door in front, I tried in vain to lie down out of sight of our persecutors. We were on a reedy flat, and could not follow our usual plan of a small stockade in which we had time to think over and concoct our plans. As I was trying to persuade my men to move on to the bank in spite of these people, a young half-caste Portuguese sergeant of militia, Cypriano di Abreu, made his appearance and gave the same advice. He had come across the Quango in search of bees'-wax. When we moved off from the chief who had been plaguing us, his people opened a fire from our sheds, and continued to blaze away some time in the direction we were going; but none of the bullets reached us. It is probable that they expected a demonstration of the abundance of ammunition they possessed would make us run; but, when we continued to move quietly to the ford, they proceeded no farther than our sleeping-place. Cypriano assisted us in making a more satisfactory arrangement with the ferryman than parting with my blanket; and as soon as we reached the opposite bank we were in the territory of the Bangala, who are subjects of the Portuguese, and often spoken of as the Cassanges or Cassantse; and happily all our difficulties with the border-tribes were at an end.

Passing with light hearts through the high grass by a narrow footpath about three miles west of the river, we came to several neat square houses, with many cleanly-looking half-caste Portuguese standing in front of them to salute us. They are all enrolled in the militia, and our friend Cypriano is the commander of a division established here

CYPRIANO'S GENEROUS HOSPITALITY.

We came to the dwelling of Cypriano after dark, and I pitched my little tent in front of it for the night. We had the company of mosquitos here. We never found them troublesome on the banks of the pure streams of Londa. On the morning of the 5th, Cypriano generously supplied my men with pumpkins and maize, and then invited me to breakfast, which consisted of groundnuts and roasted maize, then boiled manioc-roots and groundnuts, with guavas and honey as a dessert. I felt sincerely grateful for this magnificent breakfast.

At dinner Cypriano was equally bountiful, and several of his friends joined us in doing justice to his hospitality. Before eating, all had water poured on the hands by a female slave to wash them. One of the guests cut up a fowl with a knife and fork. Neither forks nor spoons were used in eating. The repast was partaken of with decency and good manners, and concluded by washing the hands as at first.

Much of the civility shown to us here was, no doubt, owing to the flattering letters of recommendation I carried from the Chevalier Du Prat, of Cape Town; but I am inclined to believe that my friend Cypriano was influenced, too, by feelings of genuine kindness, for he quite bared his garden in feeding us during the few days which I remained, anxiously expecting the clouds to disperse so far as to allow of my taking observations for the determination of the position of the Quango. He slaughtered an ox for us, and furnished his mother and her maids with manioc-roots, to prepare farina for the four or five days of our journey to Cassange, and never even hinted at payment. My wretched appearance must have excited his compassion.

We were detained by rains and a desire to ascertain our geographical position till Monday, the 10th, and only got the latitude 9° 50′ S., and, after three days' pretty hard travelling through the long grass, reached Cassange, the farthest inland station of the Portuguese in Western Africa. I made my entrance in a somewhat forlorn state as to clothing among our Portuguese allies. The first gentleman I met in the village asked if I had a passport, and said it was necessary to take me before the authorities. As I was in the same state of mind in which individuals are who commit a petty depredation in order to obtain the shelter and food of a prison, I gladly accompanied him to the house of the commandant or Chefe, Senhor de Silva Rego. Having shown my passport to this gentleman, he politely asked me to supper, and, as we had eaten nothing except the farina of Cypriano from the Quango to this, I suspect I appeared particularly ravenous to the other gentlemen around the table. They seemed, however, to understand my position pretty well, from having all travelled extensively themselves: had they not been present, I might have put some in my pocket to eat by night; for, after fever, the appetite is excessively keen, and manioc is one of the most unsatisfying kinds of food. Captain Antonio Rodrigues Neves then kindly invited me to take up my abode in his house. Next morning this generous man arrayed me in decent clothing, and continued during the whole period of my stay to treat me as if I had been his brother. I feel deeply grateful to him for his disinterested kindness. He not only attended to my wants, but also furnished food for my famishing party free of charge.

The village of Cassange (pronounced Kassanjé) is composed of thirty or forty traders' houses, slattered about, without any regularity, on an elevated flat spot in the great Quango or Cassange valley. They are built of wattle and daub, and surrounded by plantations of manioc, maize, &c. There are about forty Portuguese traders in this district, all of whom are officers in the militia, and many of them have become rich from adopting the plan of sending out pombeiros, or native traders, with large quantities of goods, to trade in the more remote parts of the country. If I might judge from the week of feasting I passed among them, they are generally prosperous.

As I always preferred to appear in my own proper character, I was an object of curiosity to these hospitable Portuguese. They evidently looked upon me as an agent of the English Government engaged in some new movement for the suppression of slavery. They could not divine what a "missionario" had to do with latitudes and longitudes, which I was intent on observing. When we became a little familiar, the questions put were rather amusing:— "Is it common for missionaries to be doctors?" "Are you a doctor of medicine and a 'doutor mathematico' too? You must be more than a missionary to know how to calculate the longitude. Come; tell us at once what rank you hold in the English army." They may have given credit to my reason for wearing the mustache, as that explains why men have beards and women have none; but that which puzzled many besides my Cassange friends was the anomaly of my being a "sacerdote," with a wife and four children! I usually got rid of the last question by putting another:—"Is it not better to have children with a wife than to have children without a wife?" But all were most kind and hospitable; and, as one of their festivals was near, they invited me to partake of the feast.

The anniversary of the Resurrection of our Savior was observed on the 16th of April as a day of rejoicing, though the Portuguese have no priests at Cassange. The colored population dressed up a figure intended to represent Judas Iscariot, and paraded him on a riding-ox about the village: sneers and maledictions were freely bestowed on the poor wretch thus represented. The slaves and free colored population, dressed in their gayest clothing, made visits to all the principal merchants, and, wishing them "a good feast," expected a present in return. This, though frequently granted in the shape of pieces of calico to make new dresses, was occasionally refused; but the rebuff did not much affect the petitioner.

At ten A.M. we went to the residence of the commandant, and, on a signal being given, two of the four brass guns belonging to the Government commenced firing, and continued some time, to the great admiration of my men, whose ideas of the power of a cannon are very exalted. The Portuguese flag was hoisted and trumpets sounded, as an expression of joy at the resurrection of our Lord. Captain Neves invited all the principal inhabitants of the place, and did what he could to feast them in a princely style. All manner of foreign preserved fruits and wine from Portugal, biscuits from America, butter from Cork, and beer from England, were displayed, and no expense spared in rendering the entertainment joyous. After the feast was over, they sat down to the common amusement of card-playing, which continued till eleven o'clock at night. As far as a mere traveller could judge, they seemed to be polite and willing to aid each other. They live in a febrile district, and many of them had enlarged spleens. They have neither doctor, apothecary, school, nor priest, and, when taken ill, trust to each other and to Providence. As men left in such circumstances must think for themselves, they have all a good idea of what ought to be done in the common diseases of the country, and what they have of either medicine or skill they freely impart to each other.

None of these gentlemen had Portuguese wives. They usually come to Africa in order to make a little money, and return to Lisbon. Hence they seldom bring their wives with them, and never can be successful colonists in consequence. It is common for them to have families by native women. It was particularly gratifying to me, who had been familiar with the stupid prejudice against color entertained only by those who are themselves becoming tawny, to view the liberality with which people of color were treated by the Portuguese. Instances, so common in the south, in which half-caste children are abandoned, are here extremely rare. They are acknowledged at table, and provided for by their fathers as if European. The colored clerks of the merchants sit at the same table with their employers without any embarrassment. The civil manners of superiors to inferiors is probably the result of the position they occupy —a few whites among thousands of blacks; but nowhere else in Africa is there so much good-will between Europeans and natives as here. If some border-colonists had the absolute certainty of our Government declining to bear them out in their arrogance, we should probably hear less of Caffre insolence. It is insolence which begets insolence.

From the village of Cassange we have a good view of the surrounding country: it is a gently-undulating plain, covered with grass and patches of forest. The western edge of the Quango valley appears, about twenty miles off, as if it were a range of lofty mountains, and passes by the name of Tala Mungongo, ("Behold the Range.") In the old Portuguese map, to which I had been trusting in planning my route, it is indicated as Talla Mugongo, or *"Castle of Rocks!"* and the Coanza is put down as rising therefrom; but here I was assured that the Coanza had its source near Bihe, far to the southwest of this, and we should not see that river till we came near Pungo Andongo. It is somewhat remarkable that more accurate information about this country has not been published. Captain Neves and others had a correct idea of the courses of the rivers, and communicated their knowledge freely; yet about this time maps were sent to Europe from Angola representing the Quango and Coanza as the same river, and Cassange placed about one hundred miles from its true position. The frequent recurrence of the same name has probably helped to increase the confusion. I have crossed several Quangos, but all insignificant except that which drains this valley. The repetition of the favorite names of chiefs, as Catendé, is also perplexing, as one Catende may be mistaken for another. To avoid this confusion as much as possible, I have refrained from introducing many names. Numerous villages are studded all over the valley; but these possess no permanence, and many more existed provious to the Portuguese expedition of 1850 to punish the Bangala.

This valley, as I have before remarked, is all fertile in the extreme. My men could never cease admiring its capability for raising their corn (*Holcus sorghum*) and despising the comparatively-limited cultivation of the inhabitants. The Portuguese informed me that no manure is ever needed, but that the more the ground is tilled the better it yields. Virgin soil does not give such a heavy crop as an old garden; and, judging from the size of the maize and manioc in the latter, I can readily believe the statement. Cattle do well, too. Viewing the valley as a whole, it may be said that its agricultural and pastoral riches are lying waste. Both the Portuguese and their descendants turn their attention almost exclusively to trade in wax and ivory; and, though the country would yield any amount of corn and dairy-produce, the native Portuguese live chiefly on manioc, and the Europeans purchase their flour, bread, butter, and cheese from the Americans.

As the traders of Cassange were the first white men we had come to, we sold the tusks belonging to Sekeletu, which had been brought to test the difference of prices in the Makololo and white men's country. The result was highly satisfactory to my companions, as the Portuguese give much larger prices for ivory than traders from the Cape can possibly give, who labor under the disadvantage of considerable overland expenses and ruinous restrictions. Two muskets, three small barrels of gunpowder, and English calico and baize sufficient to clothe my whole party, with large bunches of beads, all for one tusk, were quite delightful for those who had been accustomed to give two tusks for one gun. With another tusk we procured calico, which here is the chief currency, to pay our way down to the coast. The remaining two were sold for money to purchase a horse for Sekeletu at Loanda.

The superiority of this new market was quite astounding to the Makololo, and they began to abuse the traders by whom they had, while in their own country, been visited, and, as they now declared, "cheated." They had no idea of the value of time and carriage, and it was somewhat difficult for me to convince them that the reason of the difference of prices lay entirely in what they themselves had done in coming here, and that, if the Portuguese should carry goods to their country, they would by no means be so liberal in their prices. They imagined that, if the Cassange traders came to Linyanti, they would continue to vend their goods at Cassange prices. I believe I gave them at last a clear idea of the manner in which prices were regulated by the expenses incurred; and when we went to Loanda, and saw goods delivered at a still cheaper rate, they concluded that it would be better for them to come to that city than to turn homeward at Cassange.

Mr. Rego, the commandant, very handsomely offered me a soldier as a guard to Ambaca. My men told me that they had been thinking it would be better to turn back here, as they had been informed by the people of color at Cassange that I was leading them down to the sea-coast only to sell them, and they would be taken on board ship, fattened, and eaten, as the white men were cannibals. I asked if they had ever heard of an Englishman buying or selling people; if I had not refused to take a slave when she was offered to me by Shinte; but, as I had always behaved as an English teacher, if they now doubted my intentions, they had better not go to the coast; I, however, who expected to meet some of my countrymen there, was determined to go on. They replied that they only thought it right to tell me what had been told to them, but they did not intend to leave me, and would follow wherever I should lead the way. This affair being disposed of for the time, the commandant gave them an ox, and me a friendly dinner before parting. All the merchants of Cassange accompanied us, in their hammocks carried by slaves, to the edge of the plateau on which their village stands, and we parted with the feeling in my mind that I should never forget their disinterested kindness. They not only did every thing they could to make my men and me comfortable during our stay, but, there being no hotels in Loanda, they furnished me with letters of recommendation to their friends in that city, requesting them to receive me into their houses, for without these a stranger might find himself a lodger in the streets. May God remember them in their day of need!

The latitude and longitude of Cassange, the most easterly station of the Portuguese in Western Africa, is lat. 9° 37' 30" S and long. 17° 49' E.; consequently we had still about three hundred miles to traverse before we could reach the coast. We had a black militia-corporal as a guide. He was a native of Ambaca, and, like nearly all the inhabitants of that district, known by the name of Ambakistas, could both read and write. He had three slaves with him, and was carried by them in a "tipoia," or hammock slung to a pole.

Having left Cassange on the 21st, we passed across the remaining portion of this excessively-fertile valley to the foot of Tala Mungongo. We crossed a fine little stream called the Lui on the 22d, and another named the Luare on the 24th, and then slept at the bottom of the height, which is from a thousand to fifteen hundred feet.

Situated a few miles from the edge of the descent, we found the village of Tala Mungongo, and were kindly accommodated with a house to sleep in,—which was very welcome, as we were all both wet and cold. We found that the greater altitude and the approach of winter lowered the temperature so much that many of my men suffered severely from colds. At this, as at several other Portuguese stations, they have been provident enough to erect travellers' houses on the same principle as khans or caravanserais of the East. They are built of the usual wattle and daub, and have benches of rods for the wayfarer to make his bed on; also chairs, and a table, and a large jar of water. These benches, though far from luxurious couches, were better than the ground under the rotten fragments of my gypsy-tent, for we had still showers occasionally, and the dews were very heavy. I continued to use them for the sake of the shelter they afforded, until I found that they were lodgings also for certain inconvenient bedfellows.

27th.—Five hours' ride through a pleasant country of forest and meadow, like those of Londa, brought us to a village of Basongo, a tribe living in subjection to the Portuguese. We crossed several little streams, which were flowing in the westerly direction in which we were marching, and unite to form the Quize, a feeder of the Coanza. The Basongo were very civil, as indeed all the tribes were who had been conquered by the Portuguese. The Basongo and Bangala are yet only partially subdued. The farther west we go from this the less independent we find the black population, until we reach the vicinity of Loanda, where the free natives are nearly identical in their feelings toward the Government with the slaves. But the governors of Angola wisely accept the limited allegiance and tribute rendered by the more distant tribes as better than none.

We spent Sunday, the 30th of April, at Ngio, close to the ford of the Quize as it crosses our path to fall into the Coanza. The country becomes more open, but is still abundantly fertile, with a thick crop of grass between two and three feet high. It is also well wooded and watered. Villages of Basongo are dotted over the landscape, and frequently a square house of wattle and daub, belonging to native Portuguese, is placed beside them for the purposes of trade.

Pitsane and another of the men had violent attacks of fever, and it was no wonder; for the dampness and evaporation from the ground was excessive. When at any time I attempted to get an observation of a star, if the trough of mercury were placed on the ground, so much moisture was condensed on the inside of the glass roof over it that it was with difficulty the reflection of the star could be seen. When the trough was placed on a box to prevent the moisture entering from below, so much dew was deposited on the outside of the roof that it was soon necessary, for the sake of distinct vision, to wipe the glass. This would not have been of great consequence, but a short exposure to this dew was so sure to bring on a fresh fever that I was obliged to give up observation by night altogether. The inside of the only covering I now had was not much better, but under the blanket one is not so liable to the chill which the dew produces.

It would have afforded me pleasure to have cultivated a more intimate acquaintance with the inhabitants of this part of the country, but the vertigo produced by frequent fevers made it as much as I could do to stick on the ox and crawl along in misery. In crossing the Lombe, my ox Sinbad, in the indulgence of his propensity to strike out a new path for himself, plunged overhead into a deep hole, and so soused me that I was obliged to move on to dry my clothing without calling on the Europeans who live on the bank. This I regretted, for all the Portuguese were very kind, and, like the Boers placed in similar circumstances, feel it a slight to be passed without a word of salutation. But we went on to a spot where orange-trees had been planted by the natives themselves, and where abundance of that refreshing fruit was exposed for sale.

On entering the district of Ambaca, we found the landscape enlivened by the appearance of lofty mountains in the distance, the grass comparatively short, and the whole country at this time looking gay and verdant. We crossed the Lucalla by means of a large canoe kept there by a man who farms the ferry from the Government and charges about a penny per head. A few miles beyond the Lucalla we came to the village of Ambaca, an important place in former times, but now a mere paltry village, beautifully situated on a little elevation in a plain surrounded on all hands by lofty mountains. It has a jail, and a good house for the commandant, but neither fort nor church, though the ruins of a place of worship are still standing.

We were most kindly received by the commandant of Ambaca, Arsenio de Carpo, who spoke a little English. He recommended wine for my debility, and here I took the first glass of that beverage I had taken in Africa. I felt much refreshed, and could then realize and meditate on the weakening effects of the fever. They were curious even to myself; for, though I had tried several times since we left Ngio to take lunar observations, I could not avoid confusion of time and distance, neither could I hold the instrument steady, nor perform a simple calculation: hence many of the positions of this part of the route were left till my return from Loanda. Often, on getting up in the mornings, I found my clothing as wet from perspiration as if it had been dipped in water. In vain had I tried to learn or collect words of the Bunda, or dialect spoken in Angola. I forgot the days of the week and the names of my companions, and, had I been asked, I probably could not have told my own. The complaint itself occupied many of my thoughts. One day I supposed that I had got the true theory of it, and would certainly cure the next attack, whether in myself or companions; but some new symptoms would appear and scatter all the fine speculations which had sprung up, with extraordinary fertility, in one department of my brain.

This district is said to contain upward of 40,000 souls. Some ten or twelve miles to the north of the village of Ambaca there once stood the missionary station of Cahenda· and it is now quite astonishing to observe the great numbers who can read and write in this district. This is the fruit of the labors of the Jesuit and Capuchin missionaries, for they taught the people of Ambaca; and ever since the expulsion of the teachers by the Marquis of Pombal the natives have continued to teach each other. These devoted men are still held in high estimation throughout the country to this day. All speak well of them, (os padres Jesuitas;)

and, now that they are gone from this lower sphere, I could not help wishing that these our Roman Catholic fellow-Christians had felt it to be their duty to give the people the Bible, to be a light to their feet when the good men themselves were gone.

When sleeping in the house of the commandant, an insect, well known in the southern country by the name tampan, bit my foot. It is a kind of tick, and chooses by preference the parts between the fingers or toes for inflicting its bite. It is seen from the size of a pin's head to that of a pea, and is common in all the native huts in this country. It sucks the blood until quite full, and is then of a dark-blue color, and its skin so tough and yielding that it is impossible to burst it by any amount of squeezing with the fingers. I had felt the effects of its bite in former years, and eschewed all native huts ever after; but, as I was here again assailed in a European house, I shall detail the effects of the bite. These are a tingling sensation of mingled pain and itching, which commences ascending the limb until the poison imbibed reaches the abdomen, where it soon causes violent vomiting and purging. Where these effects do not follow, as we found afterward at Tete, fever sets in; and I was assured by intelligent Portuguese there that death has sometimes been the result of this fever. The anxiety my friends at Tete manifested to keep my men out of the reach of the tampans of the village made it evident that they had seen cause to dread this insignificant insect. The only inconvenience I afterward suffered from this bite was the continuance of the tingling sensation in the point bitten for about a week.

May 12.—As we were about to start this morning, the commandant, Senhor Arsenio, provided bread and meat most bountifully for my use on the way to the next station, and sent two militia-soldiers as guides, instead of our Cassange corporal, who left us here. About mid-day we asked for shelter from the sun in the house of Senhor Mellot, at Zangu; and, though I was unable to sit and engage in conversation, I found, on rising from his couch, that he had at once proceeded to cook a fowl for my use; and at parting he gave me a glass of wine, which prevented the violent fit of shivering I expected that afternoon. The universal hospitality of the Portuguese was most gratifying, as it was quite unexpected; and even now, as I copy my journal, I remember it all with a glow of gratitude.

We spent Sunday, the 14th of May, at Cabinda, which is one of the stations of the sub-commandants, who are placed at different points in each district of Angola as assistants of the head-commandant, or chefe. It is situated in a beautiful glen, and surrounded by plantations of bananas and manioc.

We met numbers of Mambari on their way back to Bihe Some of them had belonged to the parties which had penetrated as far as Linyanti, and foolishly showed their displeasure at the prospect of the Makololo preferring to go to the coast-markets themselves to intrusting them with their ivory. The Mambari repeated the tale of the mode in which the white men are said to trade. "The ivory is left on the shore in the evening, and next morning the seller finds a quantity of goods placed there in its stead by the white men who live on the sea." "Now," added they to my men, "how can you Makolo trade with these 'mermen'? Can you enter into the sea and tell them to come ashore?" It was remarkable to hear this idea repeated so near the sea as we now were. My men replied that they only wanted to see for themselves; and, as they were now getting some light on the nature of the trade carried on by the Mambari, they were highly amused on perceiving the reasons why the Mambari would rather have met them on the Zambesi than so near the sea-coast.

There is something so exhilarating to one of Highland blood in being near or on high mountains, that I forgot my fever as we wended our way among the lofty tree-covered masses of mica schist which form the highlands around the romantic residence of the chefe of Golungo Alto. (Lat. 9°

8′ 30″ S., long. 15° 2′ E.) The whole district is extremely beautiful. The hills are all bedecked with trees of various hues of foliage, and among them towers the graceful palm, which yields the oil of commerce for making our soaps and the intoxicating toddy.

We were most kindly received by the commandant, Lieutenant Antonio Canto e Castro, a young gentleman whose whole subsequent conduct will ever make me regard him with great affection. Like every other person of intelligence whom I had met, he lamented deeply the neglect with which this fine country had been treated. This district contained, by the last census, 26,000 hearths or fires; and, if to each hearth we reckon four souls, we have a population of 104,000. The number of carregadores (carriers) who may be ordered out at the pleasure of Government to convey merchandise to the coast is in this district alone about 6000; yet there is no good road in existence. This system of compulsory carriage of merchandise was adopted in consequence of the increase in numbers and activity of our cruisers which took place in 1845. Each trader who went, previous to that year, into the interior, in the pursuit of his calling, proceeded on the plan of purchasing ivory and bees'-wax, and a sufficient number of slaves to carry these commodities. The whole were intended for exportation as soon as the trader reached the coast. But when the more stringent measures of 1845 came into operation, and rendered the exportation of slaves almost impossible, there being no roads proper for the employment of wheel-conveyances, this new system of compulsory carriage of ivory and bees'-wax to the coast was resorted to by the Government of Loanda. A trader who requires two or three hundred carriers to convey his merchandise to the coast now applies to the general Government for aid. An order is sent to the commandant of a district to furnish the number required. Each head-man of the villages to whom the order is transmitted must furnish from five to twenty or thirty men, according to the proportion that his people bear to the entire population of the district. For this accommodation the trader must pay a tax to the Government of one thousand reis, or about three shillings, per load carried. The trader is obliged to pay the carrier also the sum of fifty reis, or about twopence a day, for his sustenance. And, as a day's journey is never more than from eight to ten miles, the expense which must be incurred for this compulsory labor is felt to be heavy by those who were accustomed to employ slave-labor alone. Yet no effort has been made to form a great line of road for wheel-carriages. The first great want of a country has not been attended to, and no development of its vast resources has taken place. The fact, however, of a change from one system of carriage to another, taken in connection with the great depreciation in the price of slaves near this coast, proves the effectiveness of our efforts at repressing the slave-trade on the ocean.

The latitude of Golungo Alto, as observed at the residence of the commandant, was 9° 8' 30" S., longitude 15° 2' E. A few days' rest with this excellent young man enabled me to regain much of my strength, and I could look with pleasure on the luxuriant scenery before his door. We were quite shut in among green hills, many of which were cultivated up to their tops with manioc, coffee, cotton, groundnuts, bananas, pineapples, guavas, papaws, custard-apples, pitangas, and jambos,—fruits brought from South America by the former missionaries.

We left Golungo Alto on the 24th of May,—the winter in those parts. Every evening clouds come rolling in great masses over the mountains in the west, and pealing thunder accompanies the fall of rain during the night or early in the morning. The clouds generally remain on the hills till the morning is well spent, so that we become familiar with the morning mists,—a thing we never once saw at Kolobeng. The thermometer stands at 80° by day, but sinks as low as 76° by night.

In going westward we crossed several fine little gushing

streams which never dry. They unite in the Luinha (pronounced Lueenya) and Lucalla. As they flow over many little cascades, they might easily be turned to good account; but they are all allowed to run on idly to the ocean. We passed through forests of gigantic timber, and, at an open space named Cambondo, about eight miles from Golungo Alto, found numbers of carpenters converting these lofty trees into planks, in exactly the same manner as was followed by the illustrious Robinson Crusoe. A tree of three or four feet in diameter and forty or fifty feet up to the nearest branches was felled. It was then cut into lengths of a few feet, and split into thick junks, which again were reduced to planks an inch thick by persevering labor with the axe. The object of the carpenters was to make little chests, and they drive a constant trade in them at Cambondo. When finished with hinges, lock, and key, all of their own manufacture, one costs only a shilling and eightpence. My men were so delighted with them that they carried several of them on their heads all the way to Linyanti.

At Trombeta we were pleased to observe a great deal of taste displayed by the sub-commandant in the laying out of his ground and adornment of his house with flowers. This trifling incident was the more pleasing, as it was the first attempt at neatness I had seen since leaving the establishment of Mozinkwa in Londa. Rows of trees had been planted along each side of the road, with pineapples and flowers between. This arrangement I had an opportunity of seeing in several other districts of this country, for there is no difficulty in raising any plant or tree if it is only kept from being choked by weeds.

This gentleman had now a fine estate, which but a few years ago was a forest and cost him only £16. He had planted about nine hundred coffee-trees upon it, and as these begin to yield in three years from being planted, and in six attain their maximum, I have no doubt but that ere now his £13 yields him sixty-fold. All sorts of fruit-trees and grape-vines yield their fruit twice in each year, without any labor or irrigation being bestowed on them. All grains and vegetables, if only sown, do the same; and, if advantage is taken of the mists of winter, even three crops of pulse may be raised. Cotton was now standing in the pods in his fields, and he did not seem to care about it. I understood him to say that this last plant flourishes, but the wet of one of the two rainy seasons with which this country is favored sometimes proves troublesome to the grower. I am not aware whether wheat has ever been tried, but I saw both figs and grapes bearing well. The great complaint of all cultivators is the want of a good road to carry their produce to market. Here all kinds of food are remarkably cheap.

Farther on we left the mountainous country, and, as we descended toward the west coast, saw the lands assuming a more sterile, uninviting aspect. On our right ran the river Senza, which nearer the sea takes the name of Bengo It is about fifty yards broad, and navigable for canoes The low plains adjacent to its banks are protected from inundation by embankments, and the population is entirely occupied in raising food and fruits for exportation to Loanda by means of canoes. The banks are infested by myriads of the most ferocious mosquitos I ever met. Not one of our party could get a snatch of sleep. I was taken into the house of a Portuguese, but was soon glad to make my escape and lie across the path on the lee side of the fire, where the smoke blew over my body. My host wondered at my want of taste, and I at his want of feeling; for, to our astonishment, he and the other inhabitants had actually become used to what was at least equal to a nail through the heel of one's boot, or the toothache.

As we were now drawing near to the sea, my companions were looking at every thing in a serious light. One of them asked me if we should all have an opportunity of watching each other at Loanda. "Suppose one went for water: would the others see if he were kidnapped?" I replied, "I see what you are driving at; and if you suspect me you may return, for I am as ignorant of Loanda as you are; but nothing will happen to you but what happens to myself. We have stood by each other hitherto, and will do so to the last." The plains adjacent to Loanda are somewhat elevated and comparatively sterile. On coming across these we first beheld the sea: my companions looked upon the boundless ocean with awe. On describing their feelings afterward, they remarked that "we marched along with our father, believing that what the ancients had always told us was true, that the world has no end; but all at once the world said to us, 'I am finished: there is no more of me!'" They had always imagined that the world was one extended plain without limit.

They were now somewhat apprehensive of suffering want, and I was unable to allay their fears with any promise of supply, for my own mind was depressed by disease and care. The fever had induced a state of chronic dysentery so troublesome that I could not remain on the ox more than ten minutes at a time; and as we came down the declivity above the city of Loanda on the 31st of May, I was laboring under great depression of spirits, as I understood that, in a population of twelve thousand souls, there was but one genuine English gentleman. I naturally felt anxious to know whether he were possessed of good-nature, or was one of those crusty mortals one would rather not meet at all.

This gentleman, Mr. Gabriel, our commissioner for the suppression of the slave-trade, had kindly forwarded an invitation to meet me on the way from Cassange, but, unfortunately, it crossed me on the road. When we entered his porch, I was delighted to see a number of flowers cultivated carefully, and inferred from this circumstance that he was, what I soon discovered him to be, a real whole-hearted Englishman.

Seeing me ill, he benevolently offered me his bed. Never shall I forget the luxurious pleasure I enjoyed in feeling myself again on a good English couch, after six months' sleeping on the ground. I was soon asleep; and Mr. Gabriel, coming in almost immediately, rejoiced at the soundness of my repose.

CHAPTER XX.

DR. LIVINGSTONE COMMENCES HIS GREAT JOURNEY ACROSS AFRICA.

In the hope that a short enjoyment of Mr. Gabriel's generous hospitality would restore me to my wonted vigor, I continued under his roof; but, my complaint having been caused by long exposure to malarious influences, I became much more reduced than ever, even while enjoying rest. Several Portuguese gentlemen called on me shortly after my arrival; and the Bishop of Angola, the Right Reverend Joaquim Moreira Reis, then the acting governor of the province, sent his secretary to do the same, and likewise to offer the services of the Government physician.

Some of her majesty's cruisers soon came into the port, and, seeing the emaciated condition to which I was reduced, offered to convey me to St. Helena or homeward; but, though I had reached the coast, I had found that, in consequence of the great amount of forest, rivers, and marsh, there was no possibility of a highway for wagons, and I had brought a party of Sekeletu's people with me, and found the tribes near the Portuguese settlement so very unfriendly that it would be altogether impossible for my men to return alone. I therefore resolved to decline the tempting offers of my naval friends, and take back my Makololo companions to their chief, with a view of trying to make a path from his country to the east coast by means of the great river Zambesi or Leeambye.

I, however, gladly availed myself of the medical assistance of Mr. Cockin, the surgeon of the "Polyphemus,' at the suggestion of his commander, Captain Phillips. Mr. Cockin's treatment, aided by the exhilarating presence of the warm-hearted naval officers, and Mr. Gabriel's un wearied hospitality and care, soon brought me round again. On the 14th I was so far well as to call on the bishop, in company with my party, who were arrayed in new robes of striped cotton cloth and red caps, all presented to them by Mr. Gabriel. He received us, as head of the provisional Government, in the grand hall of the palace. He put many intelligent questions respecting the Makololo, and then gave them free permission to come to Loanda as often as they pleased. This interview pleased the Makololo extremely.

Every one remarked the serious deportment of the Makololo. They viewed the large stone houses and churches in the vicinity of the great ocean with awe. A house with two stories was, until now, beyond their comprehension. In explanation of this strange thing, I had always been obliged to use the word for hut; and, as huts are constructed by the poles being let into the earth, they never could comprehend how the poles of one hut could be founded upon the roof of another, or how men could live, in the upper story, with the conical roof of the lower one in the middle. Some Makololo, who had visited my little house at Kolobeng, in trying to describe it to their countrymen at Linyanti, said, "It is not a hut: it is a mountain with several caves in it."

Commander Bedingfeld and Captain Skene invited them to visit their vessels, the "Pluto" and "Philomel." Knowing their fears, I told them that no one need go if he entertained the least suspicion of foul play. Nearly the whole party went; and, when on deck, I pointed to the sailors, and said, "Now, these are all my countrymen, sent by our queen for the purpose of putting down the trade of those that buy and sell black men." They replied, "Truly! they are just like you!" and all their fears seemed to vanish at once, for they went forward among the men, and the jolly tars, acting much as the Makololo would have done in similar circumstances, handed them a share of the bread and beef which they had for dinner. The commander allowed them to fire off a cannon; and, having the most exalted ideas of its power, they were greatly pleased when I told them, "That is what they put down the slave-trade with." The size of the brig-of-war amazed them. "It is not a canoe at all: it is a town!" The sailors' deck they named "the kotla;" and then, as a climax to their description of this great ark, added, "And what sort of a town is it that you must climb up into with a rope?"

The effect of the politeness of the officers and men on their minds was most beneficial. They had behaved with the greatest kindness to me all the way from Linyanti, and I now rose rapidly in their estimation; for, whatever they may have surmised before, they now saw that I was respected among my own countrymen, and always afterward treated me with the greatest deference.

On the 15th there was a procession and service of the mass in the Cathedral; and, wishing to show my men a place of worship, I took them to the church, which now serves as the chief one of the see of Angola and Congo. There is an impression on some minds that a gorgeous ritual is better calculated to inspire devotional feelings than the simple forms of the Protestant worship. But here the frequent genuflexions, changing of positions, burning of incense, with the priests' back turned to the people, the laughing, talking, and manifest irreverence of the singers, with firing of guns, &c., did not convey to the minds of my men the idea of adoration. I overheard them, in talking to each other, remark that "they had seen the white men charming their demons;" a phrase identical with one they had used when seeing the Balonda beating drums before their idols.

In the beginning of August I suffered a severe relapse.

which reduced me to a mere skeleton. I was then unable to attend to my men for a considerable time; but, when in convalescence from this last attack, I was thankful to find that I was free from that lassitude which, in my first recovery, showed the continuance of the malaria in the system. I found that my men, without prompting, had established a brisk trade in firewood. They sallied forth at cock-crowing in the morning, and by daylight reached the uncultivated parts of the adjacent country, collected a bundle of firewood, and returned to the city. It was then divided into smaller fagots, and sold to the inhabitants; and, as they gave larger quantities than the regular wood-carriers, they found no difficulty in selling. A ship freighted with coal for the cruisers having arrived from England, Mr. Gabriel procured them employment in unloading her at sixpence a day. They continued at this work for upward of a month; and nothing could exceed their astonishment at the vast amount of cargo one ship contained. As they themselves always afterward expressed it, they had labored every day from sunrise to sunset for a moon and a half, unloading, as quickly as they could, "stones that burn," and were tired out, still leaving plenty in her. With the money so obtained they purchased clothing, beads, and other articles to take back to their own country. Their ideas of the value of different kinds of goods rather astonished those who had dealt only with natives on the coast. Hearing it stated with confidence that the Africans preferred the thinnest fabrics, provided they had gaudy colors and a large extent of surface, the idea was so new to my experience in the interior that I dissented, and, in order to show the superior good sense of the Makololo, took them to the shop of Mr. Schut. When he showed them the amount of general goods which **they might procure at Loanda for a single tusk, I requested them, without assigning any reason, to point out the fabrics they prized most.** They all at once selected the strongest **pieces** of English calico and other cloths, showing that they had regard to strength without reference to color. I believe that most of the Bechuana nation would have done the same. But I was assured that the people near the coast, with whom the Portuguese have to deal, have not so much regard to durability. *This probably arises from calico being the chief circulating-medium,—quantity being then of more importance than quality.

During the period of my indisposition, the bishop sent frequently to make inquiries, and as soon as I was able to walk I went to thank him for his civilities. His whole conversation and conduct showed him to be a man of great benevolence and kindness of heart. Alluding to my being a Protestant, he stated that he was a Catholic from conviction; and though sorry to see others, like myself, following another path, he entertained no uncharitable feelings, nor would he ever sanction persecuting measures. He compared the various sects of Christians, in their way to heaven, to a number of individuals choosing to pass down the different streets of Loanda to one of the churches: all would arrive at the same point at last. His good influence, both in the city and the country, is universally acknowledged: he was promoting the establishment of schools, which, though formed more on the monastic principle than Protestants might approve, will no doubt be a blessing. He was likewise successfully attempting to abolish the non-marriage custom of the country; and several marriages had taken place in Loanda among those who, but for his teaching, would have been content with concubinage.

St. Paul de Loanda has been a very considerable city, but is now in a state of decay. It contains about twelve thousand inhabitants, most of whom are people of color.*

---

* From the census of 1850–51 we find the population of this city arranged thus:—830 whites, only 160 of whom are females. This is the largest collection of whites in the country, for Angola itself contains only about 1000 whites. There are 2400 half-castes in Loanda, and only 120 of them slaves; and there are 9000 blacks, more than 5000 of whom are slaves

There are various evidences of its former magnificence, especially two cathedrals, one of which, once a Jesuit college, is now converted into a workshop; and in passing the other we saw with sorrow a number of oxen feeding within its stately walls. Three forts continue in a good state of repair. Many large stone houses are to be found. The palace of the governor and Government offices are commodious structures, but nearly all the houses of the native inhabitants are of wattle and daub. Trees are planted all over the town for the sake of shade, and the city presents an imposing appearance from the sea. It is provided with an effective police, and the custom-house department is extremely well managed. All parties agree in representing the Portuguese authorities as both polite and obliging; and, if ever any inconvenience is felt by strangers visiting the port, it must be considered the fault of the system, and not of the men.

The harbor is formed by the low, sandy island of Loanda, which is inhabited by about 1300 souls, upward of 600 of whom are industrious native fishermen, who supply the city with abundance of good fish daily. The space between it and the mainland, on which the city is built, is the station for ships. When a high southwest wind blows, the waves of the ocean dash over part of the island, and, driving large quantities of sand before them, gradually fill up the harbor. Great quantities of soil are also washed in the rainy season from the heights above the city, so that the port, which once contained water sufficient to float the largest ships close to the custom-house, is now at low-water dry. The ships are compelled to anchor about a mile north of their old station. Nearly all the water consumed in Loanda is brought from the river Bengo by means of launches, the only supply that the city affords being from some deep wells of slightly-brackish water. Unsuccessful attempts have been made by different governors to finish a canal which the Dutch, while in possession of Loanda during the seven years preceding 1648, had begun, to bring water from the river Coanza to the city. There is not a single English merchant at Loanda, and only two American. This is the more remarkable as nearly all the commerce is carried on by means of English calico brought hither *viá* Lisbon. Several English houses attempted to establish a trade about 1845, and accepted bills on Rio de Janeiro in payment for their goods; but the increased activity of our cruisers had such an effect upon the mercantile houses of that city that most of them failed. The English merchants lost all, and Loanda got a bad name in the commercial world in consequence.

One of the arrangements of the custom-house may have had some influence in preventing English trade. Ships coming here must be consigned to some one on the spot; the consignee receives one hundred dollars per mast, and he generally makes a great deal more for himself by putting a percentage on boats and men hired for loading and unloading, and on every item that passes through his hands. The port-charges are also rendered heavy by twenty dollars being charged as a perquisite of the secretary of Government, with a fee for the chief physician, something for the hospital, custom-house officers, guards, &c. &c. But, with all these drawbacks, the Americans carry on a brisk and profitable trade in calico, biscuit, flour, butter, &c. &c.

The Portuguese home Government has not generally received the credit for sincerity in suppressing the slave-trade which I conceive to be its due. In 1839, my friend Mr. Gabriel saw thirty-seven slave-ships lying in this harbor, waiting for their cargoes, under the protection of the guns of the forts. At that time slavers had to wait many months at a time for a human freight, and a certain sum per head was paid to the Government for all that were exported. The duties derived from the exportation of slaves far exceeded those from other commerce, and, by agreeing to the suppression of this profitable traffic, the Government actually sacrificed the chief part of the export-revenue. Since that period, however, the revenue from lawful commerce has very much exceeded that on slaves. The intentions of the home Portuguese Government, however good, cannot be fully carried out under the present system. The pay of the officers is so very small that they are nearly all obliged to engage in trade; and, owing to the lucrative nature of the slave-trade, the temptation to engage in it is so powerful that the philanthropic statesmen of Lisbon need hardly expect to have their humane and enlightened views carried out. The law, for instance, lately promulgated for the abolition of the carrier-system (carregadores) is but one of several equally humane enactments against this mode of compulsory labor, but there is very little probability of the benevolent intentions of the legislature being carried into effect.

Loanda is regarded somewhat as a penal settlement, and those who leave their native land for this country do so with the hope of getting rich in a few years and then returning home. They have thus no motive for seeking the permanent welfare of the country. The Portuguese law preventing the subjects of any other nation from holding landed property unless they become naturalized, the country has neither the advantage of native nor foreign enterprise, and remains very much in the same state as our allies found it in 1575. Nearly all the European soldiers sent out are convicts, and, contrary to what might be expected from men in their position, behave remarkably well. A few riots have occurred, but nothing at all so serious as have taken place in our own penal settlements. It is a remarkable fact that the whole of the arms of Loanda are every night in the hands of those who have been convicts. Various reasons for this mild behavior are assigned by the officers, but none of these, when viewed in connection with our own experience in Australia, appear to be valid. Religion seems to have no connection with the change. Perhaps the climate may have some influence in subduing their turbulent disposition, for the inhabitants generally are a timid race: they are not half so brave as our Caffres

The people of Ambriz ran away like a flock of sheep, and allowed the Portuguese to take possession of their coppermines and country without striking a blow. If we must have convict-settlements, attention to the climate might be of advantage in the selection. Here even bulls are much tamer than with us. I never met with a ferocious one in this country, and the Portuguese use them generally for riding: an ox is seldom seen.

The objects which I had in view in opening up the country, as stated in a few notes of my journey published in the newspapers of Angola, so commended themselves to the general Government and merchants of Loanda, that, at the instance of his excellency the bishop, a handsome present for Sekeletu was granted by the Board of Public Works, (Junta da Fazenda Publica.) It consisted of a colonel's complete uniform and a horse for the chief, and suits of clothing for all the men who accompanied me. The merchants also made a present, by public subscription, of handsome specimens of all their articles of trade, and two donkeys, for the purpose of introducing the breed into his country, as tsetse cannot kill this beast of burden. These presents were accompanied by letters from the bishop and merchants; and I was kindly favored with letters of recommendation to the Portuguese authorities in Eastern Africa.

I took with me a good stock of cotton cloth, fresh supplies of ammunition and beads, and gave each of my men a musket. As my companions had amassed considerable quantities of goods, they were unable to carry mine; but the bishop furnished me with twenty carriers, and sent forward orders to all the commandants of the districts through which we were to pass to render me every assistance in their power. Being now supplied with a good new tent made by my friends on board the Philomel, we left Loanda on the 20th of September, 1854, and passed round by sea to the mouth of the river Bengo. Ascending this river, we went through the district in which stand the ruins of the Convent of St. Antonio; thence into Icollo i Bengo, which contains a population of 6530 blacks, 172 mulattoes, and 11 whites, and is so named from having been the residence of a former native king. The proportion of slaves is only 3.38 per cent. of the inhabitants. The commandant of this place, Laurence José Marquis, is a frank old soldier and a most hospitable man: he is one of the few who secure the universal approbation of their fellow-men for stern unflinching honesty, and has risen from the ranks to be a major in the army. We were accompanied thus far by our generous host, Edmund Gabriel, Esq., who, by his unwearied attentions to myself, and liberality in supporting my men, had become endeared to all our hearts. My men were strongly impressed with a sense of his goodness, and often spoke of him in terms of admiration all the way to Linyanti.

28th September, Kalungwembo.—We were still on the same path by which we had come, and, there being no mosquitos, we could now better enjoy the scenery. Ranges of hills occupy both sides of our path, and the fine level road is adorned with a beautiful red flower named Bolcamaria The markets or sleeping-places are well supplied with provisions by great numbers of women, every one of whom is seen spinning cotton with a spindle and distaff exactly like those which were in use among the ancient Egyptians. A woman is scarcely ever seen going to the fields—though with a pot on her head, a child on her back, and the hoe over her shoulder—but she is employed in this way. The cotton was brought to the market for sale, and I bought a pound for a penny. This was the price demanded, and probably double what they ask from each other. We saw the cotton growing luxuriantly all around the market-places from seeds dropped accidentally. It is seen also about the native huts, and, so far as I could learn, it was the American cotton, so influenced by climate as to be perennial. We met in the road natives passing with bundles of cops, or spindles full of cotton thread, and these they were carrying to other parts to be woven into cloth. The women are the spinners, and the men perform the weaving. Each web is about five feet long, and fifteen or eighteen inches wide. The loom is of the simplest construction, being nothing but two beams placed one over the other, the web standing perpendicularly. The threads of the web are separated by means of a thin wooden lath, and the woof passed through by means of the spindle on which it has been wound in spinning.

Numbers of other articles are brought for sale to these sleeping-places. The native smiths there carry on their trade. I bought ten very good table-knives, made of country iron, for twopence each.

Labor is extremely cheap, for I was assured that even carpenters, masons, smiths, &c. might be hired for fourpence a day; and agriculturists would gladly work for half that sum.

Being anxious to obtain some more knowledge of this interesting country and its ancient missionary-establishments than the line of route by which we had come afforded, I resolved to visit the town of Massangano, which is situated to the south of Golungo Alto and at the confluence of the rivers Lucalla and Coanza. This led me to pass through the district of Cazengo, which is rather famous for the abundance and excellence of its coffee. Extensive coffee-plantations were found to exist on the sides of the several lofty mountains that compose this district. They were not planted by the Portuguese. The Jesuit and other missionaries are known to have brought some of the fine old Mocha seed, and these have propagated themselves far and wide: hence the excellence of the Angola coffee. Some have asserted that, as new plantations were constantly discovered even during the period of our visit, the coffee-tree was indigenous; but the fact that pineapples, bananas, yams, orange-trees, custard-apple-trees, pitangas, guavas, and other South American trees were found by me in the same localities with the recently-discovered coffee would seem to indicate that all foreign trees must have been introduced by the same agency. It is known that the

Jesuits also introduced many other trees for the sake of their timber alone. Numbers of these have spread over the country; some have probably died out and others failed to spread, like a lonely specimen that stands in what was the Botanic Garden of Loanda, and, though most useful in yielding a substitute for frankincense, is the only one of the kind in Africa.

Accompanied by the commandant of Cazengo, who was well acquainted with this part of the country, I proceeded in a canoe down the river Lucalla to Massangano. This river is about eighty-five yards wide, and navigable for canoes from its confluence with the Coanza to about six miles above the point where it receives the Luinha. Near this latter point stand the strong, massive ruins of an iron-foundry erected in the times (1768) and by the order of the famous Marquis of Pombal. The whole of the buildings were constructed of stone cemented with oil and lime. The dam for water-power was made of the same materials, and twenty-seven feet high. This had been broken through by a flood, and solid blocks, many yards in length, were carried down the stream, affording an instructive example of the transporting-power of water. There was nothing in the appearance of the place to indicate unhealthiness; but eight Spanish and Swedish workmen, being brought hither for the purpose of instructing the natives in the art of smelting iron, soon fell victims to disease and "irregularities." The effort of the marquis to improve the mode of manufacturing iron was thus rendered abortive. Labor and subsistence are, however, so very cheap that almost any amount of work can be executed at a cost that renders expensive establishments unnecessary.

A party of native miners and smiths are still kept in the employment of the Government, who, working the rich, black, magnetic iron-ore, produce for the Government from 480 to 500 bars of good malleable iron every month. They are supported by the appropriation of a few thousands of a small fresh-water fish, called "Cacusu," a portion of the tax levied upon the fishermen of the Coanza. This fish is so much relished in the country that those who do not wish to eat them can easily convert them into money. The commandant of the district of Massangano, for instance, has a right to a dish of three hundred every morning, as part of his salary. Shell-fish are also found in the Coanza, and the "Peixemulher," or woman-fish of the Portuguese, which is probably a Manatee.

We found the town of Massangano on a tongue of rather high land formed by the left bank of the Lucalla and right bank of the Coanza, and received true Portuguese hospitality from Senhor Lubata. The town has more than a thousand inhabitants: the district has 28,063, with only 315 slaves.

Massangano district is well adapted for sugar and rice, while Cambambe is a very superior field for cotton; but the bar at the mouth of the Coanza would prevent the approach of a steamer into this desirable region, though a small one could ply on it with ease when once in.

The latitude of the town and fort of Massangano is 9° 37′ 46″ S., being nearly the same as that of Cassange. The country between Loanda and this point being comparatively flat, a railroad might be constructed at small expense. The level country is prolonged along the north bank of the Coanza to the edge of the Cassange basin, and a railway carried thither would be convenient for the transport of the products of the rich districts of Cassange, Pungo Andongo, Ambaca, Cambambe, Golungo Alto, Cazengo, Muchima, and Calumbo,—in a word, the whole of Angola and independent tribes adjacent to this kingdom.

Returning by ascending the Lucalla into Cazengo, we had an opportunity of visiting several flourishing coffee-plantations, and observed that several men, who had begun with no capital but honest industry, had in the course of a few years acquired a comfortable subsistence. One of these, Mr. Pinto, generously furnished me with a good supply of his excellent coffee, and my men with a breed of rabbits to carry to their own country. Their lands granted by Government, yielded, without much labor, coffee sufficient for all the necessaries of life.

On returning to Golungo Alto, I found several of my men laid up with fever. One of the reasons for my leaving them there was that they might recover from the fatigue of the journey from Loanda, which had much more effect upon their feet than hundreds of miles had on our way westward. They had always been accustomed to moisture in their own well-watered land, and we certainly had a superabundance of that in Loanda. The roads, however, from Loanda to Golungo Alto were both hard and dry, and they suffered severely in consequence; yet they were composing songs to be sung when they should reach home. The Argonauts were nothing to them; and they remarked very impressively to me, "It was well you came with Makololo; for no tribe could have done what we have accomplished in coming to the white man's country: we are the true ancients, who can tell wonderful things." Two of them now had fever in the continued form, and became jaundiced, the whites or conjunctival membrane of their eyes becoming as yellow as saffron; and a third suffered from an attack of mania. He came to his companions one day, and said, "Remain well. I am called away by the gods!" and set off at the top of his speed. The young men caught him before he had gone a mile, and bound him. By gentle treatment and watching for a few days he recovered. I have observed several instances of this kind in the country, but very few cases of idiocy; and I believe that continued insanity is rare.

CHAPTER XXI.

DR LIVINGSTONE VISITS PUNGO ANDONGO.

WHILE waiting for the recovery of my men, I visited, in company with my friend Mr. Canto, the deserted Convent of St. Hilarion, at Bango, a few miles northwest of Golungo Alto. It is situated in a magnificent valley, containing a population numbering 4000 hearths. This is the abode of the Sova, or Chief Bango, who still holds a place of authority under the Portuguese. The garden of the convent, the church, and dormitories of the brethren are still kept in a good state of repair. I looked at the furniture, couches, and large chests for holding the provisions of the brotherhood with interest, and would fain have learned something of the former occupants; but all the books and sacred vessels had lately been removed to Loanda, and even the graves of the good men stand without any record: their resting-places are, however, carefully tended. All speak well of the Jesuits and other missionaries, as the Capuchins, &c., for having attended diligently to the instruction of the children. They were supposed to have a tendency to take the part of the people against the Government, and were supplanted by priests, concerning whom no regret is expressed that they were allowed to die out. In viewing the present fruits of former missions, it is impossible not to feel assured that, if the Jesuit teaching has been so permanent, that of Protestants, who leave the Bible in the hands of their converts, will not be less abiding.

The chief recreations of the natives of Angola are marriages and funerals. When a young woman is about to be married, she is placed in a hut alone and anointed with various unguents, and many incantations are employed in order to secure good fortune and fruitfulness. Here, as almost everywhere in the south, the height of good fortune is to bear sons. They often leave a husband altogether if they have daughters only. In their dances, when any one may wish to deride another, in the accompanying song a line is introduced, "So and so has no children, and never will get any." She feels the insult so keenly that it is not uncommon for her to rush away and commit suicide. After some days the bride elect is taken to another hut, and adorned with all the richest clothing and ornaments that the relatives can either lend or borrow. She is then placed in a public situation, saluted as a lady, and presents made by all her acquaintances are placed around her. After this she is taken to the residence of her husband, where she has a hut for herself, and becomes one of several wives,—for polygamy is general. Dancing, feasting, and drinking on such occasions are prolonged for several days. In case of separation, the woman returns to her father's family, and the husband receives back what he gave for her. In nearly all cases a man gives a price for the wife, and in cases of mulattoes as much as £60 is often given to the parents of the bride. This is one of the evils the bishop was trying to remedy.

In cases of death the body is kept several days; and there is a grand concourse of both sexes, with beating of drums, dances, and debauchery, kept up with feasting, &c., according to the means of the relative. The great ambition of many of the blacks of Angola is to give their friends an expensive funeral. Often, when one is asked to sell a pig, he replies, "I am keeping it in case of the death of any of my friends." A pig is usually slaughtered and eaten on the last day of the ceremonies, and its head thrown into the nearest stream or river. A native will sometimes appear intoxicated on these occasions, and, if blamed for his intemperance, will reply, "Why, my mother is dead!" as if he thought it a sufficient justification. The expenses of funerals are so heavy that often years elapse before they can defray them.

These people are said to be very litigious and obstinate

constant disputes are taking place respecting their lands A case came before the weekly court of the commandant involving property in a palm-tree worth twopence. The judge advised the pursuer to withdraw the case, as the more expenses of entering it would be much more than the cost of the tree. "Oh, no," said he; "I have a piece of calico with me for the clerk, and money for yourself. It's my right: I will not forego it." The calico itself cost three or four shillings. They rejoice if they can say of an enemy, "I took him before the court."

My friend Mr. Canto, the commandant, being seized with fever in a severe form, it afforded me much pleasure to attend *him* in his sickness who had been so kind to *me* in mine He was for some time in a state of insensibility; and I, having the charge of his establishment, had thus an opportunity of observing the workings of slavery. When a master is ill, the slaves run riot among the eatables. I did not know this until I observed that every time the sugar-basin came to the table it was empty. On visiting my patient by night, I passed along a corridor, and unexpectedly came upon the washerwoman eating pineapples and sugar. All the sweetmeats were devoured, and it was difficult for me to get even bread and butter until I took the precaution of locking the pantry-door. Probably the slaves thought that, as both they and the luxuries were the master's property, there was no good reason why they should be kept apart.

Debarred by my precaution from these sources of enjoyment, they took to killing the fowls and goats, and, when the animal was dead, brought it to me, saying, "We found this thing lying out there." They then enjoyed a feast of flesh. A feeling of insecurity prevails throughout this country. It is quite common to furnish visitors with the keys of their rooms. When called on to come to breakfast or dinner, each locks his door and puts the key in his pocket. At Kolobeng we never locked our doors by night or by day for months together; but there slavery is unknown. The Portuguese do not seem at all bigoted in their attachment to slavery, nor yet in their prejudices against color. Mr. Canto gave an entertainment in order to draw all classes together and promote general good-will Two sovas or native chiefs were present, and took their places without the least appearance of embarrassment. The Sova of Kilombo appeared in the dress of a general, and the Sova of Bango was gayly attired in a red coat profusely ornamented with tinsel. The latter had a band of musicians with him, consisting of six trumpeters and four drummers, who performed very well. These men are fond of titles, and the Portuguese Government humors them by conferring honorary captaincy, &c.: the Sova of Bango was at present anxious to obtain the title of "Major of all the Sovas." At the tables of other gentlemen I observed the same thing constantly occurring. At this meeting Mr. Canto communicated some ideas which I had written out on the dignity of labor and the superiority of free over slave labor. The Portuguese gentlemen present were anxiously expecting an arrival of American cotton-seed from Mr. Gabriel. They are now in the transition-state from unlawful to lawful trade, and turn eagerly to cotton, coffee, and sugar as new sources of wealth. Mr. Canto had been commissioned by them to purchase three sugar-mills. Our cruisers have been the principal agents in compelling them to abandon the slave-trade; and our Government, in furnishing them with a supply of cotton-seed, showed a generous intention to aid them in commencing a more honorable course. It can scarcely be believed, however, that after Lord Clarendon had been at the trouble of procuring fresh cotton-seed through our minister at Washington, and had sent it out to the care of H. M. Commissioner at Loanda, probably from having fallen into the hands of a few incorrigible slave-traders, it never reached its destination. It was most likely cast into the sea of Ambriz, and my friends at Golungo Alto were left without the means of commencing a new enterprise.

Mr. Canto mentioned that there is now much more cotton in the country than can be consumed; and if he had possession of a few hundred pounds he would buy up all the oil and cotton at a fair price, and thereby bring about a revolution in the agriculture of the country. These commodities are not produced in greater quantity, because the people have no market for those which now spring up almost spontaneously around them. The above was put down in my journal when I had no idea that enlarged supplies of cotton from new sources were so much needed at home.

It is common to cut down cotton-trees as a nuisance, and cultivate beans, potatoes, and manioc sufficient only for their own consumption. I have the impression that cotton, which is deciduous in America, is perennial here; for the plants I saw in winter were not dead, though going by the name Algodão Americana, or American cotton. The rents paid for gardens belonging to the old convents are merely nominal, varying from one shilling to three pounds per annum. The higher rents being realized from those in the immediate vicinity of Loanda, none but Portuguese or half-castes can pay them.

When about to start, the horse which the governor had kindly presented for Sekeletu was seized with inflammation, which delayed us some time longer; and we ultimately lost it.

November 20.—An eclipse of the sun, which I had anxiously hoped to observe with a view of determining the longitude, happened this morning, and, as often took place in this cloudy climate, the sun was covered four minutes before it began. When it shone forth, the eclipse was in progress, and a few minutes before it should (according to my calculations) have ended the sun was again completely obscured. The greatest patience and perseverance are required if one wishes to ascertain his position when it is the rainy season.

Before leaving, I had an opportunity of observing a

curious insect, which inhabits trees of the fig family, (*Ficus*,) upward of twenty species of which are found here. Seven or eight of them cluster round a spot on one of the smaller branches, and there keep up a constant distillation of a clear fluid, which, dropping to the ground, forms a little puddle below. If a vessel is placed under them in the evening, it contains three or four pints of fluid in the morning. The natives say that if a drop falls into the eyes it causes inflammation of these organs. To the question, whence is this fluid derived, the people reply that the insects suck it out of the tree; and our own naturalists give the same answer. I have never seen an orifice, and it is scarcely possible that the tree can yield so much. A similar but much smaller homopterous insect, of the family *Cercopidæ*, is known in England as the frog-hopper, (*Aphrophora spumaria*,) when full grown and furnished with wings, but while still in the pupa state it is called "*Cuckoo-spit*," from the mass of froth in which it envelops itself. The circulation of sap in plants in our climate, especially of the graminaceæ, is not quick enough to yield much moisture. The African species is five or six times the size of the English. In the case of branches of the fig-tree, the point the insects congregate on is soon marked by a number of incipient roots, such as are thrown out when a cutting is inserted in the ground for the purpose of starting another tree. I believe that both the English and African insects belong to the same family, and differ only in size, and that the chief part of the moisture is derived from the atmosphere. I leave it for naturalists to explain how these little creatures distil both by night and day as much water as they please, and are more independent than her majesty's steamships with their apparatus for condensing steam; for, without coal, their abundant supplies of sea-water are of no avail. I tried the following experiment. Finding a colony of these insects busily distilling on a branch of the *Ricinus communis*, or castor-oil plant, I denuded about twenty inches of the bark on the tree side of the insects, and scraped away the inner bark, so as to destroy all the ascending vessels. I also cut a hole in the side of the branch, reaching to the middle, and then cut out the pith and internal vessels. The distillation was then going on at the rate of one drop each sixty-seven seconds, or about 2 ounces 5½ drachms in twenty-four hours. Next morning the distillation, so far from being affected by the attempt to stop the supplies, supposing they had come up through the branch from the tree, was increased to a drop every five seconds, or twelve drops per minute, making one pint (16 ounces) in every twenty-four hours. I then cut the branch so much that, during the day, it broke; but they still went on at the rate of a drop every five seconds, while another colony on a branch of the same tree gave a drop every seventeen seconds only, or at the rate of about 10 ounces 4⅜ drachms in twenty-four hours. I finally cut off the branch; but this was too much for their patience, for they immediately decamped, as insects will do from either a dead branch or a dead animal,—which Indian hunters soon know when they sit down on a recently-killed bear. The presence of greater moisture in the air increased the power of these distillers: the period of greatest activity was in the morning, when the air and every thing else was charged with dew.

Having but one day left for experiment, I found again that another colony on a branch denuded in the same way yielded a drop every two seconds, or 4 pints 10 ounces in twenty-four hours, while a colony on a branch untouched yielded a drop every eleven seconds, or 16 ounces 2$\frac{18}{18}$ drachms in twenty-four hours. I regretted somewhat the want of time to institute another experiment, namely, to cut a branch and place it in water, so as to keep it in life, and then observe if there was any diminution of the quantity of water in the vessel. This alone was wanting to make it certain that they draw water from the atmosphere. I imagine that they have some power of which we are not aware, besides that nervous influence which caus.s constant motion to our own involuntary muscles, the power of life-long action without fatigue. The reader will remember, in connection with this insect, the case of the ants already mentioned.

December 14.—Both myself and men having recovered from severe attacks of fever, we left the hospitable residence of Mr. Canto with a deep sense of his kindness to us all, and proceeded on our way to Ambaca. (Lat. 9° 16′ 35″ S., long. 15° 23′ E.)

Owing to the weakness of the men who had been sick, we were able to march but short distances. Three hours and a half brought us to the banks of the Caloi, a small stream which flows into the Senza.

We found, on reaching Ambaca, that the gallant old soldier, Laurence José Marquis, had, since our passing Icollo i Bengo, been promoted, on account of his stern integrity, to the government of this important district. The office of commandant is much coveted by the officers of the line who come to Angola, not so much for the salary as for the perquisites, which, when managed skilfully, in the course of a few years make one rich.

Before leaving Ambaca we received a present of ten head of cattle from Mr. Schut of Loanda; and, as it shows the cheapness of provisions here, I may mention that the cost was only about a guinea per head.

On crossing the Lucalla we made a détour to the south, in order to visit the famous rocks of Pungo Andongo. As soon as we crossed the rivulet Lotete, a change in the vegetation of the country was apparent. We found trees identical with those to be seen south of the Chobe. The grass, too, stands in tufts, and is of that kind which the natives consider to be best adapted for cattle. Two species of grape-bearing vines abound everywhere in this district, and the influence of the good pasturage is seen in the plump condition of the cattle. In all my previous inquiries respecting the vegetable products of Angola, I was invariably

directed to Pungo Andongo. "Do you grow wheat?"—
"Oh, yes, in Pungo Andongo." "Grapes, figs, or peaches?"
—"Oh, yes, in Pungo Andongo." "Do you make butter,
cheese, &c.?" The uniform answer was, "Oh, yes: there
is abundance of all these in Pungo Andongo." But when
we arrived here we found that the answers all referred to
the activity of one man, Colonel Manuel Antonio Pires.
The presence of the wild grape shows that vineyards might
be cultivated with success; the wheat grows well without
irrigation; and any one who tasted the butter and cheese
at the table of Colonel Pires would prefer them to the
stale produce of the Irish dairy in general use throughout
that province. The cattle in this country are seldom
milked, on account of the strong prejudice which the Portuguese entertain against the use of milk. They believe
that it may be used with safety in the morning, but, if
taken after mid-day, that it will cause fever. It seemed
to me that there was not much reason for carefully avoiding a few drops in their coffee after having devoured ten
times the amount in the shape of cheese at dinner.

The fort of Pungo Andongo (lat. 9° 42′ 14″ S., long. 15°
30′ E.) is situated in the midst of a group of curious
columnar-shaped rocks, each of which is upward of three
hundred feet in height. They are composed of conglomerate, made up of a great variety of rounded pieces in a
matrix of dark red sandstone. They rest on a thick stratum of this last rock, with very few of the pebbles in its
substance. On this a fossil palm has been found, and if of
the same age as those on the eastern side of the continent
on which similar palms now lie, there may be coal underneath this, as well as under that of Tete. The asserted
existence of petroleum-springs at Dande, and near Cambambe, would seem to indicate the presence of this useful
mineral, though I am not aware of any one having actually
seen a seam of coal tilted up to the surface in Angola, as
we have at Tete. The gigantic pillars of Pungo Andongo
have been formed by a current of the sea coming from the

s

S.S.E.; for, seen from the top, they appear arranged in that direction, and must have withstood the surges of the ocean at a period of our world's history when the relations of land and sea were totally different from what they are now, and long before "the morning stars sang together, and all the sons of God shouted for joy to see the abodes prepared which man was soon to fill." The embedded pieces in the conglomerate are of gneiss, clay shale, mica and sandstone schists, trap, and porphyry, most of which are large enough to give the whole the appearance of being the only remaining vestiges of vast primeval banks of shingle. Several little streams run among these rocks, and in the central part of the pillars stands the village, completely environed by wellnigh-inaccessible rocks. The pathways into the village might be defended by a small body of troops against an army; and this place was long the stronghold of the tribe called Jinga, the original possessors of the country.

In former times the Portuguese imagined that this place was particularly unhealthy, and banishment to the black rocks of Pungo Andongo was thought by their judges to be a much severer sentence than transportation to any part of the coast; but this district is now well known to be the most healthy part of Angola. The water is remarkably pure, the soil is light, and the country open and undulating, with a general slope down toward the river Coanza, a few miles distant. That river is the southern boundary of the Portuguese, and beyond, to the S. and S.W., we see the high mountains of the Libollo. On the S.E. we have also a mountainous country, inhabited by the Kimbonda or Ambonda, who are said by Colonel Pires to be a very brave and independent people, but hospitable and fair in their dealings. They are rich in cattle, and their country produces much bees'-wax, which is carefully collected and brought to the Portuguese, with whom they have always been on good terms.

The Ako, (Hako,) a branch of this family, inhabit the

left bank of the Coanza above this village, who, instead of bringing slaves for sale, as formerly, now occasionally bring wax for the purchase of a slave from the Portuguese. I saw a boy sold for twelve shillings: he said that he belonged to the country of Matiamvo. Here I bought a pair of well-made boots, of good tanned leather, which reached above the knee, for five shillings and eightpence, and that was just the price given for one pound of ivory by Mr. Pires: consequently, the boy was worth two pairs of boots, or two pounds of ivory. The Libollo on the south have not so good a character; but the Coanza is always deep enough to form a line of defence. Colonel Pires is a good example of what an honest, industrious man in this country may become. He came as a servant in a ship, and, by a long course of persevering labor, has raised himself to be the richest merchant in Angola. He possesses some thousands of cattle, and, on any emergency, can appear in the field with several hundred armed slaves.

While enjoying the hospitality of this merchant-prince in his commodious residence, which is outside the rocks and commands a beautiful view of all the adjacent country, I learned that all my despatches, maps, and journal had gone to the bottom of the sea in the mail-packet "Forerunner." I felt so glad that my friend Lieutenant Bedingfeld, to whose care I had committed them, though in the most imminent danger, had not shared a similar fate, that I was at once reconciled to the labor of rewriting. I availed myself of the kindness of Colonel Pires, and remained till the end of the year reproducing my lost papers.

Colonel Pires having another establishment on the banks of the Coanza, about six miles distant, I visited it with him about once a week for the purpose of recreation. The difference of temperature caused by the lower altitude was seen in the cashew-trees; for while, near the rocks, these trees were but coming into flower, those at the lower station were ripening their fruit. Cocoanut-trees and bananas bear well at the lower station, but yield little or no fruit at the upper. The difference indicated by the thermometer was 7°. The general range near the rocks was 67° at 7 A.M., 74° at mid-day, and 72° in the evening.

A slave-boy belonging to Colonel Pires, having stolen and eaten some lemons in the evening, went to the river to wash his mouth, so as not to be detected by the flavor. An alligator seized him and carried him to an island in the middle of the stream: there the boy grasped hold of the reeds, and baffled all the efforts of the reptile to dislodge him, till his companions, attracted by his cries, came to his assistance. The alligator at once let go his hold; for when out of his own element he is cowardly. The boy had many marks of the teeth in his abdomen and thigh, and those of the claws on his legs and arms.

The slaves in Colonel Pires' establishments appeared more like free servants than any I had elsewhere seen. Every thing was neat and clean,—while generally, where slaves are the only domestics, there is an aspect of slovenliness, as if they went on the principle of always doing as little for their masters as possible.

In the country near to this station were a large number of the ancient burial-places of the Jinga. These are simply large mounds of stone, with drinking and cooking vessels of rude pottery on them. Some are arranged in a circular form, two or three yards in diameter, and shaped like a haycock. There is not a single vestige of any inscription. The natives of Angola generally have a strange predilection for bringing their dead to the sides of the most frequented paths. They have a particular anxiety to secure the point where cross-roads meet. On and around the graves are planted tree-euphorbias and other species of that family. On the grave itself they also place waterbottles, broken pipes, cooking-vessels, and sometimes a little bow and arrow.

The Portuguese Government, wishing to prevent this custom affixed a penalty on any one burying in the roads, and appointed places of public sepulture in every district in the country. The people persist, however, in spite of the most stringent enforcement of the law, to follow their ancient custom.

The country between the Coanza and Pungo Andongo is covered with low trees, bushes, and fine pasturage. In the latter we were pleased to see our old acquaintances, the gaudy gladiolus, Amaryllis toxicaria, hymanthus, and other bulbs, in as flourishing a condition as at the Cape.

It is surprising that so little has been done in the way of agriculture in Angola. Raising wheat by means of irrigation has never been tried; no plough is ever used; and the only instrument is the native hoe, in the hands of slaves. The chief object of agriculture is the manioc, which does not contain nutriment sufficient to give proper stamina to the people. The half-caste Portuguese have not so much energy as their fathers. They subsist chiefly on the manioc; and, as that can be eaten either raw, roasted, or boiled, as it comes from the ground, or fermented in water, and then roasted or dried after fermentation, and baked or pounded into fine meal, or rasped into meal and cooked as farina, or made into confectionary with butter and sugar, it does not so soon pall upon the palate as one might imagine when told that it constitutes their principal food. The leaves boiled make an excellent vegetable for the table; and, when eaten by goats, their milk is much increased. The wood is a good fuel, and yields a large quantity of potash. If planted in a dry soil, it takes two years to come to perfection, requiring during that time one weeding only. It bears drought well, and never shrivels up like other plants when deprived of rain. When planted in low, alluvial soils, and either well supplied with rain or annually flooded, twelve, or even ten, months are sufficient to bring it to maturity The root rasped while raw, placed upon a cloth, and rubbed with the hands while water is poured upon it, parts with its starchy glutinous matter, and this, when it settles at the bottom of the vessel and the water poured off, is placed in the sun till nearly dry, to form tapioca. The process of drying is completed on an iron plate over a slow fire, the mass being stirred meanwhile with a stick, and when quite dry it appears agglutinated into little globules, and is in the form we see the tapioca of commerce. This is never eaten by weevils, and so little labor is required in its cultivation that on the spot it is extremely cheap. Throughout the interior parts of Angola, fine manioc-meal, which could with ease have been converted either into superior starch or tapioca, is commonly sold at the rate of about ten pounds for a penny. All this region, however, has no means of transport to Loanda other than the shoulders of the carriers and slaves over a footpath.

Cambambe, to which the navigation of the Coanza reaches, is reported to be thirty leagues below Pungo Andongo. A large waterfall is the limit on that side; and another exists higher up, at the confluence of the Lombe, (lat. 9° 41' 26" S. and about long. 16° E.,) over which hippopotami and elephants are sometimes drawn and killed. The river between is rapid, and generally rushes over a rocky bottom. Its source is pointed out as S.E. or S.S.E. of its confluence with the Lombe, and near Bihe. The situation of Bihe is not well known. When at Sanza, we were assured that it lies nearly south of that point, and eight days distant. This statement seemed to be corroborated by our meeting many people going to Matiamvo and to Loanda from Bihe. Both parties had come to Sanza, and then branched off, one to the east, the other to the west. The source of the Coanza is thus probably not far from Sanza.

I had the happiness of doing a little good in the way of administering to the sick; for there are no doctors in the interior of Angola. Notwithstanding the general healthiness of this fine district and its pleasant temperature, I was attacked by the fever myself. While confined to my room, a gentleman of color, a canon of the Church, kindly paid me a visit. He was on a tour of visitation in the different interior districts for the purpose of baptizing and marrying He had lately been on a visit to Lisbon in company with the Prince of Congo, and had been invested with an order of honor by the King of Portugal as an acknowledgment of his services. He had all the appearance of a true negro, but commanded the respect of the people; and Colonel P., who had known him for thirty years, pronounced him to be a good man. There are only three or four priests in Loanda, —all men of color, but educated for the office. About the time of my journey in Angola, an offer was made to any young men of ability who might wish to devote themselves to the service of the Church to afford them the requisite education at the University of Coimbra in Portugal. I was informed, on what seemed good authority, that the Prince of Congo is professedly a Christian, and that there are no fewer than twelve churches in that kingdom, the fruits of the mission established in former times at San Salvador, the capital. These churches are kept in partial repair by the people, who also keep up the ceremonies of the Church, pronouncing some gibberish over the dead in imitation of the Latin prayers which they had formerly heard. Many of them can read and write. When a king of Congo dies, the body is wrapped up in a great many folds of cloth until a priest can come from Loanda to consecrate his successor. The King of Congo still retains the title of Lord of Angola, which he had when the Jinga, the original possessors of the soil, owed him allegiance; and, when he writes to the Governor of Angola, he places his own name first, as if addressing his vassal. The Jinga paid him tribute annually in cowries, which were found on the island that shelters Loanda Harbor, and, on refusing to continue payment, the King of Congo gave over the island to the Portuguese, and thus their dominion commenced in this quarter.

There is not much knowledge of the Christian religion in either Congo or Angola; yet it is looked-upon with a certain degree of favor. The prevalence of fever is probably the reason why no priest occupies a post in any part of the interior. They come on tours of visitation like that mentioned, and it is said that no expense is incurred, for all the people are ready not only to pay for their services, but also to furnish every article in their power gratuitously. In view of the desolate condition of this fine missionary-field, it is more than probable that the presence of a few Protestants would soon provoke the priests, if not to love, to good works.

CHAPTER XXII.

DR. LIVINGSTONE REACHES THE LOAJIMA RIVER.

January 1, 1855.—HAVING, through the kindness of Colonel Pires, reproduced some of my lost papers, I left Pungo Andongo the first day of this year, and at Candumba slept in one of the dairy-establishments of my friend, who had sent forward orders for an ample supply of butter, cheese, and milk. Our path lay along the right bank of the Coanza. This is composed of the same sandstone rock, with pebbles, which forms the flooring of the country. The land is level, has much open forest, and is well adapted for pasturage.

On reaching the confluence of the Lombe, we left the river, and proceeded in a northeasterly direction, through a fine open green country, to the village of Malange, where we struck into our former path. A few miles to the west of this a path branches off to a new district named the Duke Braganza. This path crosses the Lucalla and several of its feeders. The whole of the country drained by these is described as extremely fertile. The territory west of Braganza is reported to be mountainous, well wooded and watered; wild coffee is abundant, and the people even to their huts of coffee-trees. The rivers Dande, Senza, and Lucalla are said to rise in one mountain-range. Numerous tribes inhabit the country to the north, who are all independent. The Portuguese power extends chiefly over the tribes through whose lands we have passed. It may be said to be firmly seated only between the rivers Dande and Coanza. It extends inland about three hundred miles to the river Quango; and the population, according to the imperfect data afforded by the census given annually by the commandants of the fifteen or sixteen districts into which it is divided, cannot be under 600,000 souls.

Leaving Malange, we passed quickly, without deviation, along the path by which we had come. At Sanza (lat. 9° 37′ 46″ S., long. 16° 59′ E.) we expected to get a little seed-wheat, but this was not now to be found in Angola.

While at Tala Mungongo, we met a native of Bihe who has visited the country of Shinte three times for the purposes of trade. He gave us some of the news of that distant part, but not a word of the Makololo, who have always been represented in the countries to the north as a desperately-savage race, whom no trader could visit with safety. The half-caste traders whom we met at Shinte's had returned to Angola with sixty-six slaves and upward of fifty tusks of ivory. As we came along the path, we daily met long lines of carriers bearing large square masses of bees' wax, each about a hundred pounds' weight, and number of elephants' tusks, the property of Angolese merchants. Many natives were proceeding to the coast also on their own account, carrying bees'-wax, ivory, and sweet oil. They appeared to travel in perfect security; and at different parts of the road we purchased fowls from them at a penny each. My men took care to celebrate their own daring in having actually entered ships, while the natives of these parts, who had endeavored to frighten them on their way down, had only seen them at a distance. Poor fellows! they were more than ever attentive to me; and as they were not obliged to erect sheds for themselves, in consequence of finding them already built at the different sleeping-places, all their care was bestowed in making me comfortable. Mashauana, as usual, made his bed with his head close to my feet, and never during the entire journey did I have to call him twice for any thing I needed.

January 15, 1855.—We descended in one hour from the heights of Tala Mungongo. I counted the number of paces made on the slope downward, and found them to be sixteen hundred, which may give a perpendicular height of from twelve to fifteen hundred feet.

Before we reached Cassange we were overtaken by the commandant, Senhor Carvalho, who was returning, with a detachment of fifty men and a field-piece, from an unsuccessful search after some rebels. The rebels had fled, and all he could do was to burn their huts. He kindly invited me to take up my residence with him; but, not wishing t pass by the gentleman (Captain Neves) who had so kindly received me on my first arrival in the Portuguese possessions, I declined. Senhor Rego had been superseded in his command, because the Governor Amaral, who had come into office since my departure from Loanda, had determined that the law which requires the office of commandant to be exclusively occupied by military officers of the line should once more come into operation. I was again most kindly welcomed by my friend Captain Neves, whom I found laboring under a violent inflammation and abscess of the hand. There is nothing in the situation of this village to indicate unhealthiness, except, perhaps, the rank luxuriance of the vegetation. Nearly all the Portuguese inhabitants suffer from enlargement of the spleen, the effects of frequent intermittents, and have generally a sickly appearance. Thinking that this affection of the hand was simply an effort of nature to get rid of malarious matter from the system, I recommended the use of quinine. He himself applied the leaf of a plant called cathory, famed among the natives as an excellent remedy for ulcers. The cathory-leaves, when boiled, exude a gummy juice, which effectually shuts out the external air. Each remedy, of course, claimed the merit of the cure.

Many of the children are cut off by fever. A fine boy of Captain Neves' had, since my passage westward, shared a similar fate. Another child died during the period of my visit.

The intercourse which the natives have had with white men does not seem to have much ameliorated their condition. A great number of persons are reported to lose their lives annually in different districts of Angola by the cruel superstitions to which they are addicted, and the Portuguese authorities either know nothing of them or are unable to prevent their occurrence. The natives are bound to secrecy by those who administer the ordeal, which generally causes the death of the victim. A person, when accused of witchcraft, will often travel from distant districts in order to assert her innocency and brave the test. They come to a river on the Cassange called Dua, drink the infusion of a poisonous tree, and perish unknown.

The same superstitious ideas being prevalent through the whole of the country north of the Zambesi seems to indicate that the people must originally have been one. All believe that the souls of the departed still mingle among the living and partake in some way of the food they consume.

The chieftainship is elective from certain families. Among the Bangalas of the Cassange valley the chief is chosen from three families in rotation. A chief's brother inherits in preference to his son. The sons of a sister belong to her brother; and he often sells his nephews to pay his debts. By this and other unnatural customs, more than by war, is the slave-market supplied.

While here, I reproduced the last of my lost papers and maps; and, as there is a post twice a month from Loanda, I had the happiness to receive a packet of the "*Times*," and, among other news, an account of the Russian war up to the terrible charge of the light cavalry. The intense anxiety I felt to hear more may be imagined by every true patriot; but I was forced to brood on in silent thought, and utter my poor prayers for friends who perchance were now no more, until I reached the other side of the continent.

A considerable trade is carried on by the Cassange merchants with all the surrounding territory by means of native traders, whom they term "pombeiros." Two of these, called in the history of Angola "the trading blacks," (os feirantes pretos,) Pedro João Baptista and Antonio José, having been sent by the first Portuguese trader that lived at Cassange, actually returned from some of the Portuguese possessions in the East with letters from the governor of Mozambique in the year 1815, proving, as is remarked, "the possibility of so important a communication between Mozambique and Loanda." This is the only instance of native Portuguese subjects crossing the continent. No European ever accomplished it, though this fact has lately been quoted as if the men had been "*Portuguese.*"

Captain Neves was now actively engaged in preparing a present, worth about fifty pounds, to be sent by pombeiros to Matiamvo. It consisted of great quantities of cotton cloth, a large carpet, an arm-chair with a canopy and curtains of crimson calico, an iron bedstead, mosquito-curtains, beads, &c., and a number of pictures rudely painted in oil by an embryo black painter at Cassange.

Matiamvo, like most of the natives in the interior of the country, has a strong desire to possess a cannon, and had sent ten large tusks to purchase one; but, being Government property, it could not be sold: he was now furnished with a blunderbuss mounted as a cannon, which would probably please him as well.

Senhor Graça and some other Portuguese have visited this chief at different times; but no European resides beyond the Quango: indeed, it is contrary to the policy of the Government of Angola to allow their subjects to penetrate farther into the interior. The present would have been a good opportunity for me to have visited that chief, and I felt strongly inclined to do so, as he had expressed dissatisfaction respecting my treatment by the Chiboque, and even threatened to punish them. As it would be improper to force my men to go thither, I resolved to wait and see whether the proposition might not emanate from themselves. When I can get the natives to agree in the propriety of any step, they go to the end of the affair without a murmur. I speak to them and treat them as rational beings, and generally get on well with them in consequence.

February 20.—On the day of starting from Cassange the westerly wind blew strongly, and on the day following we were brought to a stand by several of our party being laid up with fever. This complaint is the only serious drawback Angola possesses. It is in every other respect an agreeable land, and admirably adapted for yielding a rich abundance of tropical produce for the rest of the world. Indeed, I have no hesitation in asserting that, had it been in the possession of England, it would now have been yielding as much or more of the raw material for her manufactures as an equal extent of territory in the cotton-growing States of America. A railway from Loanda to this valley would secure the trade of most of the interior of South Central Africa.

As soon as we could move toward the Quango we did so, meeting in our course several trading-parties, both native and Portuguese. We met two of the latter carrying a tusk weighing 126 lbs. The owner afterward informed us that its fellow on the left side of the same elephant was 130 lbs. It was 8 feet 6½ inches long, and 21 inches in circumference at the part on which the lip of the animal rests. The elephant was rather a small one, as is common in this hot central region. Some idea may be formed of the strength of his neck when it is recollected that he bore a weight of 256 lbs. The ivory which comes from the east and northeast of Cassange is very much larger than any to be found farther south. Captain Neves had one weighing 120 lbs.; and this weight is by no means uncommon. They have been found weighing even 158 lbs.

Before reaching the Quango we were again brought to a stand, by fever in two of my companions, close to the residence of a Portuguese who rejoiced in the name of William Tell and who lived here in spite of the prohibition of the Government. We were using the water of a pond; and this gentleman, having come to invite me to dinner, drank a little of it, and caught fever in consequence. If malarious matter existed in water, it would have been a wonder had we escaped; for, travelling in the sun, with the thermometer from 96° to 98° in the shade, the evaporation from our bodies causing much thirst, we generally partook of every water we came to. We had probably thus more disease than others might suffer who had better shelter.

Mr. Tell remarked that his garden was rather barren, being still, as he said, wild; but when more worked it would become better, though no manure be applied. My men were busy collecting a better breed of fowls and pigeons than those in their own country. Mr. Tell presented them with some large specimens from Rio Janeiro. Of these they were wonderfully proud, and bore the cock in triumph through the country of the Balonda, as evidence of having been to the sea. But when at the village of Shinte a hyena came into our midst when we were all sound asleep, and picked out the giant in his basket from eighty-four others, and he was lost, to the great grief of my men. The anxiety these people have always shown to improve the breed of their domestic animals is, I think, a favorable point in their character.

On coming back to Cypriano's village on the 28th, we found his step-father had died after we had passed, and, according to the custom of the country, he had spent more than his patrimony in funeral orgies. He acted with his wonted kindness, though, unfortunately, drinking has got him so deeply in debt that he now keeps out of the way of his creditors. He informed us that the source of the Quango is eight days, or one hundred miles, to the south of this, and in a range called Mosamba, in the country of the Basongo. We can see from this a sort of break in the high land which stretches away round to Tala Mongongo, through which the river comes.

A death had occurred in a village about a mile off, and the people were busy beating drums and firing guns. The funeral rites are half festive, half mourning, partaking somewhat of the character of an Irish wake. There is nothing more heart-rending than their death-wails. When the natives turn their eyes to the future world, they have a view cheerless enough of their own utter helplessness and hopelessness. They fancy themselves completely in the power of the disembodied spirits, and look upon the prospect of following them as the greatest of misfortunes. Hence they are constantly deprecating the wrath of departed souls, believing that, if they are appeased, there is no other cause of death but witchcraft, which may be averted by charms.

We were informed that a chief named Gando, living on the other side of the river, having been accused of witchcraft, was killed by the ordeal, and his body thrown into the Quango.

The ferrymen demanded thirty yards of calico, but received six thankfully. The canoes were wretched, carrying only two persons at a time; but, my men being well acquainted with the water, we all got over in about two hours and a half. They excited the admiration of the inhabitants by the manner in which they managed the cattle and donkeys in crossing.

On the eastern side of the Quango we passed on, without visiting our friend of the conical head-dress, to the residence of some Ambakistas who had crossed the river in order to secure the first chances of trade in wax. I have before remarked on the knowledge of reading and writing that these Ambakistas possess; they are famed for their love of all sorts of learning within their reach, a knowledge of the history of Portugal, Portuguese law, &c. &c. They are remarkably keen in trade, and are sometimes called the Jews of Angola. They are employed as clerks and writers, their feminine delicacy of constitution enabling them to write a fine lady's hand, a kind of writing much esteemed among the Portuguese. They are not physically equal to the European Portuguese, but possess considerable ability; and it is said that half-castes, in the course of a few generations, return to the black color of the maternal ancestor.

The Bashinje, in whose country we now are, seem to possess more of the low negro character and physiognomy than either the Balonda or Basongo; their color is generally dirty black, foreheads low and compressed, noses flat and much expanded laterally, though this is partly owing to the alæ spreading over the cheeks, by the custom of inserting bits of sticks or reeds in the septum; their teeth are deformed by being filed to points; their lips are large. They make a nearer approach to a general negro appearance than any tribes I met; but I did not notice this on my way down. They cultivate pretty largely, and rely upon their agricultural products for their supplies of salt, flesh, tobacco, &c. from Bangalas. Their clothing consists of pieces of skin hung loosely from the girdle in front and behind. They plait their hair fantastically. We saw some women coming with their hair woven into the form of a European hat, and it was only by a closer inspection that its nature was detected. Others had it arranged in tufts, with a threefold cord along the edge of each tuft; while others, again, follow the ancient Egyptian fashion, having the whole mass of wool plaited into cords, all hanging down as far as the shoulders. This mode, with the somewhat Egyptian cast of countenance in other parts of Londa, reminded me strongly of the paintings of that nation in the British Museum.

We had now rain every day, and the sky seldom presented that cloudless aspect and clear blue so common in the dry lands of the south. The heavens are often overcast by large white motionless masses, which stand for hours in the same position; and the intervening spaces are filled with a milk-and-water-looking haze. Notwithstanding these unfavorable circumstances, I obtained good observations for the longitude of this important point on both sides of the Quango, and found the river running in 9° 50' S. lat., 18° 33' E. long.

On proceeding to our former station near Sansawe's village, he ran to meet us with wonderful urbanity, asking if we had seen Moene Put, king of the white men, (or Portuguese,) and added, on parting, that he would come to receive his dues in the evening. I replied that, as he had treated us so scurvily, even forbidding his people to sell us any food, if he did not bring us a fowl and some eggs as part of his duty as a chief, he should receive no present from me. When he came, it was in the usual Londa way of showing the exalted position he occupies, mounted on the shoulders of his spokesman, as schoolboys sometimes do in England, and as was represented to have been the case in the southern islands when Captain Cook visited them. My companions, amused at his idea of dignity, greeted him with a hearty laugh. He visited the native traders first, and then came to me with two cocks as a present. I spoke to him about the impolicy of treatment we had received at his hands, and quoted the example of the Bangalas, who had been conquered by the Portuguese for their extortionate demands of payment for firewood, grass, water, &c., and concluded by denying his right to any payment for simply passing through uncultivated land. To all this he agreed; and then I gave him, as a token of friendship, a pannikin of coarse powder, two iron spoons, and two yards of coarse printed calico. He looked rather

T

saucily at these articles, for he had just received a barrel containing eighteen pounds of powder, twenty-four yards of calico, and two bottles of brandy, from Senhor Pascoal the pombeiro. Other presents were added the next day, but we gave nothing more; and the pombeiros informed me that it was necessary to give largely, because they are accompanied by slaves and carriers who are no great friends to their masters; and, if they did not secure the friendship of these petty chiefs, many slaves and their loads might be stolen while passing through the forests. It is thus a sort of black-mail that these insignificant chiefs levy; and the native traders, in paying, do so simply as a bribe to keep them honest. This chief was a man of no power, but in our former ignorance of this he plagued us a whole day in passing.

Finding the progress of Senhor Pascoal and the other pombeiros excessively slow, I resolved to forego his company to Cabango after I had delivered to him some letters to be sent back to Cassange. I went forward with the intention of finishing my writing and leaving a packet for him at some village. We ascended the eastern acclivity that bounds the Cassange valley, which has rather a gradual ascent up from the Quango, and we found that the last ascent, though apparently not quite so high as that at Tala Mungongo, is actually much higher. The top is about 5000 feet above the level of the sea, and the bottom 3500 feet; water boiling on the heights at 202°, the thermometer in the air showing 96°, and at the bottom at 205°, the air being 75°. We had now gained the summit of the western subtending ridge, and began to descend toward the centre of the country, hoping soon to get out of the Chiboque territory, which, when we ascended from the Cassange valley, we had entered; but, on the 19th of April, the intermittent, which had begun on the 16th of March, was changed into an extremely severe attack of rheumatic fever. This was brought on by being obliged to sleep on an extensive plain covered with water The rain poured down incessantly; but we formed our beds by dragging up the earth into oblong mounds, somewhat like graves in a country churchyard, and then placing grass upon them. The rain continuing to deluge us, we were unable to leave for two days; but as soon as it became fair we continued our march. The heavy dew upon the high grass was so cold as to cause shivering, and I was forced to lie by for eight days, tossing and groaning with violent pain in the head. This was the most severe attack I had endured. It made me quite unfit to move, or even know what was passing outside my little tent. Senhor Pascoal, who had been detained by the severe rain at a better spot, at last came up, and, knowing that leeches abounded in the rivulets, procured a number, and applied some dozens to the nape of the neck and the loins. This partially relieved the pain. He was then obliged to move forward, in order to purchase food for his large party. After many days, I began to recover, and wished to move on, but my men objected to the attempt on account of my weakness. When Senhor Pascoal had been some time at the village in front, as he had received instructions from his employer, Captain Neves, to aid me as much as possible, and being himself a kindly-disposed person, he sent back two messengers to invite me to come on, if practicable.

It happened that the head-man of the village where I had lain twenty-two days, while bargaining and quarrelling in my camp for a piece of meat, had been struck on the mouth by one of my men. My principal men paid five pieces of cloth and a gun as an atonement; but the more they yielded the more exorbitant he became, and he sent word to all the surrounding villages to aid him in avenging the affront of a blow on the beard. As their courage usually rises with success, I resolved to yield no more, and departed. In passing through a forest in the country beyond, we were startled by a body of men rushing after us. They began by knocking down the burdens of the hindermost of my men, and several shots were fired, each party spreading out on both sides of the path. I fortunately had a six-barrelled revolver, which my friend Captain Henry Need, of her majesty's brig "Linnet," had considerately sent to Golungo Alto after my departure from Loanda. Taking this in my hand, and forgetting fever, I staggered quickly along the path with two or three of my men, and fortunately encountered the chief. The sight of the six barrels gaping into his stomach, with my own ghastly visage looking daggers at his face, seemed to produce an instant revolution in his martial feelings, for he cried out, "Oh, I have only come to speak to you, and wish peace only." Mashauana had hold of him by the hand, and found him shaking. We examined his gun, and found that it had been discharged. Both parties crowded up to their chiefs. One of the opposite party coming too near, one of mine drove him back with a battle-axe. The enemy protested their amicable intentions, and my men asserted the fact of having the goods knocked down as evidence of the contrary. Without waiting long, I requested all to sit down; and Pitsane, placing his hand upon the revolver, somewhat allayed their fears. I then said to the chief, "If you have come with peaceable intentions, we have no other: go away home to your village." He replied, "I am afraid lest you shoot me in the back." I rejoined, "If I wanted to kill you, I could shoot you in the face as well." Mosantu called out to me, "That's only a Makalaka trick: don't give him your back." But I said, "Tell him to observe that I am not afraid of him," and, turning, mounted my ox. There was not much danger in the fire that was opened at first, there being so many trees. The enemy probably expected that the sudden attack would make us forsake our goods and allow them to plunder with ease. The villagers were no doubt pleased with being allowed to retire unscathed, and we were also glad to get away without having shed a drop of blood or having compromised ourselves for any future visit. My men were delighted with their own bravery, and made the woods ring with telling each other how "brilliant their conduct before the enemy" would have been, had hostilities not been brought to a sudden close.

I do not mention this little skirmish as a very frightful affair. The negro character in these parts, and in Angola, is essentially cowardly, except when influenced by success. A partial triumph over any body of men would induce the whole country to rise in arms; and this is the chief danger to be feared. These petty chiefs have individually but little power, and with my men, now armed with guns, I could have easily beaten them off singly; but, being of the same family, they would readily unite in vast numbers if incited by prospects of successful plunder. They are by no means equal to the Cape Caffres in any respect whatever.

In the evening we came to Moena Kikanje, and found him a sensible man. He is the last of the Chiboque chiefs in this direction, and is in alliance with Matiamvo, whose territory commences a short distance beyond. His village is placed on the east bank of the Quilo, which is here twenty yards wide and breast deep.

The country was generally covered with forest, and we slept every night at some village. I was so weak, and had become so deaf from the effects of the fever, that I was glad to avail myself of the company of Senhor Pascoal and the other native traders. Our rate of travelling was only two geographical miles per hour, and the average number of hours three and a half per day, or seven miles. Two-thirds of the month was spent in stoppages, there being only ten travelling-days in each month. The stoppages were caused by sickness, and the necessity of remaining in different parts to purchase food; and also because when one carrier was sick the rest refused to carry his load.

We crossed the Loange, a deep but narrow stream, by a bridge. It becomes much larger, and contains hippopotami, lower down. It is the boundary of Londa on the west. We slept also on the banks of the Pezo, now flooded, and could not but admire their capabilities for easy irrigation. On reaching the river Chikapa, (lat. 10° 10′ S., long. 19° 42′ E.,) the 25th of March, we found it fifty or sixty yards wide, and flowing E.N.E. into the Kasai. The adjacent country is of the same level nature as that part of Londa formerly described; but, having come farther to the eastward than our previous course, we found that all the rivers had worn for themselves much deeper valleys than at the points we had formerly crossed them.

Surrounded on all sides by large gloomy forests, the people of these parts have a much more indistinct idea of the geography of their country than those who live in hilly regions. It was only after long and patient inquiry that I became fully persuaded that the Quilo runs into the Chikapa. As we now crossed them both considerably farther down, and were greatly to the eastward of our first route, there can be no doubt that these rivers take the same course as the others, into the Kasai, and that I had been led into a mistake in saying that any of them flowed to the westward. Indeed, it was only at this time that I began to perceive that all the western feeders of the Kasai, except the Quango, flow first from the western side toward the centre of the country, then gradually turn, with the Kasai itself, to the north, and, after the confluence of the Kasai with the Quango, an immense body of water, collected from all these branches, finds its way out of the country by means of the river Congo or Zaire, on the west coast.

The people living along the path we are now following were quite accustomed to the visits of native traders, and did not feel in any way bound to make presents of food except for the purpose of cheating: thus, a man gave me a fowl and some meal, and after a short time returned. I offered him a handsome present of beads; but these he declined, and demanded a cloth instead, which was far more than the value of his gift. They did the same with my men, until we had to refuse presents altogether. Others made high demands because I slept in a "house of cloth" and must be rich. They seemed to think that they had a perfect right to payment for simply passing through the country.

Beyond the Chikapa we crossed the Kamáue, a small, deep stream proceeding from the S.S.W. and flowing into the Chikapa.

On the 30th of April we reached the Loajima, where we had to form a bridge to effect our passage. This was not so difficult an operation as some might imagine; for a tree

A LONDA LADY'S MODE OF WEARING HER HAIR.

was growing in a horizontal position across part of the stream, and, there being no want of the tough climbing plants which admit of being knitted like ropes, Senhor P. soon constructed a bridge. The Loajima was here about twenty-five yards wide, but very much deeper than where I had crossed before on the shoulders of Mashauana. The last rain of this season had fallen on the 28th, and had suddenly been followed by a great decrease of the temperature. The people in these parts seemed more slender in form, and their color a lighter olive, than any we had hitherto met. The mode of dressing the great masses of woolly hair which lay upon their shoulders, together with their general features, again reminded me of the ancient Egyptians. Several were seen with the upward inclination of the outer angles of the eye; but this was not general.

LADY'S HEAD-DRESS OF WOVEN HAIR.

A few of the ladies adopt a curious custom of attaching the hair to a hoop which encircles the head, giving it somewhat the appearance of the glory round the head of the Virgin, as shown on p. 295. Some have a small hoop behind that represented in the wood-cut. Others wear an ornament of woven hair and hide adorned with beads. The hair of the tails of buffaloes, which are to be found farther east, is sometimes added; while others weave their own hair on pieces of hide into the form of buffalo-horns, or make a single horn in front. Many tattoo their bodies by inserting some black substance beneath the skin, which leaves an elevated cicatrix about half an inch long: these are made in the form of stars and other figures of no particular beauty.

LADY'S HEAD-DRESS IN

CHAPTER XXIII.

DR. LIVINGSTONE VISITS THE COUNTRY OF THE BALONDA.

WE made a little detour to the southward, in order to get provisions i cheaper market. This led us along the rivulet called Tamba, where we found the people, who had not been visited so frequently by the slave-traders as the rest, rather timid and very civil.

We reached the river Moamba (lat. 9° 38′ S., long. 20° 13′ 34″ E.) on the 7th May. This is a stream of thirty yards wide, and, like the Quilo, Loange, Chikapa, and Loajima, contains both alligators and hippopotami. We crossed it by means of canoes.

We crossed two small streams, the Kanesi and Fombeji, before reaching Cabango, a village situated on the banks of the Chihombo. The country was becoming more densely peopled as we proceeded, but it bears no population compared to what it might easily sustain.

Cabango (lat. 9° 31′ S., long. 20° 31′ or 32′ E.) is the dwelling-place of Muanzánza, one of Matiamvo's subordinate chiefs. His village consists of about two hundred huts and ten or twelve square houses, constructed of poles with grass interwoven. The latter are occupied by half-caste Portuguese from Ambaca, agents for the Cassange traders. The cold in the mornings was now severe to the feelings, the therm   ing from 58° to 60°,   standing as high as   well up, the thermom   in the evenings it is

Havin   an accident to one of my eyes by a blow from a branch in passing through a forest, I remained some days here, endeavoring, though with much pain, to draw a sketch of the country thus far, to be sent back to

Mr. Gabriel at Loanda. I was always anxious to transmit an account of my discoveries on every possible occasion, lest, any thing happening in the country to which I was going, they should be entirely lost. I also fondly expected a packet of letters and papers which my good angel at Loanda would be sure to send if they came to hand; but I afterward found that, though he had offered a large sum to any one who would return with an assurance of having delivered the last packet he sent, no one followed me with it to Cabango. The unwearied attentions of this good Englishman, from his first welcome to me, when, a weary, dejected, and worn-down stranger, I arrived at his residence, and his whole subsequent conduct, will be held in lively remembrance by me to my dying day

As we thought it best to strike away to the S.E. from Cabango to our old friend Katema, I asked a guide from Muanzanza. He agreed to furnish one, and also accepted a smaller present from me than usual, when it was re presented to him by Pascoal and Faria that I was not a trader.

We were forced to prepay our guide and his father too; and he went but one day, although he promised to go with us to Katema.

The reason why we needed a guide at all was to secure the convenience of a path, which, though generally no better than a sheep-walk, is much easier than going straight in one direction through tangled forests and tropical vegetation. We knew the general direction we ought to follow, and also if any deviation occurred from our proper route; but, to avoid impassable forests and untreadable bogs, and to get to the proper fords of the rivers, we always tried to procure a guide, and he always followed the common path from one village to another when that lay in the direction we were going.

After leaving Cabango, on the 21st, we crossed several little streams running into the Chihombo on our left.

On the 28th we reached the village of the chief Bango,

(lat. 12° 22' 53" S., long. 20° 58' E.,) who brought us a handsome present of meal and the meat of an entire pallah. We here slaughtered the last of the cows presented to us by Mr. Schut, which I had kept milked until it gave only a teaspoonful at a time. My men enjoyed a hearty laugh when they found that I had given up all hope of more, for they had been talking among themselves about my perseverance.

May 30.—We left Bango, and proceeded to the river Loembwe, which flows to the N.N.E. and abounds in hippopotami. It is about sixty yards wide and four feet deep, but usually contains much less water than this, for there are fishing-weirs placed right across it. Like all the African rivers in this quarter, it has morasses on each bank; yet the valley in which it winds, when seen from the high lands above, is extremely beautiful.

Having passed the Loembwe, we were in a more open country, with every few hours a small valley, through which ran a little rill in the middle of a bog. These were always difficult to pass, and, being numerous, kept the lower part of the person constantly wet.

On the evening of the 2d of June we reached the village of Kawawa,—rather an important personage in these parts. This village consists of forty or fifty huts, and is surrounded by forest. Drums were beating over the body of a man who had died the preceding day, and some women were making a clamorous wail at the door of his hut, and addressing the deceased as if alive.

In the morning we had agreeable intercourse with Kawawa: he visited us, and we sat and talked nearly the whole day with him and his people. When we visited him in return, we found him in his large court-house, which, though of a bee-hive shape, was remarkably well built. As I had shown him a number of curiosities, he now produced a jug, of English ware, shaped like an old man holding a can of beer in his hand, as the greatest curiosity he had to exhibit.

We exhibited the pictures of the magic lantern in the evening, and all were delighted except Kawawa himself. He showed symptoms of dread, and several times started up as if to run away, but was prevented by the crowd behind. Some of the more intelligent understood the explanations well, and expatiated eloquently on them to the more obtuse. Nothing could exceed the civilities which had passed between us during this day; but Kawawa had heard that the Chiboque had forced us to pay an ox, and now thought he might do the same. When, therefore, I sent next morning to let him know that we were ready to start, he replied, in his figurative way, "If an ox come in the way of a man, ought he not to eat it? I had given one to the Chiboque, and must give him the same, together with a gun, gunpowder, and a black robe, like that he had seen spread out to dry the day before; that, if I refused an ox, I must give one of my men, and a book by which he might see the state of Matiamvo's heart toward him, and which would forewarn him should Matiamvo ever resolve to cut off his head." Kawawa came in the coolest manner possible to our encampment after sending this message, and told me he had seen all our goods and must have all he asked, as he had command of the Kasai in our front, and would prevent us from passing it unless we paid this tribute. I replied that the goods were my property and not his; that I would never have it said that a white man had paid tribute to a black, and that I should cross the Kasai in spite of him. He ordered his people to arm themselves, and when some of my men saw them rushing for their bows, arrows, and spears, they became somewhat panic-stricken. I ordered them to move away, and not to fire unless Kawawa's people struck the first blow. I took the lead, and expected them all to follow, as they usually had done; but many of my men remained behind. When I knew this, I jumped off the ox and made a rush to them with the revolver in my hand. Kawawa ran away among his people, and they turned their backs too. I shouted to my men to take up their luggage and march: some did so with alacrity, feeling that they had disobeyed orders by remaining; but one of them refused, and was preparing to fire at Kawawa, until I gave him a punch on the head with the pistol and made him go too. I felt here, as elsewhere, that subordination must be maintained at all risks. We all moved into the forest, the people of Kawawa standing about a hundred yards off, gazing, but not firing a shot or an arrow. It is extremely unpleasant to part with these chieftains thus, after spending a day or two in the most amicable intercourse, and in a part where the people are generally civil. This Kawawa, however, is not a good specimen of the Balonda chiefs, and is rather notorious in the neighborhood for his folly. We were told that he has good reason to believe that Matiamvo will some day cut off his head for his disregard of the rights of strangers.

Kawawa was not to be balked of his supposed rights by the unceremonious way in which we had left him; for, when we had reached the ford of the Kasai, about ten miles distant, we found that he had sent four of his men with orders to the ferrymen to refuse us passage. We were here duly informed that we must deliver up all the articles mentioned, and one of our men besides. This demand for one of our number always nettled every heart. The canoes were taken away before our eyes, and we were supposed to be quite helpless without them, at a river a good hundred yards broad, and very deep. Pitsane stood on the bank, gazing with apparent indifference on the stream, and made an accurate observation of where the canoes were hidden among the reeds. The ferrymen casually asked one of my Batoka if they had rivers in his country, and he answered, with truth, "No; we have none." Kawawa's people then felt sure we could not cross. I thought of swimming when they were gone; but, after it was dark, by the unasked loan of one of the hidden canoes, we soon were snug in our bivouac on the southern bank of the Kasai. I left some beads as payment for some meal which had been presented by the ferrymen; and, the canoe having been left on their own side of the river, Pitsane and his companions laughed uproariously at the disgust our enemies would feel, and their perplexity as to who had been our paddler across. They were quite sure that Kawawa would imagine that we had been ferried over by his own people and would be divining to find out who had done the deed. When ready to depart in the morning, Kawawa's people appeared on the opposite heights, and could scarcely believe their eyes when they saw us prepared to start away to the south. At last one of them called out, "Ah! ye are bad;" to which Pitsane and his companions retorted, "Ah! ye are good, and we thank you for the loan of your canoe." We were careful to explain the whole of the circumstances to Katema and the other chiefs, and they all agreed that we were perfectly justifiable under the circumstances, and that Matiamvo would approve our conduct. When any thing that might bear an unfavorable construction happens among themselves, they send explanations to each other. The mere fact of doing so prevents them from losing their character, for there is public opinion even among them.

CHAPTER XXIV.

DR. LIVINGSTONE RETURNS TO THE COUNTRY OF THE MAKOLOLO.

AFTER leaving the Kasai, we entered upon the extensive level plains which we had formerly found in a flooded condition. The water on them was not yet dried up, as it still remained in certain hollow spots. Vultures were seen floating in the air, showing that carrion was to be found; and, indeed, we saw several of the large game, but so exceedingly wild as to be unapproachable.

During our second day on this extensive plain I suffered from my twenty-seventh attack of fever, at a part where no surface-water was to be found. We never thought it necessary to carry water with us in this region; and now, when I was quite unable to move on, my men soon found water to allay my burning thirst by digging with sticks a few feet beneath the surface. We had thus an opportunity of observing the state of these remarkable plains at different seasons of the year. Next day we pursued our way, and on the 8th of June we forded the Lotembwa to the N.W. of Dilolo, and regained our former path.

After crossing the Northern Lotembwa, we met a party of the people of Kangenke, who had treated us kindly on our way to the north, and sent him a robe of striped calico, with an explanation of the reason for not returning through his village. We then went on to the Lake Dilolo. It is a fine sheet of water, six or eight miles long and one or two broad, and somewhat of a triangular shape. A branch proceeds from one of the angles and flows into the Southern Lotembwa.

We found Moene Dilolo (Lord of the Lake) a fat, jolly fellow, who lamented that when they had no strangers they had plenty of beer, and always none when they came. He gave us a handsome present of meal and putrid buffalo's flesh. Meat cannot be too far gone for them, as it is used only in small quantities, as a sauce to their tasteless manioc.

June 14.—We reached the collection of straggling villages over which Katema rules, and were thankful to see old familiar faces again. Shakatwala performed the part of a chief by bringing forth abundant supplies of food in his master's name. He informed us that Katema, too, was out hunting skins for Matiamvo.

On the 15th Katema came home from his hunting, having heard of our arrival. He desired me to rest myself and eat abundantly, for, being a great man, I must feel tired, and took good care to give the means of doing so. All the people in these parts are exceedingly kind and liberal with their food, and Katema was not behindhand. When he visited our encampment, I presented him with a cloak of red baize, ornamented with gold tinsel, which cost thirty shillings, according to the promise I had made in going to Londa; also a cotton robe, both large and small beads, an iron spoon, and a tin pannikin containing a quarter of a pound of powder. He seemed greatly pleased with the liberality shown, and assured me that the way was mine, and that no one should molest me in it if he could help it.

Leaving Katema's town on the 19th, and proceeding four miles to the eastward, we forded the southern branch of Lake Dilolo. We found it a mile and a quarter broad; and, as it flows into the Lotembwa, the lake would seem to be a drain of the surrounding flats, and to partake of the character of a fountain. The ford was waist deep, and very difficult, from the masses of arum and rushes through which we waded. Going to the eastward about three miles, we came to the Southern Lotembwa itself, running in a valley two miles broad. It is here eighty or ninety yards wide, and contains numerous islands covered with dense sylvan vegetation.

We traversed the extended plain on the north bank of the Leeba, and crossed this river a little farther on at Kanyonke's village, which is about twenty miles west of the Peri Hills, our former ford. The first stage beyond the Leeba was at the rivulet Loamba, by the village of Chebende, nephew of Shinte; and next day we met Chebende himself returning from the funeral of Samoana, his father. He was thin and haggard-looking compared to what he had been before,—the probable effect of the orgies in which he had been engaged.

We reached our friend Shinte, and received a hearty welcome from this friendly old man, and abundant provisions of the best he had. On hearing a report of the journey given by my companions, and receiving a piece of cotton cloth about two yards square, he said, "These Mambari cheat us by bringing little pieces only; but the next time you pass I shall send men with you to trade for me in Loanda." When I explained the use made of the slaves he sold, and that he was just destroying his own tribe by selling his people, and enlarging that of the Mambari for the sake of these small pieces of cloth, it seemed to him quite a new idea.

We parted on the best possible terms with our friend Shinte, and proceeded by our former path to the village of his sister Nyamoana, who is now a widow. She received us with much apparent feeling, and said, "We had removed from our former abode to the place where you found us, and had no idea then that it was the spot where my husband was to die." She had come to the river Lofuje, as they never remain in a place where death has once visited them. We received the loan of five small canoes from her, and also one of those we had left here before, to proceed down the Leeba.

Having despatched a message to our old friend Manenko, we waited a day opposite her village, which was about fifteen miles from the river. Her husband was instantly despatched to meet us with liberal presents of food, she being unable to travel in consequence of a burn on the foot. Sambanza gave us a detailed account of the political affairs of the country, and of Kolimbota's evil doings.

A short distance below the confluence of the Leeba and Lecambye we met a number of hunters belonging to the tribe called Mambowe, who live under Masiko. They had dried flesh of hippopotami, buffaloes, and alligators. This party had been sent by Masiko to the Makololo for aid to repel their enemy, but, afraid to go thither, had spent the time in hunting. They have a dread of the Makololo, and hence the joy they expressed when peace was proclaimed.*

---

* The Masiko were terrible warriors, but the atrocities committed by them in war will hardly bear comparison with those committed even in time of peace by the Zulus (Zooloos) under Chaka. Here is a specimen given by Captain Harris:—"Umnante, the queen-mother, died, and every subject in the realm was expected to proceed, according to esta-

The Mambowe hunters were much alarmed until my name
was mentioned. They then joined our party, and on the
following day discovered a hippopotamus dead, which they
had previously wounded. This was the first feast of flesh
my men had enjoyed, for, though the game was wonderfully abundant, I had quite got out of the way of shooting,
and missed perpetually. Once I went with the determination of getting so close that I should not miss a zebra.
We went along one of the branches that stretch out from the
river in a small canoe, and two men, stooping down as low
as they could, paddled it slowly along to an open space near
to a herd of zebras and pokus. Peering over the edge of
the canoe, the open space seemed like a patch of wet ground,
such as is often seen on the banks of a river, made smooth
as the resting-place of alligators. When we came within
a few yards of it, we found by the precipitate plunging of
the reptile that this was a large alligator itself. Although
I had been most careful to approach near enough, I unfortunately only broke the hind-leg of a zebra. My two men
pursued it, but the loss of a hind-leg does not prevent this
animal from a gallop. As I walked slowly after the men
on an extensive plain covered with a great crop of grass,

---

tished custom, to the king's residence, there to mourn for the illustrious
deceased. Umnante had been repudiated by Essenzinconyarna, and had
afterward been guilty of signal infidelity to the nation by cohabiting with
a commoner of her father's tribe. Whether in consequence of this lapse,
or from some other circumstance, the usual etiquette was somewhat laxly
observed, and there ensued an appalling tragedy, which had never been
exceeded, either in brutality or foulness, by any of the black and inhu-
man exploits detailed in the long and bloody catalogue of Chaka's crimes.
Upon the grounds that 'some of the subjects must have been accessary
by witchcraft to the death of the queen-mother, and did not therefore
attend to mourn,' several kraals and villages were fired; men, women,
and children, having first been cruelly tortured, were roasted alive in the
flames by the ferocious agents of a still more fiendish master; this act
of unprecedented barbarity being followed up by a general massacre
throughout the realm,—the tide of blood flowing for a whole fortnight,
and reeking of cruelties too revolting to narrate."—*Ed.*

which was *laid* by its own weight, I observed that a solitary buffalo, disturbed by others of my own party, was coming to me at a gallop. I glanced around, but the only tree on the plain was a hundred yards off, and there was no escape elsewhere. I therefore cocked my rifle, with the intention of giving him a steady shot in the forehead when he should come within three or four yards of me. The thought flashed across my mind, " What if your gun misses fire ?" I placed it to my shoulder as he came on at full speed, and that is tremendous, though generally he is a lumbering-looking animal in his paces. A small bush and bunch of grass fifteen yards off made him swerve a little, and exposed his shoulder. I just heard the ball crack there as I fell flat on my face. The pain must have made him renounce his purpose, for he bounded close past me on to the water, where he was found dead. In expressing my thankfulness to God among my men, they were much offended with themselves for not being present to shield me from this danger. The tree near me was a camel-thorn, and reminded me that we had come back to the land of thorns again, for the country we had left is one of evergreens.

July 27.—We reached the town of Libonta, and were received with demonstrations of joy such as I had never witnessed before. The women came forth to meet us, making their curious dancing gestures and loud lulliloos. Some carried a mat and stick, in imitation of a spear and shield. Others rushed forward and kissed the hands and cheeks of the different persons of their acquaintance among us, raising such a dust that it was quite a relief to get to the men assembled and sitting with proper African decorum in the kotla. We were looked upon as men risen from the dead, for the most skilful of their diviners had pronounced us to have perished long ago. After many expressions of joy at meeting, I arose, and, thanking them, explained the causes of our long delay, but left the report to be made by their own countrymen Formerly I had been the chief speaker, now I would leave the task of speaking to them. Pitsane then delivered a speech of upward of an hour in length, giving a highly-flattering picture of the whole journey, of the kindness of the white men in general, and of Mr. Gabriel in particular. He concluded by saying that I had done more for them than they expected; that I had not only opened up a path for them to the other white men, but conciliated all the chiefs along the route. The oldest man present rose and answered this speech, and, among other things, alluded to the disgust I felt at the Makololo for engaging in marauding-expeditions against Lechulatebe and Sebolamakwaia, of which we had heard from the first persons we met, and which my companions most energetically denounced as "mashue hela," entirely bad. He entreated me not to lose heart, but to reprove Sekeletu as my child. Another old man followed with the same entreaties. The following day we observed as our thanksgiving to God for his goodness in bringing us all back in safety to our friends. My men decked themselves out in their best, and I found that, although their goods were finished, they had managed to save suits of European clothing, which, being white, with their red caps, gave them rather a dashing appearance. They tried to walk like the soldiers they had seen in Loanda, and called themselves my "braves," (batlabani.) During the service they all sat with their guns over their shoulders, and excited the unbounded admiration of the women and children. I addressed them all on the goodness of God in preserving us from all the dangers of strange tribes and disease. We had a similar service in the afternoon. The men gave us two fine oxen for slaughter, and the women supplied us abundantly with milk, meal, and butter. It was all quite gratuitous, and I felt ashamed that I could make no return. My men explained the total expenditure of our means, and the Libontese answered, gracefully, "It does not matter: you have opened a path for us, and we shall have sleep." Strangers came flocking from a distance, and seldom empty-handed. Their presents I distributed among my men.

Our progress down the Barotse valley was just like this. Every village gave us an ox, and sometimes two. The people were wonderfully kind. I felt, and still feel, most deeply grateful, and tried to benefit them in the only way I could, by imparting the knowledge of that Savior who can comfort and supply them in the time of need; and my prayer is that he may send his good Spirit to instruct them and lead them into his kingdom. Even now I earnestly long to return and make some recompense to them for their kindness. In passing them on our way to the north, their liberality might have been supposed to be influenced by the hope of repayment on our return, for the white man's land is imagined to be the source of every ornament they prize most. But, though we set out from Loanda with a considerable quantity of goods, hoping both to pay our way through the stingy Chiboque and to make presents to the kind Balonda and still more generous Makololo, the many delays caused by sickness made us expend all my stock, and all the goods my men procured by their own labor at Loanda, and we returned to the Makololo as poor as when we set out. Yet no distrust was shown, and my poverty did not lessen my influence. They saw that I had been exerting myself for their benefit alone, and even my men remarked, "Though we return as poor as we went, we have not gone in vain." They began immediately to collect tusks of hippopotam and other ivory for a second journey.

CHAPTER XXV.

DR LIVINGSTONE PREPARES FOR HIS JOURNEY TO THE EAST COAST.

On the 31st of July we parted with our kind Libonta friends. We planted some of our palm-tree seeds in different villages of this valley. They began to sprout even while we were there; but, unfortunately, they were always destroyed by the mice which swarm in every hut.

At Chitlane's village we collected the young of a colony of the linkololo (*Anastomus lamalligerus,*) a black, long-legged bird, somewhat larger than a crow, which lives on shell-fish (*Ampullaria*) and breeds in society at certain localities among the reeds. These places are well known, as they continue there from year to year, and belong to the chiefs, who at particular times of the year gather most of the young. The produce of this "harvest," as they call it, which was presented to me, was a hundred and seventy-five unfledged birds. They had been rather late in collecting them, in consequence of waiting for the arrival of Mpololo, who acts the part of chief, but gave them to me, knowing that this would be pleasing to him, otherwise this colony would have yielded double the amount. The old ones appear along the Leeambye in vast flocks, and look lean and scraggy. The young are very fat, and, when roasted, are esteemed one of the dainties of the Barotse valley. In presents of this kind, as well as of oxen, it is a sort of feast of joy, the person to whom they are presented having the honor of distributing the materials of the feast. We generally slaughtered every ox at the village where it was presented, and then our friends and we rejoiced together.

The village of Chitlane is situated, like all others in the Barotse valley, on an eminence, over which floods do not rise; but this last year the water approached nearer to an entire submergence of the whole valley than has been known in the memory of man. Great numbers of people were now suffering from sickness, which always prevails when the waters are drying up, and I found much demand for the medicines I had brought from Loanda. The great variation of the temperature each day must have a trying effect upon the health. At this village there is a real Indian banian-tree, which has spread itself over a considerable space by means of roots from its branches; it has been termed, in consequence, "the tree with legs," (more oa maotu.) It is curious that trees of this family are looked upon with veneration, and all the way from the Barotse to Loanda are thought to be preservatives from evil.

On reaching Naliele on the 1st of August we found Mpololo in great affliction on account of the death of his daughter and her child. She had been lately confined; and her father naturally remembered her when an ox was slaughtered, or when the tribute of other food, which he receives in lieu of Sekeletu, came in his way, and sent frequent presents to her. This moved the envy of one of the Makololo who hated Mpololo, and, wishing to vex him, he entered the daughter's hut by night, and strangled both her and her child. He then tried to make fire in the hut and burn it, so that the murder might not be known; but the squeaking noise of rubbing the sticks awakened a servant, and the murderer was detected. Both he and his wife were thrown into the river,—the latter having "known of her husband's intentions, and not revealing them." She declared she had dissuaded him from the crime, and, had any one interposed a word, she might have been spared.

Mpololo exerted himself in every way to supply us with other canoes, and we left Shinte's with him. The Mambowe were well received, and departed with friendly messages to their chief Masiko. My men were exceedingly delighted with 'the cordial reception we met with every where; but a source of annoyance was found where it was not expected. Many of their wives had married other men during our two years' absence. Mashauana's wife, who had borne him two children, was among the number. He wished to appear not to feel it much, saying, "Why, wives are as plentiful as grass, and I can get another: she may go;" but he would add, "If I had that fellow, I would open his ears for him." As most of them had more wives than one, I tried to console them by saying that they had still more than I had, and that they had enough yet; but they felt the reflection to be galling that, while they were toiling, another had been devouring their corn. Some of their wives came with very young infants in their arms. This excited no discontent; and for some I had to speak to the chief to order the men, who had married the only wives some of my companions ever had, to restore them.

Sunday, August 5.—A large audience listened most attentively to my morning address. Surely some will remember the ideas conveyed, and pray to our merciful Father, who would never have thought of him but for this visit. The invariably kind and respectful treatment I have received from these and many other heathen tribes in this central country, together with the attentive observations of many years, have led me to the belief that, if one exerts himself for their good, he will never be ill treated. There may be opposition to his doctrine, but none to the man himself.

While still at Naliele, a party which had been sent after me by Masiko arrived. He was much disappointed because I had not visited him. They brought an elephant's tusk, two calabashes of honey, two baskets of maize, and one of groundnuts, as a present. Masiko wished to say that he had followed the injunction which I had given as the will of God, and lived in peace until his brother Limboa came, captured his women as they went to their gardens, and then appeared before his stockade. Masiko offered to lead his men out; but they objected, saying, "Let us servants be killed: you must not be slain." Those who said this were young Barotse who had been drilled to fighting by Sebituane, and used shields of ox-hide. They beat off the party of Limboa, ten being wounded, and ten slain in the engagement. Limboa subsequently sent three slaves as a self-imposed fine to Masiko for attacking him. I succeeded in getting the Makololo to treat the messengers of Masiko well, though, as they regarded them as rebels, it was somewhat against the grain at first to speak civilly to them.

Mpololo, attempting to justify an opposite line of conduct, told me how they had fled from Sebituane, even though he had given them numbers of cattle after their subjection by his arms, and was rather surprised to find that I was disposed to think more highly of them for having asserted their independence, even at the loss of milk. For this food all who have been accustomed to it from infancy in Africa have an excessive longing. I pointed out how they might be mutually beneficial to each other by the exchange of canoes and cattle.

There are some very old Barotse living here, who were the companions of the old chief Santuru. These men, protected by their age, were very free in their comments on the "upstart" Makololo. One of them, for instance, interrupted my conversation one day with some Makololo gentlemen with the advice "not to believe them, for they were only a set of thieves;" and it was taken in quite a good-natured way. It is remarkable that none of the ancients here had any tradition of an earthquake having occurred in this region. Their quick perception of events recognizable by the senses, and retentiveness of memory, render it probable that no perceptible movement of the earth has taken place between 7° and 27° S. in the centre of the continent during the last two centuries at least There is no appearance of recent fracture or disturbance of rocks to be seen in the central country, except the falls

Boat Capsized by a Hippopotamus Robbed of her Young.

of Gonye; nor is there any evidence or tradition of hurricanes.

I left Nalicle on the 13th of August, and, when proceeding along the shore at mid-day, a hippopotamus struck the canoe with her forehead, lifting one-half of it quite out of the water, so as nearly to overturn it. The force of the butt she gave tilted Mashauana out into the river; the rest of us sprang to the shore, which was only about ten yards off. Glancing back, I saw her come to the surface a short way off and look to the canoe, as if to see if she had done much mischief. It was a female, whose young one had been speared the day before. No damage was done, except wetting person and goods. This is so unusual an occurrence, when the precaution is taken to coast along the shore, that my men exclaimed, "Is the beast mad?" There were eight of us in the canoe at the time, and the shake it received shows the immense power of this animal in the water.

August 22.—This is the end of winter. The trees which line the banks begin to bud and blossom, and there is some show of the influence of the new sap, which will soon end in buds that push off the old foliage by assuming a very bright orange color. This orange is so bright that I mistook it for masses of yellow blossom. There is every variety of shade in the leaves,—yellow, purple, copper, liver-color, and even inky black.

Having got the loan of other canoes from Mpololo, and three oxen as provision for the way, which made the number we had been presented with in the Barotse valley amount to thirteen, we proceeded down the river toward Sesheke, and were as much struck as formerly with the noble river. The whole scenery is lovely, though the atmosphere is murky in consequence of the continuance of the smoky tinge of winter.

The amount of organic life is surprising. At the time the river begins to rise, the *Ibis religiosa* comes down in flocks of fifties, with prodigious numbers of other waterfowl. Some of the sand-banks appear whitened during the day with flocks of pelicans; I once counted three hundred; others are brown with ducks, (*Anas histrionica,*)—I got fourteen of these by one shot,—(*Querquedula Hottentota,* Smith,) and other kinds. Great numbers of gulls, (*Procellaria turtur,* Smith,) and several others, float over the surface. The vast quantity of small birds which feed on insects show that the river teems also with specimens of minute organic life. In walking among bushes on the banks, we are occasionally stung by a hornet, which makes its nest in form like that of our own wasp, and hangs it on the branches of trees. The breeding στοργη is so strong in this insect that it pursues any one twenty or thirty yards who happens to brush too closely past its nest. The sting, which it tries to inflict near the eye, is more like a discharge of electricity from a powerful machine, or a violent blow, than aught else. It produces momentary insensibility, and is followed by the most pungent pain. Yet this insect is quite timid when away from its nest It is named Murotuani by the Bechuanas.

We have tsetse between Nameta and Sekhosi. An insect of prey, about an inch in length, long-legged and gaunt-looking, may be observed flying about and lighting upon the bare ground. It is a tiger in its way, for it springs upon tsetse and other flies, and, sucking out their blood, throws the bodies aside.

Long before reaching Sesheke we had been informed that a party of Matebele, the people of Mosilikatse, had brought some packages of goods for me to the south bank of the river, near Victoria Falls, and, though they declared they had been sent by Mr. Moffat, the Makololo had refused to credit the statement of their sworn enemies. They imagined the parcels were directed to me as a mere trick whereby to place witchcraft-medicine in the hands of the Makololo. When the Matebele on the south bank called to the Makololo on the north to come over in canoes and receive the goods sent by Moffat to "Nake," the Makololo replied, "Go along with you: we know better than that. How could he tell Moffat to send his things here, he having gone away to the north?" The Matebele answered, "Here are the goods: we place them now before you, and if you leave them to perish the guilt wil. be yours." When they had departed, the Makololo thought better of it, and, after much divination, went over with fear and trembling, and carried the packages carefully to an island in the middle of the stream; then, building a hut over them to protect them from the weather, they left them; and there I found they had remained from September, 1854. till September, 1855, in perfect safety. Here, as I had often experienced before, I found the news was very old, and had lost much of its interest by keeping; but there were some good eatables from Mrs. Moffat. Among other things, I discovered that my friend Sir Roderick Murchison, while in his study in London, had arrived at the same conclusion respecting the form of the African continent as I had lately come to on the spot; and that from the attentive study of the geological map of Mr. Bain and other materials, some of which were furnished by the discoveries of Mr. Oswell and myself, he had not only clearly enunciated the peculiar configuration as a hypothesis in his discourse before the Geographical Society in 1852, but had even the assurance to send me out a copy for my information! There was not much use in nursing my chagrin at being thus fairly "cut out" by the man who had foretold the existence of the Australian gold before its discovery; for here it was in black and white. In his easy-chair he had forestalled me by three years, though I had been working hard through jungle, marsh, and fever, and, since the light dawned on my mind at Dilolc, had been cherishing the pleasing delusion that I should be the first to suggest the idea that the interior of Africa was a watery plateau of less elevation than flanking hilly ranges.

Having waited a few days at Sesheke till the horses

which we had left at Linyanti should arrive, we proceeded to that town, and found the wagon, and every thing we had left in November, 1853, perfectly safe. A grand meeting of all the people was called to receive our report and the articles which had been sent by the governor and merchants of Loanda. I explained that none of these were my property, but that they were sent to show the friendly feelings of the white men, and their eagerness to enter into commercial relations with the Makololo. I then requested my companions to give a true account of what they had seen. The wonderful things lost nothing in the telling, the climax always being that they had finished the whole world, and had turned only when there was no more land. One glib old gentleman asked, "Then you reached Ma Robert [Mrs. L.]?" They were obliged to confess that she lived a little beyond the world. The presents were received with expressions of great satisfaction and delight; and on Sunday, when Sekeletu made his appearance at church in his uniform, it attracted more attention than the sermon; and the kind expressions they made use of respecting myself were so very flattering that I felt inclined to shut my eyes. Their private opinion must have tallied with their public report, for I very soon received offers from volunteers to accompany me to the east coast. They said they wished to be able to return and relate strange things like my recent companions; and Sekeletu immediately made arrangements with the Arab Ben Habid to conduct a fresh party with a load of ivory to Loanda. These, he said, must go with him and learn to trade; they were not to have any thing to do in the disposal of the ivory, but simply look and learn. My companions were to remain and rest themselves, and then return to Loanda when the others had come home. Sekeletu consulted me as to sending presents back to the governor and merchants of Loanda; but, not possessing much confidence in this Arab, I advised him to send a present by Pitsane, as he knew who ought to receive it

Since my arrival in England, information has been received from Mr. Gabriel that this party had arrived on the west coast, but that the ivory had been disposed of to some Portuguese merchants in the interior, and the men had been obliged to carry it down to Loanda. They had not been introduced to Mr. Gabriel, but that gentleman, having learned that they were in the city, went to them and pronounced the names Pitsane, Mashauana, when all started up and crowded round him. When Mr. G. obtained an interpreter, he learned that they had been ordered by Sekeletu to be sure and go to my brother, as he termed him. Mr. G. behaved in the same liberal manner as he had done to my companions, and they departed for their distant home after bidding him a formal and affectionate adieu.

During the time of our absence at Loanda, the Makololo had made two forays and captured large herds of cattle One to the lake was in order to punish Lechulatebe for the insolence he had manifested after procuring some firearms; and the other to Sebola Makwaia, a chief living far to the N.E. This was most unjustifiable, and had been condemned by all the influential Makololo.

In accordance with the advice of my Libonta friends, I did not fail to reprove "my child Sekeletu" for his marauding. This was not done in an angry manner, for no good is ever achieved by fierce denunciations. Motibe, his father-in-law, said to me, "Scold him much, but don't let others hear you."

The Makololo expressed great satisfaction with the route we had opened up to the west, and soon after our arrival a "picho" was called, in order to discuss the question of removal to the Barotse valley, so that they might be nearer the market. Some of the older men objected to abandoning the line of defence afforded by the rivers Chobe and Zambesi against their southern enemies the Matebele. The Makololo generally have an aversion to the Barotse valley, on account of the fevers which are annually engendered in it as the waters dry up. They prefer it only as a cattle-station; for, though the herds are frequently thinned by an endemic disease, (*peripneumon'a,*) they breed so fast that the osses are soon made good. Wherever else the Makololo go, they always leave a portion of their stock in the charge of herdsmen in that prolific valley. Some of the younger men objected to removal because the rankness of the grass at the Barotse did not allow of their running fast, and because there "it never becomes cool"

Sekeletu at last stood up, and, addressing me, said, "I am perfectly satisfied as to the great advantages for trade of the path which you have opened, and think that we ought to go to the Barotse, in order to make the way from us to Loanda shorter; but with whom am I to live there? If you were coming with us, I would remove to-morrow; but now you are going to the white man's country to bring Ma Robert, and when you return you will find me near to the spot on which you wish to dwell." I had then no idea that any healthy spot existed in the country, and thought only of a convenient central situation, adapted for intercourse with the adjacent tribes and with the coast, such as that near to the confluence of the Leeba and Leeambye.

During the whole of my stay with the Makololo, Sekeletu supplied my wants abundantly, appointing some cows to furnish me with milk, and, when he went out to hunt, sent home orders for slaughtered oxen to be given. That the food was not given in a niggardly spirit may be inferred from the fact that when I proposed to depart on the 20th of October he protested against my going off in such a hot sun. "Only wait," said he, "for the first shower, and then I will let you go." This was reasonable, for the thermometer, placed upon a deal box in the sun, rose to 138°. It stood at 108° in the shade by day, and 96° at sunset.

I still possessed some of the coffee which I had brought from Angola, and some of the sugar which I had left in my wagon. So long as the sugar lasted, Sekeletu favored me with his company at meals; but the sugar soon came to a close. The Makololo, as formerly mentioned, were well acquainted with the sugarcane, as it is cultivated by the Barotse, but never knew that sugar could be got from it When I explained the process by which it was produced, Sekeletu asked if I could not buy him an apparatus for the purpose of making sugar. He said he would plant the cane largely if he only had the means of making the sugar from it. I replied that I was unable to purchase a mill, when he instantly rejoined, "Why not take ivory to buy it?" As I had been living at his expense, I was glad of the opportunity to show my gratitude by serving him; and when he and his principal men understood that I was willing to execute a commission, Sekeletu gave me an order for a sugar-mill, and for all the different varieties of clothing that he had ever seen, especially a mohair coat, a good rifle, beads, brass wire, &c. &c., and wound up by saying, "And any other beautiful thing you may see in your own country." As to the quantity of ivory required to execute the commission, I said I feared that a large amount would be necessary. Both he and his councillors replied, "The ivory is all your own: if you leave any in the country it will be your own fault." He was also anxious for horses. The two I had left with him when I went to Loanda were still living, and had been of great use to him in hunting the giraffe and eland; and he was now anxious to have a breed. This, I thought, might be obtained at the Portuguese settlements. All were very much delighted with the donkeys we had brought from Loanda. As we found that they were not affected by the bite of the tsetse, and there was a prospect of the breed being continued, it was gratifying to see the experiment of their introduction so far successful. The donkeys came as frisky as kids all the way from Loanda until we began to descend the Leeambye. There we came upon so many interlacing branches of the river, and were obliged to drag them through such masses of tangled aquatic plants, that we half drowned them, and were at last obliged to leave them, somewhat exhausted, at Naliele. They excited the unbounded admiration of my men by their knowledge of the different kinds of plants, which, as they remarked, "the animals had never before seen in their own country;" and when the donkeys indulged in their music they startled the inhabitants more than if they had been lions We never rode them, nor yet the horse which had beer given by the bishop, for fear of hurting them by any work.

Although the Makololo were so confiding, the reader must not imagine that they would be so to every individual who might visit them. Much of my influence depended upon the good name given me by the Bakwains, and that I secured only through a long course of tolerably good conduct. No one ever gains much influence in this country without purity and uprightness. The acts of a stranger are keenly scrutinized by both young and old; and seldom is the judgment pronounced, even by the heathen, unfair or uncharitable. I have heard women speaking in admiration of a white man because he was pure and never was guilty of any secret immorality. Had he been, they would have known it, and, untutored heathen though they be, would have despised him in consequence. Secret vice becomes known throughout the tribe; and, while one unacquainted with the language may imagine a peccadillo to be hidden, it is as patent to all as it would be in London had he a placard on his back.

27th October, 1855.—The first continuous rain of the season commenced during the night, the wind being from the N.E., as it always was on like occasions at Kolobeng. The rainy season was thus begun, and I made ready to go The mother of Sekeletu prepared a bag of groundnuts, by frying them with cream with a little salt, as a sort of sandwiches for my 'journey. This is considered food fit for a chief. Others ground the maize from my own garden into meal, and Sekeletu pointed out Sekwébu and Kanyata as the persons who should head the party intended to form my company. Sekwebu had been captured by the Matebele when a little boy, and the tribe in which he was a captive had migrated to the country near Toto; he had travelled along both banks of the Zambesi several times, and was intimately acquainted with the dialects spoken there. I found him to be a person of great prudence and sound judgment, and his subsequent loss at the Mauritius has been, ever since, a source of sincere regret. He at once recommended our keeping well away from the river, on account of the tsetse and rocky country, assigning also as a reason for it that the Leeambye beyond the falls turns round to the N.N.E. Mamire, who had married the mother of Sekeletu, on coming to bid me farewell before starting, said, "You are now going among people who cannot be trusted, because we have used them badly; but you go with a different message from any they ever heard before, and Jesus will be with you and help you, though among enemies; and if he carries you safely, and brings you and Ma Robert back again, I shall say he has bestowed a great favor upon me. May we obtain a path whereby we may visit and be visited by other tribes and by white men!" On telling him my fears that he was still inclined to follow the old marauding system, which prevented intercourse, and that he, from his influential position, was especially guilty in the late forays, he acknowledged all rather too freely for my taste, but seemed quite aware that the old system was far from right. Mentioning my inability to pay the men who were to accompany me, he replied, "A man wishes, of course, to appear among his friends, after a long absence, with something of his own to show: the whole of the ivory in the country is yours, so you must take as much as you can, and Sekeletu will furnish men to carry it." These remarks of Mamire are quoted literally, in order to show the state of mind of the most influential in the tribe. And, as I wish to give the reader a fair idea of the other side of the question as well, it may be mentioned that Motibe parried the imputation of the guilt of marauding by every possible subterfuge. He would not admit that they had done wrong, and laid the guilt of the wars in which the Makololo had engaged on the Boers, the Matebele, and every other tribe except his own. When quite a youth, Motibe's family had been attacked by a party of Boers: he hid himself in an ant-eater's hole, but was drawn out and thrashed with a whip of hippopotamus-hide. When enjoined to live in peace, he would reply, "Teach the Boers to lay down their arms first." Yet Motibe, on other occasions, seemed to feel the difference between those who are Christians indeed and those who are so only in name. In all our discussions we parted good friends.

CHAPTER XXVI.

DR. LIVINGSTONE DISCOVERS THE FALLS OF VICTORIA.

On the 3d of November we bade adieu to our friends at Linyanti, accompanied by Sekeletu and about 200 followers. We were all fed at his expense, and he took cattle for this purpose from every station we came to. The principal men of the Makololo, Lebeóle, Ntlarié, Nkwatléle, &c. were also of the party. We passed through the patch of the tsetse, which exists between Linyanti and Sesheke, by night. The majority of the company went on by daylight, in order to prepare our beds. Sekeletu and I, with about forty young men, waited outside the tsetse till dark. We then went forward, and about ten o'clock it became so pitchy dark that both horses and men were completely blinded. The lightning spread over the sky, forming eight or ten branches at a time, in shape exactly like those of a tree. This, with great volumes of sheet-lightning, enabled us at times to see the whole country. The intervals between the flashes were so densely dark as to convey the idea of stone-blindness. The horses trembled, cried out, and turned round, as if searching for each other, and every new flash revealed the men taking different directions, laughing, and stumbling against each other. The thunder was of that tremendously-loud kind only to be heard in tropical countries, and which friends from India have assured me is louder in Africa than any they have ever heard elsewhere. Then came a pelting rain, which completed our confusion. After the intense heat of the day, we soon felt miserably cold, and turned aside to a fire we saw in the distance. This had been made by some people on their march; for this path is seldom without numbers of strangers passing to and from the capital. My clothing having gone on, I lay down on the cold ground, expecting to spend a miserable night; but Sekeletu kindly covered me with his own blanket and lay uncovered himself. I was much affected by this act of genuine kindness. If such men must perish by the advance of civilization, as certain races of animals do before others, it is a pity. God grant that ere this time comes they may receive that gospel which is a solace for the soul in death!

While at Seshcke, Sekeletu supplied me with twelve oxen,—three of which were accustomed to being ridden upon,—hoes, and beads to purchase a canoe when we should strike the Leeambye beyond the falls. He likewise presented abundance of good fresh butter and honey, and did every thing in his power to make me comfortable for the journey. I was entirely dependent on his generosity; for the goods I originally brought from the Cape were all expended by the time I set off from Linyanti to the west coast. I there drew £70 of my salary, paid my men with it, and purchased goods for the return-journey to Linyanti. These being now all expended, the Makololo again fitted me out, and sent me on to the east coast. I was thus dependent on their bounty and that of other Africans for the means of going from Linyanti to Loanda, and again from Linyanti to the east coast, and I feel deeply grateful to them. Coin would have been of no benefit, for gold and silver are quite unknown. We were here joined by

Moriantsár.e, uncle of Sekeletu and head-man of Seshéke; and, entering canoes on the 13th, some sailed down the river to the confluence of the Chobe, while others drove the cattle along the banks, spending one night at Mparia, the island at the confluence of the Chobe, which is composed of trap having crystals of quartz in it coated with a pellicle of green copper-ore. Attempting to proceed down the river next day, we were detained some hours by a strong east wind raising waves so large as to threaten to swamp the canoe. The river here is very large and deep, and contains two considerable islands, which from either bank seem to be joined to the opposite shore.

Having descended about ten miles, we came to the island of Nampéne, at the beginning of the rapids, where we were obliged to leave the canoes and proceed along the banks on foot. The next evening we slept opposite the island of Chondo, and, then crossing the Lekóne or Lek-wine, early the following morning were at the island of Sekóte, called Kalái. This Sekote was the last of the Batoka chiefs whom Sebituane rooted out.

As this was the point from which we intended to strike off to the northeast, I resolved on the following day to visit the falls of Victoria, called by the natives Mosioa-tunya, or, more anciently, Shongwe. Of these we had often heard since we came into the country: indeed, one of the questions asked by Sebituane was, "Have you smoke that sounds in your country?" They did not go near enough to examine them, but, viewing them with awe at a distance, said, in reference to the vapor and noise, "Mosi oa tunya," (smoke does sound there.) It was previously called Shongwe, the meaning of which I could not ascertain. The word for a "pot" resembles this, and it may mean a seething caldron; but I am not certain of it. Being persuaded that Mr. Oswell and myself were the very first Europeans who ever visited the Zambesi in the centre of the country, and that this is the connecting-link between the known and unknown portions of that river, I decided to use the same liberty as the Makololo did, and gave the only English name I have affixed to any part of the country. No better proof of previous ignorance of this river could be desired than that an untravelled gentleman, who had spent a great part of his life in the study of the geography of Africa and knew every thing written on the subject from the time of Ptolemy downward, actually asserted in the "Athenæum," while I was coming up the Red Sea, that this magnificent river, the Leeambye, "had no connection with the Zambesi, but flowed under the Kalahari Desert and became lost;" and "that, as all the old maps asserted, the Zambesi took its rise in the very hills to which we have now come." This modest assertion smacks exactly as if a native of Timbuctoo should declare that the "Thames" and the "Pool" were different rivers, he having seen neither the one nor the other. Leeambye and Zambesi mean the very same thing,—viz., the RIVER.

Sekeletu intended to accompany me; but, one canoe only having come instead of the two he had ordered, he resigned it to me. After twenty minutes' sail from Kalai we came in sight, for the first time, of the columns of vapor appropriately called "smoke," rising at a distance of five or six miles, exactly as when large tracts of grass are burned in Africa. Five columns now arose, and, bending in the direction of the wind, they seemed placed against a low ridge covered with trees; the tops of the columns at this distance appeared to mingle with the clouds. They were white below, and higher up became dark, so as to simulate smoke very closely. The whole scene was extremely beautiful. The banks and islands dotted over the river are adorned with sylvan vegetation of great variety of color and form. At the period of our visit several trees were spangled over with blossoms. Trees have each their own physiognomy. There, towering over all, stands the great burly baobab, each of whose enormous arms would form the trunk of a large tree, besides groups of graceful palms, which, with their feathery-shaped leaves depicted on the sky, lend their beauty to the scene. As a hieroglyphic they always mean "far from home," for one can never get over their foreign air in a picture or landscape. The silvery mohonono—which in the tropics is in form like the cedar of Lebanon—stands in pleasing contrast with the dark color of the motsouri, whose cypress-form is dotted over at present with its pleasant scarlet fruit. Some trees resemble the great spreading oak; others assume the character of our own elms and chestnuts; but no one can imagine the beauty of the view from any thing witnessed in England. It had never been seen before by European eyes; but scenes so lovely must have been gazed upon by angels in their flight. The only want felt is that of mountains in the background. The falls are bounded on three sides by ridges three hundred or four hundred feet in height, which are covered with forest, with the red soil appearing among the trees. When about half a mile from the falls, I left the canoe by which we had come down thus far, and embarked in a lighter one, with men well acquainted with the rapids, who, by passing down the centre of the stream in the eddies and still places caused by many jutting rocks, brought me to an island situated in the middle of the river and on the edge of the lip over which the water rolls. In coming hither there was danger of being swept down by the streams which rushed along on each side of the island; but the river was now low, and we sailed where it is totally impossible to go when the water is high. But, though we had reached the island, and were within a few yards of the spot a view from which would solve the whole problem, I believe that no one could perceive where the vast body of water went: it seemed to lose itself in the earth, the opposite lip of the fissure into which it disappeared being only eighty feet distant. At least I did not comprehend it until, creeping with awe to the verge, I peered down into a large rent which had been made from bank to bank of the broad Zambesi, and saw that a stream of a thousand yards broad leaped down a hundred feet and then became suddenly compressed into a space of fifteen or twenty yards. The entire falls are simply a crack made in a hard basaltic rock from the right to the left bank of the Zambesi, and then prolonged from the left bank away through thirty or forty miles of hills. If one imagines the Thames filled with low, tree-covered hills immediately beyond the tunnel, extending as far as Gravesend, the bed of black basaltic rock instead of London mud, and a fissure made therein from one end of the tunnel to the other down through the keystones of the arch, and prolonged from the left end of the tunnel through thirty miles of hills, the pathway being one hundred feet down from the bed of the river instead of what it is, with the lips of the fissure from eighty to one hundred feet apart, then fancy the Thames leaping boldly into the gulf, and forced there to change its direction and flow from the right to the left bank and then rush boiling and roaring through the hills, he may have some idea of what takes place at this, the most wonderful sight I had witnessed in Africa. In looking down into the fissure on the right of the island, one sees nothing but a dense white cloud, which, at the time we visited the spot, had two bright rainbows on it. (The sun was on the meridian, and the declination about equal to the latitude of the place.) From this cloud rushed up a great jet of vapor exactly like steam, and it mounted two hundred or three hundred feet high; there, condensing, it changed its hue to that of dark smoke, and came back in a constant shower, which soon wetted us to the skin. This shower falls chiefly on the opposite side of the fissure, and a few yards back from the lip there stands a straight hedge of evergreen trees, whose leaves are always wet. From their roots a number of little rills run back into the gulf; but, as they flow down the steep wall there, the column of vapor, in its ascent, licks them up clean off the rock, and away they mount again. They are constantly running down, but never reach the bottom.

On the left of the island we see the water at the bottom, a white rolling mass moving away to the prolongation of the fissure, which branches off near the left bank of the river. A piece of the rock has fallen off a spot on the left of the island, and juts out from the water below, and from it I judged the distance which the water falls to be about one hundred feet. The walls of this gigantic crack are perpendicular, and composed of one homogeneous mass of rock. The edge of that side over which the water falls is worn off two or three feet, and pieces have fallen away, so as to give it somewhat of a serrated appearance. That over which the water does not fall is quite straight, except at the left corner, where a rent appears and a piece seems inclined to fall off. Upon the whole, it is nearly in the state in which it was left at the period of its formation. The rock is dark brown in color, except about ten feet from the bottom, which is discolored by the annual rise of the water to that or a greater height. On the left side of the island we have a good view of the mass of water which causes one of the columns of vapor to ascend, as it leaps quite clear of the rock, and forms a thick unbroken fleece all the way to the bottom. Its whiteness gave the idea of snow, a sight I had not seen for many a day. As it broke into (if I may use the term) pieces of water all rushing on in the same direction, each gave off several rays of foam, exactly as bits of steel, when burned in oxygen gas, give off rays of sparks. The snow-white sheet seemed like myriads of small comets rushing on in one direction, each of which left behind its nucleus-rays of foam. I never saw the appearance referred to noticed elsewhere. It seemed to be the effect of the mass of water leaping at once clear of the rock and but slowly breaking up into spray.

I have mentioned that we saw five columns of vapor ascending from this strange abyss. They are evidently formed by the compression suffered by the force of the water's own fall into an unyielding wedge-shaped space. Of the five columns, two on the right and one on the left of the island were the largest, and the streams which formed them seemed each to exceed in size the falls of the Clyde at Stonebyres when that river is in flood. This was the period of low-water in the Leeambye; but, as far as I could guess, there was a flow of five or six hundred yards of water, which, at the edge of the fall, seemed at least three feet deep.

Having feasted my eyes long on the beautiful sight, I returned to my friends at Kalai, and, saying to Sekeletu that he had nothing else worth showing in his country, his curiosity was excited to visit it the next day. I returned with the intention of taking a lunar observation from the island itself; but the clouds were unfavorable, consequently all my determinations of position refer to Kalai. (Lat. 17° 51′ 54″ S., long. 25° 41′ E.) Sekeletu acknowledged to feeling a little nervous at the probability of being sucked into the gulf before reaching the island. His companions amused themselves by throwing stones down, and wondered to see them diminishing in size, and even disappearing, before they reached the water at the bottom.

I had another object in view in my return to the island. I observed that it was covered with trees, the seeds of which had probably come down with the stream from the distant north, and several of which I had seen nowhere else, and every now and then the wind wafted a little of the condensed vapor over it, and kept the soil in a state of moisture, which caused a sward of grass, growing as green as on an English lawn. I selected a spot—not too near the chasm, for there the constant deposition of the moisture nourished numbers of polypi of a mushroom shape and fleshy consistence, but somewhat back—and made a little garden. I there planted about a hundred peach and apricot stones, and a quantity of coffee-seeds. I had attempted fruit-trees before, but, when left in charge of my Makololo friends, they were always allowed to wither, after having vegetated, by being forgotten. I bargained for a hedge with one of the Makololo, and, if he is faithful, I have great hopes of Mosioatunya's abilities as a nursery-man. My only source of fear is the hippopotami, whose footprints I saw on the island. When the garden was prepared, I cut my initials on a tree, and the date 1855. This was the only instance in which I indulged in this piece of vanity. The garden stands in front, and, were there no hippopotami, I have no doubt but this will be the parent of all the gardens which may yet be in this new country. We then went up to Kalai again.

20th November.—Sekeletu and his large party having conveyed me thus far, and furnished me with a company of one hundred and fourteen men to carry the tusks to the coast, we bade adieu to the Makololo and proceeded northward to the Lekone. The country around is very beautiful, and was once well peopled with Batoka, who possessed enormous herds of cattle. When Sebituane came in former times, with his small but warlike party of Makololo, to this spot, a general rising took place of the Batoka through the whole country, in order to "eat him up;" but his usual success followed him, and, dispersing them, the Makololo obtained so many cattle that they could not take any note of the herds of sheep and goats. The tsetse has been brought by buffaloes into some districts where formerly cattle abounded. This obliged us to travel the first few stages by night. We could not well detect the nature of the country in the dim moonlight: the path, however, seemed to lead along the high bank of what may have been the ancient bed of the Zambesi before the fissure was made. The Lekone now winds in it in an opposite direction to that in which the ancient river must have flowed.

24th.—We remained a day at the village of Moyara. Here the valley in which the Lekone flows trends away to the eastward, while our course is more to the northeast. The country is rocky and rough, the soil being red sand, which is covered with beautiful green trees, yielding abundance of wild fruits. The father of Moyara was a powerful chief; but the son now sits among the ruins of the town.

with four or five wives and very few people. At his hamlet a number of stakes are planted in the ground, and I counted fifty-four human skulls hung on their points. These were Matebele, who, unable to approach Sebituane on the island of Loyéla, had returned sick and famishing. Moyara's father took advantage of their reduced condition, and, after putting them to death, mounted their heads in the Batoka fashion. The old man who perpetrated this deed now lies in the middle of his son's huts, with a lot of rotten ivory over his grave. One cannot help feeling thankful that the reign of such wretches is over. They inhabited the whole of this side of the country, and were probably the barrier to the extension of the Portuguese commerce in this direction. When looking at these skulls, I remarked to Moyara that many of them were those of mere boys. He assented readily, and pointed them out as such. I asked why his father had killed boys. "To show his fierceness," was the answer. "Is it fierceness to kill boys?" "Yes: they had no business here." When I told him that this would probably insure his own death if the Matebele came again, he replied, "When I hear of their coming I shall hide the bones." He was evidently proud of these trophies of his father's ferocity; and I was assured by other Batoka that few strangers ever returned from a visit to this quarter. If a man wished to curry favor with a Batoka chief, he ascertained when a stranger was about to leave, and waylaid him at a distance from the town, and when he brought his head back to the chief it was mounted as a trophy, the different chiefs vieing with each other as to which should mount the greatest number of skulls in his village.

Next day we came to Namilanga, or "The Well of Joy." It is a small well dug beneath a very large fig-tree, the shade of which renders the water delightfully cool. The temperature through the day was 104° in the shade and 94° after sunset, but the air was not at all oppressive. This well receives its name from the fact that, in former times, marauding-parties, in returning with cattle, sat down here and were regaled with boyaloa, music, and the lullilooing of the women from the adjacent towns.

All the surrounding country was formerly densely peopled, though now desolate and still. The old head-man of the place told us that his father once went to Bambala, where white traders lived, when our informant was a child, and returned when he had become a boy of about ten years He went again, and returned when it was time to knock out his son's teeth. As that takes place at the age of puberty, he must have spent at least five years in each journey. He added that many who went there never returned, because they liked that country better than this. They had even forsaken their wives and children; and children had been so enticed and flattered by the finery bestowed upon them there that they had disowned their parents and adopted others. The place to which they had gone, which they named Bambala, was probably Dambarari, which was situated close to Zumbo. This was the first intimation we had of intercourse with the whites. The Barotse, and all the other tribes in the central valley, have no such tradition as this; nor have either the one or the other any account of a trader's visit to them in ancient times.

All the Batoka tribes follow the curious custom of knocking out the upper front teeth at the age of puberty. This is done by both sexes; and though the under teeth, being relieved from the attrition of the upper, grow long and somewhat bent out and thereby cause the under lip to protrude in a most unsightly way, no young woman thinks herself accomplished until she has got rid of the upper incisors. This custom gives all the Batoka an uncouth, old-man-like appearance. Their laugh is hideous; yet they are so attached to it that even Sebituane was unable to eradicate the practice. He issued orders that none of the children living under him should be subjected to the custom by their parents, and disobedience to his mandates was usually punished with severity; but, notwithstanding this, the children would appear in the streets without their incisors, and no one would confess to the deed. When questioned respecting the origin of this practice, the Batoka reply that their object is to be like oxen, and those who retain their teeth they consider to resemble zebras. Whether this is the true reason or not it is difficult to say; but it is noticeable that the veneration for oxen which prevails in many tribes should be associated with hatred to the zebra, as among the Bakwains, that this operation is performed at the same age that circumcision is in other tribes, and that here that ceremony is unknown. The custom is so universal that a person who has his teeth is considered ugly; and occasionally, when the Batoka borrowed my looking-glass, the disparaging remark would be made respecting boys or girls who still retained their teeth, "Look at the great teeth!" Some of the Makololo give a more facetious explanation of the custom: they say that, the wife of a chief having in a quarrel bitten her husband's hand, he, in revenge, ordered her front teeth to be knocked out, and all the men in the tribe followed his example: but this does not explain why they afterward knocked out their own.

The Batoka of the Zambesi are generally very dark in color and very degraded and negro-like in appearance, while those who live on the high lands we are now ascending are frequently of the color of coffee and milk. We had a large number of the Batoka of Mokwiné in our party, sent by Sekeletu to carry his tusks. Their greater degradation was probably caused by the treatment of their chiefs,—the barbarians of the islands. I found them more difficult to manage than any of the rest of my companions, being much less reasonable and impressible than the others. My party consisted of the head-men aforementioned, Sekwebu, and Kanyata. We were joined at the falls by another head-man of the Makololo, named Monahin, in command of the Batoka. We had also some of the Banajoa under Mosisinyane, and, last of all, a small party of Bashubia and Barotse under Tuba Mokoro, which had been furnished by Sekeletu because of their ability to swim. They carried their paddles with them, and, as the Makololo suggested, were able to swim over the rivers by night and steal canoes if the inhabitants should be so unreasonable as to refuse to lend them. These different parties assorted together into messes: any orders were given through their head-man, and when food was obtained he distributed it to the mess. Each party knew its own spot in the encampment; and, as this was always placed so that our backs should be to the east, the direction from whence the prevailing winds came, no time was lost in fixing the sheds of our encampment. They each took it in turn to pull grass to make my bed; so I lay luxuriously.

November 26.—As the oxen could only move at night, in consequence of a fear that the buffaloes in this quarter might have introduced the tsetse, I usually performed the march by day on foot, while some of the men brought on the oxen by night. On coming to the villages under Marimba, an old man, we crossed the Unguesi, a rivulet which, like the Lekone, runs backward. It falls into the Leeambye a little above the commencement of the rapids.

We passed the remains of a very large town, which, from the only evidence of antiquity afforded by ruins in this country, must have been inhabited for a long period: the millstones of gneiss, trap, and quartz were worn down two and a half inches perpendicularly. The ivory gravestones soon rot away. Those of Moyara's father, who must have died not more than a dozen years ago, were crumbling into powder; and we found this to be generally the case all over the Batoka country. The region around is pretty well covered with forest; but there is abundance of open pasturage, and, as we are ascending in altitude, we find the grass to be short and altogether unlike the tangled herbage of the Barotse valley.

CHAPTER XXVII.

THE BATOKA COUNTRY—DR. LIVINGSTONE VISITS THE CHIEF MONZE.

November 27.—STILL at Marimba's. In the adjacent country palms abound, but none of that species which yields the oil: indeed, that is met with only near the coast. There are numbers of flowers and bulbs just shooting up from the soil. The surface is rough and broken into gullies; and, though the country is parched, it has not that appearance, so many trees having put forth their fresh green leaves at the time the rains ought to have come. Among the rest stands the mola, with its dark brownish-green color and spreading oak-like form. In the distance there are ranges of low hills. On the north we have one called Kanjele, and to the east that of Kaonka, to which we proceed to-morrow. We have made a considerable détour to the north, both on account of our wish to avoid the tsetse and to visit the people. Those of Kaonka are the last Batoka we shall meet in friendship with the Makololo.

November 28.—The inhabitants of the last of Kaonka's villages complained of being plundered by the independent Batoka. The tribes in front of this are regarded by the Makololo as in a state of rebellion. I promised to speak to the rebels on the subject, and enjoined on Kaonka the duty of giving them no offence. According to Sekeletu's order, Kaonka gave us the tribute of maize-corn and groundnuts which would otherwise have gone to Linyanti. This had been done at every village, and we thereby saved the people the trouble of a journey to the capital. My own Batoka had brought away such loads of provisions from their homes that we were in no want of food.

After leaving Kaonka, we travelled over an uninhabited, gently-undulating, and most beautiful district, the border-territory between those who accept and those who reject the sway of the Makololo. The face of the country appears as if in long waves running north and south. There are no rivers, though water stands in pools in the hollows. We were now come into the country which my people all magnify as a perfect paradise. Sebituane was driven from it by the Matebele. It suited him exactly for cattle, corn, and health. The soil is dry, and often a reddish sand: there are few trees, but fine large shady ones stand dotted here and there over the country where towns formerly stood. One of the fig family I measured and found to be forty feet in circumference; the heart had been burned out, and some one had made a lodging in it, for we saw the remains of a bed and a fire. The sight of the open country, with the increased altitude we were attaining, was most refreshing to the spirits. Large game abound. We see in the distance buffaloes, elands, hartebeest, gnus, and elephants, all very tame, as no one disturbs them. Lions, which always accompany other large animals, roared about us; but, as it was moonlight, there was no danger. In the evening, while standing on a mass of granite, one began to roar at me, though it was still light. The temperature was pleasant, as the rains, though not universal, had fallen in many places. It was very cloudy, preventing observations. The temperature at 6 A.M. was 70°, at mid-day 90°, in the evening 84°. This is very pleasant on the high lands, with but little moisture in the air.

On the 30th we crossed the river Kalomo, which is about fifty yards broad, and is the only stream that never dries up on this ridge. The current is rapid, and its course is toward the south, as it joins the Zambesi at some distance below the falls. The Unguesi and Lekone, with their feeders, flow westward, this river to the south, and all those to which we are about to come take an easterly direction. We were thus at the apex of the ridge, and found that, as water boiled at 202°, our altitude above the level of the sea was over 5000 feet.

We met an elephant on the Kalomo which had no tusks. This is as rare a thing in Africa as it is to find them with tusks in Ceylon. As soon as she saw us she made off. It is remarkable to see the fear of man operating even on this huge beast. Buffaloes abound, and we see large herds of them feeding in all directions by day. When much disturbed by man, they retire into the densest parts of the forest and feed by night only. We secured a fine large bull by crawling close to a herd. When shot, he fell down, and the rest, not seeing their enemy, gazed about, wondering where the danger lay. The others came back to it, and, when we showed ourselves, much to the amusement of my companions, they lifted him up with their horns, and, half supporting him in the crowd, bore him away. All these wild animals usually gore a wounded companion and expel him from the herd; even zebras bite and kick an unfortunate or a diseased one. It is intended by this instinct that none but the perfect and healthy ones should propagate the species. In this case they manifested their usual propensity to gore the wounded; but our appearance at that moment caused them to take flight, and this, with the goring being continued a little, gave my men the impression that they were helping away their wounded companion. He was shot between the fourth and fifth ribs; the ball passed through both lungs and a rib on the opposite side, and then lodged beneath the skin. But, though it was eight ounces in weight, yet he ran off some distance, and was secured only by the people driving him into a pool of water and killing him there with their spears. The herd ran away in the direction of our camp, and then came bounding past us again. We took refuge on a large ant-hill, and as they rushed by us at full gallop I had a good opportunity of seeing that the leader of a herd of about sixty was an old cow: all the others allowed her a full half-length in their front. On her withers sat about twenty buffalo-birds, (*Textor erythrorhynchus*, Smith,) which act the part of guardian spirits to the animals. When the buffalo is quietly feeding, this bird may be seen hopping on the ground picking up food, or sitting on its back ridding it of the insects with which their skins are sometimes infested. The sight of the bird being much more acute than that of the buffalo, it is soon alarmed by the approach of any danger, and, flying up, the buffaloes instantly raise their heads to discover the cause which has led to the sudden flight of their guardian. They sometimes accompany the buffaloes in their flight on the wing; at other times they sit as above described.

Another African bird—namely, the *Buphaga Africana*—attends the rhinoceros for a similar purpose. It is called "kala" in the language of the Bechuanas. When these people wish to express their dependence upon another, they address him as "my rhinoceros," as if they were the birds. The satellites of a chief go by the same name This bird cannot be said to depend entirely on the insects on that animal, for its hard, hairless skin is a protection against all except a few spotted ticks; but it seems to be attached to the beast somewhat as the domestic dog is to man; and, while the buffalo is alarmed by the sudden flying up of its sentinel, the rhinoceros, not having keen sight, but an acute ear, is warned by the cry of its associate, the *Buphaga Africana*. The rhinoceros feeds by night, and its sentinel is frequently heard in the morning uttering its well-known call as it searches for its bulky companion. One species of this bird, observed in Angola, possesses a bill of a peculiar scoop or stone-forceps form, as if intended only to tear off insects from the skin; and its claws are as sharp as needles, enabling it to hang on to an animal's ear while performing a useful service within it. This sharpness of the claws allows the bird to cling to the nearly-insensible cuticle without irritating the nerves of pain on the true skin, exactly as a burr does to the human hand; but, in the case of the *Buphaga Africana* and *erythrorhyncha*, other food is partaken of, for we observed flocks of them roosting on the reeds in spots where neither tame nor wild animals were to be found.

The most wary animal in a herd is generally the "leader." When it is shot, the others often seem at a loss what to do and stop in a state of bewilderment. I have seen them then attempt to follow each other, and appear quite confused, no one knowing for half a minute or more where to direct the flight. On one occasion I happened to shoot the leader, a young zebra mare, which at some former time had been bitten on the hind-leg by a carnivorous animal, and, thereby made unusually wary, had, in consequence, become a leader. If they see either one of their own herd or any other animal taking to flight, wild animals invariably flee. The most timid thus naturally leads the rest. It is not any other peculiarity, but simply this provision, which is given them for the preservation of the race. The great increase of wariness which is seen to occur when the females bring forth their young, causes all the leaders to be at that time females; and there is a probability that the separation of sexes into distinct herds, which is annually observed in many antelopes, arising from the simple fact that the greater caution of the she antelopes is partaken of only by the young males, and their more frequent flights now have the effect of leaving the old males behind. I am inclined to believe this, because they are never seen in the act of expelling the males.

December 2, 1855.—We remained near a small hill, called Maundo, where we began to be frequently invited by the honey-guide, (*Cuculus indicator*.) Wishing to ascertain the truth of the native assertion that this bird is a deceiver, and by its call sometimes leads to a wild beast and not to honey, I inquired if any of my men had ever been led by this friendly little bird to any thing else than what its name implies. Only one of the one hundred and fourteen could say he had been led to an elephant instead of a hive. I am quite convinced that the majority of people who commit themselves to its guidance are led to honey, and to it alone.

On the 3d we crossed the river Mozuma, or river of Dila, having travelled through a beautifully-undulating pastoral country. To the south, and a little east of this, stands the hill Taba Cheu, or "White Mountain," from a mass of white rock, probably dolomite, on its top. But none of the hills are of any great altitude.

At the river of Dila we saw the spot where Sebituane lived, and Sekwebu pointed out the heaps of bones of cattle which the Makololo had been obliged to slaughter after performing a march with great herds captured from the Batoka through a patch of the fatal tsetse. When Sebituane saw the symptoms of the poison, he gave orders to his people to eat the cattle. He still had vast numbers; and when the Matebele, crossing the Zambesi opposite this part, came to attack him, he invited the Batoka to take repossession of their herds, he having so many as to be unable to guide them in their flight. The country was at that time exceedingly rich in cattle, and, besides pasturage, it is all well adapted for the cultivation of native produce. Being on the eastern slope of the ridge, it receives more rain than any part of the westward. Sekwebu had been instructed to point out to me the advantages of this position for a settlement, as that which all the Makololo had never ceased to regret. It needed no eulogy from Sekwebu; I admired it myself, and the enjoyment of good health in fine open scenery had an exhilarating effect on my spirits. The great want was population, the Batoka having all taken refuge in the hills. We were now in the vicinity of those whom the Makololo deem rebels, and felt some anxiety as to how we should be received.

On the 4th we reached their first village. Remaining at a distance of a quarter of a mile, we sent two men to inform them who we were and that our purposes were peaceful. The head-man came and spoke civilly, but, when nearly dark, the people of another village arrived and behaved very differently. They began by trying to spear a young man who had gone for water. Then they approached us, and one came forward howling at the top of his voice in the most hideous manner: his eyes were shot out, his lips covered with foam, and every muscle of his frame quivered. He came near to me, and, having a small battle-axe in his hand, alarmed my men lest he might do violence; but they were afraid to disobey my previous orders and to follow their own inclination by knocking him on the head. I felt a little alarmed too, but would not show fear before my own people or strangers, and kept a sharp look-out on the little battle-axe. It seemed to me a case of ecstasy or prophetic frenzy voluntarily produced. I felt it would be a sorry way to leave the world to get my head chopped by a mad savage, though that, perhaps, would be preferable to hydrophobia or delirium tremens. Sekwebu took a spear in his right hand, as if to pierce a bit of leather, but in reality to plunge it into the man if he offered violence to me. After my courage had been sufficiently tested, I beckoned with the head to the civil headman to remove him; and he did so by drawing him aside. This man pretended not to know what he was doing. I would fain have felt his pulse, to ascertain whether the violent trembling were not feigned, but had not much inclination to go near the battle-axe again. There was, however, a flow of perspiration, and the excitement continued fully half an hour, then gradually ceased. This paroxysm is the direct opposite of hypnotism, and it is singular that it has not been tried in Europe as well as clairvoyance. This second batch of visitors took no pains to conceal their contempt for our small party, saying to each other, in a tone of triumph, "They are quite a godsend!"—literally, "God has apportioned them to us." "They are lost among the tribes!" "They have wandered in order to be destroyed, and what can they do without shields among so many?" Some of them asked if there were no other parties. Sekeletu had ordered my men not to take their shields, as in the case of my first company. We were looked upon as unarmed, and an easy prey. We prepared against a night-attack by discharging and reloading our guns, which were exactly the same in number (five) as on the former occasion, as I allowed my late companions to retain those which I purchased at Loanda. We were not molested; but some of the enemy tried to lead us toward the Bashukulompo, who are considered to be the fiercest race in this quarter. As we knew our direction to the confluence of the Kafue and Zambesi, we declined their guidance, and the civil head-man of the evening before then came along with us. Crowds of natives hovered round us in the forest; but he ran forward and explained, and we were not molested. That night we slept by a little village under a low range of hills, which are called Chizamena. The country here is more woody than on the high lands we had left; but the trees are not in general large.

When we had passed the outskirting villages which alone consider themselves in a state of war with the Makololo, we found the Batoka, or Batonga, as they here call themselves, quite friendly. Great numbers of them came from all the surrounding villages with presents of maize and masuka, and expressed great joy at the first appearance of a white man and harbinger of peace. The women clothe themselves better than the Balonda, but the men go *in puris naturalibus*. They walk about without the smallest sense of shame. They have even lost the tradition of the "fig-leaf." I asked a fine, large-bodied old man if he did not think it would be better to adopt a little covering. He looked with a pitying leer, and laughed with surprise at my thinking him at all indecent: he evidently considered himself above such weak superstition. I told them that, on my return, I should have my family with me, and no one must come near us in that state. "What shall we put on? we have no clothing." It was considered a good joke when I told them that, if they had nothing else, they must put on a bunch of grass.

The farther we advanced the more we found the country swarming with inhabitants. Great numbers came to see the white man,—a sight they had never beheld before. They always brought presents of maize and masuka. Their mode of salutation is quite singular. They throw themselves on their backs on the ground, and, rolling from side to side, slap the outside of their thighs as expressions of thankfulness and welcome, uttering the words "Kina bomba." This method of salutation was to me very disagreeable, and I never could get reconciled to it. I called out, "Stop, stop! I don't want that;" but they, imagining I was dissatisfied, only tumbled about more furiously and slapped their thighs with greater vigor. The men being totally unclothed, this performance imparted to my mind a painful sense of their extreme degradation. My own Batoka were much more degraded than the Barotse, and more reckless. We had to keep a strict watch, so as not to be involved by their thieving from the inhabitants, in whose country and power we were. We had also to watch the use they made of their tongues, for some within hearing of the villagers would say, "I broke all the pots of that village," or "I killed a man there." They were eager to recount their soldier-deeds when they were in company with the Makololo in former times as a conquering army. They were thus placing us in danger by their remarks. I called them together, and spoke to them about their folly, and gave them a pretty plain intimation that I meant to insist upon as complete subordination as I had secured in my former journey, as being necessary for the safety of the party. Happily, it never was needful to resort to any other measure for their obedience, as they all believe that I would enforce it.

December 6.—We passed the night near a series of villages Before we came to a stand under our tree, a man came running to us with hands and arms firmly bound with ;ords behind his back, entreating me to release him When I had dismounted, the head-man of the village advanced, and I inquired the prisoner's offence. He stated that he had come from the Bashukulompo as a fugitive, and he had given him a wife and garden and a supply of seed; but, on refusing a demand for more, the prisoner had threatened to kill him, and had been seen the night before skulking about the village, apparently with that intention. I declined interceding unless he would confess to his father-in-law, and promise amendment. He at first refused to promise to abstain from violence, but afterward agreed. The father-in-law then said that he would take him to the village and release him; but the prisoner cried out, bitterly, "He will kill me there! don't leave me, white man." I ordered a knife, and one of the villagers released him on the spot. His arms were cut by the cords, and he was quite lame from the blows he had received.

We spent Sunday, the 10th, at Monze's village, who is considered the chief of all the Batoka we have seen. He lives near the hill Kisekise, whence we have a view of at least thirty miles of open undulating country, covered with short grass and having but few trees. These open lawns would in any other land, as well as this, be termed pastoral; but the people have no cattle, and only a few goats and fowls.

The chief Monze came to us on Sunday morning, wrapped in a large cloth, and rolled himself about in the dust, screaming "Kina bomba," as they all do. The sight of great naked men wallowing on the ground, though intended to do me honor, was always very painful: it made me feel thankful that my lot had been cast in such different circumstances from that of so many of my fellow-men. One of his wives accompanied him; she would have been comely if her teeth had been spared: she had a little battle-axe in her hand, and helped her husband to scream. She was much excited, for she had never seen a white man before We rather liked Monze, for he soon felt at home among us, and kept up conversation during much of the day. One head-man of a village after another arrived, and each of them supplied us liberally with maize, groundnuts, and corn. Monze gave us a goat and a fowl, and appeared highly satisfied with a present of some handkerchiefs I had got in my supplies left at the island. Being of printed cotton, they excited great admiration; and, when I put a gaudy-colored one as a shawl about his child, he said that he would send for all his people to make a dance about it. In telling them that my object was to open up a path whereby they might, by getting merchandise for ivory, avoid the guilt of selling their children, I asked Monze, with about one hundred and fifty of his men, if they would like a white man to live among them and teach them. All expressed high satisfaction at the prospect of the white man and his path: they would protect both him and his property. I asked the question, because it would be of great importance to have stations in this healthy region, whither agents oppressed by sickness might retire, and which would serve, moreover, as part of a chain of communication between the interior and the coast. The answer does not mean much more than what I know, by other means, to be the case,—that a white man *of good sense* would be welcome and safe in all these parts. By uprightness, and laying himself out for the good of the people, he would be known all over the country as a *benefactor* of the race. None desire Christian instruction, for of it they have no idea. But the people are now humbled by the scourgings they have received, and seem to be in a favorable state for the reception of the gospel. The gradual restoration of their former prosperity in cattle, simultaneously with instruction, would operate beneficially upon their minds. The language is a dialect of the other negro languages in the great valley; and, as many of the Batoka living under the Makololo understand both it and the Sichuana, missionaries could soon acquire it through that medium.

Monze had never been visited by any white man, but had seen black native traders, who, he said, came for ivory, not for slaves. He had heard of white men passing far to the east of him to Cazembe,—referring, no doubt, to Pereira, Lacerda, and others, who have visited that chief.

Monze came on Monday morning, and, on parting, presented us with a piece of a buffalo which had been killed the day before by lions. We crossed the rivulet Makoo, which runs westward into the Kafue, and went northward in order to visit Semalembue, an influential chief there. We slept at the village of Monze's sister, who also passes by the same name. Both he and his sister are feminine in their appearance, but disfigured by the foolish custom of knocking out the upper front teeth.

It is not often that jail-birds turn out well; but the first person who appeared to welcome us at the village of Monze's sister was the prisoner we had released in the way. He came with a handsome present of corn and meal, and, after praising our kindness to the villagers who had assembled around us, asked them, "What do you stand gazing at? Don't you know that they have mouths like other people?" He then set off and brought large bundles of grass and wood for our comfort, and a pot to cook our food in.

December 12.—The morning presented the appearance of a continuous rain from the north,—the first time we had seen it set in from that quarter in such a southern latitude. In the Bechuana country, continuous rains are always from the northeast or east, while in Londa and Angola they are from the north. At Pungo Andongo, for instance, the whitewash is all removed from the north side of the houses. It cleared up, however, about mid-day, and Monze's sister conducted us a mile or two upon the road. On parting, she said that she had forwarded orders to a distant village to send food to the point where we should sleep. In expressing her joy at the prospect of living in peace, she said it would be so pleasant " to sleep without dreaming of any one pursuing them with a spear."

In our front we had ranges of hills called Chamai, covered

with trees. We crossed the river Nuckachinta, flowing westward into the Kafue, and then passed over ridges of rocks of the same mica schist which we found so abundant in Golungo Alto: here they were surmounted by reddish porphyry and finely-laminated feldspathic grit with trap.

As we passed along, the people continued to supply us with food in great abundance. They had by some means or other got a knowledge that I carried medicine, and, somewhat to the disgust of my men, who wished to keep it all to themselves, brought their sick children for cure. Some of them I found had hooping-cough, which is one of the few epidemics that range through this country.

CHAPTER XXVIII.

DR. LIVINGSTONE DESCENDS THE ZAMBESI RIVER TO ITS CONFLUENCE WITH THE LOANGWA.

13th.—The country is becoming very beautiful, and furrowed by deep valleys; the underlying rocks, being igneous, have yielded fertile soil. There is great abundance of large game. The buffaloes select open spots, and often eminences, as standing-places through the day. We crossed the Mbai, and found in its bed rocks of pink marble. Some little hills near it are capped by marble of beautiful whiteness, the underlying rock being igneous. Violent showers occur frequently on the hills, and cause such sudden sweeping floods in these rivulets that five of our men, who had gone to the other side for firewood, were obliged to swim back. The temperature of the air is lowered considerably by the daily rains. Several times the thermometer at sunrise has been as low as 68°, and 74° at sunset. Generally, however, it stood at from 72° to 74° at sunrise, 90° to 96° at mid-day, and

80° to 84° at sunset. The sensation, however, as before remarked, was not disagreeable.

14th.—We entered a most beautiful valley, abounding in large game. Finding a buffalo lying down, I went to secure him for our food. Three balls did not kill him, and, as he turned round as if for a charge, we ran for the shelter of some rocks. Before we gained them, we found that three elephants, probably attracted by the strange noise, had cut off our retreat on that side: they, however, turned short off, and allowed us to gain the rocks. We then saw that the buffalo was moving off quite briskly, and, in order not to be entirely balked, I tried a long shot at the last of the elephants, and, to the great joy of my people, broke his fore-leg. The young men soon brought him to a stand, and one shot in the brain despatched him. I was right glad to see the joy manifested at such an abundant supply of meat.

On the following day, while my men were cutting up the elephant, great numbers of the villagers came to enjoy the feast. We were on the side of a fine green valley, studded here and there with trees and cut by numerous rivulets. I had retired from the noise, to take an observation among some rocks of laminated grit, when I beheld an elephant and her calf at the end of the valley, about two miles distant. The calf was rolling in the mud, and the dam was standing fanning herself with her great ears. As I looked at them through my glass, I saw a long string of my own men appearing on the other side of them, and Sekwebu came and told me that these men had gone off, saying, "Our father will see to-day what sort of men he has got." I then went higher up the side of the valley, in order to have a distinct view of their mode of hunting. The goodly beast, totally unconscious of the approach of an enemy, stood for some time suckling her young one, which seemed about two years old: they then went into a pit containing mud, and smeared themselves all over with it, the little one frisking about his dam, flapping his ears

Female Elephant, Pierced with Javelins, Protecting her Young.

and tossing his trunk incessantly, in elephantine fashion
She kept flapping her ears and wagging her tail, as if in
the height of enjoyment. Then began the piping of her
enemies, which was performed by blowing into a tube, or
the hands closed together, as boys do into a key. They
call out to attract the animal's attention :—

> "O chief! chief! we have come to kill you.
> O chief! chief! many more will die besides you," &c.
> "The gods have said it," &c. &c.

Both animals expanded their ears and listened, then left
their bath as the crowd rushed toward them. The little
one ran forward toward the end of the valley, but, seeing
the men there, returned to his dam. She placed herself on
the danger-side of her calf, and passed her proboscis over it
again and again, as if to assure it of safety. She frequently
looked back to the men, who kept up an incessant shouting,
singing, and piping; then looked at her young one and
ran after it, sometimes sideways, as if her feelings were
divided between anxiety to protect her offspring and desire
to revenge the temerity of her persecutors. The men kept
about a hundred yards in her rear, and some that distance
from her flanks, and continued thus until she was obliged
to cross a rivulet. The time spent in descending and getting up the opposite bank allowed of their coming up to
the edge and discharging their spears at about twenty
yards' distance. After the first discharge she appeared with
her sides red with blood, and, beginning to flee for her own
life, seemed to think no more of her young. I had previously sent off Sekwebu with orders to spare the calf. It
ran very fast, but neither young nor old ever enter into a
gallop: their quickest pace is only a sharp walk. Before
Sekwebu could reach them, the calf had taken refuge in
the water, and was killed. The pace of the dam gradually
became slower. She turned with a shriek of rage, and
made a furious charge back among the men. They
vanished at right angles to her course, or sideways, and,
as she ran straight on, she went through the whole party

but came near no one except a man who wore a piece of cloth on his shoulders. Bright clothing is always dangerous in these cases. She charged three or four times, and, except in the first instance, never went farther than one hundred yards. She often stood after she had crossed a rivulet, and faced the men, though she received fresh spears. It was by this process of spearing and loss of blood that she was killed; for at last, making a short charge, she staggered round and sank down dead in a kneeling posture. I did not see the whole hunt, having been tempted away by both sun and moon appearing unclouded. I turned from the spectacle of the destruction of noble animals, which might be made so useful in Africa, with a feeling of sickness; and it was not relieved by the recollection that the ivory was mine, though that was the case. I regretted to see them killed, and more especially the young one, the meat not being at all necessary at that time; but it is right to add that I did not feel sick when my own blood was up the day before. We ought, perhaps, to judge those deeds more leniently in which we ourselves have no temptation to engage. Had I not been previously guilty of doing the very same thing, I might have prided myself on superior humanity when I experienced the nausea in viewing my men kill these two.

Passing the rivulet Losito, and through the ranges of hills, we reached the residence of Semalembue on the 18th. His village is situated at the bottom of ranges through which the Kafue finds a passage, and close to the bank of that river. The Kafue, sometimes called Kahowhe or Bashukulompo River, is upward of two hundred yards wide here, and full of hippopotami, the young of which may be seen perched on the necks of their dams. At this point we had reached about the same level as Linyanti.

Semalembue paid us a visit soon after our arrival, and said that he had often heard of me, and, now that he had the pleasure of seeing me, he feared that I should sleep the first night at his village hungry. This was considered the handsome way of introducing a present, for he then handed five or six baskets of meal and maize, and an enormous one of groundnuts. Next morning he gave me about twenty baskets more of meal. I could make but a poor return for his kindness; but he accepted my apologies politely, saying that he knew there were no goods in the country from which I had come, and, in professing great joy at the words of peace I spoke, he said, "Now I shall cultivate largely, in the hope of eating and sleeping in peace." It is noticeable that all whom we have yet met eagerly caught up the idea of living in peace as the probable effect of the gospel. They require no explanation of the existence of the Deity. Sekwebu makes use of the term "Reza," and they appear to understand at once. Like negroes in general, they have a strong tendency to worship; and I heard that Semalembue gets a good deal of ivory from the surrounding tribes on pretence of having some supernatural power. He transmits this to some other chiefs on the Zambesi, and receives in return English cotton goods which come from Mozambique by Babisa traders. My men here began to sell their beads and other ornaments for cotton cloth. Semalembue was accompanied by about forty people, all large men. They have much wool on their heads, which is sometimes drawn all together up to the crown and tied there in a large tapering bunch. The forehead and round by the ears is shaven close to the base of this tuft. Others draw out the hair on one side and twist it into little strings. The rest is taken over and hangs above the ear, which gives the appearance of having a cap cocked jauntily on the side of the head.

The mode of salutation is by clapping the hands. Various parties of women came from the surrounding villages to see the white man, but all seemed very much afraid. Their fear, which I seldom could allay, made them, when addressed, clap their hands with increasing vigor. Sekwebu was the only one of the Makololo who knew this part of the country; and this was the region which to his mind was best adapted for the residence of a tribe. The natives generally have a good idea of the nature of the soil and pasturage, and Sekwebu expatiated with great eloquence on the capabilities of this part for supplying the wants of the Makololo. There is certainly abundance of room at present in the country for thousands and thousands more of population.

We passed near the Losito, a former encampment of the Matebele, with whom Sekwebu had lived. At the sight of the bones of the oxen they had devoured, and the spot where savage dances had taken place, though all deserted now, the poor fellow burst out into a wild Matebele song. He pointed out also a district, about two days and a half west of Semalembue, where Sebituane had formerly dwelt. There is a hot fountain on the hills there named "Nakalombo," which may be seen at a distance emitting steam. "There," said Sekwebu, "had your Molekanè [Sebituane] been alive, he would have brought you to live with him. You would be on the bank of the river; and, by taking canoes, you would at once sail down to the Zambesi and visit the white people at the sea."

The Kafue enters a narrow gorge close by the village of Semalembue: as the hill on the north is called Bolengwe, I apply that name to the gorge, (lat. 15° 48' 19" S., long. 28° 22' E.) Semalembue said that he ought to see us over the river; so he accompanied us to a pass about a mile south of his village, and when we entered among the hills we found the ford of the Kafue. On parting with Semalembue 1 put on him a shirt, and he went away with it apparently much delighted.

The ford was at least 250 yards broad, but rocky and shallow. After crossing it in a canoe, we went along the left bank, and were completely shut in by high hills.

Semalembue intended that we should go a little to the northeast, and pass through the people called Babimpe, and we saw some of that people, who invited us to come that way on account of its being smoother; but, feeling anxious to get back to the Zambesi again, we decided to cross the hills toward its confluence with the Kafue. The distance, which in a straight line is but small, occupied three days. The precipitous nature of the sides of this mass of hills knocked up the oxen and forced us to slaughter two, one of which—a very large one, and ornamented with upward of thirty pieces of its own skin detached and hanging down—Sekeletu had wished us to take to the white people as a specimen of his cattle. We saw many elephants among the hills, and my men ran off and killed three. When we came to the top of the outer range of the hills, we had a glorious view. At a short distance below us we saw the Kafue, wending away over a forest-clad plain to the confluence, and on the other side of the Zambesi, beyond that, lay a long range of dark hills. A line of fleecy clouds appeared lying along the course of that river at their base. The plain below us, at the left of the Kafue, had more large game on it than anywhere else I had seen in Africa. Hundreds of buffaloes and zebras grazed on the open spaces, and there stood lordly elephants feeding majestically, nothing moving apparently but the proboscis. I wished that I had been able to take a photograph of a scene so seldom beheld, and which is destined, as guns increase, to pass away from earth. When we descended, we found all the animals remarkably tame. The elephants stood beneath the trees, fanning themselves with their large ears, as if they did not see us at 200 or 300 yards' distance. The number of animals was quite astonishing, and made me think that here I could realize an image of that time when Megatheria fed undisturbed in the primeval forests.

We tried to leave one morning, but the rain, coming on afresh, brought us to a stand, and after waiting an hour, wet to the skin, we were fain to retrace our steps to our sheds. These rains were from the east, and the clouds might be seen on the hills exactly as the "Table-cloth" on Table Mountain. This was the first wetting we had got since we left Seshoke, for I had gained some experience in travelling. In Londa we braved the rain, and, as I despised being carried in our frequent passage through running water, I was pretty constantly drenched; but now, when we saw a storm coming, we invariably halted. The men soon pulled grass sufficient to make a little shelter for themselves by placing it on a bush, and, having got my camp-stool and umbrella, with a little grass under my feet, I kept myself perfectly dry. We also lighted large fires, and the men were not chilled by streams of water running down their persons and abstracting the heat, as they would have been had they been exposed to the rain. When it was over they warmed themselves by the fires, and we travelled on comfortably. The effect of this care was that we had much less sickness than with a smaller party in journeying to Loanda. Another improvement made from my experience was avoiding an entire change of diet. In going to Loanda I took little or no European food, in order not to burden my men and make them lose spirit, but trusted entirely to what might be got by the gun and the liberality of the Balonda; but on this journey I took some flour which had been left in the wagon, with some got on the island, and baked my own bread all the way in an extemporaneous oven made by an inverted pot. With these precautions, aided, no doubt, by the greater healthiness of the district over which we passed, I enjoyed perfect health.

When we left the Chipongo on the 30th, we passed among the range of hills on our left, which are composed of mica and clay slate. At the bottom we found a forest of large silicified trees, all lying as if the elevation of the range had made them fall away from it and toward the river. The numbers of large game were quite astonishing. I never saw elephants so tame as those near the Chiponga: they stood close to our path without being the least afraid. This is different from their conduct where they have been accustomed to guns, for there they take alarm at the distance of a mile, and begin to run if a shot is fired even at a longer distance. My men killed another here, and rewarded the villagers of the Chiponga for their liberality in meal by loading them with flesh. We spent a night at a baobab, which was hollow and would hold twenty men inside. It had been used as a lodging-house by the Babisa.

As we approached nearer the Zambesi, the country became covered with broad-leaved bushes, pretty thickly planted, and we had several times to shout to elephants to get out of our way. At an open space, a herd of buffaloes came trotting up to look at our oxen; and it was only by shooting one that I made them retreat. The meat is very much like that of an ox, and this one was very fine. The only danger we actually encountered was from a female elephant, with three young ones of different sizes. Charging through the centre of our extended line, and causing the men to throw down their burdens in a great hurry, she received a spear for her temerity. I never saw an elephant with more than one calf before. We knew that we were near our Zambesi again, even before the great river burst upon our sight, by the numbers of waterfowl we met. I killed four geese with two shots, and, had I followed the wishes of my men, could have secured a meal of waterfowl for the whole party. I never saw a river with so much animal life around and in it, and, as the Barotse say, "Its fish and fowl are always fat." When our eyes were gladdened by a view of its goodly broad waters, we found it very much larger than it is even above the falls. One might try to make his voice heard across it in vain. Its flow was more rapid than near Seshcke, being often four and a half miles an hour; and, what I never saw before, the water was discolored and of a deep brownish red. In the great valley the Leeambye never becomes of this color. The adjacent country, so far north as is known, is all level, and the soil, being generally covered with dense herbage, is not abraded; but on the eastern ridge the case is different: the grass is short, and, the elevation being great, the soil is washed down by the streams, and hence the discoloration which we now view. The same thing was observed on the western ridge. We never saw discoloration till we reached the Quango: that obtained its matter from the western slope of the western ridge, just as this part of the Zambesi receives its soil from the eastern slope of the eastern ridge. It carried a considerable quantity of wreck of reeds, sticks, and trees. We struck upon the river about eight miles east of the confluence with the Kafue, and thereby missed a sight of that interesting point. The cloudiness of the weather was such that but few observations could be made for determining our position; so, pursuing our course, we went down the left bank, and came opposite the island of Menye makaba. The Zambesi contains numerous islands: this was about a mile and a half or two miles long and upward of a quarter of a mile broad. Besides human population, it has a herd of buffaloes that never leave it. In the distance they seemed to be upward of sixty. The human and brute inhabitants understand each other; for when the former think they ought to avenge the liberties committed on their gardens, the leaders of the latter come out boldly to give battle. They told us that the only time in which they can thin them is when the river is full and part of the island flooded. They then attack them from their canoes. The comparatively small space to which they have confined themselves shows how luxuriant the vegetation of this region is; for were they in want of more pasture, as buffaloes can swim well, and the distance from this bank to the island is not much more than 200 yards, they might easily remove hither. The opposite bank is much more distant.

Ranges of hills appear now to run parallel with the Zambesi, and are about fifteen miles apart. Those on the north approach nearest to the river. The inhabitants on that side are the Batonga, those on the south bank are the Banyai. The hills abound in buffaloes, and elephants are numerous; and many are killed by the people on both banks. They erect stages on high trees overhanging the paths by which the elephants come, and then use a large spear with a handle nearly as thick as a man's wrist, and four or five feet long. When the animal comes beneath they throw the spear, and if it enters between the ribs above, as the blade is at least twenty inches long by two broad, the motion of the handle, as it is aided by knocking against the trees, makes frightful gashes within and soon causes death. They kill them also by means of a spear inserted in a beam of wood, which being suspended on a branch of a tree by a cord attached to a latch fastened in the path and intended to be struck by the animal's foot, leads to the fall of the beam, and, the spear being poisoned, causes death in a few hours.

We were detained by continuous rains several days at this island. The clouds rested upon the tops of the hills as they came from the eastward, and then poured down plenteous showers on the valleys below. As soon as we could move, Tomba Nyama, the head-man of the island, volunteered the loan of a canoe to cross a small river, called the Chongwe, which we found to be about fifty or sixty yards broad and flooded. All this part of the country was well known to Sekwebu; and he informed us that, when he passed through it as a boy, the inhabitants possessed abundance of cattle and there were no tsetse. The existence of the insect now shows that it may return in company with the larger game. The vegetation along the bank was exceedingly rank, and the bushes so tangled that it was difficult to get on. The paths had been made by the wild animals alone, for the general pathway of the people is the river, in their canoes. We usually followed the footpaths of the game; and of these there was no lack. Buffaloes, zebras, pallahs, and waterbucks abound; and there is also a great abundance of wild pigs, koodoos, and the black antelope. We got one buffalo as he was rolling himself in a pool of mud. He had a large piece of skin torn out of his flank, it was believed, by an alligator.

We were struck by the fact that, as soon as we came

between the ranges of hills which flank the Zambesi, the rains felt warm. At sunrise the thermometer stood at from 82° to 86°; at mid-day in the coolest shade, namely, in my little tent under a shady tree, at 96° to 98°; and at sunset it is 86°. This is different from any thing we experienced in the interior; for these rains always bring down the mercury to 72° or even 68°. There, too, we found a small, black coleopterous insect, which stung like the mosquito but injected less poison: it puts us in mind of that insect, which does not exist in the high lands we had left.

January 6, 1856.—Each village we passed furnished us with a couple of men to take us on to the next. They were useful in showing us the parts least covered with jungle. When we came near a village, we saw men, women, and children employed in weeding their gardens, they being great agriculturists. Most of the men are muscular, and have large ploughman-hands. Their color is the same admixture—from very dark to light olive— that we saw in Londa. Though all have thick lips and flat noses, only the more degraded of the population possess the ugly negro physiognomy. They mark themselves by a line of little raised cicatrices, each of which is a quarter of an inch long: they extend from the tip of the nose to the root of the hair on the forehead. It is remarkable that I never met with an albino in crossing Africa, though, from accounts published by the Portuguese, I was led to expect that they were held in favor as doctors by certain chiefs. I saw several in the south: one at Kuruman is a full-grown woman, and a man having this peculiarity of skin was met with in the colony. Their bodies are always blistered on exposure to the sun, as the skin is more tender than that of the blacks. The Kuruman woman lived some time at Kolobeng, and generally had on her bosom and shoulders the remains of large blisters. She was most anxious to be made black; but nitrate of silver, taken internally, did not produce its usual effect. During the time I resided at Mabotsa, a woman came to the station with a fine boy, an albino. The father had ordered her to throw him away; but she clung to her offspring for many years. He was remarkably intelligent for his age. The pupil of the eye was of a pink color, and the eye itself was unsteady in vision. The hair, or rather wool, was yellow, and the features were those common among the Bechuanas. After I left the place, the mother is said to have become tired of living apart from the father, who refused to have her while she retained the son. She took him out one day and killed him close to the village of Mabotsa, and nothing was done to her by the authorities. From having met with no albinos in Londa, I suspect they are there also put to death. We saw one dwarf only in Londa, and brands on him showed he had once been a slave; and there is one dwarf woman at Linyanti. The general absence of deformed persons is partly owing to their destruction in infancy, and partly to the mode of life being a natural one so far as ventilation and food are concerned. They use but few unwholesome mixtures as condiments, and, though their undress exposes them to the vicissitudes of the temperature, it does not harbor vomites. It was observed that, when smallpox and measles visited the country, they were most severe on the half-castes who were clothed. In several tribes, a child which is said to "tlola" (transgress) is put to death. "Tlolo," or transgression, is ascribed to several curious cases. A child who cut the upper front teeth before the under was always put to death among the Bakaa, and, I believe, also among the Bakwains. In some tribes, a case of twins renders one of them liable to death; and an ox which, while lying in the pen, beats the ground with its tail, is treated in the same way. It is thought to be calling death to visit the tribe. When I was coming through Londa, my men carried a great number of fowls, of a larger breed than any they had at home. If one crowed before midnight, it had been guilty of "tlolo," and was killed. The men often carried them sitting on their guns, and, if one began to crow in a forest, the owner would give it a beating, by way of teaching it not to be guilty of crowing at unseasonable hours.

The women here are in the habit of piercing the upper lip and gradually enlarging the orifice until they can insert a shell. The lip then appears drawn out beyond the perpendicular of the nose, and gives them a most ungainly aspect. Sekwebu remarked, "These women want to make their mouths like those of ducks;" and, indeed, it does appear as if they had the idea that female beauty of lip had been attained by the *Ornithorhynchus paradoxus* alone. This custom prevails throughout the country of the Maravi, and no one could see it without confessing that fashion had never led women to a freak more mad. We had rains now every day, and considerable cloudiness; but the sun often burst through with scorching intensity. All call out against it then, saying, "Oh, the sun! that is rain again." It is worth noticing that my companions never complained of the heat while on the highlands; but when we descended into the lowlands of Angola, and here also, they began to fret on account of it. I myself felt an oppressive steaminess in the atmosphere which I had not experienced on the higher lands.

As the game was abundant and my party very large, I had still to supply their wants with the gun. We slaughtered the oxen only when unsuccessful in hunting. We always entered into friendly relations with the head-men of the different villages, and they presented grain and other food freely. One man gave a basinful of rice,—the first we met with in the country. It is never seen in the interior. He said he knew it was "white man's corn," and, when I wished to buy some more, he asked me to give him a slave. This was the first symptom of the slave-trade on this side of the country. The last of these friendly head men was named Mobala; and, having passed him in peace, we had no anticipation of any thing else; but after a few hours we reached Selole or Chilole, and found that he not only considered us enemies, but had actually sent an express to raise the tribe of Mburúma against us. All the women of Selole had fled, and the few people we met exhibited signs of terror. An armed party had come from Mburuma in obedience to the call; but the head-man of the company, being Mburuma's brother, suspecting that it was a hoax, came to our encampment and told us the whole. When we explained our objects, he told us that Mburuma, he had no doubt, would receive us well. The reason why Selole acted in this foolish manner we afterward found to be this: an Italian named Simoens, and nicknamed Siriatomba, (don't eat tobacco,) had married the daughter of a chief called Sekokole, living north of Tete. He armed a party of fifty slaves with guns, and, ascending the river in canoes some distance beyond the island Moya makaba, attacked several inhabited islands beyond, securing a large number of prisoners and much ivory. On his return, the different chiefs—at the instigation of his father-in-law, who also did not wish him to set up as chief—united, attacked and dispersed the party of Simoens, and killed him while trying to escape on foot. Selole imagined that I was another Italian, or, as he expressed it, "Siriatomba risen from the dead." In his message to Mburuma he even said that Mobala, and all the villages beyond, were utterly destroyed by our fire-arms; but the sight of Mobala himself, who had come to the village of Selole, led the brother of Mburuma to see at once that it was all a hoax. But for this the foolish fellow Selole might have given us trouble.

We saw many of the liberated captives of this Italian among the villages here, and Sekwebu found them to be Matebele. The brother of Mburuma had a gun, which was the first we had seen in coming eastward. Before we reached Mburuma, my men went to attack a troop of elephants, as they were much in need of meat. When the troop began to run, one of them fell into a hole, and before he could extricate himself an opportunity was afforded for all the men to throw their spears. When he rose he was like a huge porcupine, for each of the seventy or eighty men had discharged more than one spear at him. As they had no more, they sent for me to finish him. In order to put him at once out of pain, I went to within twenty yards, there being a bank between us which he could not readily climb. I rested the gun upon an ant-hill, so as to take a steady aim; but, though I fired twelve two-ounce bullets (all I had) into different parts, I could not kill him. As it was becoming dark, I advised my men to let him stand, being sure of finding him dead in the morning; but, though we searched all the next day, and went more than ten miles, we never saw him again. I mention this to young men who may think that they will be able to hunt elephants on foot by adopting the Ceylon practice of killing them by one ball in the brain. I believe that in Africa the practice of standing before an elephant, expecting to kill him with one shot, would be certain death to the hunter; and I would add for the information of those who may think that, because I met with a great abundance of game here, they also might find rare sport, that the tsetse exists all along both banks of the Zambesi, and there can be no hunting by means of horses. Hunting on foot in this climate is such excessively hard work that I feel certain the keenest sportsman would very soon turn away from it in disgust. I myself was rather glad, when furnished with the excuse that I had no longer any balls, to hand over all the hunting to my men, who had no more love for the sport than myself, as they never engaged in it except when forced by hunger.

Some of them gave me a hint to melt down my plate by asking if it were not lead. I had two pewter plates and a piece of zinc, which I now melted into bullets. I also spent the remainder of my handkerchiefs in buying spears for them. My men frequently surrounded herds of buffaloes and killed numbers of the calves. I, too, exerted myself greatly; but, as I am now obliged to shoot with the left arm, I am a bad shot, and this, with the lightness of the bullets, made me very unsuccessful. The more the hunger, the less my success, invariably

I may here add an adventure with an elephant of one who has had more narrow escapes than any man living, but whose modesty has always prevented him from publishing any thing about himself. When we were on the banks of the Zouga in 1850, Mr. Oswell pursued one of these animals into the dense, thick, thorny bushes met with on the margin of that river, and to which the elephant usually flees for safety. He followed through a narrow pathway by lifting up some of the branches and forcing his way through the rest; but, when he had just got over this difficulty, he saw the elephant, whose tail he had but got glimpses of before, now rushing toward him. There was then no time to lift up branches; so he tried to force the horse through them. He could not effect a passage; and, as there was but an instant between the attempt and failure, the hunter tried to dismount, but in doing this one foot was caught by a branch, and the spur drawn along the animal's flank; this made him spring away and throw the rider on the ground with his face to the elephant, which, being in full chase, still went on. Mr. Oswell saw the huge fore-foot about to descend on his legs, parted them, and drew in his breath as if to resist the pressure of the other foot, which he expected would next descend on his body. He saw the whole length of the under part of the enormous brute pass over him: the horse got away safely. I have heard of but one other authentic instance in which an elephant went over a man without injury, and, for any one who knows the nature of the bush in which this occurred, the very thought of an encounter in it with such a foe is appalling. As the thorns are placed in pairs on opposite sides of the branches, and these turn round on being pressed against, one pair brings the other exactly into the position in which it must pierce the intruder. They cut like knives. Horses dread this bush extremely; indeed, most of them refuse to face its thorns.

On reaching Mburuma's village, his brother came to meet us. We explained the reason of our delay, and he told us that we were looked upon with alarm. He said that Siriatomba had been killed near the village of Selole and hence that man's fears. He added that the Italian had come talking of peace, as we did, but had kidnapped children and bought ivory with them, and that we were supposed to be following the same calling. I pointed to my men, and asked if any of these were slaves, and if we had any children among them, and I think we satisfied him that we were true men. Referring to our ill success in hunting the day before, he said, "The man at whose village you remained was in fault in allowing you to want meat, for he had only to run across to Mburuma; he would have given him a little meal, and, having sprinkled that on the ground as an offering to the gods, you would have found your elephant." The chiefs in these parts take upon themselves an office somewhat like the priesthood, and the people imagine that they can propitiate the Deity through them In illustration of their ideas, it may be mentioned that, when we were among the tribes west of Semalembue, several of the people came forward and introduced themselves,—one as a hunter of elephants, another as a hunter of hippopotami, a third as a digger of pitfalls,—apparently wishing me to give them medicine for success in their avocations, as well as to cure the diseases of those to whom I was administering the drugs. I thought they attributed supernatural power to them, for, like all Africans, they have unbounded faith in the efficacy of charms; but I took pains to let them know that they must pray and trust to another power than mine for aid. We never saw Mburuma himself, and the conduct of his people indicated very strong suspicions, though he gave us presents of meal, maize, and native corn. His people never came near us except in large bodies and fully armed. We had to order them to place their bows, arrows, and spears at a distance before entering our encampment. We did not, however, care much for a little trouble now, as we hoped that, if we could pass this time without much molestation we might yet be able to return with ease, and without meeting sour, suspicious looks.

Mburuma sent two men as guides to the Loangwa. These men tried to bring us to a stand, at a distance of about six miles from the village, by the notice, "Mburuma says you are to sleep under that tree." On declining to do this, we were told that we must wait at a certain village for a supply of corn. As none appeared in an hour, I proceeded on the march. It is not quite certain that their intentions were hostile; but this seemed to disarrange their plans, and one of them was soon observed running back to Mburuma. They had first of all tried to separate our party by volunteering the loan of a canoe to convey Sekwebu and me, together with our luggage, by way of the river, and, as it was pressed upon us, I thought that this was their design. The next attempt was to detain us in the pass; but, betraying no suspicion, we civilly declined to place ourselves in their power in an unfavorable position. We afterward heard that a party of Babisa traders, who came from the northeast, bringing English goods from Mozambique, had been plundered by this same people.

At the village of Ma Mburuma, (mother of Mburuma,) the guides, who had again joined us, gave a favorable report, and the women and children did not flee. Ma Mburuma promised us canoes to cross the Loangwa in our front. It was pleasant to see great numbers of men, women, and boys come, without suspicion, to look at the books, watch, looking-glass, revolver, &c. They are a strong, muscular race, and both men and women are seen cultivating the ground.

We were obliged to hurry along, for the oxen were bitten daily by the tsetse, which, as I have before remarked, now inhabits extensive tracts which once supported herds of cattle that were swept off by Mpakane and other marauders, whose devastations were well known to Sekwebu, for he himself had been an actor in the scenes. When he told me of them he always lowered his voice, in order that the guides might not hear that he had been one of their enemies. But that we were looked upon with suspicion, on account of having come in the footsteps of invaders, was evident from our guides remarking to men in the gardens through which we passed, "They have words of peace—all very fine; but lies only, as the Bazunga are great liars." They thought we did not understand them; but Sekwebu knew every word perfectly; and, without paying any ostensible attention to these complimentary remarks, we always took care to explain ever afterward that we were not Bazunga, but Makoa, (English.)

CHAPTER XXIX.

DR. LIVINGSTONE DESCENDS THE ZAMBESI TO CHICOVA.

14th.—We reached the confluence of the Loangwa and the Zambesi, most thankful to God for his great mercies in helping us thus far. Mburuma's people had behaved so suspiciously, that, though we had guides from him, we were by no means sure that we should not be attacked in crossing the Loangwa. We saw them here collecting in large numbers, and, though professing friendship, they kept at a distance from our camp. They refused to lend us more canoes than two, though they have many. They have no intercourse with Europeans except through the Babisa. They tell us that this was formerly the residence of the Bazunga, and maintain silence as to the cause of their leaving it. I walked about some ruins I discovered, built of stone, and found the remains of a church, and on one side lay a broken bell, with the letters I. H. S. and a cross, but no date. There were no inscriptions on stone, and the people could not tell what the Bazunga called their place. We found afterward it was Zumbo.

I felt some turmoil of spirit in the evening at the prospect of having all my efforts for the welfare of this great region and its teeming population knocked on the head by savages to-morrow, who might be said to "know not what they do." It seemed such a pity that the important fact of the existence of the two healthy ridges which I had discovered should not become known in Christendom, for a confirmation would thereby have been given to the idea that Africa is not open to the gospel. But I read that Jesus said, "All power is given unto me in heaven and on earth: go ye, therefore, and teach all nations; . . . and lo, *I am with you alway, even unto the end of the world.*" I took this as His word of honor, and went out to take observations for latitude and longitude, which, I think, were very successful. (The church: lat. 15° 37′ 22″ S., long. 30° 32′ E.)

15th.—The natives of the surrounding country collected around us this morning, all armed. The women and children were sent away, and one of Mburuma's wives, who lives in the vicinity, was not allowed to approach, though she had come from her village to pay me a visit. Only one canoe was lent to us, though we saw two others tied to the bank. The part we crossed was about a mile from the confluence, and, as it was now flooded, it seemed upward of half a mile in breadth. We passed all our goods first on to an island in the middle, then the remaining cattle and men; occupying the post of honor, I, as usual, was the last to enter the canoe. A number of the inhabitants stood armed all the time we were embarking. I showed them my watch, lens, and other things to keep them amused, until there only remained those who were to enter the canoe with me. I thanked them for their kindness, and wished them peace. After all, they may have been influenced only by the intention to be ready in case I should play them some false trick, for they have reason to be distrustful of the whites. The guides came over to bid us adieu, and we sat under a mango-tree fifteen feet 'n cir cumference. We found them more communicative now They said that the land on both sides belonged to the Bazunga, and that they had left of old, on the approach of Changamera, Ngaba, and Mpakane. Sekwebu was with the last-named, but he maintained that they never came to the confluence, though they carried off all the cattle of Mburuma. The guides confirmed this by saying that the Bazunga were not attacked, but fled in alarm on the approach of the enemy. This mango-tree he knew by its proper name, and we found seven others and several tamarinds, and were informed that the chief Mburuma sends men annually to gather the fruit, but, like many Africans whom I have known, has not had patience to propagate more trees. I gave them some little presents for themselves, a handkerchief and a few beads; and they were highly pleased with a cloth of red baize for Mburuma, which Sekeletu had given me to purchase a canoe. We were thankful to part good friends.

The situation of Zumbo was admirably well chosen as a site for commerce. Looking backward, we see a mass of high, dark mountains covered with trees; behind us rises the fine high hill Mazanzwe, which stretches away northward along the left bank of the Loangwa; to the S.E. lies an open country, with a small round hill in the distance called Tofulo The merchants, as they sat beneath the verandahs in front of their houses, had a magnificent view of the two rivers at their confluence, of their church at the angle, and of all the gardens which they had on both sides of the rivers. In these they cultivated wheat without irrigation, and, as the Portuguese assert, of a grain twice the size of that at Tete. From the guides we learned that the inhabitants had not imbibed much idea of Christianity, for they used the same term for the church-bell which they did for a diviner's drum. From this point the merchants had water-communication in three directions beyond, namely, from the Loangwa to the N.N.W., by the Kafue to the W., and by the Zambesi to the S W. Their attention, however, was chiefly attracted to the N., or Londa; and the principal articles of trade were ivory and slaves. Private enterprise was always restrained, for, the colonies of the Portuguese being strictly military, and the pay of the commandants being very small, the officers have always been obliged to engage in trade; and had they not employed their power to draw the trade to themselves by preventing private traders from making bargains beyond the villages, and only at regulated prices, they would have had no trade, as they themselves were obliged to remain always at their posts.

Several expeditions went to the north as far as to Cazembe, and Dr. Lacerda, himself commandant of Tete, went to that chief's residence. Unfortunately, he was cut off while there, and his papers, taken possession of by a Jesuit who accompanied him, were lost to the world. This Jesuit probably intended to act fairly and have them published; but soon after his return he was called away by death himself, and the papers were lost sight of. Dr. Lacerda had a strong desire to open up communication with Angola, which would have been of importance then, as affording a speedier mode of communication with Portugal than by the way of the Cape; but since the opening of the overland passage to India a quicker transit is effected from Eastern Africa to Lisbon by way of the Red Sea. Besides Lacerda, Cazembe was visited by Pereira, who gave a glowing account of that chief's power, which none of my inquiries have confirmed. The people of Matiamvo stated to me that Cazembe was a vassal of their chief; and, from all the native visitors whom I have seen, he appears to be exactly like Shinte and Katema, only a little more powerful. The term "Emperor," which has been applied to him, seems totally inappropriate. The statement of Pereira that twenty negroes were slaughtered in a day was not confirmed by any one else, though numbers may have been killed on some particular occasion during the time of his visit, for we find throughout all the country north of 20°, which I consider to be real negro, the custom of slaughtering victims to accompany the departed soul of a chief; and human sacrifices are occasionally offered, and certain parts of the bodies are used as charms. It is on account of the existence of such rites, with the similarity of the language, and the fact that the names of rivers are repeated again and again from north to south through all that region, that I consider them to have been originally one family. The last expedition to Cazembe was somewhat of the same nature as the others, and failed in establishing a commerce because the people of Cazembe, who had come to Tete to invite the Portuguese to visit them, had not been allowed to trade with whom they might. As it had not been free trade there, Cazembe did not see why it should be free trade at his town: he accordingly would not allow his people to furnish the party with food except at his price; and the expedition, being half starved in consequence, came away voting unanimously that Cazembe was a great bore.

When we left the Loangwa, we thought we had got rid of the hills; but there are some behind Mazanzwe, though five or six miles off from the river. Tsetse and the hills had destroyed two riding-oxen, and, when the little one that I now rode knocked up, I was forced to march on foot. The bush being very dense and high, we were going along among the trees, when three buffaloes, which we had unconsciously passed above the wind, thought that they were surrounded by men, and dashed through our line. My ox set off at a gallop, and when I could manage to glance back I saw one of the men up in the air about five feet above a buffalo which was tearing along with a stream of blood running down his flank. When I got back to the poor fellow, I found that he had lighted on his face, and, though he had been carried on the horns of the buffalo about twenty yards before getting the final toss, the skin was not pierced, nor was a bone broken. When the beasts appeared, he had thrown down his load and stabbed one in the side. It

The Travelling-Procession Interrupted.

turned suddenly upon him, and, before he could use a tree for defence, carried him off. We shampooed him well, and then went on, and in about a week he was able to engage in the hunt again.

On the morning of the 17th we were pleased to see a person coming from the island of Shibanga with jacket and hat on. He was quite black, but had come from the Portuguese settlement at Tete or Nyungwé; and now, for the first time, we understood that the Portuguese settlement was on the other bank of the river, and that they had been fighting with the natives for the last two years. We had thus got into the midst of a Caffre war, without any particular wish to be on either side. He advised us to cross the river at once, as Mpende lived on this side. We had been warned by the guides of Mburuma against him, for they said that if we could get past Mpende we might reach the white men, but that he was determined that no white man should pass him. Wishing to follow this man's advice, we proposed to borrow his canoes; but, being afraid to offend the lords of the river, he declined. The consequence was, we were obliged to remain on the enemy's side. The next island belonged to a man named Zungo, a fine, frank fellow, who brought us at once a present of corn, bound in a peculiar way in grass. He freely accepted our apology for having no present to give in return, as he knew that there were no goods in the interior, and, besides, sent forward a recommendation to his brother-in-law Pangola.

18*th*.—Pangola visited us and presented us with food. In few other countries would one hundred and fourteen sturdy vagabonds be supported by the generosity of the head-men and villagers and whatever they gave be presented with politeness. My men got pretty well supplied individually, for they went into the villages and commenced dancing. The young women were especially pleased with the new steps they had to show, though I suspect many of them were invented for the occasion, and would say. "Dance for me, and I will grind corn for you" At every fresh instance of liberality, Sekwebu said, "Did not I tell you that these people had hearts, while we were still at Linyanti?" All agreed that the character he had given was true, and some remarked, "Look! although we have been so long away from home, not one of us has become lean." It was a fact that we had been all well supplied either with meat by my gun or their own spears, or food from the great generosity of the inhabitants. Pangola promised to ferry us across the Zambesi, but failed to fulfil his promise. He seemed to wish to avoid offending his neighbor Mpende by aiding us to escape from his hands; so we proceeded along the bank. Although we were in doubt as to our reception by Mpende, I could not help admiring the beautiful country as we passed along. Finding no one willing to aid us in crossing the river, we proceeded to the village of the chief Mpende. When we came to Mpende's village, he immediately sent to inquire who we were, and then ordered the guides who had come with us from the last village to go back and call their masters. He sent no message to us whatever. We had travelled very slowly up to this point, the tsetse-stricken oxen being now unable to go two miles an hour. We were also delayed by being obliged to stop at every village and send notice of our approach to the head-man, who came and received a little information and gave some food. If we had passed on without taking any notice of them, they would have considered it impolite, and we should have appeared more as enemies than friends. I consoled myself for the loss of time by the thought that these conversations tended to the opening of our future path.

23d.—This morning, at sunrise, a party of Mpende's people came close to our encampment, uttering strange cries and waving some bright-red substance toward us. They then lighted a fire with charms in it, and departed, uttering the same hideous screams as before. This was intended to render us powerless, and probably also to frighten us

Ever since dawn, parties of armed men have been seen collecting from all quarters, and numbers passed us while it was yet dark. Had we moved down the river at once, it would have been considered an indication of fear or defiance, and so would a retreat. I therefore resolved to wait, trusting to Him who has the hearts of all men in his hands. They evidently intended to attack us, for no friendly message was sent; and, when three of the Batoka the night before entered the village to beg food, a man went round about each of them, making a noise like a lion The villagers then called upon them to do homage, and, when they complied, the chief ordered some chaff to be given them, as if it had been food. Other things also showed unmistakable hostility. As we were now pretty certain of a skirmish, I ordered an ox to be slaughtered, as this is a means which Sebituane employed for inspiring courage. I have no doubt that we should have been victorious: indeed, my men, who were far better acquainted with fighting than any of the people on the Zambesi, were rejoicing in the prospect of securing captives to carry the tusks for them. "We shall now," said they, "get both corn and clothes in plenty." They were in a sad state, poor fellows; for the rains we had encountered had made their skin-clothing drop off piecemeal, and they were looked upon with disgust by the well-fed and well-clothed Zambesians. They were, however, veterans in marauding; and the head-men, instead of being depressed by fear, as the people of Mpende intended should be the case in using their charms, hinted broadly to me that I ought to allow them to keep Mpende's wives. The roasting of meat went on fast and furious, and some of the young men said to me, "You have seen us with elephants, but you don't know yet what we can do with men." I believe that, had Mpende struck the first blow, he would soon have found out that he never made a greater mistake in his life.

His whole tribe was assembled at about the distance of

half a mile As the country is covered with trees, we did not see them; but every now and then a few came about us as spies, and would answer no questions. I handed a leg of the ox to two of these, and desired them to take it to Mpende. After waiting a considerable time in suspense two old men made their appearance and said they had come to inquire who I was. I replied, "I am a Lekoa," (an Englishman.) They said, "We don't know that tribe. We suppose you are a Mozunga, the tribe with which we have been fighting." As I was not yet aware that the term Mozunga was applied to a Portuguese, and thought they meant half-castes, I showed them my hair and the skin of my bosom, and asked if the Bazunga had hair and skin like mine. As the Portuguese have the custom of cutting the hair close, and are also somewhat darker than we are, they answered, "No; we never saw skin so white as that," and added, "Ah! you must be one of that tribe that loves [literally, *has heart to*] the black men." I, of course, gladly responded in the affirmative. They returned to the village, and we afterward heard that there had been a long discussion between Mpende and his councillors, and that one of the men with whom we had remained to talk the day before had been our advocate. He was named Sandeso Oaléa. When we were passing his village, after some conversation, he said to his people, "Is that the man whom they wish to stop after he has passed so many tribes? What can Mpende say to refusing him a passage?" It was owing to this man, and the fact that I belonged to the "friendly white tribe," that Mpende was persuaded to allow us to pass. When we knew the favorable decision of the council, I sent Sekwebu to speak about the purchase of a canoe, as one of my men had become very ill, and I wished to relieve his companions by taking him in a canoe. Before Sekwebu could finish his story, Mpende remarked, "That white man is truly one of our friends. See how he lets me know his afflictions!" Sekwebu adroitly took advantage of this turn in the conversation, and said, "Ah! if you only knew him as well as we do who have lived with him, you would understand that he highly values your friendship and that of Mburuma, and, as he is a stranger, he trusts in you to direct him." He replied, "Well, he ought to cross to the other side of the river, for this bank is hilly and rough, and the way to Tete is longer on this than on the opposite bank." "But who will take us across if you do not?" "Truly," replied Mpende, "I only wish you had come sooner to tell me about him; but you shall cross" Mpende said frequently he was sorry he had not known me sooner, but that he had been prevented by his enchanter from coming near me; and he lamented that the same person had kept him from eating the meat which I had presented. He did every thing he could afterward to aid us on our course, and our departure was as different as possible from our approach to his village. I was very much pleased to find the English name spoken of with such great respect so far from the coast, and most thankful that no collision occurred to damage its influence.

24th.—Mpende sent two of his principal men to order the people of a large island below to ferry us across. The river is very broad, and, though my men were well acquainted with the management of canoes, we could not all cross over before dark. It is 1200 yards from bank to bank, and between 700 and 800 of deep water, flowing at the rate of 3¼ miles per hour. We landed first on an island, then, to prevent our friends playing false with us, hauled the canoes up to our bivouac and slept in them. The next morning we all reached the opposite bank in safety.

29th.—I was most sincerely thankful to find myself on the south bank of the Zambesi; and, having nothing else, I sent back one of my two spoons and a shirt as a thank-offering to Mpende. The different head-men along this river act very much in concert, and if one refuses passage they all do, uttering the sage remark, "If so-and-so did not lend his canoes, he must have had some good reason." The next island we came to was that of a man named Mozinkwa. Here we were detained some days by continuous rains.

We were detained here so long that my tent became again quite rotten. One of my men, after long sickness, which I did not understand, died here. He was one of the Batoka, and when unable to walk I had some difficulty in making his companions carry him. They wished to leave him to die when his case became hopeless. Another of them deserted to Mozinkwa. He said that his motive for doing so was that the Makololo had killed both his father and mother, and, as he had neither wife nor child, there was no reason why he should continue longer with them. I did not object to his statements, but said if he should change his mind he would be welcome to rejoin us, and intimated to Mozinkwa that he must not be sold as a slave

February 1.—We met some native traders; and, as many of my men were now in a state of nudity, I bought some American calico, marked "Lawrence Mills, Lowell," with two small tusks, and distributed it among the most needy. After leaving Mozinkwa's, we came to the Zingesi, a sand-rivulet in flood, (lat. 15° 38' 34" S., long. 31° 1' E.) It was sixty or seventy yards wide, and waist deep. Like all these sand-rivers, it is for the most part dry; but, by digging down a few feet, water is to be found, which is percolating along the bed on a stratum of clay.

February 4.—We were much detained by rains, a heavy shower without wind falling every morning about daybreak: it often cleared up after that, admitting of our moving on a few miles. A continuous rain of several hours then set in.

On the 6th we came to the village of Boroma, which is situated among a number of others, each surrounded by extensive patches of cultivation. . On the opposite side of the river we have a great cluster of conical hills, called Chorichori. Boroma did not make his appearance, but sent a substitute, who acted civilly. I sent Sekwebu in the morning to state that we intended to move on: his mother rep'ed that, as she had expected that we should remain, no food was ready; but she sent a basket of corn and a fowl. As an excuse why Boroma did not present himself, she said that he was seized this morning by the Barimo,—which probably meant that his lordship was drunk.

We marched along the river to a point opposite the hill Pinkwo, (lat. 15° 39′ 11″ S., long. 32° 5′ E.;) but the late abundant rains now flooded the Zambesi again, and great quantities of wreck appeared upon the stream.

This flood having filled the river, we found the numerous rivulets which flow into it filled also, and when going along the Zambesi we lost so much time in passing up each little stream till we could find a ford about waist deep, and then returning to the bank, that I resolved to leave the river altogether and strike away to the southeast. We accordingly struck off when opposite the hill Pinkwe, and came into a hard Mopane country.

This Chicova is not a kingdom, as has been stated, but a level tract, a part of which is annually overflowed by the Zambesi, and is well adapted for the cultivation of corn. It is said to be below the northern end of the hill Bungwe. I was very much pleased in discovering a small specimen of such a precious mineral as coal. I saw no indication of silver; and, if it ever was worked by the natives, it is remarkable that they have entirely lost the knowledge of it, and cannot distinguish between silver and tin. Our path lay along the bed of the Nake for some distance, the banks being covered with impenetrable thickets. The villages are not numerous; but we went from one to the other, and were treated kindly. Here they call themselves Bambiri, though the general name of the whole nation is Banyái. One of our guides was an inveterate talker, always stopping and asking for pay, that he might go on with a merry heart. I thought that he led us in the most difficult paths in order to make us feel his value, for, after passing through one thicket after another, we always came into the bed of the Nake again; and as that was full of coarse sand, and the water only ankle deep, and as hot as a foot-bath from the powerful rays of the sun, we were all completely tired out. He likewise gave us a bad character at every village we passed, calling to them that they were to allow him to lead us astray, as we were a bad set. Sekwebu knew every word he said, and, as he became intolerable, I dismissed him, giving him six feet of calico I had bought from native traders, and telling him that his tongue was a nuisance. It is in general best, when a scolding is necessary, to give it in combination with a present, and then end it by good wishes. This fellow went off smiling; and my men remarked, "His tongue is cured now."

13th.—The head-man of these parts is named Nyampungo. I sent the last fragment of cloth we had, with a request that we should be furnished with a guide to the next chief. After a long conference with his council, the cloth was returned with a promise of compliance and a request for some beads only. This man is supposed to possess the charm for rain, and other tribes send to him to beg it. This shows that what we inferred before was correct,—that less rain falls in this country than in Londa. Nyampungo behaved in quite a gentlemanly manner, presented me with some rice, and told my people to go among all the villages and beg for themselves. An old man, father-in-law of the chief, told me that he had seen books before, but never knew what they meant. They pray to departed chiefs and relatives, but the idea of praying to God seemed new, and they heard it with reverence. As this was an intelligent old man, I asked him about the silver; but he was as ignorant of it as the rest, and said, "We never dug silver, but we have washed for gold in the sands of the rivers Mazoe and Luia, which unite in the Luenya." I think that this is quite conclusive on the question of no silver having been dug by the natives of this district. Nyampungo is afflicted with a kind of disease called Se senda, which I imagine to be a species of leprosy common in this quarter,—though they are a cleanly people. They never had cattle. The chief's father had always lived in their present position, and, when I asked him why he did not possess these useful animals, he said, "Who would give us the medicine to enable us to keep them?" I found out the reason afterward in the prevalence of tsetse; but of this he was ignorant, having supposed that he could not keep cattle because he had no medicine.

CHAPTER XXX.

DR. LIVINGSTONE REACHES TETE.

14th.—WE left Nyampungo this morning. The path wound up the Molinge, another sand-river which flows into the Nake. When we got clear of the tangled jungle which covers the banks of these rivulets, we entered the Mopane country, where we could walk with comfort. When we had gone on a few hours, my men espied an elephant, and were soon in full pursuit. They were in want of meat, having tasted nothing but grain for several days. The desire for animal food made them all eager to slay him, and, though an old bull, he was soon killed. The people of Nyampungo had never seen such desperadoes before. One rushed up and hamstrung the beast, while still standing, by a blow with an axe. Some Banyai elephant-hunters happened to be present when my men were fighting with him. One of them took out his snuff-box and poured out all its contents at the root of a tree, as an offering to the Barimo for success. As soon as the animal fell, the whole of my party engaged in a wild, savage dance round the body, which quite frightened the Banyai, and he who made the offering said to me, "I see you are travelling with people who don't know how to pray: I therefore offered the only thing I had in their behalf, and the elephant soon fell." One of Nyampungo's men, who remained with me, ran a little forward, when an opening in the trees gave us a view of the chase, and uttered loud prayers for success in the combat. I admired the devout belief they al. possessed in the actual existence of unseen beings, and prayed that they might yet know that benignant One who views us all as his own. My own people, who are rather a degraded lot, remarked to me, as I came up, "God gave it to us. He said to the old beast, 'Go up there: men are come who will kill and eat you.'" These remarks are quoted to give the reader an idea of the native mode of expression.

As we were now in the country of stringent game-laws, we were obliged to send all the way back to Nyampungo, to give information to a certain person who had been left there by the real owner of this district to watch over his property, the owner himself living near the Zambesi. The side upon which the elephant fell had a short, broken tusk; the upper one, which was ours, was large and thick. The Banyai remarked on our good luck. The men sent to give notice came back late in the afternoon of the following day. They brought a basket of corn, a fowl, and a few strings of handsome beads, as a sort of thank-offering for our having killed it on their land, and said they had thanked the Barimo besides for our success, adding, "There it is: eat it and be glad." Had we begun to cut it up before we got this permission, we should have lost the whole. They brought a large party to eat their half, and they divided it with us in a friendly way. My men were delighted with the feast, though, by lying unopened a whole day, the carcass was pretty far gone. An astonishing number of hyenas collected round and kept up a loud laughter for two whole nights. Some of them do make a very good imitation of a laugh. I asked my men what the hyenas were laughing at, as they usually give animals credit for a share of intelligence. They said that they were laughing because we could not take the whole, and that they would have plenty to eat as well as we.

On coming to the part where the elephant was slain, we passed through grass so tall that it reminded me of that in the valley of Cassango. Insects are very numerous as as the rains commence. While waiting by the elephant, I observed a great number of insects, like grains of fine sand, moving on my boxes. On examination with a glass, four species were apparent: one of green and gold preening its wings, which glanced in the sun with metallic lustre; another clear as crystal; a third of the color of vermilion; and a fourth black. These are probably some of those which consume the seeds of every plant that grows. Almost every kind has its own peculiar insect, and when the rains are over very few seeds remain untouched. The rankest poisons, as the kongwhano and euphorbia, are soon devoured; the former has a scarlet insect; and even the fiery bird's-eye pepper, which will keep off many others from their own seeds, is itself devoured by a maggot. I observed here, what I had often seen before, that certain districts abound in centipedes. Here they have light reddish bodies and blue legs: great myriapedes are seen crawling everywhere. Although they do no harm, they excite in man a feeling of loathing. Perhaps our appearance produces a similar feeling in the elephant and other large animals. Where they have been much disturbed, they certainly look upon us with great distrust, as the horrid biped that ruins their peace. In the quietest parts of the forest there is heard a faint but distinct hum, which tells of insect joy. One may see many whisking about in the clear sunshine in patches among the green glancing leaves; but there are invisible myriads working with never-tiring mandibles on leaves and stalks and beneath the soil. They are all brimful of enjoyment. Indeed, the universality of organic life may be called a mantle of happy existence encircling the world, and imparts the idea of its being caused by the consciousness of our benignant Father's smile on all the works of his hands.

The birds of the tropics have been described as generally wanting in power of song. I was decidedly of opinion that this was not applicable to many parts in Londa, though birds there are remarkably scarce. Here the chorus, or body of song, was not much smaller in volume than it is in England. It was not so harmonious, and sounded always as if the birds were singing in a foreign tongue. Some resemble the lark, and, indeed, there are several of that family; two have notes not unlike those of the thrush. One brought the chaffinch to my mind, and another the robin; but their songs are intermixed with several curious abrupt notes unlike any thing English. One utters deliberately "peek, pak, pok;" another has a single note like a stroke on a violin-string. The mokwa reza gives forth a screaming set of notes like our blackbird when disturbed, then concludes with what the natives say is "pula, pula," (rain, rain,) but more like "weep, weep, weep." Then we have the loud cry of francolins, the "pumpuru, pumpuru," of turtle-doves, and the "chiken, chiken, chik, churr, churr," of the honey-guide. Occasionally, near villages, we have a kind of mocking-bird, imitating the calls of domestic fowls. These African birds have not been wanting in song: they have only lacked poets to sing their praises, which ours have had from the time of Aristophanes downward. Ours have both a classic and a modern interest to enhance their fame. In hot, dry weather, or at mid-day when the sun is fierce, all are still: let, however, a good shower fall, and all burst forth at once into merry lays and loving courtship. The early mornings and the cool evenings are their favorite times for singing. There are comparatively few with gaudy plumage, being totally unlike, in this respect, the birds of the Brazils. The majority have decidedly a sober dress, though collectors, having generally selected the gaudiest as the most valuable, have conveyed the idea that the birds of the tropics for the most part possess gorgeous plumage.

15th.—Several of my men have been bitten by spiders and other insects, but no effect except pain has followed. A large caterpillar is frequently seen, called lezuntabuca. It is covered with long gray hairs, and, the body being

dark, it resembles a porcupine in miniature. If one
it, the hairs run into the pores of the skin, and
there, giving sharp pricks. There are others wh
a similar means of defence; and when the hand
across them, as in passing a bush on which they happen to
be, the contact resembles the stinging of nettle
the great number of caterpillars seen, we have a
able variety of butterflies. One particular kind fi
like a swallow than a butterfly. They are not rer
for the gaudiness of their colors.

In passing along, we crossed the hills Vungue or Mvung-
we, which we found to be composed of various eruptive
rocks. At one part we have breccia of altered marl or slate
in quartz, and various amygdaloids. It is curious to observe
the different forms which silica assumes. We have it in clay-
stone porphyry here, no larger than turnip-seed, dotted
thickly over the matrix; or crystallized round the walls of
cavities once filled with air or other elastic fluid; or it may
appear in similar cavities as tufts of yellow asbestos, or as
red, yellow, or green crystals, or in laminæ so arranged as to
appear like fossil wood. Vungue forms the watershed between those sand-rivulets which run to the N.E., and others
which flow southward, as the Kapopo, Ue, and Due, which
run into the Luia.

We found that many elephants had been feeding on the
fruit called mokoronga. This is a black-colored plum,
having purple juice. We all ate it in large quantities, as
we found it delicious. The only defect it has is the great
size of the seed in comparison with the pulp. This is the
chief fault of all uncultivated wild fruits. The mokoronga exists throughout this part of the country most
abundantly, and the natives eagerly devour it, as it is said
to be perfectly wholesome, or, as they express it, "It is
pure fat," and fat is by them considered the best of food.
Though only a little larger than a cherry, we found that the
elephants had stood picking them off patiently by the hour.
We observed the footprints of a black rhinoceros (*Rhino-*

ceros bicornis, Linn.) and her calf. We saw other footprints among the hills of Semalembue; but the black rhinoceros is remarkably scarce in all the country north of the Zambesi. The white rhinoceros (*Rhinoceros simus* of Burchell,) or Mohóhu of the Bechuanas, is quite extinct here, and will soon become unknown in the country to the south. It feeds almost entirely on grasses, and is of a timid, unsuspecting disposition: this renders it an easy prey, and they are slaughtered without mercy on the introduction of fire-arms. The black possesses a more savage nature, and, like the ill-natured in general, is never found with an ounce of fat in its body. From its greater fierceness and wariness, it holds its place in a district much longer than its more timid and better-conditioned neighbor. Mr. Oswell was once stalking two of these beasts, and, as they came slowly to him, he, knowing that there is but little chance of hitting the small brain of this animal by a shot in the head, lay expecting one of them to give his shoulder till he was within a few yards. The hunter then thought that by making a rush to his side he might succeed in escaping; but the rhinoceros, too quick for that, turned upon him, and, though he discharged his gun close to the animal's head, he was tossed in the air. My friend was insensible for some time, and, on recovering, found large wounds on the thigh and body: I saw that on the former part still open, and five inches long. The white, however, is not always quite safe, for one, even after it was mortally wounded, attacked Mr. Oswell's horse, and thrust the horn through to the saddle, tossing at the time both horse and rider. I once saw a white rhinoceros give a buffalo, which was gazing intently at myself, a poke in the chest, but it did not wound it, and seemed only a hint to get out of the way. Four varieties of the rhinoceros are enumerated by naturalists, but my observation led me to conclude that there are but two, and that the extra species have been formed from differences in their sizes, ages, and the direction of the horns; as if we should reckon the short-horned cattle a different species from the Alderneys or the Highland breed. I was led to this from having once seen a black rhinoceros with a horn bent downward like that of the kuabaoba, and also because the animals of the two great varieties differ very much in appearance at different stages of their growth. I find, however, that Dr. Smith, the best judge in these matters, is quite decided as to the propriety of the subdivision into three or four species. For common readers it is sufficient to remember that there are two well-defined species, that differ entirely in appearance and food. The absence of both these rhinoceroses among the reticulated rivers in the central valley may easily be accounted for, they would be such an easy prey to the natives in their canoes at the periods of inundation; but one cannot so readily account for the total absence of the giraffe and ostrich on the high open lands of the Batoka north of the Zambesi, unless we give credence to the native report which bounds the country still farther north by another network of waters near Lake Shuia, and suppose that it also prevented their progress southward. The Batoka have no name for the giraffe or the ostrich in their language; yet, as the former exists in considerable numbers in the angle formed by the Leeambye and Chobe, they may have come from the north along the western ridge. The Chobe would seem to have been too narrow to act as an obstacle to the giraffe, supposing it to have come into that district from the south; but the broad river into which that stream flows seems always to have presented an impassable barrier to both the giraffe and the ostrich, though they abound on its southern border, both in the Kalahari Desert and the country of Mashona.

The honey-guides were very assiduous in their friendly offices, and enabled my men to get a large quantity of honey. But, though bees abound, the wax of these parts forms no article of trade. In Londa it may be said to be fully cared for, as you find hives placed upon trees in the most lonesome forests. We often met strings of carriers known with large blocks of this substance, each eighty or a hundred pounds in weight, and pieces were offered to us for sale at every village; but here we never saw a single artificial hive. The bees were always found in the natural cavities of mopane-trees. It is probable that the good market for wax afforded to Angola by the churches of Brazil led to the gradual development of that branch of commerce there. I saw even on the banks of the Quango as much as sixpence paid for a pound. In many parts of the Batoka country bees exist in vast numbers, and the tribute due to Sekeletu is often paid in large jars of honey; but, having no market nor use for the wax, it is thrown away. This was the case also with ivory at the Lake Ngami at the period of its discovery.

Though we are now approaching the Portuguese settlement, the country is still full of large game. My men killed six buffalo-calves out of a herd we met. The abundance of these animals, and also of antelopes, shows the insufficiency of the bow and arrow to lessen their numbers. There are also a great many lions and hyenas, and there is no check upon the increase of the former, for the people, believing that the souls of their chiefs enter into them, never attempt to kill them: they even believe that a chief may metamorphose himself into a lion, kill any one he chooses, and then return to the human form: therefore, when they see one, they commence clapping their hands, which is the usual mode of salutation here. The consequence is that lions and hyenas are so abundant that we see little huts made in the trees, indicating the places where some of the inhabitants have slept when benighted in the fields. As numbers of my men frequently left the line of march in order to take out the korwes from their nests or follow the honey-guides, they excited the astonishment of our guides, who were constantly warning them of the danger they thereby incurred from lions. I was often considerably ahead of the main body of my men on this account, and was obliged to stop every hour or two; but, the sun being excessively hot by day, I was glad of the excuse for resting. We could make no such prodigious strides as officers in the Arctic regions are able to do. Ten or twelve miles a day were a good march for both the men and myself; and it was not the length of the marches, but continuing day after day to perform the same distance, that was so fatiguing. It was in this case much longer than appears on the map, because we kept out of the way of villages. I drank less than the natives when riding; but all my clothing was now constantly damp from the moisture which was imbibed in large quantities at every pond. One does not stay on these occasions to prepare water with alum or any thing else, but drinks any amount without fear. I never felt the atmosphere so steamy as on the low-lying lands of the Zambesi; and yet it was becoming cooler than it was on the highlands.

We crossed the rivulets Kapopo and Ue, now running but usually dry. There are great numbers of wild grape-vines growing in this quarter: indeed, they abound everywhere along the banks of the Zambesi. In the Batoka country there is a variety which yields a black grape of considerable sweetness. The leaves are very large and harsh, as if capable of withstanding the rays of this hot sun; but the most common kinds—one with a round leaf and a greenish grape, and another with a leaf closely resembling that of the cultivated varieties and with dark or purple fruit—have large seeds, which are strongly astringent and render it a disagreeable fruit. The natives eat all the varieties; and I tasted vinegar made by a Portuguese from these grapes. Probably a country which yields the wild vines so very abundantly might be a fit one for the cultivated species. At this part of the journey so many of the vines had run across the little footpath we followed that one had to be constantly on the watch to avoid being tripped. The ground was covered with rounded shingle, which was not easily seen among the grass. Pedestrianism may be all very well for those whose obesity requires much exercise;

but for one who was becoming as thin as a lath, through the constant perspiration caused by marching day after day in the hot sun, the only good I saw in it was that it gave an honest sort of a man a vivid idea of the tread mill.

Although the rains were not quite over, great numbers of pools were drying up, and the ground was in many parts covered with small green cryptogamous plants, which gave it a mouldy appearance and a strong smell. As we sometimes pushed aside the masses of rank vegetation which hung over our path, we felt a sort of hot blast on our faces. Every thing looked unwholesome; but we had no fever. The Ue flows between high banks of a soft red sandstone streaked with white, and pieces of tufa. The crumbling sandstone is evidently alluvial, and is cut into twelve feet deep. In this region, too, we met with potholes six feet deep and three or four in diameter. In some cases they form convenient wells; in others they are full of earth; and in others still the people have made them into graves for their chiefs.

On the 20th we came to Monina's village, (close to the sand-river Tangwe, latitude 16° 13′ 38″ south, longitude 32° 32′ east.) This man is very popular among the tribes, on account of his liberality. Boróma, Nyampúngo, Monína, Jira, Katolósa, (Monomotápa,) and Súsa, all acknowledge the supremacy of one called Nyatéwe, who is reported to decide all disputes respecting land.

When we told Monina that we had nothing to present but some hoes, he replied that he was not in need of those articles, and that he had absolute power over the country in front, and if he prevented us from proceeding no one would say any thing to him. His little boy Borómo having come to the encampment to look at us, I gave him a knife, and he went off and brought a pint of honey for me. The father came soon afterward, and I offered him a shirt. He remarked to his councillors, "It is evident that this man has nothing, for, if he had, his people would be buying provisions, but we don't see them going about for that purpose." His council did not agree in this. They evidently believed that we had goods but kept them hid, and we felt it rather hard to be suspected of falsehood. It was probably at their suggestion that in the evening a war-dance was got up about a hundred yards from our encampment, as if to put us in fear and force us to bring forth presents. Some of Monina's young men had guns, but most were armed with large bows, arrows, and spears. They beat their drums furiously, and occasionally fired off a gun. As this sort of dance is never got up unless there is an intention to attack, my men expected an assault. We sat and looked at them for some time, and then, as it became dark, lay down all ready to give them a warm reception. But an hour or two after dark the dance ceased, and, as we then saw no one approaching us, we went to sleep. During the night, one of my head-men, Monahin, was seen to get up, look toward the village, and say to one who was half awake, "Don't you hear what these people are saying? Go and listen." He then walked off in the opposite direction, and never returned. We had no guard set, but every one lay with his spear in his hand. The man to whom he spoke appears to have been in a dreamy condition, for it did not strike him that he ought to give the alarm. Next morning I found to my sorrow that Monahin was gone, and not a trace of him could be discovered. He had an attack of pleuritis some weeks before, and had recovered, but latterly complained a little of his head. I observed him in good spirits on the way hither, and in crossing some of the streams, as I was careful not to wet my feet, he aided me, and several times joked at my becoming so light. In the evening he sat beside my tent until it was dark, and did not manifest any great alarm. It was probably either a sudden fit of insanity, or, having gone a little way out from the camp, he may have been carried off by a lion, as this part of the country is full of them. I incline to the former opinion, because sudden insanity occurs when there is any unusual strain upon their minds. Monahin was in command of the Batoka of Mokwiné in my party, and he was looked upon with great dislike by all that chief's subjects. The only difficulties I had with them arose in consequence of being obliged to give orders through him. They said Mokwine is reported to have been killed by the Makololo, but Monahin is the individual who put forth his hand and slew him. When one of these people kills in battle, he seems to have no compunction afterward; but when he makes a foray on his own responsibility, and kills a man of note, the common people make remarks to each other, which are reported to him and bring the affair perpetually to his remembrance. This iteration on the conscience causes insanity, and, when one runs away in a wide country like this, the fugitive is never heard of. Monahin had lately become afraid of his own party from overhearing their remarks, and said more than once to me, "They want to kill me." I believe if he ran to any village they would take care of him. I felt his loss greatly, and spent three days in searching for him. He was a sensible and most obliging man. I sent in the morning to inform Monina of this sad event, and he at once sent to all the gardens around, desiring the people to look for him, and, should he come near, to bring him home. He evidently sympathized with us in our sorrow, and, afraid lest we might suspect him, added, "We never catch nor kidnap people here. It is not our custom. It is considered as guilt among all the tribes." I gave him credit for truthfulness, and he allowed us to move on without further molestation.

After leaving his village, we marched in the bed of a sand-river a quarter of a mile broad, called Tangwe. Walking on this sand is as fatiguing as walking on snow. The country is flat, and covered with low trees; but we see high hills in the distance. A little to the south we have those of the Lobole. This region is very much infested by lions, and men never go any distance into the woods alone. Having turned aside on one occasion at mid-day, and gone a short distance among grass a little taller than myself, an animal sprang away from me which was certainly not an antelope, but I could not distinguish whether it was a lion or a hyena. This abundance of carnivora made us lose all hope of Monahin. We saw footprints of many black rhinoceroses, buffalos, and zebras.

After a few hours we reached the village of Nyakoba. Two men who accompanied us from Monina to Nyakoba's would not believe us when we said that we had no beads. It is very trying to have one's veracity doubted; but, on opening the boxes, and showing them that all I had was perfectly useless to them, they consented to receive some beads off Sekwebu's waist, and I promised to send four yards of calico from Tete. As we came away from Monina's village, a witch-doctor, who had been sent for, arrived, and all Monina's wives went forth into the fields that morning fasting. There they would be compelled to drink an infusion of a plant named "goho," which is used as an ordeal. This ceremony is called "muavi," and is performed in this way. When a man suspects that any of his wives has bewitched him, he sends for the witch-doctor, and all the wives go forth into the field and remain fasting till that person has made an infusion of the plant. They all drink it, each one holding up her hand to heaven in attestation of her innocency. Those who vomit it are considered innocent, while those whom it purges are pronounced guilty, and put to death by burning. The innocent return to their homes, and slaughter a cock as a thank-offering to their guardian spirits. The practice of ordeal is common among all the negro nations north of the Zambesi. This summary procedure excited my surprise, for my intercourse with the natives here had led me to believe that the women were held in so much estimation that the men would not dare to get rid of them thus. But the explanation I received was this. The slightest imputation makes them eagerly desire the test; they are conscious of being innocent, and have the fullest faith in the muavi detecting the guilty alone: hence they go willingly, and even eagerly, to drink it. When in Angola, a half-caste was pointed out to me who is one of the most successful merchants in that country; and the mother of this gentleman, who was perfectly free, went, of her own accord, all the way from Ambaca to Cassange, to be killed by the ordeal, her rich son making no objection. The same custom prevails among the Barotse, Bashubia, and Batoka, but with slight variations. The Barotse, for instance, pour the medicine down the throat of a cock or of a dog, and judge of the innocence or guilt of the person accused according to the vomiting or purging of the animal. I happened to mention to my own men the water-test for witches formerly in use in Scotland: the supposed witch, being bound hand and foot, was thrown into a pond: if she floated, she was considered guilty, taken out, and burned; but if she sank and was drowned, she was pronounced innocent. The wisdom of my ancestors excited as much wonder in their minds as their custom did in mine.

The person whom Nyakoba appointed to be our guide, having informed us of the decision, came and bargained that his services should be rewarded with a hoe. I had no objection to give it, and showed him the article: he was delighted with it, and went off to show it to his wife. He soon afterward returned, and said that, though he was perfectly willing to go, his wife would not let him. I said, "Then bring back the hoe;" but he replied, "I want it." "Well, go with us, and you shall have it." "But my wife won't let me." I remarked to my men, "Did you ever hear such a fool?" They answered, "Oh, that is the custom of these parts: the wives are the masters." And Sekwebu informed me that he had gone to this man's house, and heard him saying to his wife, "Do you think that I would ever leave you?" then, turning to Sekwebu, he asked, "Do you think I would leave this pretty woman? Is she not pretty?" Sekwebu had been making inquiries among the people, and had found that the women indeed possessed a great deal of influence. We questioned the guide whom we finally got from Nyakoba, an intelligent young man, who had much of the Arab features, and found the statements confirmed. When a young man takes a liking for a girl of another village, and the parents have no objection to the match, he is obliged to come and live at their village. He has to perform certain services for the mother-in-law, such as keeping her well supplied with firewood; and when he comes into her presence he is obliged to sit with his knees in a bent position, as putting out his feet toward the old lady would give her great offence. If he becomes tired of living in this state of vassalage, and wishes to return to his own family, he is obliged to leave all his children behind: they belong to the wife. This is only a more stringent enforcement of the law from which emanates the practice which prevails so very extensively in Africa, known to Europeans as "buying wives." Such virtually it is; but it does not appear quite in that light to the actors. So many head of cattle or goats are given to the parents of the girl "to give her up," as it is termed, —*i.e.* to forego all claim on her offspring and allow an entire transference of her and her seed into another family. If nothing is given, the family from which she has come can claim the children as part of itself: the payment is made to sever this bond. In the case supposed, the young man has not been able to advance any thing for that purpose; and, from the temptations placed here before my men, I have no doubt that some prefer to have their daughters married in that way, as it leads to the increase of their own village. My men excited the admiration of the Bambiri, who took them for a superior breed on account of their bravery in elephant-hunting, and wished to get them as sons-in-law on the conditions named; but none yielded to the temptation.

We were informed that there is a child belonging to a

half-caste Portuguese in one of these tribes, and the father had tried in vain to get him from the mother's parents. We saw several things to confirm the impression of the higher position which women hold here; and, being anxious to discover if I were not mistaken, when we came among the Portuguese I inquired of them, and was told that they had ascertained the same thing; and that, if they wished a man to perform any service for them, he would reply, "Well, I shall go and ask my wife." If she consented, he would go and perform his duty faithfully; but no amount of coaxing or bribery would induce him to do it if she refused. The Portuguese praised the appearance of the Banyai; and they certainly are a fine race.

We got on better with Nyakoba than we expected. He has been so much affected by the sesenda that he is quite decrepit, and requires to be fed. I at once showed his messenger that we had nothing whatever to give. Nyakoba was offended with him for not believing me, and he immediately sent a basket of maize and another of corn, saying that he believed my statement, and would send men with me to Tete who would not lead me to any other village.

The birds here sing very sweetly, and I thought I heard the canary, as in Londa. We had a heavy shower of rain; and I observed that the thermometer sank 14° in one hour afterward. From the beginning of February we experienced a sensible diminution of temperature. In January the lowest was 75°, and that at sunrise; the average at the same hour (sunrise) being 79°; at 3 P.M., 90°; and at sunset, 82°. In February it fell as low as 70° in the course of the night, and the average height was 88°. Only once did it rise to 91°, and a thunder-storm followed this; yet the sensation of heat was greater now than it had been at much higher temperatures on more elevated lands.

We passed several villages by going roundabout ways through the forest. We saw the remains of a lion that had been killed by a buffalo, and the horns of a putokwane, (black antelope,) the finest I had ever seen, which had met its death by a lion. The drums, beating all night in one village near which we slept, showed that some person in it had finished his course. On the occasion of the death of a chief, a trader is liable to be robbed, for the people consider themselves not amenable to law until a new one is elected. We continued a very winding course, in order to avoid the chief Katolosa, who is said to levy large sums upon those who fall into his hands. One of our guides was a fine, tall young man, the very image of Ben Habib the Arab. They were carrying dried buffalo's meat to the market at Tete as a private speculation.

A great many of the Banyai are of a light coffee-and-milk color, and, indeed, this color is considered handsome throughout the whole country, a fair complexion being as much a test of beauty with them as with us. As they draw out their hair into small cords a foot in length, and entwine the inner bark of a certain tree round each separate cord, and dye this substance of a reddish color, many of them put me in mind of the ancient Egyptians. The great mass of dressed hair which they possess reaches to the shoulders, but when they intend to travel they draw it up to a bunch and tie it on the top of the head. They are cleanly in their habits.

As we did not come near human habitations, and could only take short stages on account of the illness of one of my men, I had an opportunity of observing the expedients my party resorted to in order to supply their wants. Large white edible mushrooms are found on the ant-hills, and are very good. The mokuri, a tuber which abounds in the Mopane country, they discovered by percussing the ground with stones; and another tuber, about the size of a turnip, called "bonga," is found in the same situations. It does not determine to the joints like the mokuri, and in winter has a sensible amount of salt in it. A fruit called "ndongo" by the Makololo, "dongolo" by the Bambiri, resembles in appearance a small plum, which becomes black when ripe, and is good food; as the seeds are small. Many trees are known by tradition, and one receives curious bits of information in asking about different fruits that are met with. A tree named "shekabakádzi" is superior to all others for making fire by friction. As its name implies, women may even readily make fire by it when benighted.

We were tolerably successful in avoiding the villages, and slept one night on the flanks of the hill Zimika, where a great number of deep pot-holes afforded an abundant supply of good rain-water. Here, for the first time, we saw hills with bare, smooth, rocky tops, and we crossed over broad dikes of gneiss and syenitic porphyry: the directions in which they lay were N. and S. As we were now near to Tete, we were congratulating ourselves on having avoided those who would only have plagued us; but next morning some men saw us, and ran off to inform the neighboring villages of our passing. A party immediately pursued us, and, as they knew we were within call of Katolósa, (Monomotápa,) they threatened to send information to that chief of our offence in passing through the country without leave. We were obliged to give them two small tusks; for, had they told Katolosa of our supposed offence, we should in all probability have lost the whole. We then went through a very rough, stony country without any path. Being pretty well tired out in the evening of the 2d of March, I remained at about eight miles' distance from Tete, Tétte, or Nyungwé. My men asked me to go on: I felt too fatigued to proceed, but sent forward to the commandant the letters of recommendation with which I had been favored in Angola by the bishop and others, and lay down to rest. Our food having been exhausted, my men had been subsisting for some time on roots and honey. About two o'clock in the morning of the 3d we were aroused by two officers and a company of soldiers, who had been sent with the materials for a civilized breakfast and a "mashcela" to bring me to Tete. (Commandant's house;

lat 16° 9' 3" S., long. 33° 28' E.) My companions thought that we were captured by the armed men, and called me in alarm. When I understood the errand on which they had come, and had partaken of a good breakfast, though I had just before been too tired to sleep, all my fatigue vanished. It was the most refreshing breakfast I ever partook of, and I walked the last eight miles without the least feeling of weariness, although the path was so rough that one of the officers remarked to me, "This is enough to tear a man's life out of him." The pleasure experienced in partaking of that breakfast was only equalled by the enjoyment of Mr. Gabriel's bed on my arrival at Loanda. It was also enhanced by the news that Sebastopol had fallen and the war was finished.

CHAPTER XXXI.

DR. LIVINGSTONE'S RESIDENCE AT TETE.

I WAS most kindly received by the commandant, Tito Augusto d'Araujo Sicard, who did every thing in his power to restore me from my emaciated condition; and, as this was still the unhealthy period at Kilimane, he advised me to remain with him until the following month. He also generously presented my men with abundant provisions of millet; and, by giving them lodgings in a house of his own until they could erect their own huts, he preserved them from the bite of the tampans, here named Carapatos. We had heard frightful accounts of this insect while among the Banyai; and Major Sicard assured me that to strangers its bite is more especially dangerous, as it sometimes causes fatal fever. It may please our homœopathic friends to learn that, in curing the bite of the tampan, the natives administer one of the insects bruised in the medicine employed.

The village of Tete is built on a long slope down to the

river, the fort being close to the water. The rock beneath is gray sandstone, and has the appearance of being crushed away from the river: the strata have thus a crumpled form. The hollow between each crease is a street, the houses being built upon the projecting fold. The rocks at the top of the slope are much higher than the fort, and, of course, completely command it. There is then a large valley, and beyond that an oblong hill called Karucira. There are about thirty European houses: the rest are native, and of wattle and daub. A wall about ten feet high is intended to enclose the village; but most of the native inhabitants prefer to live on different spots outside. There are about twelve hundred huts in all, which with European households would give a population of about four thousand five hundred souls. Only a small proportion of these, however, live on the spot; the majority are engaged in agricultural operations in the adjacent country. Generally there are not more than two thousand people resident, for, compared with what it was, Tete is now a ruin. The number of Portuguese is very small; if we exclude the military, it is under twenty. Lately, however, one hundred and five soldiers were sent from Portugal to Senna, where in one year twenty-five were cut off by fever. They were then removed to Tete; and here they enjoy much better health, though, from the abundance of spirits distilled from various plants, wild fruits, and grain, in which pernicious beverage they largely indulge, besides partaking chiefly of unwholesome native food, better health could scarcely have been expected. The natives here understand the method of distillation by means of gun-barrels and a succession of earthen pots filled with water to keep them cool. The general report of the fever here is that, while at Kilimane the fever is continuous, at Tete a man recovers in about three days. The mildest remedies only are used at first, and, if that period be passed, then the more severe.

The fort of Tete has been the salvation of the Portuguese

power in this quarter. It is a small square building, with a thatched apartment for the residence of the troops; and, though there are but few guns, they are in a much better state than those of any fort in the interior of Angola. The cause of the decadence of the Portuguese power in this region is simply this:—In former times, considerable quantities of grain, as wheat, millet, and maize, were exported; also coffee, sugar, oil, and indigo, besides gold-dust and ivory. The cultivation of grain was carried on by means of slaves, of whom the Portuguese possessed a large number. The gold-dust was procured by washing at various points on the north, south, and west of Tete. A merchant took all his slaves with him to the washings, carrying as much calico and other goods as he could muster. On arriving at the washing-place, he made a present to the chief of the value of about a pound sterling. The slaves were then divided into parties, each headed by a confidential servant, who not only had the supervision of his squad while the washing went on, but bought dust from the inhabitants and made a weekly return to his master. When several masters united at one spot, it was called a "Bara;" and they then erected a temporary church, in which a priest from one of the missions performed mass. Both chiefs and people were favorable to these visits, because the traders purchased grain for the sustenance of the slaves with the goods they had brought. They continued at this labor until the whole of the goods were expended; and by this means about one hundred and thirty pounds of gold were annually produced. Probably more than this was actually obtained, but, as it was an article easily secreted, this alone was submitted to the authorities for taxation. At present the whole amount of gold obtained annually by the Portuguese is from eight to ten pounds only. When the slave-trade began, it seemed to many of the merchants a more speedy mode of becoming rich to sell off the slaves than to pursue the slow mode of gold-washing and agriculture, and they continued to export them until they had neither hands to labor nor to fight for them. It was just the story of the goose and the golden egg. The coffee and sugar plantations and gold-washings were abandoned, because the labor had been exported to the Brazils. Many of the Portuguese then followed their slaves, and the Government was obliged to pass a law to prevent further emigration, which, had it gone on, would have depopulated the Portuguese possessions altogether. A clever man of Asiatic (Goa) and Portuguese extraction, called Nyaude, now built a stockade at the confluence of the Luenya and Zambesi; and, when the commandant of Tete sent an officer with his company to summon him to his presence, Nyaude asked permission of the officer to dress himself, which being granted, he went into an inner apartment, and the officer ordered his men to pile their arms. A drum of war began to beat a note which is well known to the inhabitants. Some of the soldiers took the alarm on hearing this note; but the officer, disregarding their warning, was, with his whole party, in a few minutes disarmed and bound hand and foot. The commandant of Tete then armed the whole body of slaves and marched against the stockade of Nyaude; but when they came near to it there was the Luenya still to cross. As they did not effect this speedily, Nyaude despatched a strong party under his son Bonga across the river below the stockade, and up the left bank of the Zambesi until they came near to Tete. They then attacked Tete, which was wholly undefended save by a few soldiers in the fort, plundered and burned the whole town except the house of the commandant and a few others, with the church and fort. The women and children fled into the church; and it is a remarkable fact that none of the natives of this region will ever attack a church. Having rendered Tete a ruin, Bonga carried off all the cattle and plunder to his father. News of this having been brought to the army before the stockade, a sudden panic dispersed the whole; and, as the fugitives took roundabout ways in their flight, Katolosa, who and hitherto pretended to be friendly with the Portuguese sent out his men to capture as many of them as they could. They killed many for the sake of their arms. This is the account which both natives and Portuguese give of the affair.

The merchants were unable to engage in trade, and commerce, which the slave-trade had rendered stagnant, was now completely obstructed. The present commandant of Tete, Major Sicard, having great influence among the natives, from his good character, put a stop to the war more than once by his mere presence on the spot. We heard of him among the Banyai as a man with whom they would never fight, because "he had a good heart." Had I come down to this coast instead of going to Loanda in 1853, I should have come among the belligerents while the war was still raging, and should probably have been cut off. My present approach was just at the conclusion of the peace; and when the Portuguese authorities here were informed, through the kind offices of Lord Clarendon and Count de Lavradio, that I was expected to come this way, they all declared that such was the existing state of affairs that no European could possibly pass through the tribes. Some natives at last came down the river to Tete and said, alluding to the sextant and artificial horizon, that "the Son of God had come," and that he was "able to take the sun down from the heavens and place it under his arm!" Major Sicard then felt sure that this was the man mentioned in Lord Clarendon's despatch.

On mentioning to the commandant that I had discovered a small seam of coal, he stated that the Portuguese were already aware of nine such seams, and that five of them were on the opposite bank of the river. As soon as I had recovered from my fatigue I went to examine them. We proceeded in a boat to the mouth of the Lofúbu or Revúbu which is about two miles below Tete and on the opposite or northern bank. Ascending this about four miles against a strong current of beautifully-clear water, we landed near a small cataract, and walked about two miles through very fertile gardens to the seam, which we found to be in one of the feeders of the Lofubu, called Muatize or Motize. The seam is in the perpendicular bank, and dips into the rivulet, or in a northerly direction. There is, first of all, a seam ten inches in diameter, then some shale, below which there is another seam, fifty-eight inches of which are seen, and, as the bottom touches the water of the Muatize, it may be more. This part of the seam is about thirty yards long. There is then a fault. About one hundred yards higher up the stream, black vesicular trap is seen, penetrating in thin veins the clay shale of the country, converting it into porcellanite, and partially crystallizing the coal with which it came into contact. On the right bank of the Lofubu there is another feeder entering that river near its confluence with the Muatize, which is called the Morongózi, in which there is another and still larger bed of coal exposed. Farther up the Lofubu there are other seams in the rivulets Inyavu and Makare; also several spots in the Maravi country have the coal cropping out. This has evidently been brought to the surface by volcanic action at a later period than the coal-formation.

I also went up the Zambesi, and visited a hot spring called Nyamborónda, situated in the bed of a small rivulet named Nyaondo, which shows that igneous action is not yet extinct. We landed at a small rivulet called Mokorozi, then went a mile or two to the eastward, where we found a hot fountain at the bottom of a high hill. A little spring bubbles up on one side of the rivulet Nyaondo, and a great quantity of acrid steam rises up from the ground adjacent, about twelve feet square of which is so hot that my companions could not stand on it with their bare feet. There are several little holes from which the water trickles; but the principal spring is in a hole a foot in diameter and about the same in depth. Numbers of bubbles are constantly rising. The steam feels acrid in the throat, but is not inflammable, as it did not burn when I held a bunch of lighted grass over the bubbles. The mercury rises to 158° when the thermometer is put into the water in the hole; but after a few seconds it stands steadily at 160°. Even when flowing over the stones the water is too hot for the hand. Little fish frequently leap out of the stream in the bed of which the fountain rises, into the hot water, and get scalded to death. We saw a frog which had performed the experiment and was now cooked. The stones over which the water flows are incrusted with a white salt, and the water has a saline taste. The ground has been dug out near the fountain by the natives, in order to extract the salt it contains. It is situated among rocks of syenitic porphyry in broad dikes, and gneiss tilted on edge and having a strike to the N.E. There are many specimens of half-formed pumice, with greenstone and lava. Some of the sandstone strata are dislocated by a hornblende rock and by basalt, the sandstone nearest to the basalt being converted into quartz.

The country around, as indeed all the district lying N. and N.W. of Tete, is hilly, and, the hills being covered with trees, the scenery is very picturesque. The soil of the valleys is very fruitful and well cultivated. There would not be much difficulty in working the coal. The Lofubu is about sixty yards broad: it flows perennially, and at its very lowest period, which is after September, there is water about eighteen inches deep, which could be navigated in flat-bottomed boats. At the time of my visit it was full, and the current was very strong. If the small cataract referred to were to be avoided, the land-carriage beyond would only be about two miles. The other seams farther up the river may, after passing the cataract, be approached more easily than that in the Muatize: as the seam, however, dips down into the stream, no drainage of the mine would be required. For if water were come to it would run into the stream. I did not visit the others, but I was informed that there are seams in the independent native territory as well as in that of the Portuguese. The in the Nake is in the Banyai country; and, indeed, I have no doubt but that the whole country between Zumbo and Lupata is a coal-field of at least two and a half degrees of latitude in breadth, having many faults, made during the time of the igneous action. The gray sandstone rock, having silicified trees lying on it, is of these dimensions. The plantation in which the seam of coal exists would be valued among the Portuguese at about 60 dollars, or £12; but much more would probably be asked if a wealthy purchaser appeared. They could not, however, raise the price very much higher, because estates containing coal might be had from the native owners at a much cheaper rate. The wages of free laborers, when employed in such work as gold-washing, agriculture, or digging coal, is two yards of unbleached calico per day. They might be got to work much cheaper if engaged by the moon, or for about sixteen yards per month. For masons and carpenters even, the ordinary rate is two yards per day. This is called one braça. Tradesmen from Kilimane demand four braças, or eight yards, per day. English or American unbleached calico is the only currency used. The carriage of goods up the river to Tete adds about ten per cent. to their cost. The usual conveyance is by means of very large canoes and launches built at Senna.

The amount of merchandise brought up during the five months of peace previous to my visit was of the value of 30,000 dollars, or about £6000. The annual supply of goods for trade is about £15,000,—being calico, thick brass wire, beads, gunpowder, and guns. The quantity of the latter is, however, small, as the Government of Mozambique made that article contraband after the commencement of the war. Goods, when traded with in the tribes around the Portuguese, produce a profit of only about ten per cent., the articles traded in being ivory and gold-dust. A little oil and wheat are exported, but nothing else. Trade with the tribes beyond the exclusive ones is much better. Thirty brass rings cost 10s. at Senna, £1 at Tete, and £2 beyond the tribes in the vicinity of Tete: these are a good price for a penful of gold-dust of the value of £2. The plantations of coffee, which, previous to the commencement of the slave-trade, yielded one material for exportation, are now deserted, and it is difficult to find a single tree. The indigo (*Indigofera argentea*, the common wild indigo of Africa) is found growing everywhere, and large quantities of the senna-plant* grow in the village of Tete and other parts; but neither indigo nor senna is collected. Calumba-root, which is found in abundance in some parts farther down the river, is bought by the Americans, it is said, to use as a dye-stuff. A kind of sarsaparilla, or a plant which is believed by the Portuguese to be such, is found from Londa to Senna, but has never been exported.

The price of provisions is low, but very much higher than previous to the commencement of the war. Two yards of calico are demanded for six fowls: this is considered very dear, because before the war the same quantity of calico was worth twenty-four fowls. Grain is sold in little bags made from the leaves of the palmyra, like those in which we receive sugar. They are called panjas; and each panja weighs between thirty and forty pounds. The panja of wheat at Tete is worth a dollar, or five shillings; but the native grain may be obtained among the islands below Lupata at the rate of three panjas for two yards of calico. The highest articles of consumption are tea and coffee, the tea being often as high as fifteen shillings a pound. Food is cheaper down the river below Lupata, and previous to the war the islands which stud the Zambesi were all inhabited, and, the soil being exceedingly fertile, grain and fowls could be got to any amount. The inhabitants disappeared before their enemies the Landeens, but are beginning

---

* These appear to belong to *Cassia acutifolia*, or true senna of commerce, found in various parts of Africa and India.—*Dr. Hooker.*

to return since the peace. They have no cattle, the only place where we found no tsetse being the district of Tete itself; and the cattle in the possession of the Portuguese are a mere remnant of what they formerly owned.

When visiting the hot fountain, I examined what were formerly the gold-washings in the rivulet Mokoroze, which is nearly on the 16th parallel of latitude. The banks are covered with large groves of fine mango-trees, among which the Portuguese lived while superintending the washing for the precious metal. The process of washing is very laborious and tedious. A quantity of sand is put into a wooden bowl with water: a half-rotatory motion is given to the dish, which causes the coarser particles of sand to collect on one side of the bottom. These are carefully removed with the hand, and the process of rotation renewed until the whole of the sand is taken away and the gold alone remains. It is found in very minute scales, and, unless I had been assured to the contrary, I should have taken it to be mica; for, knowing the gold to be of greater specific gravity than the sand, I imagined that a stream of water would remove the latter and leave the former; but here the practice is to remove the whole of the sand by the hand. This process was no doubt a profitable one to the Portuguese, and it is probable that, with the improved plan by means of mercury, the sands would be lucrative. I had an opportunity of examining the gold-dust from different parts to the east and northeast of Tete. There are six well-known washing-places. These are called Mashinga, Shindúndo, Missála, Kapáta, Máno, and Jáwa. From the description of the rock I received, I suppose gold is found both in clay shale and in quartz. At the range Mushinga to the N.N.W. the rock is said to be so soft that the women pound it into powder in wooden mortars previous to washing.

Round toward the westward, the old Portuguese indicate a station which was near to Zumbo on the river Panyáme, and called Dambarári, near which much gold was found

Farther west lay the now unknown kingdom of Abútua, which was formerly famous for the metal; and then, coming round toward the east, we have the gold-washings of the Mashóna, or Bazizúlu, and, farther east, that of Manica, where gold is found much more abundantly than in any other part, and which has been supposed by some to be the Ophir of King Solomon. I saw the gold from this quarter as large as grains of wheat, that found in the rivers which run into the coal-field being in very minute scales. If we place one leg of the compasses at Tete, and extend the other three and a half degrees, bringing it round from the northeast of Tete by west, and then to the southeast, we nearly touch or include all the known gold-producing country. As the gold on this circumference is found in coarser grains than in the streams running toward the centre or Tete, I imagine that the real gold-field lies round about the coal-field; and, if I am right in the conjecture, then we have coal encircled by a gold-field, and abundance of wood, water, and provisions,—a combination not often met with in the world. The inhabitants are not unfavorable to washings conducted on the principle formerly mentioned. At present they wash only when in want of a little calico. They know the value of gold perfectly well; for they bring it for sale in goose-quills, and demand twenty-four yards of calico for one penful.

Major Sicard, the commandant, whose kindness to me and my people was unbounded, presented a rosary made of the gold of the country, the workmanship of a native of Tete, to my little daughter,—also specimens of the gold-dust of three different places, which, with the coal of Muatize and Morongoze, are deposited in the Museum of Practical Geology, Jermyn Street, London.

All the cultivation is carried on with hoes in the native manner, and considerable quantities of *Holcus sorghum*, maize, *Pennisetum typhoïdeum*, or lotsa of the Balonda, millet, rice, and wheat are raised, as also several kinds of beans,—one of which, called "litloo" by the Bechuanas, yields under ground, as well as the *Arachis hypogœa*, or groundnut; with cucumbers, pumpkins, and melons. The wheat is sown in low-lying places which are annually flooded by the Zambesi. When the waters retire, the women drop a few grains in a hole made with a hoe, then push back the soil with the foot. One weeding alone is required before the grain comes to maturity. This simple process represents all our sub-soil ploughing, liming, manuring, and harrowing, for in four months after planting a good crop is ready for the sickle, and has been known to yield a hundred-fold. It flourished still more at Zumbo. No irrigation is required, because here there are gentle rains, almost like mist, in winter, which go by the name of "wheat-showers," and are unknown in the interior, where no winter rain ever falls. The rains at Tete come from the east, though the prevailing winds come from the S.S.E. The finest portion of the flour does not make bread nearly so white as the seconds, and here the boyaloa, (pombe,) or native beer, is employed to mix with the flour instead of yeast. It makes excellent bread. At Kilimane, where the cocoanut-palm abounds, the toddy from it, called "sura," is used for the same purpose, and makes the bread still lighter.

As it was necessary to leave most of my men at this place, Major Sicard gave them a portion of land on which to cultivate their own food, generously supplying them with corn in the mean time. He also said 'that my young men might go and hunt elephants in company with his servants, and purchase goods with both the ivory and dried meat, in order that they might have something to take with them on their return to Sekeletu. The men were delighted with his liberality, and soon sixty or seventy of them set off to engage in this enterprise. There was no calico to be had at this time in Tete, but the commandant handsomely furnished my men with clothing. I was in a state of want myself; and, though I pressed him to take payment in ivory for both myself and men, he refused all recompense

I shall ever remember his kindness with deep gratitude. He has written me, since my arrival in England, that my men had killed four elephants in the course of two months after my departure.

On the day of my arrival I was visited by all the gentlemen of the village, both white and colored, including the padre. Not one of them had any idea as to where the source of the Zambesi lay. They sent for the best-travelled natives; but none of them knew the river even as far as Kansála. The father of one of the rebels who had been fighting against them had been a great traveller to the southwest, and had even heard of our visit to Lake Ngami; but he was equally ignorant with all the others that the Zambesi flowed in the centre of the country. They had, however, more knowledge of the country to the north of Tete than I had. One man, who had gone to Cazembe with Major Monteiro, stated that he had seen the Luapúra or Loapula flowing past the town of that chieftain into the Luaméji or Leeambye, but imagined that it found its way, somehow or other, into Angola. The fact that sometimes rivers were seen to flow like this toward the centre of the country led geographers to the supposition that Inner Africa was composed of elevated sandy plains, into which rivers ran and were lost. One of the gentlemen present, Senhor Candido, had visited a lake forty-five days to the N.N.W. of Tete, which is probably the Lake Maravi of geographers, as in going thither they pass through the people of that name. The inhabitants of its southern coast are named Shiva, those on the north, Mujao; and they call the lake Nyanja or Nyanje, which simply means a large water, or bed of a large river. A high mountain stands in the middle of it, called Murómbo or Murombola, which is inhabited by people who have much cattle. He stated that he crossed the Nyanja at a narrow part, and was thirty-six hours in the passage. The canoes were punted the whole way, and, if we take the rate about two miles per hour, it may be sixty or seventy miles in breadth. The country all round was composed of level plains covered with grass, and, indeed, in going thither they travelled seven or eight days without wood, and cooked their food with grass and stalks of native corn alone. The people sold their cattle at a very cheap rate. From the southern extremity of the lake two rivers issue forth: one, named after itself, the Nyanja, which passes into the sea on the east coast under another name; and the Shire, which flows into the Zambesi a little below Senna. The Shire is named Shirwa at its point of departure from the lake, and Senhor Candido was informed, when there, that the lake was simply an expansion of the river Nyanja, which comes from the north and encircles the mountain Murómbo, the meaning of which is junction or union, in reference to the water having parted at its northern extremity and united again at its southern. The Shire flows through a low, flat, marshy country, but abounding in population, and they are said to be brave. The Portuguese are unable to navigate the Shire up to the Lake Nyanja, because of the great abundance of a water-plant which requires no soil, and which they name "alfacinya" (*Pistia stratiotes*) from its resemblance to a lettuce. This completely obstructs the progress of canoes. In confirmation of this, I may state that, when I passed the mouth of the Shire, great quantities of this same plant were floating from it into the Zambesi, and many parts of the banks below were covered with the dead plants.

Senhor Candido stated that slight earthquakes have happened several times in the country of the Maravi, and at no great distance from Tete. The motion seems to come from the eastward and never to have lasted more than a few seconds. They are named in the Maravi tongue "shiwo," and in that of the people of Tete "shitakotéko," or "*shivering.*" This agrees exactly with what has taken place in the coast of Mozambique,—a few slight shocks of short duration, and all appearing to come from the east. At Senna, too, a single shock has been felt several times.

which shook the doors and windows and made the lasses
jingle. Both Tete and Senna have hot springs i. thei-
vicinity, but the shocks seemed to come, not from them,
but from the east, and proceed to the west. They **s e** probably connected with the active volcanoes in the isl and of
Bourbon.

Having waited a month for the commencement of the
healthy season at Kilimane, I would have started at the
beginning of April, but tarried a few days, in order that the
moon might make her appearance and enable me to take
lunar observations on my way down the river. A sudden
change of temperature happening on the 4th, simultaneously with the appearance of the new moon, the commandant and myself, with nearly every person in the house,
were laid up with a severe attack of fever. I soon recovered by the use of my wonted remedies; but Major
Sicard and his little boy were confined much longer.
There was a general fall of 4° of temperature from the
middle of March, 84° at 9 A.M., and 87° at 9 P.M.,—the
greatest heat being 90° at mid-day, and the lowest 81° at
sunrise. It afforded me pleasure to attend the invalids in
their sickness,—though I was unable to show a tithe of the
gratitude I felt for the commandant's increasing kindness.

The commandant provided for the journey most abundantly, and gave orders to Lieutenant Miranda that I
should not be allowed to pay for any thing all the way to
the coast, and sent messages to his friends Senhors Ferrão,
Isidore, Asevedo, and Nunes, to treat me as they would
himself. From every one of these gentlemen I am happy
to acknowledge that I received most disinterested kindness, and I ought to speak well forever of Portuguese hospitality. I have noted each little act of civility received,
because, somehow or other, we have come to hold the Portuguese character in rather a low estimation. This may
have arisen partly from the pertinacity with which some
of them have pursued the slave-trade, and partly from the
contrast which they now offer to their illustrious ancestors,

—the foremost navigators of the world. If my specification of their kindnesses will tend to engender a more respectful feeling to the nation, I shall consider myself well rewarded. We had three large canoes in the company which had lately come up with goods from Senna. They are made very large and strong, much larger than any we ever saw in the interior, and might strike with great force against a rock and not be broken. The men sit at the stern when paddling, and there is usually a little shed made over a part of the canoe to shade the passengers from the sun. The boat in which I went was furnished with such a covering; so I sat quite comfortably.

CHAPTER XXXII.

DR. LIVINGSTONE REACHES THE EAST COAST AND RETURNS TO ENGLAND.

We left Tete at noon on the 22d, and in the afternoon arrived at the garden of Senhor A. Manoel de Gomez, son-in-law and nephew of Bonga. The Commandant of Tete had sent a letter to the rebel Bonga, stating that he ought to treat me kindly, and he had deputed his son-in-law to be my host. Bonga is not at all equal to his father Nyaude, who was a man of great ability. He is also in bad odor with the Portuguese, because he receives all runaway slaves and criminals. He does not trust the Portuguese, and is reported to be excessively superstitious. I found his son-in-law, Manoel, extremely friendly, and able to converse in a very intelligent manner. He was in his garden when we arrived, but soon dressed himself respectably and gave us a good tea and dinner. After a breakfast of tea, roasted eggs, and biscuits next morning, he presented six fowls and three goats as provision for the journey.

When we parted from him, we passed the stockade of Bonga at the confluence of the Luenya, but did not go near it, as he is said to be very suspicious. The Portuguese advised me not to take any observation, as the instruments might awaken fears in Bonga's mind, but Manoel said I might do so if I wished: his garden, however, being above the confluence, could not avail as a geographical point There are some good houses in the stockade. The trees of which it is composed seemed to me to be living, and could not be burned. It was strange to see a stockade menacing the whole commerce of the river in a situation where the guns of a vessel would have full play on it; but it is a formidable affair for those who have only muskets. On one occasion, when Nyaude was attacked by Kisaka, they fought for weeks; and, though Nyaude was reduced to cutting up his copper anklets for balls, his enemies were not able to enter the stockade.

We sailed on quickly with the current of the river, and found that it spread out to more than two miles in breadth: it is, however, full of islands, which are generally covered with reeds, and which previous to the war were inhabited and yielded vast quantities of grain. We usually landed to cook breakfast, and then went on quickly.

Next day we landed at Shiramba for breakfast, having sailed eight and a half hours from Lupata. This was once the residence of a Portuguese brigadier, who spent large sums of money in embellishing his house and gardens: these we found in entire ruin, as his half-caste son had destroyed all, and then rebelled against the Portuguese, but with less success than either Nyaude or Kisaka, for he had been seized and sent a prisoner to Mozambique a short time before our visit. All the southern shore has been ravaged by the Caffres, who are here named Landeens; and most of the inhabitants who remain acknowledge the authority of Bonga and not of the Portuguese. When at breakfast, the people of Shiramba commenced beating the drum of war Lieutenant Miranda, who was well acquainted with the customs of the country, immediately started to his feet and got all the soldiers of our party under arms: he then demanded of the natives why the drum was beaten while we were there. They gave an evasive reply; and, as they employ this means of collecting their neighbors when they intend to rob canoes, our watchfulness may have prevented their proceeding further.

We spent the night of the 26th on the island called Nkuesi, opposite a remarkable saddle-shaped mountain, and found that we were just on the seventeenth parallel of latitude. The sail down the river was very fine; the temperature becoming low, it was pleasant to the feelings; but, the shores being flat and far from us, the scenery was uninteresting. We breakfasted on the 27th at Pita, and found some half-caste Portuguese had established themselves there, after fleeing from the opposite bank to escape Kisaka's people, who were now ravaging all the Maganja country. On the afternoon of the 27th we arrived at Senna. (Commandant Isidore's house, three hundred yards S.W. of the mud-fort on the banks of the river: lat. 17° 27′ 1″ S., long. 35° 10′ E.) We found Senna to be twenty-three and a half hours' sail from Tete.

I thought the state of Tete quite lamentable; but that of Senna was ten times worse. At Tete there is some life: here every thing is in a state of stagnation and ruin. The fort, built of sun-dried bricks, has the grass growing over the walls, which have been patched in some places by paling. The Landeens visit the village periodically and levy fines upon the inhabitants, as they consider the Portuguese a conquered tribe, and very rarely does a native come to trade. Senhor Isidore, the commandant, a man of considerable energy, had proposed to surround the whole village with palisades as a protection against the Landeens, and the villagers were to begin this work the day after I left. It was sad to look at the ruin manifest in every building; but the half-castes appear to be in league with the rebels and Landeens; for when any attempt is made by the Portuguese to coerce the enemy or defend themselves, information is conveyed at once to the Landeen camp, and, though the commandant prohibits the payment of tribute to the Landeens, on their approach the half-castes eagerly ransom themselves.

The village of Senna stands on the right bank of the Zambesi. There are many reedy islands in front of it, and there is much bush in the country adjacent. The soil is fertile; but the village, being in a state of ruin, and having several pools of stagnant water, is very unhealthy.

The most pleasant sight I witnessed at Senna was the negroes of Senhór Isidoro building boats after the European model, without any one to superintend their operations. They had been instructed by a European master, but now go into the forest and cut down the motondo-trees, lay down the keel, fit in the ribs, and make very neat boats and launches, valued at from £20 to £100. Senhor Isidoro had some of them instructed also in carpentry at Rio Janeiro, and they constructed for him the handsomest house in Kilimane, the woodwork being all of country trees, some of which are capable of a fine polish, and very durable.

On the 9th of May sixteen of my men were employed to carry Government goods in canoes up to Tete. They were much pleased at getting this work. On the 11th the whole of the inhabitants of Senna, with the commandant, accompanied us to the boats. A venerable old man, son of a judge, said they were in much sorrow on account of the miserable state of decay into which they had sunk, and of the insolent conduct of the people of Kisaka now in the village. We were abundantly supplied with provisions by the commandant and Senhor Ferrão, and sailed pleasantly down the broad river. About thirty miles below Senna we passed the mouth of the river Zangwe on our right, which farther up goes by the name of Pungwe; and about five miles farther on our left, close to the end of a low range into which Morumbala merges, we crossed the mouth of the Shire, which seemed to be about two hundred yards broad.

A few miles beyond the Shire we left the hills entirely and sailed between extensive flats. The banks soon in the distance are covered with trees. We slept on a large inhabited island, and then came to the entrance of the river Mutu, (latitude 18° 3′ 37″ S., longitude 35° 46′ E. :) the point of departure is called Mazáro, or "mouth of the Mutu."

I was seized by a severe tertian fever at Mazaro, but went along the right bank of the Mutu to the N.N.E. and E. for about fifteen miles. We then found that it was made navigable by a river called the Pangázi, which comes into it from the north.

My fever became excessively severe in consequence of travelling in the hot sun, and the long grass blocking up the narrow path so as to exclude the air. The pulse beat with amazing force, and felt as if thumping against the crown of the head. The stomach and spleen swelled enormously,—giving me, for the first time, an appearance which I had been disposed to laugh at among the Portuguese. At Interra we met Senhor Asevedo, a man who is well known by all who ever visited Kilimane, and who was presented with a gold chronometer watch by the Admiralty for his attentions to English officers. He immediately tendered his large sailing-launch, which had a house in the stern. This was greatly in my favor, for it anchored in the middle of the stream, and gave me some rest from the mosquitos, which in the whole of the delta are something frightful. Sailing comfortably in this commodious launch along the river of Kilimane, we reached that village (latitude 17° 53′ 8″ S., longitude 36° 40′ E.) on the 20th of May, 1856, which wanted only a few days of being four years since I started from Cape Town. Here I was received into the house of Colonel Galdina José Nunes, one of the best men in the country. I had been three years without hearing from my family,—letters having been frequently sent, but somehow or other, with but a single exception, they never reached me. I received, however, a letter from Admiral Trotter, conveying information of their welfare, and some newspapers, which were a treat indeed. Her majesty's brig the "Frolic" had called to inquire for me in the November previous, and Captain Nolluth, of that ship, had most considerately left a case of wine; and his surgeon, Dr. James Walsh, divining what I should need most, left an ounce of quinine. These gifts made my heart overflow. I had not tasted any liquor whatever during the time I had been in Africa; but, when reduced in Angola to extreme weakness, I found much benefit from a little wine, and took from Loanda one bottle of brandy in my medicine-chest, intending to use it if it were again required; but the boy who carried it whirled the box upside-down and smashed the bottle, so that I cannot give my testimony either in favor of or against the brandy.

But my joy on reaching the east coast was sadly embittered by the news that Commander MacLune, of H.M. brigantine "Dart," on coming in to Kilimane to pick me up, had, with Lieutenant Woodruffe and five men, been lost on the bar. I never felt more poignant sorrow. It seemed as if it would have been easier for me to have died for them than that they should all be cut off from the joys of life in generously attempting to render me a service. I would here acknowledge my deep obligations to the Earl of Clarendon, to the admiral at the Cape, and others, for the kind interest they manifested in my safety: even the inquiries made were very much to my advantage. I also refer with feelings of gratitude to the Governor of Mozambique for offering me a passage in the schooner "Zambesi," belonging to that province; and I shall never forget the generous hospitality of Colonel Nunes and his nephew, with whom I remained. One of the discoveries I have made is that there are vast numbers of good people in the world; and I do most devoutly tender my unfeigned thanks to that Gracious One who mercifully watched over me in every position and influenced the hearts of both black and white to regard me with favor.

If the reader has accompanied me thus far, he may perhaps be disposed to take an interest in the objects I propose to myself should God mercifully grant me the honor of doing something more for Africa. As the highlands on the borders of the central basin are comparatively healthy, the first object seems to be to secure a permanent path thither, in order that Europeans may pass as quickly as possible through the unhealthy region near the coast. The river has not been surveyed, but at the time I came down there was abundance of water for a large vessel; and this continues to be the case during four or five months of each year. The months of low water still admit of navigation by launches, and would permit small vessels equal to the Thames steamers to ply with ease in the deep channel. If a steamer were sent to examine the Zambesi, I would recommend one of the lightest draught, and the months of May, June, and July for passing through the delta; and this not so much for fear of want of water as the danger of being grounded on a sand or mud bank and the health of the crew being endangered by the delay.

In the months referred to, no obstruction would be incurred in the channel below Tete. Twenty or thirty miles above that point we have a small rapid, of which I regret my inability to speak, as (mentioned already) I did not visit it. But, taking the distance below this point, we have, in round numbers, three hundred miles of navigable river. Above this rapid we have another reach of three hundred miles, with sand, but no mud-banks in it, which brings us to the foot of the eastern ridge. Let it not, however, be thought that a vessel by going thither would return laden with ivory and gold-dust. The Portuguese of Tete pick up all the merchandise of the tribes in their vicinity; and, though I came out by traversing the people with whom the Portuguese had been at war, it does not follow that it will be perfectly safe for others to go in whose goods may be a stronger temptation to cupidity than any thing I possessed. When we get beyond the hostile population mentioned, we reach a very different race. On the latter my chief hopes at present rest. All of them, however, are willing and anxious to engage in trade, and, while eager for this, none have ever been encouraged to cultivate the raw materials of commerce. Their country is well adapted for cotton; and I venture to entertain the hope that by distributing seeds of better kinds than that which is found indigenous, and stimulating the natives to cultivate it by affording them the certainty of a market for all they may produce, we may engender a feeling of mutual dependence between them and ourselves. I have a twofold object in view, and believe that, by guiding our missionary labors so as to benefit our own country, we shall thereby more effectually and permanently benefit the heathen. Seven years were spent at Kolobeng in instructing my friends there; but, the country being incapable of raising materials for exportation, when the Boers made their murderous attack and scattered the tribe for a season, none sympathized except a few Christian friends. Had the people of Kolobeng been in the habit of raising the raw materials of English commerce, the outrage would have been felt in England; or, what is more likely to have been the case, the people would have raised themselves in the scale by barter, and have become, like the Basutos of Moshesh and people of Kuruman, possessed of fire-arms, and the Boers would never have made the attack at all. We ought to encourage the Africans to cultivate for our markets, as the most effectual means, next to the gospel, of their elevation.

It is in the hope of working out this idea that I propose the formation of stations on the Zambesi beyond the Portuguese territory but having communication through them with the coast. A chain of stations admitting of easy and speedy intercourse, such as might be formed along the flank of the eastern ridge, would be in a favorable position for carrying out the objects in view. The London Missionary

Society has resolved to have a station among the Makololo on the north bank, and another on the south among the Matebele. The Church—Wesleyan, Baptist, and that most energetic body, the Free Church—could each find desirable locations among the Batoka and adjacent tribes. The country is so extensive there is no fear of clashing. All classes of Christians find that sectarian rancor soon dies out when they are working together among and for the real heathen. Only let the healthy locality be searched for and fixed upon, and then there will be free scope to work in the same cause in various directions, without that loss of men which the system of missions on the unhealthy coast entails. While respectfully submitting the plan to these influential societies, I can positively state that, when fairly in the interior, there is perfect security for life and property among a people who will at least listen and reason.

Eight of my men begged to be allowed to come as far as Kilimane, and, thinking that they would there see the ocean, I consented to their coming, though the food was so scarce in consequence of a dearth that they were compelled to suffer some hunger. They would fain have come farther; for when Sekeletu parted with them his orders were that none of them should turn until they had reached Ma Robert and brought her back with them. On my explaining the difficulty of crossing the sea, he said, "Wherever you lead, they must follow." As I did not know well how I should get home myself, I advised them to go back to Tete, where food was abundant, and there await my return. I bought a quantity of calico and brass wire with ten of the smaller tusks which we had in our charge, and sent the former back as clothing to those who remained at Tete. As there were still twenty tusks left, I deposited them with Colonel Nunes, that, in the event of any thing happening to prevent my return, the impression might not be produced in the country that I had made away with Sekeletu's ivory. I instructed Colonel Nunes, in case of my death, to sell the tusks and deliver the proceeds to my men; but I intended, if my life should be prolonged, to purchase the goods ordered by Sekeletu in England with my own money, and pay myself on my return out of the price of the ivory. This I explained to the men fully, and they, understanding the matter, replied, "Nay, father, you will not die; you will return to take us back to Sekeletu." They promised to wait till I came back; and, on my part, I assured them that nothing but death would prevent my return. This I said, though while waiting at Kilimane a letter came from the Directors of the London Missionary Society stating that "they were restricted in their power of aiding plans connected only remotely with the spread of the gospel, and that the financial circumstances of the society were not such as to afford any ground of hope that it would be in a position, within any definite period, to enter upon untried, remote, and difficult fields of labor." This has been explained since as an effusion caused by temporary financial depression; but, feeling perfect confidence in my Makololo friends, I was determined to return and trust to their generosity. The old love of independence, which I had so strongly before joining the society, again returned. It was roused by a mistaken view of what this letter meant; for the directors, immediately on my reaching home, saw the great importance of the opening, and entered with enlightened zeal on the work of sending the gospel into the new field. It is to be hoped that their constituents will not only enable them to begin, but to carry out their plans, and that no material depression will ever again be permitted, nor appearances of spasmodic benevolence recur. While I hope to continue the same cordial co-operation and friendship which have always characterized our intercourse, various reasons induce me to withdraw from pecuniary dependence on any society. I have done something for the heathen; but for an aged mother, who has still more sacred claims than they, I have been able to do nothing, and a continuance of the connection would be a perpetuation of my inability to make any provision for her declining years. In addition to "clergyman's sore throat," which partially disabled me from the work, my father's death imposed new obligations; and, a fresh source of income having been opened to me without my asking, I had no hesitation in accepting what would enable me to fulfil my duty to my aged parent as well as to the heathen.

The village of Kilimane stands on a great mud-bank, and is surrounded by extensive swamps and rice-grounds. The banks of the river are lined with mangrove-bushes, the roots of which, and the slimy banks on which they grow, are alternately exposed to the tide and sun. The houses are well built of brick and lime, the latter from Mozambique. If one digs down two or three feet in any part of the site of the village, he comes to water: hence the walls built on this mud-bank gradually subside; pieces are sometimes sawn off the doors below, because the walls in which they are fixed have descended into the ground, so as to leave the floors higher than the bottom of the doors. It is almost needless to say that Kilimane is very unhealthy. A man of plethoric temperament is sure to get fever, and concerning a stout person one may hear the remark, "Ah, he will not live long; he is sure to die."

After waiting about six weeks at this unhealthy spot, in which, however, by the kind attentions of Colonel Nunes and his nephew, I partially recovered from my tertian, H.M. brig "Frolic" arrived off Kilimane. As the village is twelve miles from the bar, and the weather was rough, she was at anchor ten days before we knew of her presence about seven miles from the entrance to the port. She brought abundant supplies for all my need, and £150 to pay my passage home, from my kind friend Mr. Thompson, the Society's agent at the Cape. The admiral at the Cape kindly sent an offer of a passage to the Mauritius, which I thankfully accepted. Sekwebu and one attendant alone remained with me now. He was very intelligent, and had been of the greatest service to me: indeed, but for his

good sense, tact, and command of the language of the
tribes through which we passed, I believe we should
scarcely have succeeded in reaching the coast. I naturally
felt grateful to him; and as his chief wished *all* my companions to go to England with me, and would probably be
disappointed if none went, I thought it would be beneficial
for him to see the effects of civilization and report them to
his countrymen. I wished also to make some return for his
very important services. Others had petitioned to come,
but I explained the danger of a change of climate and food,
and with difficulty restrained them. The only one who
now remained begged so hard to come on board ship that I
greatly regretted that the expense prevented my acceding
to his wish to visit England. I said to him, "You will die
if you go to such a cold country as mine." "That is
nothing," he reiterated; "let me die at your feet."

When we parted from our friends at Kilimane, the sea
on the bar was frightful even to the seamen. This was the
first time Sekwebu had seen the sea. Captain Peyton had
sent two boats in case of accident. The waves were so high
that, when the cutter was in one trough and we in the
pinnace in another, her mast was hid. We then mounted
to the crest of the wave, rushed down the slope, and
struck the water again with a blow which felt as if she
had struck the bottom. Boats must be singularly well constructed to be able to stand these shocks. Three breakers
swept over us. The men lift up their oars, and a wave
comes sweeping over all, giving the impression that the
boat is going down; but she only goes beneath the top of
the wave, comes out on the other side, and swings down
the slope and a man bales out the water with a bucket.
Poor Sekwebu looked at me when these terrible seas broke
over, and said, "Is this the way you go? Is this the way
you go?" I smiled and said, "Yes; don't you see it is?"
and tried to encourage him. He was well acquainted with
canoes, but never had seen aught like this. When we
reached the ship,—a fine, large brig of sixteen guns and a

crew of one hundred and thirty,—she was rolling so that we could see a part of her bottom. It was quite impossible for landsmen to catch the ropes and climb up; so a chair was sent down, and we were hoisted in as ladies usually are, and received so hearty an English welcome from Captain Peyton and all on board that I felt myself at once at home in every thing except my own mother-tongue. I seemed to know the language perfectly, but the words I wanted would not come at my call. When I left England I had no intention of returning, and directed my attention earnestly to the languages of Africa, paying none to English composition. With the exception of a short interval in Angola, I had been three and a half years without speaking English, and this, with thirteen years of previous partial disuse of my native tongue, made me feel sadly at a loss on board the "Frolic."

We left Kilimane on the 12th of July, and reached the Mauritius on the 12th of August, 1856. Sekwebu was picking up English, and becoming a favorite with both men and officers. He seemed a little bewildered, every thing on board a man-of-war being so new and strange; but he remarked to me several times, "Your countrymen are very agreeable," and, "What a strange country this is!—all water together!" He also said that he now understood why I used the sextant. When we reached the Mauritius a steamer came out to tow us into the harbor. The constant strain on his untutored mind seemed now to reach a climax, for during the night he became insane. I thought at first that he was intoxicated. He had descended into a boat, and, when I attempted to go down and bring him into the ship, he ran to the stern and said, "No! no! it is enough that I die alone. You must not perish; if you come, I shall throw myself into the water." Perceiving that his mind was affected, I said, "Now, Sekwebu, we are going to Ma Robert." This struck a chord in his bosom, and he said, "Oh, yes! where is she, and where is Robert?" and he seemed to recover The officers proposed to secure him by putting him in irons; but, being a gentleman in his own country, I objected, knowing that the insane often retain an impression of ill-treatment, and I could not bear to have it said in Sekeletu's country that I had chained one of his principal men as they had seen slaves treated. I tried to get him on shore by day, but he refused. In the evening a fresh accession of insanity occurred: he tried to spear one of the crew, then leaped overboard, and, though he could swim well, pulled himself down hand under hand by the chain-cable. We never found the body of poor Sekwebu.

At the Mauritius I was most hospitably received by Major-General C. M. Hay, and he generously constrained me to remain with him till, by the influence of the good climate and quiet English comfort, I got rid of an enlarged spleen from African fever. In November I came up the Red Sea, escaped the danger of shipwreck through the admirable management of Captain Powell, of the Peninsular and Oriental Steam-Company's ship "Candia," and on the 12th of December was once more in dear old England. The Company most liberally refunded my passage-money. I have not mentioned half the favors bestowed; but I may just add that no one has cause for more abundant gratitude to his fellow-men and to his Maker than I have; and may God grant that the effect on my mind be such that I may be more humbly devoted to the service of the Author of all our mercies!

HISTORICAL NOTICES OF DISCOVERIES IN AFRICA

In the time of Herodctus, and long afterward, the general opinion was that Africa did not extend so far south as the equatorial line. There existed, however, a tradition that Africa had been circumnavigated by the Phœnicians about six centuries before the Christian era; but, if the southern promontory of Africa had really been reached, it is difficult to conceive how so erroneous an impression could have prevailed as to the extent of the continent. It is, therefore, most probable that such a voyage had never succeeded; and, indeed, the circumstances under which it was prosecuted, according to the accounts which have come down to us, only add an additional feature of improbability to the story. Turning to modern times, we find, at the commencement of the fifteenth century, that Europeans were only acquainted with that portion of the western coast of Africa which extends from the Straits of Gibraltar to Cape Nun,—a line of coast not exceeding six hundred miles in length. The Portuguese had the honor of extending this limited acquaintance with the outline of the African continent. Their zeal for discovery in this direction became truly a national passion, and the sovereigns and princes of Portugal prosecuted this object with singular enthusiasm. By the year 1471 the Portuguese navigators had advanced $2\frac{1}{2}°$ south of the Line. In 1484, Diego Cam reached 22° south latitude. The next navigator, Bartholomew Diaz, was commanded to pursue his course southward until he should reach the extremity of Africa; and to him belongs the honor of discovering the Cape of Good Hope, the name given to it at the time by the King of Portugal, though Diaz had named it Cabo Tormentoso, (the Cape of Tempests.) The Cape of Good Hope was at first frequently called the Lion of the Sea, and also the Head of Africa In 1497, Vasco de Gama set forth with the intention of reaching India by sailing round the Cape of Good Hope

After doubling the Cape, he pursued his course along the eastern coast of Africa, and then stretched across the ocean to India. The Portuguese had now ascertained the general outline of Africa and the position of many of the principal rivers and headlands. With the exception of a portion of the coast from the Straits of Bab el Mandeb to Mukdeesha, situated in 3° north latitude, the whole of the coast had been traced by the Portuguese, and their zeal and enthusiasm, which had at one period been treated with ridicule, were at length triumphantly rewarded, about four years before Columbus had achieved his great discovery, which, with that of Vasco de Gama, amply repaid a century of speculative enterprise. This interesting combination of events had a sensible effect upon the general mind of Europe. The Portuguese soon formed settlements in Africa, and began to acquire a knowledge of the interior of the country. They were followed by the French, and afterward by the English and the Dutch.

It is chiefly within the last fifty years that discoveries in the interior of Africa have been perseveringly and systematically prosecuted. In 1788, a society was established in London with the design of encouraging men of enterprise to explore the African continent. John Ledyard, an American, was the first person selected by the African Association for this task; and he set out in 1788 with the intention of traversing the widest part of the continent from east to west, in the supposed latitude of the river Niger. Unfortunately, he was seized at Cairo with a fever, of which he died. He possessed few scientific acquirements; but his vigor and powers of endurance, mental and bodily, his indifference to pain, hardship, and fatigue, would have rendered him an admirable geographical pioneer. "I have known," he said, shortly before leaving England for the last time, "hunger and nakedness to the utmost extremity of human suffering: I have known what it is to have food given as charity to a madman, and have at times been obliged to shelter myself under the miseries of that character to avoid a heavier calamity My distresses have been greater than I have ever owned, or ever will own, to any man. Such evils are terrible to bear; but they never yet had the power to turn me from my purpose.' Such was the indomitable energy of this man, the first of a long list of victims in the cause of African discovery Mr. Lucas, who was despatched by the Association to supply the place of Ledyard, was compelled to return home in consequence of several of the countries through which he would have to pass being engaged in hostilities. In 1790, Major Houghton, an officer who was acquainted with the customs of the Moors and Negroes, proceeded to Africa under the auspices of the Association, and had made considerable progress in the interior, when, after having been treacherously plundered and left in the Desert, where he endured severe privations, he reached Jarra, and died there in September, 1791, it being strongly suspected that he was murdered. The next individual on whom the Association fixed was Mungo Park, who proceeded to the river Gambia in 1795 and thence set out into the interior. The great object accomplished during his journey was that of successfully exploring the banks of the Niger, which had previously been considered identical with the river Senegal In 1804, Park set out upon his second journey, which was undertaken at the expense of the Government. The plan of former travellers had been to accompany the caravans from one part of the country to another; but in this expedition Park required a party of thirty-six Europeans, six of whom were to be seamen and the remainder soldiers it being his intention, on reaching the Niger, to build two vessels, and to follow with his party the course of the river If the Congo and the Niger were the same stream, as was then supposed, he anticipated little difficulty in his enterprise; but if, as was also maintained, the Niger terminated in swamps and morasses, many hardships and dangers were expected in their subsequent progress. Park at length reached the Niger, accompanied only by seven of his party all of whom were in a state of great weakness from the effects of the climate. They built one vessel, and, on the 17th of November, 1805, were ready to embark on the river, previous to which Park sent despatches to England His party was now reduced to five, his brother-in-law having died a few days before. Park's spirit, however, remained undaunted. "Though all the Europeans who are with me should die," said he, in his last letters to England, "and though I myself were half dead, I would still persevere; and, if I could not succeed in the object of my journey, I would at least die in the Niger." He embarked, therefore, with the intention of sailing down the river to its mouth, wherever that might be; but, after passing Timbuctoo and several other cities, he was killed in the Niger, at a place called Boussa, a short distance below Yaouri. No part of his journal after he left Sansanding has ever been recovered.

In 1797, the African Association had engaged Mr. Hornemann, a German, who left Cairo in September, 1798, with the intention of carrying into effect the objects of the Association by proceeding as far southward and westward as he could get. In his last despatches he expressed himself confident in being able to succeed in reaching a greater distance into the interior than any other European traveller; but, after reaching Bornou, no certain intelligence was ever afterward heard concerning him. Mr. Hornemann learned many particulars which had not before been known in Europe respecting the countries to the east of Timbuctoo. Mr. Nicholls, who was next engaged, arrived in the Gulf of Benin in November, 1804, and died soon afterward of the fever of the country. Another German, Bœntzen, was next sent to Africa. He had bestowed extraordinary pains in making himself acquainted with the prevailing language, and, throwing off his costume, proceeded in the character of a Mussulman, but unhappily was murdered by his guides on his way to Soudan. The next traveller sent out by the Association was Burckhardt, a Swiss. He spent several years in acquiring a knowledge of the language and customs of the people he intended to visit, and, like Mr Bœntzen, assumed the characteristics of a Mussulman. He died at Cairo in 1817, his travels having been chiefly confined to the Abyssinian countries.

In 1816, an expedition was sent out by the Government, under the command of Captain Tuckey, to the river Congo, under the idea, in which Park coincided, that it and the Niger were the same river. Captain Tuckey ascended the Congo for about two hundred and eighty miles. At the same time, Major Peddie, and, after his death, Captain Campbell, proceeded from the mouth of the river Senegal as far as Kakundy. In 1817, Mr. Bowdich explored the countries adjoining Cape Coast Castle. In 1820, Mr. Jackson communicated an interesting account of the territories of Timbuctoo and Houssa, from details which he had collected from a Mussulman merchant. In 1819 and in 1821, the expeditions of Messrs. Ritchie and Lyon, and of Major Laing, showed the strong and general interest on the subject of African geography. In 1822, the important expedition under Major Denham and Lieut. Clapperton set forth. After crossing the Desert, the travellers reached the great inland sea or lake called the Tchad, the coasts of which to the west and south were examined by Major Denham. This lake, from four hundred to six hundred feet above the level of the sea, is one of the most remarkable features in the physical geography of Africa. Lieut. Clapperton, in the mean time, proceeded through the kingdom of Bornou and the country of the Fellatahs to Sockatoo, situated on a stream supposed to run into the Niger. A great mass of information respecting the countries eastward of Timbuctoo was the result of his expedition. As to the course of the Niger, very little intelligence was obtained which could be depended upon : the natives stated that it flowed into the sea at Funda, though what place on the coast was meant still remained a conjecture. Soon after his return to England, Clapperton was sent out by the Government to conduct a new expedition, and was directed to proceed to the scene of his former adventures. Having reached the Niger at Boussa, where Park was killed, he passed through various countries, and reached Sockatoo, where he died; and Lander, his friend and servant, commenced his return to England with Clapperton's journals and papers. Major Laing, meanwhile, had visited Timbuctoo, and transmitted home accounts of this famous city, where he spent some weeks; but on his return he was murdered, and his papers have never been recovered. We have not space to allude to the many well-executed expeditions which have proceeded from Cape Town for the purpose of exploring South Africa, but have confined ourselves to those exertions which had for their object the elucidation of the question concerning the course and termination of the Niger, and were consequently directed to Central Africa.

The termination of the Niger had long been one of the most interesting problems in African geography, and we have now reached the period when, on this point, facts were substituted for conjecture and hypothesis. The river had first been seen by Park, near Sego, the capital of Bambarra. It was called by the natives the Joliba, or "Great Water;" and Park described it as "flowing slowly to the eastward." He followed the course of the river for about three hundred miles, and was told that a journey of ten days would bring him to its source. At Sockatoo, Lieut. Clapperton found that it was called the Quorra, by which name it is known in the most recent maps, it having received the name of the Niger, in the first instance, from its supposed identity with the Nigir of the ancients. The want of information concerning the course and termination of this mysterious river, until determined by actually proceeding down its channel to the sea, was, as may be supposed, a fruitful source of speculation among geographers. By some it was supposed to flow into the Nile; others imagined that a great central lake received its waters. Major Rennel, an authority of great weight, came to the conclusion that, after passing Timbuctoo, the Niger flowed a thousand miles in an easterly direction, and terminated in a lake or swamp; others supported the opinion that its waters were lost in the arid sands of the Desert; while the Congo was said by many to be its outlet. Major Laing, by ascertaining the source of the Niger to be not more than sixteen hundred feet above the level of the sea, proved that it could not flow into the Nile; and Denham and Clapperton demonstrated that it did not, as had been supposed, discharge itself into the Lake of Bornou.

Richard and John Lander, in 1830, under the auspices of the British Government, solved the long-disputed problem of the course of the Niger by sailing down on its waters from Boussa to the ocean, where it was found to terminate in what was called the Nun, or First Brass River, from the negro town of Brass situated on its banks.

An expedition under the auspices of the British Government, and headed by Dr. Henry Barth, attended by Dr. Overberg and Mr. James Richardson, was sent out in 1849 to prosecute discoveries in Northern Central Africa. Their travels and researches into the history and present state of the interior tribes were continued till 1855, and their results have recently been published by Dr. Barth. Dr. Overberg died in 1854, and was buried on the shores of Lake Tchad or Tsad. Mr. Richardson also fell a victim to the climate before the close of the expedition.

Dr. Barth visited the countries of Bornou, Kanem, Mandara, Bagirmi, and others previously explored by Denham and Clapperton, and carried his researches much farther, reaching the eighth degree of north latitude. His volumes contain much curious and minute information.

As Dr. Livingstone's researches reach only the eighth degree of north latitude, there still remains an immense region of Interior Africa, sixteen degrees broad, open to future explorers.

Since the preceding pages were written, the last two of the five octavo volumes of Dr. Barth's Journal have been published in London, and received in this country, and we have condensed it into one large 12mo., uniform with our edition of Livingstone, and illustrated, &c., with a map giving the routes of Livingstone and Barth; they should be read together. We are thus placed in possession of the whole result of Dr. Barth's explorations, and truly they are of unparalleled extent and importance. The following extract from the preface gives a summary of his travels:

"Extending over a tract of country of twenty-four degrees from north to south, and twenty degrees from east to west, in the broadest part of the continent of Africa, my travels necessarily comprise subjects of great interest and diversity.

"After having traversed vast deserts of the most barren soil, and scenes of the most frightful desolation, I met with fertile lands irrigated by large navigable rivers and extensive central lakes, ornamented with the finest timber, and producing various species of grain, rice, sesamum, ground-nuts, in unlimited abundance, the sugar-cane, &c., together with cotton and indigo, the most valuable commodities of trade. The whole of Central Africa, from Bagirmi to the east as far as Timbuctu to the west (as will be seen in my narrative), abounds in these products. The natives of these regions not only weave their own cotton, but dye their home-made shirts with their own indigo. The river, the far-famed Niger, which gives access to these regions by means of its eastern branch, the Benuwe, which I discovered, affords an uninterrupted navigable sheet of water for more than six hundred miles into the very heart of the country. Its western branch is obstructed by rapids at the distance of about three hundred and fifty miles from the coast; but even at that point it is probably not impassable in the present state of navigation, while, higher up, the river opens an immense high-road for nearly one thousand miles into the very heart of Western Africa, so rich in every kind of produce.

"The same diversity of soil and produce which the regions

traversed by me exhibit, is also observed with respect to man. Starting from Tripoli in the north, we proceed from the settlements of the Arab and the Berber, the poor remnants of the vast empires of the middle ages, into a country dotted with splendid ruins from the period of the Roman dominion, through the wild roving hordes of the Tawarek, to the Negro and half-Negro tribes, and to the very border of the South African nations. In the regions of Central Africa there exists not one and the same stock, as in South Africa, but the greatest diversity of tribes, or rather nations, prevails, with idioms entirely distinct.

"The great and momentous struggle between Islamism and Paganism is here continually going on, causing every day the most painful and affecting results, while the miseries arising from slavery and the slave trade are here revealed in their most repulsive features. We find Mohammedan learning ingrafted on the ignorance and simplicity of the black races, and the gaudy magnificence and strict ceremonial of large empires side by side with the barbarous simplicity of naked and half-naked tribes. We here trace a historical thread which guides us through this labyrinth of tribes and overthrown kingdoms; and a lively interest is awakened by reflecting on their possible progress and restoration, through the intercourse with more civilized parts of the world. Finally, we find here commerce in every direction radiating from Kano, the great emporium of Central Africa, and spreading the manufactures of that industrious region over the whole of Western Africa."

NOTICES OF THE PRESS.

From among the hundreds of favorable notices, from the most respectable journals, of our cheap edition of "Livingstone's Travels and Explorations in Africa, we take the following:

It abounds in descriptions of strange and wonderful scenes, among a people and in a country entirely new to the civilized world; and altogether we regard it as one of the most interesting books issued within the past year. The work is well printed and handsomely illustrated; and one thing which we think considerably enhances the value of this edition above all others, is the fact that the price at which it is published is sufficiently low to bring it within the reach of all classes of readers. This is done by leaving out a mass of dry scientific details, which are of use only to a very small class of the community, and which would actually only make the narrative department, now so extremely charming, tiresome and uninteresting.—*Daily Democrat, Paterson, N. J.*

The present volume is a beautiful 12mo, of 446 pages, numerously illustrated, and contains all of the original, except some of the more dry scientific details. It is emphatically an edition for the people; and, judging from the rapid sale with which it is meeting, it is fully appreciated by them.—*Christian Freeman, Boston.*

Great care has been taken to preserve all the incidents and descriptions which are essential to the interest of the work. In this way a very excellent volume has been made, which deserves a large circulation.—*New York Chronicle.*

The subjects treated of are new and strange, and take a deep hold upon popular feeling. The book is having a great run, and will be read by every reading man, woman, and child, in this, as well as other lands.—*Ashtabula (Ohio) Telegraph.*

The work is finely illustrated, well printed, and firmly bound, thus answering, in every respect, the demand for a *popular* and cheap edition of the "Journeys and Researches in South Africa." Those of our readers who would have a delightful book for reading at any hour, will not be disappointed in this work.—*United States Journal.*

The price and size of the original volume have led the publisher of this, in view of the popular interest in the travels of this great explorer, to present the main portions of Dr. Livingstone's narrative in a condensed form and at a lower price. So far as we have compared the two, not a single word of Dr. Livingstone's has been changed, and the only liberty taken with the text has been simply that of omission. The chapters of the abridgment answer to those of the original work, so that a reference to them can easily be verified. The entire course of Dr. Livingstone's journey is thus traced, and the result given in his own words.—*N. Y. Evangelist*

We commend his book to the perusal of all our friends.—*Philadelphia City Item.*

That this work *is* a work of merit, is proved by the war waged on it by the various publishers who have raised the cry of "*spurious edition*," hoping this false alarm would draw off the public attention from the cheap edition of J. W. Bradley, of Philadelphia; but we rather guess that those who want to obtain this excellent work know their own interests well enough to get not only the *cheapest* edition yet published, but at the same time get all the important facts of the narrative which, in the English edition, is sold for six dollars.—*Temperance Monitor, Aurora, Ill.*

This is an admirable abridgment of the huge volume published by Dr. Livingstone some months ago, affording to general readers all that they can possibly care for in its contents, unless they have become as Africanized as Mrs. Jellaby herself.—*Boston Daily Evening Traveler.*

This is a valuable work for the general reader, gotten up in beautiful style. A special interest is given to this volume by the addition of valuable "Historical Notices of Discoveries

(1)

NOTICES OF THE PRESS CONTINUED.

in Arms." Altogether, it would be difficult to name any work which would more completely meet the popular taste of our day. Those of our friends who have perused "our" copy, speak very highly of it —*Fort Edward Institute Monthly.*

No book of travels and personal experiences has ever appeared which has excited more interest among all classes than "Dr. Livingstone's Researches and Narrative." But the great cost of the large work placed it beyond the reach of thousands who desired it. To obviate this objection of price, the publishers have issued this volume, which contains the gist of the original work. It forms a solid 12mo of 440 pages, is given in Dr. Livingstone's own words thus sustaining all the interest which attaches to his wonderful story. The work is finely illustrated, well printed, and firmly bound, and will answer the demand for a popular and cheap edition of the "Journeys and Researches in South Africa."—*The Constitution, Erie, Pa.*

With truth we can say, that seldom is presented to the reading public a work containing such a vast amount of solid instruction as the one in question. The volume is handsomely illustrated, and presents that unique appearance of exterior for which Mr. Bradley's publications are noted —*Family Magazine.*

In this volume we have presented to us the whole of Dr. Livingstone's Travels, omitting only scientific details.—*Medical and Surgical Reporter.*

This interesting work should be in the hands of every one. Its interesting pages of adventures are full of instruction and amusement. Ten thousand copies, it is stated, have been sold in one month.—*Auburn American.*

Nothing of real importance is omitted. The general reader will prefer this to the English edition, especially as the cost is so trifling.—*Pennsylvania Inquirer.*

Dr. Livingstone's Travels and Researches in South Africa appear to great advantage in this edition, which is undoubtedly the edition most acceptable to the reader who reads for practical instruction and amusement.—*Saturday Post.*

It is a rich and valuable book for the general reader; and the admirable style in which the publisher has issued it, will commend it to the favor of thousands.—*Christian Observer.*

We cannot name thirty-two chapters which are likely to beguile time and enlarge the scope of reflection more pleasantly, and at the same time more satisfactorily, than these Livingstone adventures. A special value is given to this volume by the addition of "Historical Notices of Discoveries in Africa;" and taken altogether, it would be difficult to name any publication which more completely meets the popular taste of our time for reading matter, which is strange, new, the scene laid in far-off countries, which touches the feelings and increases our stock of useful knowledge.—*New Yorker.*

It tells the whole story, leaving out digressions and episodes.—*Legal Intelligencer.*

While it contains all the material portions, it is free from much superfluous matter inserted in the larger edition.—*Auburn Daily Advertiser.*

This edition of Dr. Livingstone's travels, published by J. W. Bradley, is just what it purports to be—the essential portions of the English editions brought within the means of all. Like all of Mr. Bradley's publications, it is excellently gotten up.—*Tioga Agitator, Pa.*

CAUTION.—The attention of the Publisher has been called to spurious editions of this work, put forth as "Narratives of Dr. Livingstone's Travels in Africa." Ours is the only cheap American edition of this great work published, and contains all the important matter of the English edition, which is sold at six dollars.

J. W. BRADLEY, Publisher,
No. 48 North Fourth Street, Philadelphia

www.ingramcontent.com/pod-product-compliance
Lightning Source LLC
Chambersburg PA
CBHW032008300426
44117CB00008B/945